The Niagara Courier
Lockport, New York
1828–1833:
Transcripts, Extracts and Indexes

THE NIAGARA COURIER
LOCKPORT, NEW YORK
1828–1833:
TRANSCRIPTS, EXTRACTS AND INDEXES

*Transcripts and extracts of articles
selected from twenty editions
of
the Niagara Courier newspaper
published between the dates,
June 26, 1828 – November 6, 1833,
with
name and subject indexes.*

compiled and edited by
Alison J. Kilpatrick

Copyright © Alison J. Kilpatrick, 2011

All rights reserved.

Any unauthorized copying, reproduction, re-use, distribution, transmission, storage, or modification, in or via any medium, in whole or in part, will constitute an infringement of copyright.

This volume consists of data that were selected for transcription or extraction; entered, catalogued, indexed, and stored in a relational database created by the compiler; and, output, assembled, and articulated for publication as an historical reference and finding aid, accompanied by the compiler's interpretive remarks, research notes, statistics, and editorial annotations.

Permission to reproduce material from this publication is granted subject to the following conditions:

1. the use must be for a non-commercial, educational or private research purpose;
2. a maximum of 10 index entries or 300 transcribed words may be used in a non-commercial, private research publication or presentation. If your proposed project requires more than this allowance, write to the publisher at the address given below;
3. provide an appropriate bibliographic citation, for example: Transcription of this article previously published in *The Niagara Courier, Lockport, New York, 1828–1833: Transcripts, Extracts and Indexes*, compiled and edited by Alison J. Kilpatrick (Clementsport, Nova Scotia, Canada: Quercus Arborealis, 2011); and,
4. this permission is not extended to transmissions, look-ups, or postings to newsgroups, bulletin boards, mailing lists, web pages or any forum on the Internet, or any sharing or social network or other medium logically or reasonably anticipated by this exclusion.

For information regarding permissions, write to the publisher at:

Quercus Arborealis Publications
PO Box 10
Clementsport, Nova Scotia
Canada   B0S 1E0
e-mail: editor@quercus-arborealis.ca

This book is for genealogists, local historians, and those who love reading stories from the past.

Some articles contain language and characterizations which may have been in common use at the time the articles or stories were written, but which are no longer acceptable. These articles do not reflect the opinions of the compiler, editor or publisher of this book.

ISBN 978-0-9868873-0-7
First Edition

For my husband,
James Pinson Ludwig,
and his brother, Frederick Edwin Ludwig II,
great-great-grandchildren of
Almeron Newman (1804–1876) and
Laura Berry (1808–1875),
residents of Ontario County and
Newfane, Niagara County, in the state of New York,
until they migrated to Portland, Michigan in 1836.

TABLE OF CONTENTS

Introduction		1
	How to use this book	3
	Abbreviations	6
1.	Transcripts and Extracts	7
2.	Index of Names	139
3.	Index of Subjects	153
4.	Supplementary Indexes:	
	4.1 Chancery	155
	4.2 Insolvent debtors	155
	4.3 Mortgage sales	155
	4.4 Sheriff's sales	155
	4.5 Wills and estates	156
	4.6 Women	156
5.	Michener Cadwallader	163
Bibliography		165

INTRODUCTION

This book presents two related compilations: first, transcriptions and extracts of articles from historic issues of the *Niagara Courier* newspaper, published in Lockport, New York between the years, 1828–1833; and second, indexes to serve as finding aids for those articles.

The dates of the surviving issues in this run of the *Niagara Courier* are summarized in Table 1, "Summary of issue dates and index entries." Though considerable gaps exist, this range of newspapers corresponds with the tenure of the first proprietor and editor of the *Niagara Courier*, Michener Cadwallader.[1]

Table 1. Summary of issue dates and index entries.	
Date of issue	No.
June 26, 1828	120
July 3, 1828	485
August 21, 1828	181
August 28, 1828	67
September 4, 1828	94
October 9, 1828	582
October 23, 1828	132
November 15, 1831	192
December 6, 1831	139
February 21, 1832	69
June 26, 1832	164
October 30, 1832	443
December 18, 1832	87
January 23, 1833	38
March 20, 1833	94
April 17, 1833	120
August 7, 1833	119
September 4, 1833	30
September 11, 1833	21
November 6, 1833	238
Total no. entries	3415

A total of 749 articles were selected from these twenty issues for transcription or extraction, yielding 3,415 index entries. Of the latter total, 3,336 contain either surnames or organization names; the remaining seventy-nine entries cite place names, only.

The most notable exclusions from this volume are articles from the editorial columns. Nevertheless, a number of Mr. Cadwallader's editorials have been included in this work, especially those that pertain to the Anti-Masonic movement, politics and elections.

Repeat advertisements were transcribed or extracted, and indexed, only once.

Several of Mr. Cadwallader's clients placed multiple ads in every issue, many of which were quite brief, often running to only two to four lines. A number of these were not transcribed and indexed in this work but have been identified in "Transcriber's notes" throughout Chapter 1, *Transcripts and Extracts*.

Even with these slight limitations in scope, advertisements made up more than half of the news articles transcribed or extracted from the *Niagara Courier*, as shown in Table 2, "Subjects of articles indexed."

Not surprisingly, many of the advertisements were mercantile and trade in nature. However, people often posted advertisements for other reasons including, for example, announcements of new ventures or dissolutions of partnerships, sales of land in the town of Lockport or farms in Niagara County, and urgent notices to customers to pay their bills. Perhaps as a sign of difficult economic times, not a few merchants expressed a great interest in taking country produce in trade.

The next largest subject category in this sample of newspapers related to legal and governmental notices. The content of notices was variable. People published cautions to the public about their stray cows, stolen horses, runaway servants, lost wallets, and eloped wives. Government proclaimed

---

[1] Chapter 5 provides a biographical sketch of Michener Cadwallader (1798–1864).

Table 2. Subjects of articles indexed.			
Subject	No.	Per cent	Rank
Advertisement	380	50.74	1
Notice	175	23.37	2
Politics	56	7.48	3
Court	17	2.27	4
Marriage	13	1.74	5
Transportation	13	1.74	5
Education	12	1.60	6
Agriculture	11	1.47	7
Temperance	11	1.47	7
Religion	10	1.34	8
Health & medicine	8	1.07	
Death	6	0.80	
Editorial	5	0.67	
Crime	4	0.53	
Miscellany	4	0.53	
Social welfare	4	0.53	
Accident	3	0.40	
Government	3	0.40	
History	2	0.27	
Manufacture	2	0.27	
Children	1	0.13	
Fire	1	0.13	
Fishing	1	0.13	
Land and property	1	0.13	
Military	1	0.13	
Natural phenomena	1	0.13	
Slavery	1	0.13	
Societies	1	0.13	
Suicide	1	0.13	
Weather	1	0.13	
Total no. articles	749	100.00	

federal and state election dates and afterwards, posted the results. The courts declared legal actions against insolvent debtors and people who had defaulted on mortgages. Often, notices of Sheriff's and mortgage sales published considerable detail about the properties put up for public auction or, in the parlance of the day, public "vendue." Notices also featured announcements about the probate of wills or the imminent sale of a deceased person's real estate.

Periodically, the various village Post Offices of Niagara County published the names of people for whom letters yet remained at the post-office, uncalled for. One imagines that many of these letters were sent to kith and kin travelling through Lockport, only to arrive after the addressees had departed, continuing their journeys either homewards or to new frontiers. This type of notice yielded more than one thousand index entries—nearly one-third of all the names indexed in this volume.

To the probable dismay of family historians, only six death and thirteen marriage notices were published in this run of the *Niagara Courier*. Very few accidents or similar calamities were reported. Local intelligence of social events, ladies' teas, and church picnics did not grace the pages of Mr. Cadwallader's paper.

Nevertheless, advertisements, notices, and news articles provide valuable insights into the lives of the people who lived and worked in, or were passing through, the town of Lockport and Niagara County during this period of rapid territorial expansion into western New York state, and beyond.

Several story lines of intense topical interest appeared in Mr. Cadwallader's publication during the period, 1828–1833, perhaps serving to distract his readers from the usual travails of day-to-day living:

- the rise of the Anti-Masonic political movement, a major proponent of which was Michener Cadwallader. Many of the articles featured the appointment of local men to Central and Vigilant Committees in the villages and towns of Niagara County (for which subject, refer to the index entries under the heading, "Anti-Masonic movement," in Chapter 3, *Index of Subjects*);
- the trial for the abduction and murder of Capt. William Morgan in 1828 (article numbers 61, 95, 119, 134, 147, 422, and 551);
- the trial and conviction of Americans at Madawaska, New Brunswick in 1831 (article numbers 184 and 192);

- the emergence, in 1832, of one of the most dreaded diseases of the nineteenth century—Cholera—and the measures taken in Niagara County to counteract its spread from places nearby, including the threat particularly perceived from the provinces of Upper and Lower Canada (article numbers 328, 332, 333, 334, 335, 336, 338), and finally, the cessation of the disease (no. 382); and,

- the early years of the Temperance movement in Niagara County (for which subject, refer to the index entries under the heading, "Temperance," in Chapter 3, *Index of Subjects*).

The *Niagara Courier* retained a distinctly local flavour. Nearly one-third of the articles transcribed and indexed pertain to the town of Lockport, and over 70% to the county of Niagara. Other parts of the state of New York account for approximately 25% of the total. The remaining articles related to other states in the United States, the provinces of Lower and Upper Canada, and other parts of British North America. Table 3, "Geographic coverage of the *Niagara Courier*, 1828–1833," provides an approximation of the distribution of geographic coverage by the newspaper, based on the index entries extracted for this volume.

HOW TO USE THIS BOOK

Transcripts and Extracts: One of the objectives in the compilation of this volume was to produce faithful transcriptions from the newspaper record. This work includes three significant exceptions to that rule: the inclusion of extracts, or partial transcriptions; occasional edits of line format or layout; and, the insertion of transcriber's notes, which are enclosed within [square parentheses].

Approximately 80% (611) of the 749 news articles presented in this book are complete transcriptions. The remaining 138 articles are extracts that, although they are abbreviated transcriptions, retain references to names of individuals, organizations, publications, and geographic places.

Table 3. Geographic coverage of the *Niagara Courier* newspaper, 1828–1833.

Place	No.	Per cent
Cambria	67	2.0
Hartland	59	1.7
Holland Co. Land	4	0.1
Le Roy	17	0.5
Lewiston	274	8.0
Lockport	1076	31.5
Middleport	21	0.6
Newfane	32	0.9
Niagara	51	1.5
Niagara County	124	3.6
Niagara Falls	130	3.8
Pendleton	120	3.5
Porter	45	1.3
Royalton	259	7.6
Somerset	31	0.9
Tonawanda	1	0.0
Wilson	32	0.9
Youngstown	77	2.3
Sub-total, Niagara Co.	2420	70.9
Albany	30	0.9
Buffalo	25	0.7
New York	41	1.2
Niagara & Niagara Falls	181	5.3
Ontario County	48	1.4
Rochester	39	1.1
Other, NY state	521	15.3
Sub-total, NY state	885	25.9
Other states in the USA	71	2.1
Upper Canada & Quebec	36	1.1
Not stated	3	0.1
Sub-total, other	110	3.2
Total index entries	3415	100.0

Extracts are indicated by the word "Extract:" placed at the beginning of the title or paragraph containing the abridged content of the original news article. Three types of edit were employed in order to compose the extracts:

1. material that has been paraphrased or digested from the original newspaper record is enclosed within [square brackets];

2. material that has been omitted and, in its place, a very brief description of the content provided, is enclosed within {curly brackets}; and,

3. material that has been omitted, without a description of the content, is marked with an ellipsis typographical symbol, that is, " ... ".

As an example of the first type of edit, the original newspaper copy for Article no. 24 contains a long and detailed listing of cabinet makers', house joiners', carpenters' and coopers' tools. Rather than enumerate all of the products published in the advertisement, the extract provides the following abridgment: [List includes a few dozen items, ranging from astrangles, nosings and ploughs, to trying squares, braces, bitts, and Coopers' Braces.]

Many of the Notices of Sheriff's Sales and Mortgage Sales feature the second type of edit. For example, an entry such as {Notice includes description of boundaries,} or {Notice includes further description of land,} indicates that the Notice, as originally published, contains additional detail about the property, or properties, for sale.

The lists of letters awaiting pick-up at the village post-offices are labelled *Extracts*, but only because the layouts of those notices have been modified by listing the surnames of the addressees alphabetically after the Post-Master's name. Otherwise, these lists of names are complete.

Another example of an Extract is Article no. 134, the report of the trial of several men for the abduction and murder of Capt. William Morgan. The original article ran to nine columns—which fact, one hopes, explains the preference for an extract over a full transcription! Yet, this Extract provides a synopsis in the form of an alphabetical list of all the individuals whose names appear in the article, together with brief descriptions of their involvement in, or connection with, the event.

Indexes: A second objective in this work was to formulate convenient and useful finding aids, by means of article numbers and indexes, in order for readers to locate news articles quickly and reliably.

Each transcript or extract in Chapter 1, *Transcripts and Extracts*, includes a reference to the original publication in the format, *Ref. Date of issue; page number; column number*. For example, the reference for Article number 192 is Ref. November 15, 1831, pg. 2, col. 4.

The indexes are sorted in two ways: by surname, organization or publication name (Chapter 2, *Index of Names*), and by subject (Chapter 3, *Index of Subjects*). Please note that the numbers listed in the index entries refer to article numbers in Chapter 1, not to page numbers.

In addition, a series of supplementary indexes have been developed from the subject heading, *Notices*, in order to direct readers' attention to different types of legal announcements and to references to women (Chapter 4, *Supplementary Indexes*). The first five supplementary indexes cross-reference surnames to article numbers for notices pertaining to the following subjects: the Court in Chancery, Sheriff's sales, mortgage sales, insolvent debtors, and wills and estates of deceased persons.

The sixth supplementary index captures 128 mentions of women from this run of the Niagara Courier. Most of these index entries (83) are attributable to notices of letters awaiting pick-up from the post-office. The remaining references to women, though scant in number, are compelling. Topics range from the new Ontario Female Seminary in Canandaigua, and one woman's plea to the public for assistance in finding her adult sons, to advertisements by enterprising seamstresses, milliners and mantua-makers.

Layout and order of text: To preserve space or to improve readability, the layout, or format, of many of the articles has been edited. Some lines have been combined; for example, rather than print an advertiser's name and the date of publication on two separate lines, as occurred frequently in the original publication, these items may appear on one line in this book. The order of words, phrases, sentences and lines has not been altered from the original.

Many words and lines, which were fully capitalized in the original record, have been transcribed in lower case in this volume.

Names of published works have been italicized, a practice not always found in the original newspaper record.

Spelling conventions: Generally, the editor, Mr. Cadwallader, employed British conventions for spelling. Examples of the British forms, as they appeared in this run of the *Niagara Courier* (with their modern American counterparts), include: acknowledgment (acknowledgement), armour (armor), authorise (authorize), behaviour (behavior), centre (center), colour (color), connexion (connection), despatch (dispatch), endeavour (endeavor), favour (favor), for ever (forever), gaol (jail), grey (gray), harbour (harbor), honour (honor), jewellery (jewelry), judgment (judgement), labour (labor), meagre (meager), neighbour (neighbor), odour (odor), offence (offense), pedlar (peddler), plough (plow), rumour (rumor), waggon (wagon), whiskey (whisky), and woollen (woolen). Consistent with the compiler's objective to provide faithful transcriptions, the British conventions, where used, have been retained in this volume.

Errors and omissions: Great care and every reasonable effort have been exercised in order to produce a comprehensive and reliable set of transcriptions, extracts and indexes, supported by useful interpretive remarks, research notes, statistics and editorial annotations. However, because this work required analysis, interpretation and judgment, errors may have occurred, for which the compiler apologizes in advance. No matter how carefully designed and assembled, this book constitutes a secondary source. When in doubt, the original source record should be consulted as the final authority. The compiler welcomes readers' comments, whether to point out errors, or to provide additional insight to the local history or publication of the *Niagara Courier* during this period.

Poems, stories, and many editorial articles were omitted from this volume. Repeat advertisements were excluded; and, where several short adverts appeared for one vendor in the same issue, these were also excluded but have been itemized in *Transcriber's Notes* throughout this volume. Most advertisements included a code appended by the editor (perhaps for bookkeeping purposes), for example, 9t6, 9–3w, 9t3, and so on: these codes were omitted from the transcripts and extracts.

:: :: ::

Whether employed in the pursuit of historical research or perused at leisure in an armchair, may this book also serve as a tribute to the memory of the people who lived and laboured in Niagara County, including—and perhaps, especially—those whose names were not immortalized in these surviving issues of the *Niagara Courier* newspaper.

ABBREVIATIONS

&c.	19th century variant of "etc."
advert	advertisement
Al. Journ.	*Albany Journal* newspaper
Albany Journ.	*Albany Journal* newspaper
Anti-Masonic Enq.	*Rochester Antimasonic Inquirer* newspaper
Att'y.	Attorney
Balance	*Lockport Balance* newspaper
Batavia Adv.	*Batavia Advertiser* newspaper
bbl.	barrel
bl.	boulevard
Buffalo Jour.	*Buffalo Journal* newspaper
Buffalo Pat.	*Buffalo Patriot* newspaper
Ch'n.	Chairman
Co.	Company, or County
Com.	Committee
Cor. Sec.	Corresponding Secretary
dec'd.	deceased
Depy.	Deputy
do.	ditto
Esq.	Esquire
Ex. Com.	Executive Committee
Fi. Fa.	*fieri facias*
Gaz.	Gazette
gro.	gross; equal to the number, 144
hdkfs.	handkerchiefs
Hhds.	hogsheads
Hon.	The Honourable
inst.	*instante mense*; in the current month
Jun., Jun'r., or Jr.	Junior
M.	one thousand
Messrs.	plural form of Mr. or Mister
N. Brunswick	New Brunswick
N.B.	*nota bene*; take note of the following...
N.Y. Com. Adv.	*New York Commercial Advertiser* newspaper
N.Y. St. T.S.	New York State Temperance Society
Nia.	Niagara
P.M.	Postmaster
pc., pce., pcs.	piece, pieces
Pres't.	President
Roch. Album	*Rochester Album* newspaper
Roch. Dai. Adv.	*Rochester Daily Advertiser* newspaper
Roch. Inq.	*Rochester Antimasonic Inquirer* newspaper
Sec'y or Sec'ry	Secretary
Shff.	Sheriff
sic	"intentionally so written;" transcribed as printed
U.C.	Upper Canada
ult.	*ultimo mense*; in the last, or previous, month
viz.	*videlicet*; that is to say, as follows
Wash. Co. Post	*Washington County Post* newspaper

1. TRANSCRIPTS AND EXTRACTS

Article no. 1   Subject: Advertisement
Ref. June 26, 1828; pg. 1, col. 1

Printed and Published Weekly by
M. CADWALLADER,
Editor and Proprietor.
Terms.

To village Subscribers, $2.50—to mail subscribers, and to those who call at the office for their papers, $2—payable half yearly in advance.

Advertisements will be inserted three times for $1 per square, and 25 cents for each subsequent insertion. A discount will be made to yearly advertisers.

All communications addressed to the editor, post paid, will be promptly attended to.

Article no. 2   Subject: Advertisement
Ref. June 26, 1828; pg. 1, col. 1

ELIAS RANSOM, Jun'r.
Attorney at Law,
May 1. Lockport, Niagara Co.

Article no. 3   Subject: Advertisement
Ref. June 26, 1828; pg. 1, col. 1

CHAPIN & HART,
Attorneys at Law,
Canal-Street—two doors east of the Post-Office,
May 1, 1828. Lockport, (Niagara County.)

Article no. 4   Subject: Advertisement
Ref. June 26, 1828; pg. 1, col. 1

BATES COOKE,
Attorney at Law,
May 8. Lewiston, N.Y.

Article no. 5   Subject: Advertisement
Ref. June 26, 1828; pg. 1, col. 1

J. CHASE, M.D.

Continues to devote his exclusive attention to the duties of his profession.

Office second door west of Jenning's Hotel, Main-street. Lockport, May 1, 1828.

Article no. 6   Subject: Advertisement
Ref. June 26, 1828; pg. 1, col. 1

Extract: GOODS ARE CHEAPER!

S. & W. PARSONS have just received, at the Yellow Store, a fashionable and extensive assortment of New Goods [List includes dry goods, bed-ticking, hats, pantaloons and vests, shirtings and sheetings, merino shawls, parasols, boots and shoes, Brazilian hair combs, hardware, cutlery, iron and steel of all sorts and sizes, nails, scythes, spades and shovels, saws, hollow-ware, crockery, and glass ware.] Their stock of Teas, Sugars, Tobacco, Pepper, Ginger, Raisins, &c., is of the first quality. The above is only a small part of their Goods, which might be named; all of which have been purchased at the best advantage, and be sold at the lowest prices. Lockport, May 1, 1828.

Article no. 7   Subject: Advertisement
Ref. June 26, 1828; pg. 1, col. 1

COPARTNERSHIP.

The subscribers have recently formed a copartnership in the business of Merchandising, under the name, style and firm of   L. FELLOWS & CO.

Are now receiving from New-York a very general assortment of Goods, peculiarly adapted to the season, and of the latest fashions. They deem it unnecessary to enumerate the variety of articles comprising their Stock of Goods, and would only invite their friends, and the public generally wishing to purchase, to call and examine for themselves, with the assurance, that the prices shall be made to suit the purchaser.

B. CAMPBELL, L. FELLOWS. Lockport, May 1.

Article no. 8   Subject: Advertisement
Ref. June 26, 1828; pg. 1, col. 1

NOW IS THE TIME!

The subscriber offers, at a bargain, a number of Lots, situated in different parts of this Village, at low prices, on accommodating terms, separately or in parcels to suit purchasers.

Since the completion of the Grand Erie Canal, experience has taught us, that money could in no way be so well invested, as in real estate located in the principal towns on its borders.—Scarcely has there been an instance where locations have been made in this village, that purchasers have not received two dollars for one.—From the great number of buildings now erecting, and other improvements, together with the daily arrival of citizens from the east and elsewhere, who are locating themselves here, reasonable expectations are entertained, that a great advance upon real estate will take place the ensuing season.

Apply at my office, opposite L.A. Spalding's.

S. OLMSTED. Lockport, May 1, 1228 [sic].

Also, to Let—A job of taking out stumps, and turnpiking several streets.

For sale—The fruit trees and rails on the place formerly occupied by J. Comstock. Apply as above.

Article no. 9 Subject: Advertisement
Ref. June 26, 1828; pg. 1, col. 1

NEW GOODS!

The subscribers are now receiving a general assortment of Goods adapted to the season, which will be offered for sale at unusually low prices.

M.H. TUCKER & CO. Lockport, May 8, 1828.

Article no. 10 Subject: Advertisement
Ref. June 26, 1828; pg. 1, col. 1

ESTATE OF ALEXANDER WATSON, Dec'd,

The subscriber has been appointed administrator, and will attend to the settlement of any business in relation to this estate when called on: all interested, will please call as early as may be.

BATES COOKE. Lewiston, May 8, 1828.

Article no. 11 Subject: Advertisement
Ref. June 26, 1828; pg. 1, col. 1

CASH!

All persons indebted to the subscriber by notes now due, and on book account of one year or longer standing, are requested to make payment without delay, and save parties trouble. And on all accounts of six months standing, and now due, payment or notes for the amount, is requested.

GEO. REYNALE. Royalton, 25th April, 1828.

Article no. 12 Subject: Advertisement
Ref. June 26, 1828; pg. 1, col. 2

PINE SHINGLES.
40M. Pine Shingles, for sale by
S. & W. PARSONS. June 12, 1828.

Article no. 13 Subject: Advertisement
Ref. June 26, 1828; pg. 1, col. 2

STAVES.

S. & W. PARSONS will pay the market price, in Cash for all kinds of Staves. June 12, 1828.

Article no. 14 Subject: Advertisement
Ref. June 26, 1828; pg. 1, col. 2

Extract: NEW GOODS.

S. DE VEAUX is just receiving a large and extensive assortment of Spring and Summer Goods, which he will sell at moderate prices. He warrants them to be as good, and the prices as low, as they are sold at any place in the country. [List includes dry goods, groceries, hardware, crockery, hollow-ware; drugs, medicine, confectionary; paints, linseed and lamp oil; window glass and putty; blistered and cast steel; whiskey by the barrel; tin and Japaned ware; ladies' and gentlemen's coarse and fine Shoes.] And almost every article usually inquired after or sold in any Country Store. Niagara Falls, May 1st, 1828.

Article no. 15 Subject: Advertisement
Ref. June 26, 1828; pg. 1, col. 2

New and Cheap GOODS!

W.H. Childs & Co. have just received, and are now opening, a general assortment of

Dry Goods, Groceries, Crockery, and Hardware,

which having been bought at the present reduced prices, will enable them to sell as cheap as in any of the villages in the western country. They not only say that their goods are of a superior quality, but they are cheap—very cheap. Not wishing the public to trust to their assertion alone, they solicit them to call and examine for themselves.

W.H.C. & Co. feel grateful for past patronage, and hope in future to merit the confidence of their customers. Niagara Falls, April 25th, 1828.

Article no. 16 Subject: Advertisement
Ref. June 26, 1828; pg. 1, col. 2

L. FELLOWS & CO.

Will pay Cash, at all times, for Black Salts of Lye, Pot and Pearl Ashes.

Goods in exchange for House and Field Ashes. May 1.

Article no. 17 Subject: Advertisement
Ref. June 26, 1828; pg. 1, col. 2

A. FIRMAN,

Dealer in Dry Goods and Groceries—manufacturer of Pot and Pearl Ashes—will pay cash for Salts of Lye, and Staves for the Quebec market.

Trunks manufactured and constantly on hand for sale: Portable Desks and Trunks made on short notice, and to any given pattern.

Lewiston, Academy Square, May 1828.

Article no. 18 Subject: Notice
Ref. June 26, 1828; pg. 1, col. 2

Extract: POST-OFFICE NOTICE. Lewiston, Niagara county, N.Y. May 8, 1828. {Closure times for Eastern, Western and Northern routes; also, for routes for mail to Lockport and Queenston, U.C.} BATES COOKE, P.M.

Article no. 19   Subject: Advertisement
Ref. June 26, 1828; pg. 1, col. 2

CASH!

The subscriber pays Cash for White Oak Pipe, Hogshead and Barrel Staves and Heading, delivered at any place on the bank of the Erie Canal, between Buffalo and Rochester, at market price—Also, for Wheat, Corn, Oats, and Pot and Pearl Ashes, delivered at his Store in Royalton.

GEO. REYNALE. Royalton, 25th April, 1828.

Article no. 20   Subject: Advertisement
Ref. June 26, 1828; pg. 1, col. 2

20,000 FEET of first rate Clear Pine Boards, just received and for sale by G. BACON. Lockport, May 1, 1828.

Article no. 21   Subject: Advertisement
Ref. June 26, 1828; pg. 1, col. 2

An article for 60 acres of first rate land lying one mile west of Molyneux', in Cambria, between the Ridge and north Ridge Road, for sale on reasonable terms. Apply to
B. COOKE. Lewiston, May 8th, 1828.

Article no. 22   Subject: Advertisement
Ref. June 26, 1828; pg. 1, col. 2

YOUNGSTOWN FERRY.

The public are informed that the Horse-boat *Union* now regularly plies between Youngstown and the Canada shore.

Persons crossing to or from Canada, with carriages or horses, will certainly find this to be decidedly the best Ferry on the River, both as regards convenience and promptness. To ensure the utmost safety to passengers and property, and to guard against delay, none but the most experienced hands are engaged in the management of the boat.

JOHN PHILLIPS, ANDREW HERON, Jr.
Youngstown, May 1st, 1828.

Article no. 23   Subject: Advertisement
Ref. June 26, 1828; pg. 1, col. 2

TO FARMERS.
The celebrated and valuable Horse,
Young Buck Rabbit,

Will be kept for the present season at the stable of the Washington House, in the village of Lockport. Terms made known at the stable.

Young Buck Rabbit is a beautiful Dappled Gray, 8 years old, 16 hands high, and for speed and bottom is not equalled by any horse in this section of country. His sire was the celebrated running horse Old Buck Rabbit, who was sired by James Edmundson's noted horse Oberon, who was sired by the imported Medley, his dam was the celebrated mare Peach Blossom, by Old Quicksilver; the Young Buck's dam was sired by Mr. James Moffat's noted horse Difidle, who was sired by Old Crack, whose sire was the Old Medley. Young Buck Rabbit was raised by John Lynch, Esq. of Monroe county, Va.

For further particulars apply to the subscriber as above.
PLATT SMITH. Lockport, May 1, 1828.

Article no. 24   Subject: Advertisement
Ref. June 26, 1828; pg. 1, col. 3

Extract: MECHANICS! TAKE NOTICE.

SPALDINGS have received, and now offer for sale, a large assortment of Cabinet-makers', House-Joiners', Carpenters' and Coopers' Tools—comprising the following, and many articles not enumerated: [List includes a few dozen items, ranging from astrangles, nosings and ploughs, to trying squares, axes, chisels, braces, bitts, and Coopers' Braces.] All of which will be sold at the manufacturers' retail prices. Mechanics are invited to call and examine them. Lockport, 6 mo. 5th, 1828.

Article no. 25   Subject: Advertisement
Ref. June 26, 1828; pg. 1, col. 3

Extract: IRON, NAILS, &c. {Advertisement includes list of stock.} Just received and for sale by House & Boughton. May 15, 1828.

Article no. 26   Subject: Advertisement
Ref. June 26, 1828; pg. 1, col. 3

NEW ESTABLISHMENT.

W.W. PRENTICE, Clock and Watch-maker, Silversmith, and Jeweller. Shop one door east of the Post-Office. Lockport, May 1, 1828.

Article no. 27   Subject: Advertisement
Ref. June 26, 1828; pg. 1, col. 3

BOOK AND JOB PRINTING.

COOLEY & LATHROP, having established an office in the village of Lockport for the purpose of doing
Book and Job Printing,
of all kinds, and having ordered a handsome variety of Type of the different sizes, and of the latest fashions, feel confident in assuring their friends, and the public generally, that all work they may be favoured with will be done in a style of neatness, accuracy and despatch not surpassed by any other office in the western part of the state.

Call at the office of 'Priest-Craft Exposed,' a few rods south of the Locks, where favours will be thankfully received, and promptly attended to.

Blanks of all kinds, for Attorneys, Justices, &c. will be kept constantly on hand, for sale in large or small quantities.

Four cents per lb. will be paid for clean linen and cotton Rags, as above. Lockport, April 30, 1828.

Article no. 28 Subject: Advertisement
Ref. June 26, 1828; pg. 1, col. 3

DYE WOODS & DYE STUFFS.

A Large and general assortment kept constantly on hand: Clothiers can at all times be supplied with any quantity of these articles at as reasonable prices as they can be purchased at other places.

S. DE VEAUX. Niagara Falls, May 1, 1828.

Article no. 29 Subject: Advertisement
Ref. June 26, 1828; pg. 1, col. 3

CHEAPER YET!

HOUSE & BOUGHTON are opening a large supply of Summer Goods, and offer them to their customers and the public generally, at unusually low rates. Their assortment is very extensive, and comprises many new and fashionable articles not heretofore offered in this section. May 15, 1828.

Article no. 30 Subject: Advertisement
Ref. June 26, 1828; pg. 1, col. 3

PAINTING.
W.T. LEWIS,
Coach, Sign, House, and Ornamental Painter,

Respectfully informs the public, that he continues the above business in the village of Lockport, in all its various branches.

Shop in Buffalo-street, opposite Main-street Bridge.

Also, Gilding, Glazing & Paper Hanging

Done in the best manner, and at the shortest notice. None but the first rate hands are employed. A share of public patronage is respectfully solicited.

Lockport, June 5, 1828.

Article no. 31 Subject: Advertisement
Ref. June 26, 1828; pg. 1, col. 3

BOOT AND SHOEMAKING.
B.H. WHITCHER

Continues to carry on the above business as usual, in the Stone Building, opposite Jennings' Hotel, Main-street, Lockport: where a good assortment of articles in the line will be kept constantly on hand for sale.

Persons indebted to the above establishment are requested to make immediate payment, and save cost. May 15, 1828.

Article no. 32 Subject: Advertisement
Ref. June 26, 1828; pg. 1, col. 3

A GENERAL ASSORTMENT OF

Drugs and Medicines, and the following Patent Medicines. Dr. Vought's Chymical Anti-Dyspeptic Medicine; do. Indian Botanical Ague Drops; do. Improved Lee's Anti-Bilious Pills; James's Anti-Dyspeptic Pills; Stearn's Opodeldoc; Dr. Waitwell's Chymical Liquid Embrocation; Hooper's Female Pills; Hamilton's worm-destroying Losenges; Dr. Cyrenius Chapin's Anti-Bilious Pills; Cephalic Snuff; Godfrey's Cordial; British and Harlaem Oil; American Cough Drops; Anderson's do.; Cologne Water.

Also—Antique Oil; Hair Restorative; Macassar Oil; Composition for colouring the Hair, &c.

These articles, and many others in the same line, for sale at the store of the subscriber.

S. DE VEAUX. Niagara Falls, May 1, 1828.

Article no. 33 Subject: Advertisement
Ref. June 26, 1828; pg. 1, col. 3

THE British Steam Packet CANADA, (Capt. Hugh Richardson,) plying twixt York and Niagara, U.C., weather permitting, leaves Niagara daily (Sunday excepted) for York, precisely at 7 o'clock, A.M.

Arrives at York, at half past 11, in the morning.

Leaves York daily (Saturday excepted) for Niagara, precisely at two in the afternoon.

Arrives at Niagara at half past 6, P.M.

FARES.
After cabin and quarter deck, $2,
Fore cabin and deck, $1.

HUGH RICHARDSON, Master and Managing Owner.

N.B. A gun will be fired and colours hoisted 28 minutes before starting. May 8.

Article no. 34 Subject: Advertisement
Ref. June 26, 1828; pg. 1, col. 4

Extract: HOUSE & BOUGHTON

Offer for sale, at the Old Stand, fronting the Bridge, on Main-street, an additional supply of Fancy & Staple Goods, Comprising as extensive an assortment as they have ever offered, or can be found in this section of country. Among their Dry Goods are [List of several dozen articles, ranging from 200 pcs. super London Fancy Prints, and French Cambrics, to Carpeting, Table Covers, and Crumb Cloths.] A large supply of Domestic Goods: [List of about a dozen articles, from Calicoes to Marseilles quilts and counterpanes.] A good assortment of Summer Goods; [List of a couple dozen articles, from Black Lasting, white and brown silk stripe, and cotton, to Silk and Cotton umbrellas & parasols.] with a complete assortment of Hardware and Crockery. {Advertisement includes short list of hardware.} Their stock of Groceries consists of every article in that line; and they will continue to keep a supply of Liquors, fresh Teas, Sugars, &c., &c.; and will supply tavern-keepers and others on good terms. May 21, 1828.

Article no. 35 Subject: Advertisement
Ref. June 26, 1828; pg. 1, col. 4

FRUIT, &c.
Lemons, Oranges;
Box and Keg Raisins;
Nutmegs; Cassia, &c.—
Just received and for sale by
HOUSE & BOUGHTON. May 21, 1828.

Article no. 36 Subject: Advertisement
Ref. June 26, 1828; pg. 1, col. 4

INDEMNITY.
Aetna Insurance Company,
of Hartford, Conn.
Capital 200,000 Dollars,
(With liberty to increase the same to half a million Dollars.)

Offer to ensure Dwelling-Houses, Stores, Mills, Manufactories, Distilleries, Barns, Ships and Vessels in port or on the stocks, Goods, and every other species of insurable personal property, against Loss or Damage by Fire, at as low rates of premium as any similar institution in good standing.

The Aetna Insurance Company was incorporated in 1819, and the reputation it has acquired for promptness and liberality in the adjustment and payment of losses, requires no additional pledge to entitle it to a liberal share of public patronage. Persons wishing to be insured, can apply to

BATES COOKE, Lewiston, N.Y.

Who is appointed agent, with full power to receive proposals, and issue Policies, without the delay necessarily attendant on an application to the Office. June, 1828.

Article no. 37 Subject: Advertisement
Ref. June 26, 1828; pg. 1, col. 4

LEGHORNS, &c.
1 Case Bolivar Hats,
1 doz. Boy's Leghorns,
1 case Straw Bonnets,
12 Misses Open Cottage do.
30 Men's Palm Leaf Hats;—For sale by
HOUSE & BOUGHTON. May 15, 1828.

Article no. 38 Subject: Notice
Ref. June 26, 1828; pg. 1, col. 4

STRAY HORSE.

Taken up by the subscriber, on the 24th day of May last, a large Bay Horse, with a small star in his forehead, left hind foot white, a white spot on his neck near the shoulder, straight-made on the back, and a natural trotter. The owner is desired to come forward, prove property, pay charges, and take him away.

THOMAS J. WORDEN.
Town of Niagara, June 12th, 1828.

Article no. 39 Subject: Notice
Ref. June 26, 1828; pg. 1, col. 5

STAVE CONTRACTS.

Staves due us on contracts, are WANTED—muddy roads to the contrary notwithstanding.

S. & W. PARSONS. June 12, 1828.

Article no. 40 Subject: Notice
Ref. June 26, 1828; pg. 1, col. 5

Extract: SHERIFF'S SALE.

By virtue of a writ of Fieri Facias, issued out of the Clerk's Office of the County of Niagara, to me directed and delivered, against the goods and chattels, lands and tenements, of Wareham M. Woodward, I have seized all those pieces or parcels of land, situate, lying and being in the town and village of Lockport, in the said county of Niagara—the first of which being part of Village Lot No. 6, on the south side of Main-street, on the west side of the Erie canal, and particularly described as the middle part of said lot No. 6, and bounded as follows: {Notice includes description of boundaries} [surveyed by Jesse P. Haines, Surveyor; bounded, in part, by James M'Kain Jun.'s west line]—and being a piece of land deeded to Woodward by Carlos B. and Corydon C. Woodward, by indenture dated 26 September 1825, and recorded in Niagara County Records, in Book of Deeds No. 3, on pages 320 and 321, to which reference is had: {Notice includes further description of the piece of land}— containing about one eighth of an acre of land, be the same more or less. And also, all the residue and remainder of said Lot No. 6, not conveyed to James M'Kain, Jun., John Lyons, Wareham W. [sic] Woodward, Carlos B. Woodward, and Corydon C. Woodward, previous to 9 August 1826: Another of which pieces or parcels of land, being part of farm Lot No. 59, in the fourteenth Township, and seventh Range, known as the west half of Village Lot No. 11, on the north side of Main-street, and on the west side of the Erie Canal {Notice includes further description of land} together with the heriditaments and appurtenances thereunto each and severally belonging; all of which I shall expose to sale at public vendue, at the house of Samuel Jennings, innkeeper, in the village of Lockport, 30 June 1828. Dated May 14th, 1828.

JOHN PHILLIPS, Sheriff.

Article no. 41   Subject: Notice
Ref. June 26, 1828; pg. 1, col. 5

BY ORDER of Robert Fleming, Esquire, First Judge of the Court of Common Pleas in and for the county of Niagara, Notice is hereby given to the creditors of Jesse G. Jones, of the town of Lockport, in the county of Niagara, an insolvent debtor, to show cause, if any they have, before the said Judge, at his office in the village of Lewiston, on the nineteenth day of August next, at one o'clock in the afternoon, why an assignment of the said insolvent's estate should not be made, and his person be exempted from imprisonment, pursuant to the act entitled "An act to abolish imprisonment for debt in certain cases," passed April 7th, 1819. Dated this 2d day of June, 1828.

Article no. 42   Subject: Notice
Ref. June 26, 1828; pg. 1, col. 5

Extract: WHEREAS Sylvester R. Hathaway, of the town of Lockport, in the county of Niagara, by Indenture of Mortgage, bearing date 28 February 1828, for securing the payment of a certain sum of money, and in the interest thereof in said Indenture mentioned, did mortgage unto Warren Sadler, of the town of Lockport aforesaid, all that certain piece or parcel of land, situate, lying and being in the town of Lockport, in the county of Niagara, being part of Lots number eleven and twelve, in the fifteenth section of township number fourteen, in the sixth range, and bounded as follows: {Notice includes further description of land} [surveyed by Jesse P. Haines, Surveyor]—containing ten acres of land, be the same more or less. And whereas default hath been made in the payment of a part of the said sum of money and the interest thereon: Therefore notice is hereby given, that pursuant to a power of sale contained in said mortgage, and according to the statute in such case made and provided, the said mortgaged premises, with the appurtenances, will be sold at public auction, at the Washington House, kept by S.B. Thompson, in the Village of Lockport, 8 November 1828. Dated May 20th, 1828.
  WARREN SADLER.
  J. CENTER, Att'y.

Article no. 43   Subject: Advertisement
Ref. June 26, 1828; pg. 1, col. 5

WHITCHER & PORTER,
Continue to carry on the Cabinet-Making Business, as usual, in the village of Lockport, directly adjoining Jennings' Hotel, where they will execute all kinds of work in their line, such as Mahogany Sideboards, Secretaries, Bureaus, &c.; together with Plain Work of every description. They invite the public to call and examine their work, and judge for themselves.

WANTED as above—An apprentice to the Cabinet-Making Business: a lad about 15 years of age, who can come well recommended, will find a good situation.
Lockport, May 15, 1828.

Article no. 44   Subject: Court
Ref. June 26, 1828; pg. 3, col. 3

David Ware.—The notorious David Ware has been sentenced to be imprisoned in the State Prison, and kept at hard labour ten years—well put on, and well deserved!—*Roch. Album.*

Article no. 45   Subject: Religion
Ref. June 26, 1828; pg. 3, col. 1

Society of Friends.—The following is taken from the Extracts of Minutes from the Yearly meeting, held in New-York, by adjournments from the 26th to the 31st of 5th month, inclusive, 1828, composed of Friends, in the States of New-York, Vermont, Connecticut, and the Province of Canada.—[*Anti-Masonic Enq.*]

"A proposition was brought up from one of the Quarterly Meetings to have a clause of discipline added, relative to such as our members as shall join the society of Free Masons, or that attend their meetings: and it appears to many Friends that our discipline was already sufficient, but for the full and clear information of all Friends relative thereto, it is the judgment of this Meeting that if any of our members do join the Free Mason Society, or attend their meetings, they are to be disowned, after suitable labour, if they do not make satisfaction."

Article no. 46   Subject: Societies
Ref. June 26, 1828; pg. 3, col. 5

Extract: "Beware of Secret Societies."
Washington's Farewell Address.
4th of July, at Le Roy, Genesee Co. N.Y.

A Convention of Seceding Masons is to be held at Le Roy, commencing on the 4th of July next, to take measures to discharge their duties to their fellow-citizens. In addition to the interest which this convention will give to the day, there will be a general celebration of our National Independence, and of the new era of equal rights; all of which will render it one of the most interesting scenes that has ever occurred since the establishment of our government. The Committee of Arrangements have the pleasure to announce the appointment of the following officers for the day: [listed, below]. {Article includes information about the convention, including time and place of procession and dinner, and issuance of a general invitation to the public.}

By order of the Committee of Arrangements, Elijah Olmstead, Chairman, Beriah B. Hotchkin, Secretary. Le Roy, June 2, 1828.
- Barlow, Jonathan K., Col.; Bethany, New York; appointed Marshall for the Convention.
- Bixby, John J., Major; Le Roy, New York; appointed Assistant Marshall for the Convention.
- Brown, Matthew, Dr., Jr.; Rochester, New York; appointed Vice-President for the Convention.
- Cary, Trumbull, Esq.; Batavia, New York; appointed Vice-President for the Convention.
- Coe, Martin O., Col.; Le Roy, New York; appointed Marshall for the Convention.
- Cooke, Bates, Esq.; Lewiston, New York; appointed Vice-President for the Convention.
- Dwight, T., Mr.; Le Roy, New York; Mr. T. Dwight and Messrs. Tuthill and Stanley to prepare a "splendid collation" at the Convention.
- Hannam, Chester, Col.; Covington, New York; appointed Assistant Marshall for the Convention.
- Hayden, Moses, Hon.; New York, New York; appointed Vice-President for the Convention.
- Hotchkin, Beriah B.; Le Roy, New York; Secretary, Committee of Arrangements.
- Hotchkin and Starr, Messrs.; Le Roy, New York; attendants at the Convention were requested to meet at the Bookstore of Messrs. Hotchkin and Starr.
- Livingston, James K.; Rochester, New York; appointed to read the Declaration of Independence at the Convention.
- Olmstead, Elijah; Le Roy, New York; Chairman, Committee of Arrangements.
- Stanley, Mr.; Le Roy, New York; Mr. T. Dwight and Messrs. Tuthill and Stanley to prepare a "splendid collation" at the Convention.
- Starr, Mr.: See Messrs. Hotchkin and Starr, above.
- Tuthill, Mr.; Le Roy, New York; Mr. T. Dwight and Messrs. Tuthill and Stanley to prepare a "splendid collation" at the Convention.
- Wadsworth, William, General; Geneseo, New York; appointed President for the Convention.

Article no. 47   Subject: Marriage
Ref. June 26, 1828; pg. 3, col. 6

MARRIED.—On Monday evening last, by E. Ransom, Jr. Esq. Mr. Cephas Hawks, to Miss Laura Blakesly, both of this village.

Article no. 48   Subject: Notice
Ref. June 26, 1828; pg. 3, col. 6

FOURTH OF JULY.

The anniversary of our National Independence will be celebrated on the 4th day of July next, at the house of John Gould, Esq., in the town of Cambria. The usual ceremonies and festivities, suited to the occasion, will be had.

The Committee of Arrangements tender an invitation to the citizens of the county as well as to others, and beg leave to request a general attendance. The procession will be formed at 11 o'clock—and a dinner will be provided, of which all who feel disposed can partake.

ALEXANDER DICKERSON,
Chairman of the Com. of Arrangements.
June 25th, 1828.

Article no. 49   Subject: Advertisement
Ref. June 26, 1828; pg. 3, col. 6

M.H. TUCKER & Co.,

Having removed to the new Brick Store, are now opening as extensive an assortment of

Dry Goods, Crockery, Hardware, Hats, &c.,

as ever offered in the county.

They have also fitted up a Room fronting the Canal, in the rear of said building, where they intend to keep, at wholesale or retail, a large stock of

Groceries, Iron, Paints,

together with many other articles in the line: and they wouldh [sic] invite Tavern-keepers and Grocers to call and examine their stock before purchasing.

Old Madeira and Port Wines, selected with care, for the sick. June 26.

Article no. 50   Subject: Advertisement
Ref. June 26, 1828; pg. 3, col. 6

WHISKEY.

Just received, and for sale very low, 4000 gallons of Leroy's best Rectified Whiskey.

G.W. ROGERS & Co. June 26.

Article no. 51   Subject: Advertisement
Ref. June 26, 1828; pg. 3, col. 6

TO LET.

The two Rooms of the second story in the Brick Building.—Also, a Room in the 3d story, 60 feet long, suitable for a large School, which is much wanted in that section of the village.—Also, a Room on the first floor, fronting the Canal.—Also, The new three story building, recently occupied by us as a Store.

M.H. TUCKER & Co. June 25, 1828.

Article no. 52   Subject: Notice
Ref. June 26, 1828; pg. 3, col. 6

CAUTION.

Ran away from the subscriber, on Sunday evening the 22d inst. an indented apprentice named JOHN McROBERTS, about 15 or 16 years of age. All persons are forbid harbouring or trusting said runaway on my account, at their peril, as they will be prosecuted if they so do. One cent will be paid to any person returning said boy, but neither thanks nor charges will be allowed.

GEORGE A. NEAL. Town of Cambria, June 25, 1828.

Article no. 53   Subject: Notice
Ref. June 26, 1828; pg. 3, col. 6

DEFAULT having been made in the payment of a sum of money, secured by Mortgage, dated June 2d, 1827, executed by Allen Skinner and Annis Skinner, on village lot Number 24, on the South side of Main-st. in the village of Lockport, on the East side of the Canal, being one chain wide in front, and extending back thirty-seven and a half chains, containing more or less. The premises will be sold by virtue of a power contained in said mortgage, at public auction, at the Court House in Lockport, on Saturday the 27th day of December next, at 10 o'clock A.M. Dated Lockport, June 26, 1828.

FESTUS NORTHAM.

Article no. 54   Subject: Notice
Ref. June 26, 1828; pg. 3, col. 6

Extract: SHERIFF'S SALE.

By virtue of two writs of Fi. Fa. issued out of the Supreme Court of Judicature against the goods and chattels, lands and tenements of Seymour Scoville, I have seized and taken the following pieces of land, viz: One of which is situated in the village of Lockport, in the County of Niagara, and may be known on a certain map of a part of said village, as village lot No. 5, and the east half of village lot No. 7, on the north side of Niagara-street, in said village, bounded as follows—{Notice includes description of boundaries}—and being the tract of land whereon the house formerly called the Niagara Hotel is situated. Also—Another piece of land, situate in the town of Lockport, and being the west part of lot No. 70, in the 14th Township, and 7th Range, and bounded as follows, viz.—{Notice includes description of boundaries}—containing 106 acres, more or less: which I shall expose for sale at public vendue, at the house now occupied by Samuel B. Thompson, commonly called the Washington Hotel, in Lockport, 11 August 1828. Dated June 24th, 1828. JOHN PHILLIPS, Sheriff.

Article no. 55   Subject: Advertisement
Ref. June 26, 1828; pg. 3, col. 6

TO JOURNEYMEN SHOEMAKERS.

Wanted, immediately, two good Workmen, to whom liberal wages will be given. Those who work at sewed work, would be preferred. Apply opposite the Lower Locks to O.H. COTTON. Lockport, June 19, 1828.

Article no. 56   Subject: Notice
Ref. June 26, 1828; pg. 4, col. 5

Extract: DEFAULT having been made in the payment of a certain sum of money, secured to be paid by a certain indenture of mortgage, dated 9 August 1826, executed by Carlos B. Woodward and Wareham M. Woodward, to one Cotton Nash, and by the said Cotton Nash duly assigned to the subscriber, Notice is hereby given, that by virtue of a power in the said mortgage contained, the premises described in said mortgage, and described therein as follows, viz.—All that certain tract or parcel of land, situate in the village of Lockport, in the county of Niagara, being part of village lot No. Six, bounded as follows—{Notice includes description of boundaries} [bounded, in part, by James M'Kean Junior's west line, and to south line of land owned by Carlos B. Woodward and Corydon C. Woodward]—containing about one eighth of an acre of land, more or less—will be sold at public vendue, at the house now occupied by William Hughes, called the Mansion House, in Lockport, 1 December 1828. Dated June 3d, 1828.

GEORGE REYNALE, Assignee.

Article no. 57   Subject: Notice
Ref. June 26, 1828; pg. 4, col. 5

Extract: DEFAULT having been made in the payment of a certain sum of money, secured to be paid by a certain indenture of mortgage, bearing date 25 December 1827, executed by Moses H. Buck (then of the town of Lockport, county of Niagara,) to Homer Kimberly, of the same place—Notice is hereby given, that by virtue of a power contained in said mortgage, and in pursuance of the statute in such case made and provided, the mortgage premises which are described in said mortgage, and, as follows to wit:—{Notice includes description of land, in the village of Lockport, being part of lot sixteen, &c.} [surveyed by Jesse P. Haines, Surveyor,] containing more or less, together with all and singular the appurtenances, hereditaments and improvements thereunto belonging or appertaining, will be sold at public auction or vendue, at the tavern now occupied by Samuel Thompson, called the Washington House, in the village of Lockport, 8 November 1828. Dated 20th May, 1828.

HOMER KIMBERLY.

By E. RANSOM, Jun., his Att'y.

Article no. 58   Subject: Advertisement
Ref. June 26, 1828; pg. 4, col. 5

Extract: American Cough Drops.

A celebrated remedy for Colds, Coughs, Asthma, and Consumptions. Scarce a case of diseased lungs occurs but may be cured by a timely application of this remedy. The proprietor does not warrant it to be a specific, but is satisfied that it approaches nearer to one than any thing of the kind which has come under his observation: it has been very extensively used, and with extraordinary success in the practice of eminent physicians. It does not like some remedies relieve for a time or only while using, but has a direct operation upon the lungs, and after using a sufficient time restores them to a healthy action. {Advert includes two testimonials or "certificates."}

N.B. This medicine is prepared from American Plants. To prevent imposition, observe that "American Cough Drops" are stamped on the bottles, and the directions signed J. Edwards.

Southmayd & Boardman, Wholesale Agents, Middletown, Conn. will supply Druggists on favourable terms. This Medicine for sale at the store of Samuel DE VEAUX. Niagara Falls, 1828.

Article no. 59   Subject: Notice
Ref. June 26, 1828; pg. 4, col. 6

BY ORDER of Hiram Gardner, Esq., Judge of the Court of Common Pleas in and for the county of Niagara, Counsellor at Law, &c., Notice is hereby given to all the creditors of Augustus Tyler, of the town of Wilson, in the county of Niagara, an insolvent debtor, to show cause, if any they have, before the said Judge, at his office in the Village of Lockport, on the nineteenth day of July next, at ten o'clock in the forenoon, why an assignment of the said insolvent's estate should not be made, and his person be exempted from imprisonment, pursuant to the act entitled "An act to abolish imprisonment for debt in certain cases," passed April 7, 1819. Dated this 26th day of May, 1828.

Article no. 60   Subject: Advertisement
Ref. July 3, 1828; pg. 1, col. 5

PINE LUMBER.

The subscribers are now receiving from Canada, a quantity of first rate Pine Lumber. They will keep a supply of the article through the season.

Dry Goods, Groceries, Crockery, and Hardware—
A splendid assortment—selling cheap.
June 26. G.W. ROGERS & Co.

Article no. 61   Subject: Religion
Ref. July 3, 1828; pg. 2, col. 4

Extract: From the *Cazenovia Monitor*.

At a meeting of several members of the Methodist Episcopal Church, in the town of Eaton, Madison co., 14 June 1828—Br. Solomon Root was chosen chairman, and John Kearn secretary. The object for which the meeting was called, was to address the Genesee Conference, at their next sitting, in behalf of said church, on the subject of Speculative Free Masonry. The following address and resolutions were unanimously agreed to {Article includes list of resolutions, a citation by the Rev. Adam Clarke re: Matt. V. 37; and, an address from A. Morton of Adams, N.Y., who mentioned the outrages that were committed on Capt. Wm. Morgan, terminating in his death.}

Article no. 62   Subject: Politics
Ref. July 3, 1828; pg. 2, col. 6

In our paper of to-day, will be found the Notice of the Anti-Masonic Central Committee of this County, calling a Convention of Delegates on the 18th inst. to nominate suitable persons to represent us at the State Convention, to be holden at Utica, on the 4th August next. We trust the friends of the good cause, in the different towns, will be on the alert to appoint their representatives to the county Convention. [Transcriber's note: This article appears in the Editorial columns.]

Article no. 63   Subject: Court
Ref. July 3, 1828; pg. 3, col. 2

The Court of Oyer and Terminer for Middlesex, Justice Ford presiding, has just closed its session in New Brunswick. On Monday last came on the trial of George B. Germain, for the murder, a short time, since, of Robert Titus. The cause, after argument, and an able and ingenious defence of the prisoner, was submitted to the Jury on Monday night, between 9 and 10 o'clock, and at 2 o'clock on Tuesday they came in with a verdict of guilty. He was sentenced to be executed on Friday the 8th day of August next.

Article no. 64   Subject: Court
Ref. July 3, 1828; pg. 3, col. 2

At the Court of Oyer and Terminer of Jefferson, held on the 20th inst. Henry Evans was convicted of the wilful murder of Joshua Rogers, and sentenced to be executed on the 22d day of August next.

It is probably in the recollection of our readers, that this man, in April last, killed two men, Joshua Rogers, and Henry Dimond, with an axe, and severely wounded a third, Wilbur Rogers, with the same deadly instrument.

The grand jury found bills against Evans, for each murder—he was only tried for one, for the murder of Rogers. The defence set up was, that Evans was acting on the defensive, having been informed that the intention of these men was to turn him and his family out of his house and massacre them. This was not however sustained by the evidence; no proof whatever being given of any forcible attempt against the prisoner. The sentence of the law was delayed, in order to give the prisoner an opportunity to apply to the Supreme Court, for their opinion, on the points raised by his counsel, in the course of the trial.—*Albany Daily Advertiser*.

Article no. 65   Subject: Politics
Ref. July 3, 1828; pg. 3, col. 4

ANTI-MASONIC COUNTY CONVENTION.

A Convention to consist of three delegates from each town in the county of Niagara, to be chosen by the inhabitants of the respective towns, opposed to Secret Societies, will be held at the house of Samuel Jennings, in the village of Lockport, on the 18th day of July inst. at 1 o'clock P.M. for the purpose of electing two delegates to represent this county in the Anti-Masonic State Convention, to be held at Utica on the 4th day of August next; and to transact such other business as may be deemed advisable.

WM. C. HOUSE,
ELIAKIM HAMMON,
ELIAS RANSOM, JR.
Anti-Masonic Central Committee.

The Central Committee respectfully invite the inhabitants of the several towns to meet and choose their delegates at an early day, and hope the Convention will be fully attended.

Article no. 66   Subject: Notice
Ref. July 3, 1828; pg. 3, col. 4

STOP THEIF [sic].

Stolen from the subscriber, in Royalton, Niagara county, on the evening of the 28th June, a large Brown Horse, 7 years old, with a white stripe the whole length of the face, part of the under lip white, one or both the hind feet white, one fore foot ancle [sic] crooked, switched tail, and is what is termed a "Reginal" horse. Fifteen Dollars will be paid for the horse alone, and Twenty-five Dollars re the theif [sic]—and all reasonable charges allowed.

JOSHUA SLAYTON. Royalton, July 3, 1828.

The publisher of the "*Gleaner*," U.C. is requested to insert the above three times, and forward his account to this office for payment.

Article no. 67   Subject: Notice
Ref. July 3, 1828; pg. 3, col. 4

NOTICE.

Strayed or stolen from the commons in this Village, about the 20th June, a Bright Bay Mare—short switch tail, ten or twelve years old, about fifteen hands high, rather low in flesh and no shoes on. Whoever will return said Mare, or give information where she may be found, shall be liberally rewarded.

RUFUS FANNING. Lewiston, June 30th, 1828.

Article no. 68   Subject: Notice
Ref. July 3, 1828; pg. 3, col. 4

NOTICE.

Taken up by the subscriber, on Sunday last, a Bay Mare, about 14 or 15 years old. The owner can have her by proving property, and paying charges.

MOSES BARNUM. Pendleton, June 27th, 1828.

Article no. 69   Subject: Notice
Ref. July 3, 1828; pg. 3, col. 4

Extract: List of letters remaining in the Post-Office at Lockport, N.Y. July 1st, 1828. [List of names, below.] N.B. Persons calling for any of the above letters, are requested to say they are advertised. G.H. Boughton, P.M.

Adams, David	Allen, Alphonso S.
Austin, James L.	Baker, Jonas
Barber, John	Barker, Abraham
Barnard, F.J.	Barnes, Collins W.
Barnum, Oris	Bass, William
Bates, Joseph S.	Bathgate, Simeon
Baxter, Eraud	Bell, Charles
Benedict, Ira	Bibbins, Joseph
Blanchard, Lovina	Blanck, Jonas
Brackenridge, Maria	Brang, Jacob
Brown, James	Bush, Stephen
Butler, D.	Calkins, James
Carl, David	Carpenter, Warren
Carr, Betsey	Clark, Erasmus D.
Clements, Whitford	Clinton, Samuel
Collins, Joseph	Compton, Randolph
Corwin, Phineas H.	Cotton, O.H.
Craig, John	Crane, Amos
Crocker, Luther	Cross, Stephen
Cudworth, David	Cullings, James
Currier, James	Curtis, Alonson
Dauchy, Wallace	Davidson, John
Davis, Lodowick L.	Doshon, Julia
Doud, Eber	Eddy, David
Edgerton, Norman	Ellsworth, Henry
Foot, Oliver	Foster, Edmund

Fowler, William
Freeman, Joel
Gaskill, George B.
Gibbs, Dan M.
Gould, Joel
Groves, Elijah
Hall, Mr.
Haven, John W.
Hawkins, Ira B.
Hawley, George
Hill, Orson
Himman, Charles
Hopkins, George
Hudson, Abraham
Hurd, Justus L.
Jenks, Abuer
Jenney, Justus
Jennings, Samuel
Johnson, Bennet
Kelley, Milton
Kidder, Hiram
Kimberley, H.
Kinsley, William
Laing, Thomas
Lathrop, N.D.
Lay, Hannah
Lemman, Ezekiel
Leslie, David
Leyburn, John
Lusk, Solomon
Matthews, Mr.
McMonagle, John
Miles, Lewis T.
Moore, John
Nelson, Charles C.
Newman, William
Northam, Festus
Olney, Whipple
Palmer, Jedediah
Parmenter, Joseph
Pattison, Elisha
Pease, Oliver C.
Phinney, Elijah G.
Pollay, Matthew
Price, Mr.
Prought, Nancy
Randall, Hose B.
Reynolds, Henry
Richards, Roswell M.
Robbins, Lysander
Root, Asahel, jun.
Ross, Wilber
Sage, Mary A.
Fox, Bryan
Garlick, Reuben
Geer, Elisha
Golden, John Y.
Graves, Frederick U.
Hackett, Joshua
Hall, Nathaniel
Haviland, Charles
Hawks, Paul
Hay, Daniel
Hillyard, William
Hollenback, Matthew
Houghton, John
Hughes, Susannah
Ingols, S.S.
Jenks, Almer
Jennings, John E.
Johnson, Doctor
Kelley, James
Kent, William
Kimball, Arial
King, James
Kizer, Coonrad
Lane, Jason
Lawrence, George A.
Leavenworth, Samuel
Lenox, Catharine
Lewis, Eason
Locke, Thomas P.
Lutten, Linus
Maynard, Joseph
Mighells, Florington
Millerd, Hiram
Moore, Levi, jun.
Nelson, Francis
Niles, John
Olds, George
Otis, James H.
Parker, Charles
Parsons, Oliver
Pearce, Ellis F., jun.
Peck, John A.
Pierce, Tisdale B.
Porter, Joel G.
Priest, A.
Quade, Christopher
Randall, Joseph
Rice, Levi
Richardson, F.G.
Rogers, John
Ross, Armintus
Rowe, Stephen
Saunders, M.O.
Scarborough, G.
Sears, Barnabas
Shaver, John P.
Shields, Andrew
Silsby, M.
Sitterington, John S.
Sloan, John
Smith, Americus
Smith, Edward J.
Snyder, John
Stahler, Isaiah
Stevens, Justus
Taylor, Levi
Thrall, Z.P.
Tibbles, Joseph C.
Tracy, Eber
Walker, Nathan
Warner, James
Warner, Jonathan
West, David
Wichell, Elder
Willits, Richard
Wilts, William H.
Woodward, Carloss B.
Scobey, John A.
Sharp, Augustus
Sherman, William
Sill, Mary
Simonds, Silas
Slade, Aaron
Smita, Aliezer
Smith, Benjamin C.
Smith, Stephen
Stahl, John
Stark, W.R.
Stranks, James
Thomss [sic], Giles B.
Thurston, Joseph
Tillotson, Turner
Tucker & Price, Messrs.
Walker & Matthews, Messrs.
Warner, James M.
Webster, Caleb
Whaley, Joshua
Williams, Eliakim
Wilmarth, Daniel
Woodard, Roswell

Article no. 70	Subject: Notice
Ref. July 3, 1828; pg. 3, col. 5	

Extract: List of letters remaining in the Post Office at Lewiston, N.Y. on the 1st day of July 1828. [List of names, below.] N.B. Persons calling for the above letters, will please say they are advertised. Bates Cook, P.M.

Anderson, Elizabeth W.
Barber, J.M.
Birdsall, Benjamin
Childs, Stephen
Churchill, Otis
Cooper, Jesse
Cusick, James
Denison, Joseph
Dimmack, Brown
Earl, David
Feenan, James
Firth, Thomas
Grinnell, George F.
Harvey, Ursen
Holmes, Leister
Hosley, J.G.
Houk, David
Howell, Col.
Jacob, Stephen
Kelly, Isaac
Lattee, John
Andrus, Asahel
Bellack, Asahel
Bronson, Mr.
Chubbuck, Samuel
Coffin, Catherine
Crooks, John
Davis, George
Dickerson, Alexander
Dunkin, Titus
Fairchild, Stephen
Firman, William
Garrison, Abraham
Hardy, Bodney H.N.
Holderman, Mr.
Holway, Sarah
Hotchkiss, Mr.
Howay, Thomas
Irwin, Arthur
Jonley, Samuel
Kent, Joseph D.P.
McLeland, William

Mehene, George
Mohr, Daniel
Mullon, James
Owen, J.P.
Pool, Aikish
Rew, William
Root, Martin
Ryen, Frank
Scarborough, John
Shepard, Ephraim
Spencer, Micha
Stone, Solomon
Sutherland, Joseph
Totton, Sally
Truman, Jacob L.
Tyler, Ebenezer F.
Wadsworth, Chester
Warren, Thomas
Weaver, Laury
Willcox, George
Willson, John
Wright, Shearman
Miller, Henry
Morehouse, Samuel
Osmer, Horace
Park, Doctor
Raymond, Caleb
Reynolds, Henry
Ross, Alanson
Sage, Sparrow S.
Seeley, Henry
Smith, Joseph
Stevenson, James
Story, Andrew
Toole, Mary S.
Townson & Bronson, Messrs.
Tryon, Amos S.
Tyler, Isaac B.
Warren, David
Washburn, —, Esq.
Willcox, Almira
Williams, Moses
Woodruff and Hotchkiss, Messrs.
Root, Chauncey
Sechler, William M.
Stocker, Aaron
Sylvant, John
Tyler, Joel
Wall, John
Williams, James
Worthington, Samuel
Ross, Samuel, Dr.
Sheldon, Elijah
Stuart, Ezekiel
Titus, Cornelius
Volentine, James
Wheeler, Noah
Worthington, Abijal B.

Article no. 72 Subject: Notice
Ref. July 3, 1828; pg. 3, col. 6

Extract: List of letters remaining in the Post Office at Niagara Falls, July 1, 1828. [List of names, below.] A. Porter, P.M.

Adams, Moses M.
Barnes, A., Miss
Bower, Benaverd B.
Bronson, William
Cabot, E.L., Miss
Cabot, Samuel
Comen, Jonathan
Crandal, Oliver
Forbs, Abraham
Gaylord, Theodosia
Green, Gardner
Green, Sarah, Miss
Grifin, William
McKnitt, Benjamin
Morrison, George
Pardee, Hannah A.
Pierce, Gad
Riff, John
Sark, E.
West, Ira
Whitewell, Samuel
Wiltsie, William H.
Workman, James
Allen, Gerald
Bomen, W.
Bradnor, William
Burr, Sally
Cabot, S.C., Miss
Charlow, Charles
Crandal, Eliza
Crawford, Isaac
Frost, James
Glime, Frederick
Green, Martha, Miss
Greenwood, Charles
Irwin, Charles
Mills, Fredus A.
Paine, Hiram
Peck, Theophilus
Rice, Gilbert
Salisbury, P.
Wellman, Emily
Whitcom, Amos
Whitney, P.
Worden, Thomas

Article no. 71 Subject: Notice
Ref. July 3, 1828; pg. 3, col. 5

Extract: List of letters remaining in the Post-Office at Royalton, Niagara co., N.Y. 30th June, 1828. [List of names, below.] G. Reynale, P.M.

Allen, Russel
Barton, Mr.
Burr, Miranda
Carrington, McRalsamon
Church, Alexander
Cook, Horace
Davis, Moses
Depuy, Rebecca, Mrs.
Driggs, Starbing, Miss
Farman, Benjamin F.
Ford, Gideon
Greenman, William
Harton, Henry W.
Heveland, Jumes
Isengham, Michael
Knight, Almira
Lee, Daniel O.
Marcy, George
McNall, John
Orton, Myron
Perry, Demas
Porter, Charles
Remele, Jacob
Roberts, Lemuel
Barmen, Nathaniel
Boots, Joseph
Carrington, Asa
Chubbock, Elijah
Clapp, Daniel
Dack, Truman
Depuy, Jacob
Depuy, William
Empry, Francis N.
Fenn, D.S., jun.
Graves, Martha M., Miss
Halcomb, Mehitable
Harwood, Maria
Holden, Anna C., Miss
Jones, William
Knox, Eligah
Makee, Abijal, Miss
McCormack, John
Merritt, John
Perrin, Stephen
Pixley, James
Ranny, Wells
Remely, Jacob
Roberts, William

Article no. 73 Subject: Notice
Ref. July 3, 1828; pg. 3, col. 6

Extract: List of letters remaining in the Post Office at Pendleton, June 30, 1828. [List of names, below.] S.P. Clarke, P.M.

Ashley, Sarah
Bissell, Daniel
Hall, Jonathan J.
Lewis, Ambrose
McNitt, Hiram
Syks, Emeline
Bartholomew, Bradley B.
Folger, Daniel
Henderson, James
Loomis, Alanson
Spooner, Stephen
Van Vothenburgh, Lambert

Article no. 74   Subject: Notice
Ref. July 3, 1828; pg. 3, col. 6

Extract: List of letters remaining in the Post Office at Youngstown, July 1, 1828. [List of names, below.] A. G. Hinman, P.M.

Armstrong, Bartholomew	Blincea, John
Brown, John	Brown, Thomas
Compton, Randolph	Crysler, Ralph M.
Doty, Ferris	Estes, Andrew
Force, David	Fowler, Joseph
Gardner, Samuel	Harrington, Uriah
King, William	McBride, Patrick
Morrison, David	Morrison, John
Ousterhout, Jeremiah	Parker, Huldah
Perry, Jonathan C.	Pierce, William L.
Putman, Christopher	Quadee, Christopher
Roberts, James T.M.	Seele, Shubal
Swain, Isaac, jun.	Thompson, John
Thompson, Seymour	Welch, William
Williams, Stephen G.	

Article no. 75   Subject: Notice
Ref. July 3, 1828; pg. 3, col. 6

Extract: List of letters remaining in the Post Office at Middle Port, July 1, 1828. [List of names, below.] James Northam, P.M.

Baker, Mr.	Bullock, Job D.
Chase, Franklin	Craig, Mr.
Craig, John	Crapsey, Jacob
Dunlap & Craig, Messrs.	Gordon, Silas W.
Lyon, Amos	Mills, Edward
Pinney, Ovid	Pratt, Samuel
Robinson, William	Sawyer, Nathan
Stevens, Phineas R.	

Article no. 76   Subject: Notice
Ref. July 3, 1828; pg. 3, col. 6

Extract: BY virtue of an Execution, issued from the Clerk's office of the County, against the goods and chattels, lands and tenements of Harvey Slayton, to me directed and delivered, I have seized and taken all that certain tract of land situate in the town of Royalton, being part of Lot No. 9, in the 4th section of township 14, and 6th range of the Holland purchase, and bounded and described as follows, viz:—{Notice includes description of land}—containing one acre and one hundred and thirty rods, more or less, I shall sell at public auction, at the Hotel kept by Samuel Jennings, in the town of Lockport, 16 August 1828. Dated Lockport, July 2, 1828.
JOHN PHILLIPS, Sheriff.

Article no. 77   Subject: Notice
Ref. July 3, 1828; pg. 3, col. 6

BY virtue of several Executions, two of which were issued from the Supreme Court of Judicature of the State of New-York, and the Court of Common Pleas of the County of Niagara, against the goods and chattels, lands and tenements of Allen Skinner, I have taken all the goods and chattels, together with the following described piece of land, situate [and] being in the town of Lockport, known as Village Lot number twenty-four, on the south side of Main Street on the east side of the Erie Canal; being one chain wide in front, along said Main Street, and eztending [sic] back two chains thirty-seven and a half links, be the same more or less. Reference, for a more particular description, may be had to a map of a part of said village of Lockport, filed in the Clerk's Office of the said County—all of which I shall expose to sale at public vendue on the 15th day of August next, at 1 o'clock in the afternoon, at the Mansion House in the village of Lockport.—Dated July 2, 1823.
ELI BRUCE, Late Sheriff.

Article no. 78   Subject: Advertisement
Ref. August 21, 1828; pg. 1, col. 1

Removal.
JOSEPH CENTER, Attorney at Law, has removed his Office to the new building adjoining the Post-Office, in the village of Lockport. July 17.

Article no. 79   Subject: Advertisement
Ref. August 21, 1828; pg. 1, col. 1

DRUGS, MEDICINES, &c.
JOHN WINER has just received a choice and genuine assortment of Drugs, Medicines, Paints, Oils, Dye woods, Dye stuffs and Groceries, &c., which will be sold as cheap for cash as at any other establishment of the kind in the country. J.W. solicits physicians and others to call and examine for themselves, before purchasing elsewhere.
Lewiston, July 10.

Article no. 80   Subject: Advertisement
Ref. August 21, 1828; pg. 1, col. 2

JOHN YOUNG
Has recently received his annual supply of Goods from England, to the amount of $100,000, which he will sell at from 30 to 50 per cent. cheaper than can be afforded in the adjacent parts of the state of New-York.

His primary object is the wholesale business, but for the accommodation of the public, he will sell by retail at a small advance above his wholesale prices.
Niagara, U.C. July 14, 1828.

Article no. 81 Subject: Notice
Ref. August 21, 1828; pg. 1, col. 2

Partnership Dissolved.

THE Copartnership heretofore existing under the firm of Smith & Gardner, Smith & Bancroft, and Smith, Bancroft & Co. in the manufacturing of Window Sash and Pails, is this day dissolved by mutual consent. As their wants imperiously demand cash, those indebted are requested to call at the Sash Factory, and settle their respective accounts, with W.P. Smith and W. Bancroft, who are duly authorised to attend to the same.

ISAAC GARDNER,
WILEY BANCROFT,
Wm. P. SMITH.
Lockport, July 17th, 1828.

The manufacturing of Window Sash will be continued at the Old Stand by the subscriber, agent for the Proprietors. WILEY BANCROFT. July 17, 1828.

Article no. 82 Subject: Advertisement
Ref. August 21, 1828; pg. 1, col. 2

WILLIAM FOX.
Barber and Hair-Dresser.

Still continues his busines [sic] at his old stand, directly opposite the Mansion-House, where he will be found at all times in readiness to wait on those who may be disposed to favour him with their custom.

Razors honed and set as usual.
Lockport, July 31, 1828.

Article no. 83 Subject: Notice
Ref. August 21, 1828; pg. 1, col. 3

Dissolution.

The copartnership heretofore existing under the firm of S. & W. PARSONS, is this day dissolved by mutual consent. All persons indebted to the firm are called upon to make immediate payment (special contracts excepted) to William Parsons, who is hereby duly authorized to settle all debts due said firm.

SETH PARSONS, WILLIAM PARSONS.
Lockport, Aug. 6, 1828.

Article no. 84 Subject: Notice
Ref. August 21, 1828; pg. 1, col. 3

LOST,

Some time within a few weeks, a due-bill for fifty dollars, dated some time in the beginning of May, and payable some time about the 8th of September, drawn by Jared Comstock, Sen. in favour of John Howder, or bearer. Whoever may have found said due-bill, will confer a favour on the subscriber by returning it; and shall receive a liberal reward.

JOHN HOWDER. Town of Cambria, Aug. 1, 1828.

Article no. 85 Subject: Notice
Ref. August 21, 1828; pg. 1, col. 3

CAUTION.

Whereas the subscriber, some time since gave a certain note of hand to a person by the name of Isaac Briggs, payable in February next, for the sum of twenty dollars; this is therefore to caution all persons from purchasing said note, as the contract, in consideration of which it was given, having never been fulfilled by said Briggs, I am determined not to pay the same.

BENJAMIN HEWITT.
Town of Lewiston, Aug. 1st, 1828.

Article no. 86 Subject: Notice
Ref. August 21, 1828; pg. 1, col. 3

LOST,

On Sunday or Monday last, between the village of Lockport and Slayton's Settlement, a Red Morocco Wallet, somewhat worn, containing an order drawn on the Subscriber by Otis Hathaway in favour of Dan Aikin, for 50 dollars; a note for $3, signed by Lyman Livingsworth, in favour of Hiram Griffiths; a number of other orders and notes, and sundry receipts, of no use to any person but the owner; and as is believed, some money. Whoever returns said Wallet, with its contents, either to the Subscriber, in the village of Lockport, or at the *Courier* Office, will be liberally rewarded. D.S. ALVERSON. July 31, 1828.

Article no. 87 Subject: Notice
Ref. August 21, 1828; pg. 1, col. 3

Extract: POST-OFFICE NOTICE. Lockport, July 1st, 1828. {Notice includes information about daily closures of the Eastern and Western Mails, and Mails for Batavia (by way of Royalton Centre and Gerrysville), Tonawanta (by way of Pendleton), Niagara Falls (by way of Mountain Ridge), and New Fane (Wright's P.O.).}

G.H. BOUGHTON, P.M.

Article no. 88 Subject: Notice
Ref. August 21, 1828; pg. 1, col. 3

Extract: POST-OFFICE NOTICE. Lewiston, Niagara county, N.Y. May 8, 1828. {Notice includes information about daily closures of the Eastern, Western and Northern mails, and the mails for Lockport (by way of Mountain Ridge) and Queenston, U.C.} This is a direct and expeditious route to the different parts of Canada.

BATES COOKE, P.M.

Article no. 89 Subject: Advertisement
Ref. August 21, 1828; pg. 1, col. 3

FOR SALE.

The subscriber now offers for sale a valuable Lot of Land, containing four and one half acres, situate on the south side of Main-st. and east of the village of Lockport, known as the former residence of John Comstock. The above mentioned Lot will be sold cheap, and the terms made easy for purchasers. For particulars inquire of the subscriber on the premises.

BENJ. K. CRANDELL. Lockport, July 24th, 1828.

Article no. 90	Subject: Advertisement
Ref. August 21, 1828; pg. 1, col. 4	

MERCHANDIZING!

The subscriber having purchased the entire stock of the late firm of S. & W. Parsons, now offers a handsome assortment of   GOODS,

upon the most reasonable terms, for Cash.

He will also receive in exchange for Goods, Staves, Wheat, Rye, Corn, Oats, Butter, Cheese, White Beans, &c.

The subscriber is fully satisfied that the course he is determined to pursue will prove satisfactory to both buyer and seller. He solicits a share of public patronage, assuring those who may favour him with their custom, that they shall not go away dissatisfied, as he will sell goods at a small advance on cost.

SETH PARSONS. Lockport, Aug. 6, 1828.

Article no. 91	Subject: Notice
Ref. August 21, 1828; pg. 1, col. 4	

PUBLIC VENDUE.

To be sold at public vendue, at the House of David Chapman, in the village of Manchester, on the 27th of September next, at 2 o'clock P.M. an Article of Land, the property of Ezekiel Hill of Niagara, deceased; distinguished by west part of Lot No. 21, ninth Range, containing twenty-five and a half acres, be the same more or less. This Lot of Land is good, and lies about one mile and a half from the village of Manchester, with three acres cleared and fenced, the rest well timbered.

ABRAHAM WITMER, Executor.
Niagara, Aug. 9th, 1828.

Article no. 92	Subject: Notice
Ref. August 21, 1828; pg. 1, col. 4	

Fair Warning!

All persons indebted to the late firm of S. & W. PARSONS, are hereby respectfully called upon for settlement and payment.

I hope this notice will be sufficient, as I have recourse to law with great reluctance.

WILLIAM PARSONS. August 14, 1828.

Article no. 93	Subject: Politics
Ref. August 21, 1828; pg. 1, col. 5	

Extract: Anti-Masonic.
From the *Anti-Masonic Enquirer*.

At a Convention of Anti-Masonic Delegates from the different counties of the state, held at the Baptist church in the village of Utica on the 4th of August, 1828, prayer by Deacon Jonathan Olmstead, the following proceedings were had. ... The resolutions adopted by the Le Roy convention in March last were then read. The following resolutions were adopted: {Article included list of resolutions.} Mr. Whittlesey reported an Address from James Hawks, President, which was read and universally adopted {Article includes the address}. [Length of news article, 7-1/2 columns.]

[Transcriber's note: Refer to key for numbered codes at the end of this list.]

- Abbey, Seth A.; Jefferson County, New York; Secretary of the Convention.
- Arnold, Andrew; Livingston County, New York
- Babcock, Charles; Oneida County, New York
- Babcock, Elijah; Otsego County, New York
- Backus, Frederick F.; County not stated, New York (1)
- Bacon, Nathaniel; Onondaga County, New York
- Ballou, Russell; Chenango County, New York
- Bascom, Ansel; Seneca County, New York (2)
- Beekman, Thomas; Madison County, New York (2)
- Bernard, David, Elder; Utica, New York; his book entitled, *Light on Masonry, &c. &c.*, was read to the Convention.
- Buel, Jonathan; Ontario County, New York
- Butler, Asa; Otsego County, New York
- Canfield, William; Ontario County, New York
- Carter, Eleazer; Cayuga County, New York
- Cary, Trumbull; Genesee County, New York
- Caten, Leonard; Onondaga County, New York
- Childs, Timothy; Monroe County, New York (2) (3)
- Clarke, Thomas E.; Oneida County, New York
- Collins, Joseph; Chenango County, New York
- Comstock, William, jun.; Otsego County, New York
- Cooke, Bates; Niagara County, New York (2) (3)
- Coon, Samuel H.; Madison County, New York
- Crandall, John G.; Monroe County, New York
- Crary, John; Washington County, New York; nominated as candidate for the office of Lieutenant-Governor of the state of New York.
- Davis, George; Montgomery County, New York (2)
- Dean, James; Oneida County, New York (4)
- Dixon, Moses; Cayuga County, New York
- Dunham, Shubael; Genesee County, New York
- Ely, Harvey; County not stated, New York (1)
- Farrel, Israel; Chenango County, New York
- Ferguson, William; Oneida County, New York

- Field, Thomas F.; Oneida County, New York
- Fitch, Timothy; Genesee County, New York (4)
- French, John; Oneida County, New York
- Gillett, Daniel M.; Madison County, New York
- Granger, Francis; Ontario County, New York; nominated as candidate for the office of Governor of the state of New York.
- Green, Thomas C.; Saratoga County, New York (2)
- Green, Thomas G.; Saratoga County, New York; Secretary of the Anti-Masonic Convention.
- Guthrie, Alfred; Jefferson County, New York (2)
- Hall, Nathaniel; Madison County, New York
- Hard, Gideon; Orleans County, New York (2)
- Hascall, John; Genesee County, New York
- Hawks, James, Hon.; Otsego County, New York; President of the Convention.
- Hawks, William; Oswego County, New York (2)
- Hazeltine, Laban; Chatauque County, New York (2)
- Hopkins, Josiah; Cayuga County, New York
- Hoskins, Laban; Cayuga County, New York
- Humphrey, Samuel; Albany County, New York (2)
- Jenks, Nathan; Ontario County, New York
- Lacy, Samuel; Monroe County, New York
- Lewis, Thomas; Tompkins County, New York (2)
- Love, Thomas C.; Eric County, New York (2)
- M'Alister, A.; Oneida County, New York
- M'Allister, A.; Utica, New York (2)
- Marvin, Mather; Seneca County, New York
- Mason, Jonathan; Ontario County, New York
- Miller, David C.; Genesee County, New York
- Moffatt, Isaac, jun.; Jefferson County, New York
- Morris, Charles; Oneida County, New York
- Morris, John C.; Otsego County, New York (3) (4)
- Mower, Timothy; Ontario County, New York
- Olmstead, Jonathan, Deacon; Madison County, New York; said prayer before the proceedings commenced.
- Parsoll, Henry, jun.; Cayuga County, New York (2)
- Peck, Calvin; Onondaga County, New York (2)
- Peckham, John S.; Oneida County, New York
- Percival, James; Livingston County, New York (2)
- Pierce, Nathan; Ontario County, New York (2)
- Ransom, Elias, jun.; Niagara County, New York
- Read, Herbert A.; Genesee County, New York (2) (3) Mr. Read read the Royal Arch degree in a plain, clear and distinct manner, and also the Knights of the Christian Mark, and Guards of the Conclave.
- Richardson, Israel J.; Wayne County, New York (2)
- Richardson, William P.; Wayne County, New York
- Robison, James; Seneca County, New York
- Sheldon, Alexander; Montgomery County, New York (4)
- Sheldon, Milton; Monroe County, New York
- Sheppard, Morris F.; Yates County, New York (2)
- Smith, Joseph; Eric County, New York
- Southwick, Solomon; Albany County, New York
- Steele, Theophilus; Oneida County, New York
- Stockham, Samuel S.; Onondaga County, New York
- Stoddard, I.N.; Oneida County, New York
- Sumner, James; Montgomery County, New York
- Sweet, S.N.; Jefferson County, New York
- Talbot, Theodore F.; Monroe County, New York (4)
- Utter, William; Otsego County, New York (2)
- Van Dyke, Benjamin W.; Orleans County, New York
- Waters, Russell; Chenango County, New York (2)
- Weed, Thurlow; County not stated, New York (1)
- Whittlesey, Frederick; Monroe County, New York (1) (3)
- Williams, Thomas; Oneida County, New York
- Works, Samuel; County not stated, New York (1)

Key:
(1) appointed to the general Central Committee of the State of New-York.
(2) appointed to a committee of one from each county represented, to report what measures ought to be adopted to counteract the influence and destroy the existence of masonic societies.
(3) appointed to a committee of five, to prepare an address to the people of this state.
(4) appointed to a committee of five to draft resolutions expressive of the sense of this meeting in relation to freemasonry.

Article no. 94   Subject: Politics
Ref. August 21, 1828; pg. 2, col. 6

From the *Le Roy Gazette*.
TO THE PUBLIC.

Having been a member of the masonic institution for more than thirty years, and having become thoroughly convinced of the impious nature of its principles, ceremonies and obligations, I feel impelled by a solemn impression of duty to God and man to declare to the world that I from this time henceforth and for ever renounce all fealty and disclaim all attachment to the order. I am now seventy-three years of age, and by the blessing of God, still retain my mental vigor; I was a soldier in the revolutionary war, and am now a professor of religion in the Methodist connexion. I united with the Free-masons in Colchester, (Conn.) where I took three degrees, and afterward took the degree of Mark Master in Pollett Lodge, (Vermont.) I have heretofore felt myself so bound to the institution, that I have hardly dared to think freely upon it, and it was not until a late perusal of a discourse by the Rev. Reuben Sanborn, entitled, "Free-masonry a Covenant with Death," that I had my eyes fully opened to the subject. I might perhaps have been convinced before, were it not that I refused to read anti-masonic papers, books, &c. I now heartily [sic] recommend to my brethren and others who are masons to take measures to inform themselves upon the subject, and see whether in upholding masonry they be not found fighting against God.

JOHN LAW. Le Roy, August 11, 1828.

Article no. 95   Subject: Politics
Ref. August 21, 1828; pg. 3, col. 3

In our last we alluded to a letter which it was said Mr. Adams had written to Mr. Oliver Heartwell of Canandaigua, and in which it was alleged he explicitly denied that he was a mason. We have accordingly given the letter in question in our paper of this day; and trust that it will for ever put to rest the charge that he is a mason: a charge solely got up for electioneering purposes.

COPY.

"Washington, 18th April, 1828.
OLIVER HEARTWELL, Esq. Canandaigua, N.Y.

Sir—In answer to your inquiry in your letter of the 31st ult. I state that I am not, never was, and never shall be, a Free Mason. I give you this answer, in the spirit of friendly return to the kindness with which you have made the inquiry. But unwilling to contribute in any manner to that excitement produced by the mysterious abduction and too probable murder of William Morgan, I request you not to give publicity to this letter. The deep and solemn feeling which pervades the community on this occasion, is founded on the purest principles of human virtue and of human rights. In the just and lawful pursuit of a signal vindication of the laws of nature and of the land, violated in his person, which has been undertaken and is yet in progress, with the authority and co-operation of your legislature, I hope and trust that the sufferer will temper with the spirit of justice, the reparation of her wrongs, and in the infliction of every penalty carefully abstain from visiting upon the innocent the misdeeds of the guilty.

I am with respect, your fellow citizen.
J.Q. ADAMS.

Article no. 96   Subject: Politics
Ref. August 21, 1828; pg. 3, col. 5

Anti-Masonic Senatorial Convention.

An Anti-Masonic Convention of delegates from the several counties in the 8th Senatorial District, will be held at the Eagle Tavern, in Batavia, Genesee county, on the 17th day of September next, at one o'clock P.M. to nominate a suitable person as Senator from said district, to supply the place of Samuel Wilkeson, whose term of service will expire on the 31st day of December next. Each county will send a number of delegates equal to the number of representatives which they may be respectively entitled to send to the Assembly; and it is confidently hoped that no county will be unrepresented. August 14, 1828.

TIMOTHY FITCH, THURLOW WEED,
CALVIN H. BRYAN, TRUMBULL CARY.
Central Committee.

Article no. 97   Subject: Religion
Ref. August 21, 1828; pg. 3, col. 5

SABBATH SCHOOL NOTICE.

The annual meeting of the Sabbath School Union will be held at the office of H. Gardner, Esq. in the village of Lockport, on the last Tuesday of August, at 11 o'clock A.M.

H. GARDNER, Pres't. F. NORTHAM, Sec'y.
Lockport, July 30th, 1828.

Article no. 98   Subject: Notice
Ref. August 21, 1828; pg. 3, col. 5

Extract: WHEREAS default has been made in the payment of a certain sum of money secured to be paid by an Indenture of Mortgage, bearing date 6 July 1826, and executed by Luke Draper, of the county of Niagara, to Lyman A. Spalding, his heirs or assigns; and whereas by an endorsement upon said Indenture of Mortgage, all the right, title and interest of said Lyman A. Spalding therein, hath been, and is assigned to me, the subscriber—Therefore notice is hereby given that by virtue of a power contained in said Mortgage, and pursuant to the Statute in such case made and provided; the premises described in said Mortgage, being all that certain tract or parcel of land, situate, lying and being in the village of Lockport, in said county, and being part or parcel of farm lot number twelve in the fourteenth township, and sixth range of townships of the Holland Land Company's land, so called, and which [on a map made by Jesse P. Haines, Surveyor, and filed in the office of the Clerk of the county of Niagara, and] is known and distinguished as village lot number three, on the north side of Niagara street, in the village of Lockport, being in the corner of said Niagara and West Second streets, {Notice includes further description of land} containing one fourth of an acre of land, more or less—will be sold at public vendue at the Washington House, now occupied by S.B. Thompson in Lockport, 7 February 1829. Dated August 21st, 1828.

CHAUNCEY LEONARD.

Article no. 99   Subject: Notice
Ref. August 21, 1828; pg. 3, col. 6

TO THE PUBLIC.

Mrs. Huldah Hoskins, who has been residing in Canada for some years past, having arrived in the village of Lockport, in search of her two sons, William and Calvin Hoskins, whom she was informed resided in or near Rochester; and of her brother-in-law, Mr. Russell Trall; if any person should have any knowledge of either of these persons, or where they may be found, will confer a favour upon the advertiser by informing her of their residence—or mentioning to them that she is now at Lockport, anxiously waiting for tidings of them. Lockport, Aug. 21, 1828.

Article no. 100	Subject: Notice
Ref. August 21, 1828; pg. 3, col. 6	

POSTPONEMENT.

The sale of Harvey Slayton's property, situate in the town of Royalton, is postponed until the 30th day of August instant, to be held at the Hotel kept by Samuel Jennings, in the town of Lockport.

JOHN PHILLIPS, Shff.

Dated Lockport, August 16th, 1832.

Article no. 101	Subject: Notice
Ref. August 21, 1828; pg. 3, col. 6	

Extract: BY virtue of an execution issued out of the Supreme Court of Judicature, of the state of New-York, to me directed and delivered, against the goods and chattels, lands and tenements of Aden Gay, Nathaniel Bolles, and Ziba Gay, I have seized and taken all that certain lot, piece or parcel of land, situate in the village of Manchester, in the town and county of Niagara, and state of New-York, and containing twenty-eight rods and sixty-four hundredths of a rod—bounded as follows {Notice includes description of boundaries} [bounded, in part, by land conveyed by Augustus Porter and Benjamin Barton to John W. Sleighton.]—Also the following described piece of land situate in the village of Manchester, and bounded as follows, to wit: {Notice includes description of boundaries} [situated near Goat Island]—together with the right and privilege of taking water in a race from the river to the northeast corner of said land in a direction from said northeast corner of south forty-two degrees east for the exclusive purpose of making and manufacturing iron into various shapes. This last described premises being subject to rent at thirty-five dollars per annum to be paid to Augustus Porter and Benjamin Barton, their heirs, executors, administrators or assigns—all which I will expose to sale, at public vendue, at the house kept by David Chapman, in the village of Manchester, 29 September 1828. Dated this 11th day of August, 1828.

JOHN PHILLIPS, Sheriff.

Article no. 102	Subject: Advertisement
Ref. August 21, 1828; pg. 3, col. 6	

Extract: Physic and Surgery.

The Subscriber presents his compliments to the inhabitants of the village of Lockport and its vicinity, and tenders them his services in the practice of Physic and Surgery in all its various branches. ...

N.B. Those afflicted with sore Eyes—Glandular swellings, Scrofulous or Cancerous affections, and many other loathsome diseases, will do well to give him a call. He has a small though well selected assortment of Medicines, and can supply the most of those who may wish to purchase by the dose or small quantity on reasonable terms.

G.W. POPE, M.D. Lockport, August 4th, 1828.

Article no. 103	Subject: Notice
Ref. August 21, 1828; pg. 4, col. 3	

CAUTION.

Whereas, Sally, my wife, has left my bed and board. [sic] I hereby forbid all persons barbouring [sic] or trusting her on my account, as I shall pay no debts of her contracting after this date.

BENJAMIN LONG. Lockport, Aug. 11th, 1828.

Article no. 104	Subject: Notice
Ref. August 21, 1828; pg. 4, col. 3	

BY virtue of two executions issued out of the Supreme Court of Judicature of the State of New-York, and one execution issued out of the Clerks [sic] office of the County of Niagara, to me directed and delivered, against the goods and chattels, lands and tenements of John Galt, I have seized and taken all that certain piece orparcel [sic] of land situate and being in the village of Lockport, being part of farm lot number 59, in the 14th township and 7th Range, and which on a map or survey of part of said lot into village lots, made for Almon H. Millard, is known as village lot number five, on the south side of Main-street in said village, containing one fourth of an acre more or less—according to said map or survey: which I shall expose for sale at public vendue, on Friday, the 26th day of September next, at the house now occupied by Samuel B. Thompson, commonly called Washington House, in the village of Lockport, at one o'clock in the afternoon of that day. Dated Aug. 11th, 1828. JOHN PHILLIPS, Sheriff.

Article no. 105	Subject: Notice
Ref. August 21, 1828; pg. 4, col. 4	

Extract: WHEREAS Sylvester R. Hathaway, of the town of Lockport, in the county of Niagara, by Indenture of Mortgage, bearing date 28 February 1828, for securing the payment of a certain sum of money, did mortgage unto Warren Sadler, of the town of Lockport aforesaid, all that certain piece or parcel of land, situate, lying and being in the town of Lockport, in the county of Niagara,

being part of Lots number eleven and twelve, in the fifteenth section of township number fourteen, in the sixth range, and bounded as follows: {Notice includes description of land} [surveyed by Jesse P. Haines, Surveyor.]—containing sixty acres of land, be the same more or less. And also that other piece or parcel of land, being a part of said above mentioned Lot number eleven, bounded and described as follows: {Notice includes description of land} [surveyed by Jesse Haines]—containing ten acres of land, be the same more or less. And whereas default hath been made in the payment of a part of the said sum of money and the interest thereon: Therefore notice is hereby given, that pursuant to a power of sale contained in said mortgage, and according to the statute in such case made and provided, the said mortgaged premises, with the appurtenances, to be sold at public auction, at the Washington House, kept by S.B. Thompson, in the Village of Lockport, 8 November 1828. Dated May 20th, 1828.
WARREN SADLER.
J. CENTER, Att'y.

Article no. 106 Subject: Notice
Ref. August 21, 1828; pg. 4, col. 4

BY order of Hiram Gardner, a Judge of the Court of Common Pleas of the County of Niagara, Counsellor, &c. notice is hereby given to all the creditors of Asahel J. Dennison of the town of Somerset in said county, an Insolvent Debtor, to appear before the said Judge at his office in the village of Lockport in said county on the 20th day of September next, at 1 o'clock in the afternoon of that day, to show cause if any they have, why an assignment of the said Insolvent's estate should not be made, and the person of the said Insolvent exempted from imprisonment, pursuant to the act entitled an act to abolish imprisonment for debt in certain cases, passed April 7, 1819. Dated August 5th, 1828.

Article no. 107 Subject: Notice
Ref. August 21, 1828; pg. 4, col. 4

Extract: DEFAULT having been made in the payment of several sums of money, secured to be paid by certain Indentures of Mortgage, one bearing date 1 October 1819, and one bearing date 9 March 1820, executed by Parkhurst Whitney of the town of Niagara, county of Niagara and state of New-York to Samuel De Veaux, of the same place, of all those certain tracts of land, situate, lying and being in the town of Niagara, county of Niagara and state of New-York viz.: Three village lots in the village of Manchester known as lots No. 26, 27, and 28, and the outlines of the said three lots are described and may be known by the following description, viz: {Notice includes description of land}.

Notice is hereby given that by virtue of a power of sale in said Mortgages contained, and in pursuance of the statute in such case made and provided, the said premises will be sold at public auction, at the store of the subscriber in Manchester, 9 February 1829. Dated this seventh day of August, 1832. S. DE VEAUX.

Article no. 108 Subject: Notice
Ref. August 21, 1828; pg. 4, col. 4

Extract: BY virtue of several executions issued out of the Supreme Court of Judicature of the state of New-York, and also one issued out of the Court of Common Pleas of the County of Niagara, to me directed and delivered, against the goods and chattels, lands and tenements of Parkhurst Whitney, I have seized, and shall expose for sale on the premises at public vendue, on 15 September 1828, at 10 o'clock in the forenoon of that day, all those certain tracts of land situate, lying and being in the town of Niagara and county of Niagara, known as village Lots number 26, 27 and 28, in the village of Manchester, and bounded as follows, viz: {Notice includes description of boundaries}—and being the premises upon which stands the elegant tavern and out buildings, now occupied by the said Whitney. Dated July 29th 1828. JOHN PHILLIPS, Sheriff.

Article no. 109 Subject: Notice
Ref. August 21, 1828; pg. 4, col. 5

Extract: BY virtue of several executions issued out of the Supreme Court of Judicature of the state of New-York, to me directed and delivered, against the goods and chattels, lands and tenements, of David Chapman and Stephen Chapman, I have seized all that certain piece or parcel of land, situate, lying and being in the Village of Manchester, in the town and county of Niagara, (near Niagara Falls,) and described as follows, viz.—{Notice includes description of boundaries}—containing about three fourths of an acre of land, more or less: Also, a certain other tract of land, in said village of Manchester, described as follows, viz.—{Notice includes description of boundaries.} On the land above mentioned is an elegant tavern, occupied by the said David Chapman, and a stone cotton and woollen factory: All of which I shall expose for sale at public vendue, at the house of David Chapman, on the premises, 15 September 1828. Dated July 29th, 1828.
JOHN PHILLIPS, Sheriff.

Article no. 110 Subject: Notice
Ref. August 21, 1828; pg. 4, col. 5

BY order of Hiram Gardner, Esq. one of the Judges of the Court of Common Pleas in and for the County of Niagara, Counsellor at Law, &c. notice is hereby given to all the creditors of William Williams, of Hartland in said County, an imprisoned and insolvent debtor, to show cause if any they have before the said Judge at his office in the village of Lockport, in the County of Niagara, on the twenty-seventh day of September next, at 10 o'clock in the forenoon of that day why an assignment of the said insolvent's estate should not be made, and his person be exempt from imprisonment, pursuant to an act entitled "An act to abolish imprisonment for debt in certain cases," passed April 7th 1819. Dated 4th August 1828.

Article no. 111   Subject: Notice
Ref. August 21, 1828; pg. 4, col. 5

BY virtue of an execution issued out of the Supreme Court of the state of New-York, to me directed and delivered, against the goods and chattels, lands and tenements, of Nathaniel Bolles and Berryhill H. White, I have seized and taken a certain triphammer, shop, forge, coal-house, &c., and the lot on which they stand, in the village of Manchester, in the town and county of Niagara, situated near the bridge that crosses to Goat Island: and also, a certain building, situate on Village Lot No. 4, in said village of Manchester, now occupied by the said White as a tailor shop: all which I shall expose for sale at public vendue, at the inn kept by Parkhurst Whitney, in said village, on the fifteenth day of September next, at 12 o'clock at noon of that day. Dated July 29th, 1828.

JOHN PHILLIPS, Sheriff.

Article no. 112   Subject: Advertisement
Ref. August 21, 1828; pg. 4, col. 5

STEARNS' APPENDIX.

A Few Copies of "An Appendix to 'An Inquiry into the nature and tendence of Speculative Freemasonry,' in which is proved the true character of Morgan's 'Illustrations of Masonry.' By John G. Stearns, Minister of the Gospel, Paris, N.Y." for sale at this office, price 12 1-2 cents.

Article no. 113   Subject: Notice
Ref. August 21, 1828; pg. 4, col. 6

BY ORDER of Hiram Gardner, Esq., Judge of the Court of Common Pleas in and for the county of Niagara, Counsellor at Law, &c. Notice is hereby given to all the creditors of Levi L. Corey, of the town of New-Fane, in the county of Niagara, an imprisoned and insolvent debtor, to show cause, if any they have, before the said Judge, at his office in the Village of Lockport, on the sixth day of October next, at ten o'clock in the forenoon, why an assignment of the said insolvent's estate should not be made, for the benefit of all his creditors, and his person be exempted from imprisonment, pursuant to the act entitled "An act to abolish imprisonment for debt in certain cases," passed April 7, 1819. Dated this 29th day of July, 1828.

Article no. 114   Subject: Notice
Ref. August 28, 1828; pg. 1, col. 2

PUBLIC VENDUE.

To be sold at public vendue, at the House of David Chapman, in the village of Manchester, on the 27th of September next, at 2 o'clock P.M. an Article of Land, the property of Ezekiel Hill of Niagara, deceased; distinguished by west part of Lot No. 21, ninth Range, containing twenty-five and a half acres, be the same more or less. This Lot of Land is good, and lies about one mile and a half from the village of Manchester, with three acres cleared and fenced, the rest well timbered.

ABRAHAM WITMER, Executor.
Niagara, Aug. 9th, 1828.

Article no. 115   Subject: Advertisement
Ref. August 28, 1828; pg. 1, col. 3

Extract: NEW ARRIVAL!

Geo. W. Rogers & Co. are now receiving, at the Green Store, large additions to their stock of Summer & Winter Goods. Dry goods, and a great variety of other Staple and Fancy articles, crockery, hardware, groceries, &c. for sale. Cash paid for Staves, Wheat, Pot and Pearl Ashes.

All debts now due must be settled by the 1st day of September next, or actual necessity will compel them to call in another shape—notwithstanding their feelings would otherwise dictate.

Article no. 116   Subject: Accident
Ref. August 28, 1828; pg. 1, col. 5

Distressing accident.—As the stage from Nashua to Peterborough, N.H. was passing through Temple, on the 11th inst. having two men, besides the driver on the driver's seat, and the seat suddenly gave way, and the three men fell to the ground. The driver was not severely injured, but the men on his right and left fell under the wheels of the carriage, which passed over them, and wounded them severely. One of them, Mr. Obadiah Perry, of Temple died of his wounds, two days after the accident. The other, Mr. Rodney Arbuckle, of Merrimack, had his jawbone broken, and was much bruised, but he is expected to recover. The horses were alarmed and ran about a mile. There was but one passenger in the stage, a female, who by great caution and presence of mind, succeeded in stopping the horses, until some persons who saw them pass came to her relief.—[*Penn. paper.*]

Article no. 117   Subject: Court
Ref. August 28, 1828; pg. 1, col. 6

From the *Canadian Courant* of Aug. 2.

Lotteries. Mr. Isaac Rouse has lately been arrested by the Solicitor General in Quebec, for vending American lottery tickets. The cause was brought forward at the Court of Appeals, at which Mr. Rouse was tried and sentenced (as we understand, according to the statute in such cases provided) to a fine of 200l. [£200] and to be imprisoned in the common jail for one year. M. Rouse appealed to the decision of the Chief Justice, who, we understand, pronounced the sentence correct. Thus it appears the Solicitor General thinks it no advantage to continue a detrimental species of gambling in this province, for the purpose of advancing the interast [sic] of the United States.

Article no. 118   Subject: Politics
Ref. August 28, 1828; pg. 2, col. 2

Extract: YOUNG MEN'S CONVENTION.

The following extracts from the proceedings of the Convention of Republican Young Men, which assembled at Utica [on] the 12th inst. contain all the resolutions adopted by the meeting: {Article contains an outline of those resolutions.} [Length, 2 columns.]

- Adams, John Quincy; Massachusetts; was given the support of the delegates, to be re-elected President of the United States.
- Bacon, Mr.; Oneida, New York; made a motion at the Convention.
- Calhoun, John C. The delegates resolved that the aspiring and vascillating character of John C. Calhoun rendered him an unsafe depository of power, &c.
- Clay, Henry; was given the support of the delegates.
- Grainger, Francis; state of New York; was given the support of the delegates, for the office of Lieutenant-Governor of the State of New York.
- Jackson, Andrew, General. The delegates at the Convention observed with deep regret the open avowal among some of the southern members of the confederacy, the most violent of the supporters of Gen. Jackson, of those principles of disorganization and dismemberment, whose tendency is to sap the foundation and overthrow the only true republic upon the face of the globe, &c. Did not recognize, in Jackson, no one of those traits which we have been taught should ever distinguish the first magistrate of a free and elective Republic, &c.
- Rush, Richard; Pennsylvania; given the support of the delegates, to be elected Vice President of the United States.
- Stow, Mr.; Jefferson, New York; made a motion at the Convention.
- Thompson, Smith; state of New York; was given the support of the delegates, for the office of Governor of the State of New York.
- Wells, Mr.; Utica, New York; on the Committee appointed to draft Resolutions; reported the resolutions drafted at the Convention.

Article no. 119   Subject: Court
Ref. August 28, 1828; pg. 2, col. 6

THE CANANDAIGUA TRIALS. The trial of Bruce, Turner and Darrow, on indictments found against them by the Grand Jury of Ontario county, for an alleged participation in the abduction of William Morgan, came on at the Court held in Canandaigua last week. Bruce was found guilty: but exceptions having been taken by his counsel to the jurisdiction of the Court, sentence has been suspended until the decision of the Supreme Court can be had. He has been recognized to the November term. Turner and Darrow got clear! by the evidence that the people relied upon for their conviction being set aside. We have received a report of the above trial, and will lay it before our readers in our next; when they can judge for themselves of the credibility and respectability of the testimony, and the strength of the grounds, upon which the evidence of Mr. Giddins was set aside. [Transcriber's note: This article appears in the Editorial columns.]

Article no. 120   Subject: Politics
Ref. August 28, 1828; pg. 3, col. 1

Extract: YOUNG MEN'S CONVENTION.

The great length of the proceedings of the Utica Convention of Young Men, precludes their insertion entire in our present publication. In a preceding column we have given the resolutions adopted by the delegates. The Convention, for number, and the talent and respectability of its members, was certainly one of the most important political assemblages that has ever been held in our state. Three hundred and fifty-six members answered to their names the first day. [Election of officers and appointments to committees, listed below.] After some further business was transacted, the Convention adjourned, after a session of two days.

- Bryan, John A.; Cattaragus County, New York; called the Convention to order.
- Burrow, L.; Orleans County, New York; appointed to the Orleans County Corresponding Committee.
- Cadwallader, M.; Niagara County, New York; appointed to the Niagara County Corresponding Committee.
- Curtis, H.R.; Orleans County, New York; appointed to the Orleans County Corresponding Committee.

- Day, D.M.; Erie County, New York; appointed to the Erie County Corresponding Committee.
- Fellows, Lathrop; Niagara County, New York; appointed to the Niagara County Corresponding Committee.
- Fleming, George W.; Orleans County, New York; appointed to the Orleans County Corresponding Committee.
- Granger, Mr.; nominated Lieutenant Governor [of the state of New York].
- Hatch, Junius H., Mr.; New York, New York; elected one of two Vice Presidents of the Convention.
- Lord, John C.; Erie County, New York; appointed to the Erie County Corresponding Committee.
- Mason, James T.; Niagara County, New York; appointed to the Niagara County Corresponding Committee.
- Mosely, William A.; Erie County, New York; appointed to the Erie County Corresponding Committee.
- Rochester, Nathaniel T., Mr.; Monroe, New York; elected one of two Vice Presidents of the Convention.
- Seward, William H., Mr.; Cayuga County, New York; elected President of the Convention.
- Shumway, Borille; Essex, New York; elected one of two Secretaries of the Convention.
- Thompson, Judge; state of New York; nominated Governor [of the state of New York].
- Wright, John C.; Scoharie, New York; elected one of two Secretaries of the Convention.

Article no. 121   Subject: Transportation
Ref. August 28, 1828; pg. 3, col. 4

Ohio Canal.—W[e] learn that the Canal from Akron to Massillon will be completed this week, and that a Canal Boat will arrive at Massillon on Monday next about 3 o'clock P.M.—*Ohio Repository.*

Article no. 122   Subject: Suicide
Ref. August 28, 1828; pg. 3, col. 4

Suicide. On the morning of the 11th inst, the body of William Parker, of Liecester [sic], (Livingston co.) was found suspended by a rope attached to the branches of a small sapling in the woods near his residence. He had been in a state of mental dejection for some time previous, and complained much of a severe pain in his head. He went out in the morning, and left word that he was going to a neighbour's house, and was found soon after by a lad, in the situation above described. A coroner's inquest was held over the body who returned a verdict of suicide. The deceased removed lately from the state of New Jersey, and was a respected citizen.—*Le Roy Gaz.*

Article no. 123   Subject: Politics
Ref. August 28, 1828; pg. 3, col. 5

At a meeting of the Central Committee of vigilance of Erie county, held at the Mansion House, in the village of Buffalo, on the 16th August, 1828, it was Resolved, That it be recommended to the citizens of the several counties of Erie, Niagara and Chatauque, friendly to the Administration, to elect five delegates from each county, to meet in convention on the 25th day of September next, at the Mansion House in the village of Buffalo, for the purpose of nominating candidates for the offices of Elector of President and Vice President, and Representative to Congress, for the 30th Congressional District.

Resolved, That the Chairman and Secretary of this Committee cause this resolution to be published in the several republican papers printed in this district.
JOSIAH TROWBRIDGE, Ch'n.
N. SARGENT, Sec'y.

Article no. 124   Subject: Religion
Ref. August 28, 1828; pg. 3, col. 5

SABBATH SCHOOL NOTICE.

The annual meeting of the Niagara County Sabbath School Union is adjourned to Tuesday the 2nd of Sept. at the Presbyterian Meeting House, at 7 o'clock, P.M.
H. GARDNER, Pres't. F. NORTHAM, Sec'y.
Lockport, August 27th, 1828.

Article no. 125   Subject: Miscellany
Ref. August 28, 1828; pg. 3, col. 6

TO MATHEMATICIANS.

Required, the sides of a triangle containing 6 acres, 1 rood and 12 perches, whose sides shall be in the proportion of 9, 8 and 6. A.F. & A.H.
[Transcriber's note: The last digit was partially obscured, and may have been an 8.]

Article no. 126   Subject: Notice
Ref. August 28, 1828; pg. 3, col. 6

ANTI-MASONIC MEETING.

A meeting of the citizens of Niagara county opposed to Secret Societies, will be held on Thursday evening, 4th day of September next, at 7 o'clock, at the house of Samuel Jennings, in Lockport, for the purpose of appointing delegates to represent the county in the Anti-Masonic Senatorial and Congressional Conventions. A full attendance is desirable.
W.C. HOUSE,
ELIAKIM HAMMOND,
ELIAS RANSOM, Jr.
Central Committee. Aug. 28th, 1828.

Article no. 127 Subject: Notice
Ref. August 28, 1828; pg. 3, col. 6

Anti-Masonic Senatorial Convention.

An Anti-Masonic Convention of delegates from the several counties in the 8th Senatorial District, will be held at the Eagle Tavern, in Batavia, Genesee county, on the 17th day of September next, at one o'clock P.M. to nominate a suitable person as Senator from said district, to supply the place of Samuel Wilkeson, whose term of service will expire on the 31st day of December next. Each county will send a number of delegates equal to the number of representatives which they may be respectively entitled to send to the Assembly; and it is confidently hoped that no county will be unrepresented. August 14, 1828.

TIMOTHY FITCH, THURLOW WEED,
CALVIN H. BRYAN, TRUMBULL CARY.
Central Committee.

Article no. 128 Subject: Notice
Ref. August 28, 1828; pg. 3, col. 6

(COPY.)
State of New-York, Secretary's Office.
Albany, August 12, 1828.
Sir,

I hereby give you notice, that at the next general election, a Governor and Lieutenant Governor are to be elected.

And also, that a Senator is to be chosen in the eighth Senatorial District, in place of Samuel Wilkeson, whose term of service will expire on the last day of December next.

And that an Elector of President and Vice President is to be chosen for the thirtieth Congressional District.

A.C. FLAGG, Secretary of State.
To the Sheriff (Clerk, or First Judge.)
of the County of Niagara.

County of Niagara, Sheriff's Office,
The above is a copy of a notice this day received by me from the Hon. A.C. Flagg, Secretary of State.
JOHN PHILLIPS, Sheriff of Niagara County.
August 25, 1828.

Article no. 129 Subject: Advertisement
Ref. August 28, 1828; pg. 3, col. 6

NOTICE.

Sore Eyes, Scald Head, Piles, Salt Rheum, Fever and Ague and Lung Complaints. Not one case perhaps in twenty but may be relieved in a very short time, by harmless remedies now in my possession. Weak Eyes relieved in twenty minutes and gradually cured in a short time. Scald Head, Salt Rheum and Piles eradicated in almost every instance. Charges low. All who take and use those articles according to directions without benefit may expect their money refunded.

I shall be at Samuel Jennings' Hotel on Saturday Sept. 6th, where further satisfaction may be obtained and all necessary information given gratis. A short Lecture on Botany, the causes and cure of diseases, will be offered to the public, to commence at 8 o'clock P.M.

H. HILL. August 26, 1828.

Article no. 130 Subject: Advertisement
Ref. August 28, 1828; pg. 3, col. 6

To Farmers!
THE Subscriber will receive
WHEAT,

At the Lockport Mills, and pay the highest price in Cash, on delivery. Should the price not be satisfactory, he will store the Wheat, and hold himself in readiness at all times, to purchase it at the market price, or deliver the quantity stored, manufactured, without deduction for wastage or charge for storage—the grinding on the usual terms being a sufficient compensation.

To those who do not wish to sell their Wheat, an opportunity is now offered of placing it in safe storage, without charge, and not subject to loss from rats or other causes (fire excepted.)

LYMAN A. SPALDING. Lockport, 8th month, 1828.

Article no. 131 Subject: Advertisement
Ref. August 28, 1828; pg. 3, col. 6

NOTICE.

The subscribers are under the necessity of calling on all persons indebted to them for immediate settlement and payment; or part payment is required of all persons indebted to them either by note or book account. Those who cannot now pay old debts, will be required to secure the same, if they wish a longer credit.

Goods

Will be sold for ready pay only, during the remainder of this year.

REYNALE & STEWART. Hartland, Aug. 26, 1828.

Article no. 132 Subject: Notice
Ref. August 28, 1828; pg. 3, col. 6

STRAYED OR STOLEN.

A yoke of Oxen, four or five years old; one Brindle, the other Red, of midling [sic] size, and formerly owned by L. Fellows & Co. Whoever will return said Oxen, or give information where they may be found, will be liberally rewarded for their trouble.

S. OLMSTED. Lockport, Aug. 26, 1828.

Article no. 133   Subject: Notice
Ref. August 28, 1828; pg. 3, col. 6

CAUTION.

Whereas the subscribers gave a note of hand to a person by the name of Isaac Briggs, dated June 5th, 1828, and payable in December next, for the sum of $50; this is therefore to caution alll [sic] persons from purchasing said note, as the alledged [sic] value for which it was given, having never been received, we are determined not to pay the same.

G.W. HAWLEY and AUGUSTUS HAWLEY.
Lewiston, Aug. 23, 1828.

Article no. 134   Subject: Court
Ref. September 4, 1828; pg. 1, col. 5

Extract: ONTARIO SESSIONS.
Wednesday, Aug. 20, 1828.

The People, vs. Eli Bruce, Orasmus Turner, Jared Darrow. Conspiracy, &c. [Judges and jurors listed, below.]

Mr. Whiting opened the cause to the Jury by relating, briefly, the history of Morgan's abduction, when he called Jeffrey Chipman [Article included other witnesses and their testimonies; synopsis provided, below.] The Jury retired, and after four hours deliberation returned a verdict of Guilty. [Length of article: 9 columns.]

- Adams, Elisha; state of New York; witness. The counsel for the defence remarked, that as Mr. Adams stood indicted for a participation in the same offence, they hoped the court would be careful that his rights were not invaded, &c.
- Adams, William H.; state of New York; made a powerful and eloquent defence.
- Agur, Mr.; state of New York; mentioned by witness, William Cooper.
- Allen, Capt.; state of New York; mentioned by witness, [name illegible].
- Allen, Nathaniel, Esq.; Ontario County, New York; one of the judges.
- Anson, Hiram; Ontario County, New York; juror.
- Atwater, Mr.; state of New York; mentioned in the case.
- Barton, Mr.; state of New York; mentioned by witness, Corydon Fox.
- Beach, —; Victor, New York; mentioned by witness, Hiram Hubbard.
- Bissel, Mr.; state of New York; mentioned by witness, Ebenezer Griffin,
- Blossom, —; state of New York; mentioned by witness, Willis Turner.
- Brae, R.W.; state of New York; mentioned by witness, Hiram Hubbard.
- Brown, Jeremiah; state of New York; mentioned by witness, Col. William Molineux.
- Bruce, Eli; Ontario County, New York; defendant.
- Cary, Nathan; Ontario County, New York; juror.
- Chesebro, Nicholas G.; Ontario County, New York; mentioned by witness, Jeffrey Chipman. Issued a civil process against William Morgan, &c. The counsel for the defendants called Chesebro, but after a consultation declined having him sworn.
- Chipman, Jeffrey; Ontario County, New York; witness. William Morgan was brought before Chipman on a charge of petit larceny, examined and discharged, &c.
- Coe, Mr.; state of New York; mentioned by witness, Hiram Hubbard.
- Cooper, William; Clarkson, New York; witness.
- Darrow, Jared; Ontario County, New York; defendant.
- Dodge, Abraham; Ontario County, New York; juror.
- Doyle, Edward; Rochester, New York; mentioned by witness, Harry Olmsted.
- Ensworth, —; state of New York; mentioned by witness, Ezra Platt.
- Farewell, Isaac; state of New York; mentioned by witness, Solomon C. Wright.
- Fleming, Robert; Lewiston, New York; witness.
- Fox, Corydon; Lewiston, New York; witness. Stage driver for Mr. Barton.
- Giddins, Edward; state of New York; witness. Mr. Griffin, counsel for the defendant, objected that Mr. Giddins did not believe in the Christian religion, and was an incompetent witness. After the arguments of counsel, the court consulted, and gave their opinion that the sentiments of Mr. Giddins rendered his testimony inadmissible.
- Gray, Robert; Niagara, Upper Canada; witness.
- Green, Evert; Ontario County, New York; juror.
- Griffin, Ebenezer; state of New York; witness.
- Griffin, Mr.; state of New York. Mr. Griffin, counsel for the defendant, objected that Mr. Giddins did not believe in the Christian religion, and was an incompetent witness. Upon this point, Mr. Griffin called David Morrison as witness.
- Hall, Mary W.; Ontario County, New York; witness; wife of the jailer.
- Hanford, —; Rochester, New York; mentioned by witness, Hiram Hubbard; also mentioned as a tavern on the Lewiston road, about three miles from Rochester.
- Hayward, Holloway; Ontario County, New York; mentioned by witness, Jeffrey Chipman, and also called as a witness; was the constable who served the warrant for larceny against William Morgan, &c.
- Hotchkiss, William; state of New York; witness.
- Howell, N.W., Hon.; Ontario County, New York; First Judge, Ontario Sessions held 20th August 1828.

- Hubbard, Hiram; Ontario County, New York; witness; kept a livery stable [in Canandaigua], September 1826; had been tried and acquitted in this case.
- Jackson, John; state of New York; witness.
- Ketchum, George; state of New York; mentioned in the case. Mr. Sibley let George Ketchum have a pair of horses to go to Batavia.
- King, Col.; state of New York; mentioned by witness, Corydon Fox. King's [place] is six miles from Lewiston.
- Kingsley, —; state of New York; mentioned by witness, Willis Turner.
- Kingsley, E.C.; Ontario County, New York; mentioned by witness, Jeffrey Chipman; swore out the warrant for larceny against William Morgan.
- Lawson, —; state of New York; mentioned by witness, Hiram Hubbard.
- Leonard, Col.; Rochester, New York; mentioned by witness, Ezra Platt; kept a tavern at Rochester.
- Lincoln, Henry; Ontario County, New York; juror.
- Loomis, Chester, Esq.; Ontario County, New York; one of the judges.
- M'Bride, Mr.; mentioned by witness, Robert Gray.
- Marvin, Gen.; Ontario County, New York; objected to so broad an examination of witness, Hiram Hubbard.
- Mather, Elihu; state of New York; mentioned in the case.
- Matthews, Gen.; state of New York; raised a question to the sufficiency of the indictment, &c.
- Maxwell, Dr.; state of New York; mentioned by witness, Elisha Adams.
- Molineux, William, Col.; Niagara County, New York; witness; lived six miles west of Wright's, where the Lockport road intercepts the bridge.
- Morgan, William; Ontario County, New York; the subject of an abduction.
- Morrison, David; state of New York; witness; said that he had known Giddins intimately since 1820, and has frequently heard him express an opinion that there was no God, &c. Cross-examined by Mr. Moseley.
- Moseley, Mr.; state of New York; cross-examined witness, David Morrison; summed up the cause for the people with much clearness and ability.
- Olmstead, Harvey, or Harry; Hanford's Landing, Greece, New York; witness; resided near Hanford's landing, September 1826.
- Osborn, Mr.; state of New York; mentioned by witness, Willis Turner.
- Parker, —; state of New York; mentioned by witness, Ezra Platt.
- Parkhurst, —; state of New York; mentioned by witness, Ezra Platt.
- Peet, Jasper W.; Ontario County, New York; juror.
- Pennell, John, jun.; Ontario County, New York; juror.
- Perry, Ebenezer; Lewiston, New York; witness; lived on a back street in Lewiston.
- Phillips, —; state of New York; mentioned in the case.
- Phillips, John; state of New York; witness.
- Platt, Ezra; Rochester, New York; mentioned by witness, Hiram Hubbard, and called as a witness; knew Hiram Hubbard. [Transcriber's note: Part of this report was illegible, due to a tear in the lower, right-hand corner of the page.]
- Price, John, Esq.; Ontario County, New York; one of the judges.
- Rawson, Samuel, Esq.; Ontario County, New York; one of the judges.
- Reed, Samuel; Ontario County, New York; juror.
- Sanders, Martin B.; Fort Niagara, New York; witness; went to Fort Niagara, where he saw Edward Giddins, &c.
- Sawyer, Col.; Ontario County, New York; mentioned by witness, Mary W. Hall. Sawyer and another man said to Mary Hall that the plaintiff, Chesebro, had consented that William Morgan should be discharged.
- Short, Daniel; Ontario County, New York; juror.
- Sibley, Mr.; state of New York; mentioned in the case. Mr. Sibley let George Ketchum have a pair of horses to go to Batavia.
- Smith, Burrage; state of New York; mentioned by witness, Silas Walker.
- Smith, Levi; Ontario County, New York; juror.
- Smith, Obed; state of New York; mentioned by witness, Elisha Adams.
- Stone, —; Pittsford, New York; mentioned by witness, Hiram Hubbard.
- Swaim, Isaac; Youngstown, New York; witness.
- Taylor, Mr.; state of New York; mentioned by witness, Willis Turner.
- Turner, Orasmus; Ontario County, New York; defendant.
- Turner, Willis; state of New York; witness.
- Waldbridge, Silas; Clarkson, New York; witness. [Transcriber's note: A portion of the report, pertaining to this individual, had been printed in the lower, left-hand corner of the page, but was torn from the original paper record.]
- Walker, Silas; state of New York; witness.
- Weed, Thurlow; state of New York; witness.
- Whiting, Mr.; Ontario County, New York; opened the cause to the Jury by relating, briefly, the history of William Morgan's abduction.
- Wright, Solomon C.; Newfane, New York; witness; kept a public house in September, 1826.

Article no. 135 Subject: Politics
Ref. September 4, 1828; pg. 3, col. 1

We have received the letter of Mr. Granger, declining the nomination for governor by the Anti-Masonic Convention of 4th August, but its length, and the very late hour in which it came to hand, preclude its insertion this week.

Mr. Granger has accepted the nomination of the Administration Convention for the office of lieutenant governor.

Article no. 136 Subject: Transportation
Ref. September 4, 1828; pg. 3, col. 5

Chesapeake and Ohio Canal.—A portion of this canal, embracing an extent of seventeen miles and three quarters, was put under contract the week before last. The number of proposals was 469, from seventy-five distinct individuals or incorporated companies. The contracts fall short of the original estimate of the U. States Engineers by $803,000. The canal is to be 60 feet wide at the surface and 45 at the bottom. Of the 34 contracts made, 18 of the heaviest were by citizens of New-York and Pennsylvania. The contracts are to be completed by the 31st of December, 1829.—*Rochester Telegraph.*

Article no. 137 Subject: Death
Ref. September 4, 1828; pg. 3, col. 5

Our readers will see with deep regret the name of the Rev. Dr. Feltus, of St. Stephen's church, recorded in our obituary of this afternoon. He expired last evening, after a short illness, having officiated the Sunday preceding. He was an able preacher, a warm friend, and an active, patriotic citizen. His death will be lamented by thousands, who have listened to his eloquence, felt his kindness, and witnessed his efforts in the cause of philanthropy.—N.Y. Statesman.

Article no. 138 Subject: Miscellany
Ref. September 4, 1828; pg. 3, col. 5

TO A.F. & A.H.

I have but little time to devote to the investigation of mathematical or other questions not immediately required of me; but having a little leisure just now, I offer you the following solution to the question contained in the article addressed to 'Mathematicians,' in the *Courier* of this week.

Find the area of the triangle whose sides are 9, 8 and 6, by Problem 5th of Gummere's Surveying, = 23.525 square perches: then, since similar triangles are to each other as the squares of their homologous sides, we have $23.526 : 1012 (6A. 1R. 12P.) :: 81 : 3484.4633$ = square of the longest side; and [the square root of] $3484.4633 = 59.029$, longest side; then, as $9 : 8 :: 59.029 : 52.47$ = second side, and $9 : 6 :: 59.029 : 39.353$ = third side of the triangle required.

J.P.H. Lockport, 30th of 8th mo. 1828.

Article no. 139 Subject: Marriage
Ref. September 4, 1828; pg. 3, col. 5

MARRIED—In Hartland, on the 28th ult., by Dexter P. Sprague, Esq., Mr. Isaac N. Cook to Miss Sarah Fick, both of Middleport, in this county.

Article no. 140 Subject: Notice
Ref. September 4, 1828; pg. 3, col. 6

Extract: The [Sale of the property, pertaining to an Execution against Harvey Slayton] is further postponed until Wednesday the 10th day of September next, at [the Hotel kept by Samuel Jennings, in the town of Lockport, at 1 o'clock in the afternoon.] Dated Aug. 30th, 1828.

JOHN PHILLIPS, Shff.

Article no. 141 Subject: Notice
Ref. October 9, 1828; pg. 1, col. 2

STOLEN!

On Sabbath evening last, 21st inst. from the pasture of the Subscriber, in the town of Royalton, near Middleport, a dark iron gray Mare, 7 years old, nearly 15 hands high, thick mane and long switch tail darker than the hair on the body, long on the back, thin between the fore shoulders, with a bunch of a pretty large size, on one of the hind feet, just above the fetlock joint; is a natural trotter, and a fast traveller. Whoever returns said Mare, or gives information where she may be found, shall receive a liberal reward, and all reasonable charges defrayed, if brought home.

ARAUNAH BENNETT. Sept. 25th, 1828.

Article no. 142 Subject: Advertisement
Ref. October 9, 1828; pg. 1, col. 3

TO LET!

A Room in the Stone Building, opposite Jennings' Hotel, on Main-st. in the village of Lockport. The Room is on the same floor with the office of the *Niagara Courier*, is well lighted, and convenient for any business whatever. For particulars inquire at this office. September 11.

Article no. 143 Subject: Notice
Ref. October 9, 1828; pg. 1, col. 3

STRAY COW.

Came into the enclosure of the Subscriber, on the 22d inst. a pale red COW, having a young calf. The owner is requested to prove property, pay all charges, and take her away.

ETHAN FENN. Town of Royalton, Sept. 25, 1828.

Article no. 144   Subject: Notice
Ref. October 9, 1828; pg. 1, col. 4

NOTICE.

The Copartnership heretofore existing under the firm of POMEROY & FORD, is this day dissolved by mutual consent. All those who are indebted to the subscribers, are requested to call and settle their accounts as soon as possible, and save cost.

JABEZ POMEROY, SIMEON FORD.

Sept. 16th, 1828.

Article no. 145   Subject: Politics
Ref. October 9, 1828; pg. 3, col. 2

We are happy in having it in our power to state that Mr. Boughton has consented to suffer his name to be used by his anti-masonic friends as a candidate for the office of senator. His election is certain.

Article no. 146   Subject: Court
Ref. October 9, 1828; pg. 3, col. 2

Joel M'Collum, Esq. of this village, has been appointed a Judge of the Court of Common Pleas of this county.

Article no. 147   Subject: Court
Ref. October 9, 1828; pg. 3, col. 2

We learn from the *Rochester Enquirer*, that Sheriff Garlinghouse has arrested John Whitney, on an indictment for kidnapping William Morgan. Whitney was held to bail, to appear at the Ontario Sessions, in the sum of $2,000.

Article no. 148   Subject: Politics
Ref. October 9, 1828; pg. 3, col. 2

Extract: At an Anti-Masonic Convention of Delegates from various towns of the county of Niagara, held at the house of Samuel Jennings, innkeeper, in the village of Lockport, in said county, on Wednesday the 8th day of October, inst. at 2 o'clock, P.M.—the following persons appeared and took their seats:

Lewiston. Jacob Townsend, John Gray, Josiah Tryon.
Porter. John Clapsaddle, William Doty, Leonard H. Walker.
Wilson. Charles Baker, James Davis, Daniel Holmes.
New-Fane. Almiron Newman, Stephen Hase, James Van Horn.
Royalton. Asher Freeman, George Reynale, Decius S. Fenn.
Hartland. Theron B. Cook, Asahel Johnson, Allen Kinyon.
Lockport. Elias Ransom, Jr.[,] John Williams, Daniel Alvord.
Cambria. Daniel Oliver, Eliakim Hammond, William Earl.
Niagara. Lorin Yerrington, Samuel De Veaux, Henry W. Clark.
Pendleton. John Schyler, Erastus Rogers.

The Convention was called to order by Elias Ransom, Jr. Esq. Jacob Townsend was chosen Chairman, and Samuel De Veaux, Secretary. The following resolutions were then adopted:

Resolved, ... we recommend [John Garnsey] to the electors of the county of Niagara as a suitable person to be supported at the ensuing election as a candidate for the member of Assembly, ...

Resolved, That like sentiments we express in proposing John Phillips as the candidate for Sheriff. ...

Resolved, That Henry Catlin, of the town of Lockport, be supported as the candidate for Clerk of the county.

Resolved, That Daniel Holmes, of the town of Wilson, Asher Saxton, of Lockport, Theron B. Cook, of Hartland, and Lathrop Cook, of Lewiston, are suitable persons to be supported as Coroners.

Resolved, That the nomination of our fellow citizen George B. Boughton, of this county, as a candidate for the Senate, and that of Ebenezer F. Norton, of the county of Erie, for member of Congress, meet our cordial approbation.

Resolved, That we approve the nomination of Solomon Southwick as the candidate for Governor, and that of John Crary for Lieutenant Governor, ...

Resolved, That the following persons constitute the committees of vigilance of the several towns of this county, and that they be authorised to call meetings in their respective towns at any time they may think proper in promoting the anti-masonic cause: (The names of the persons composing the committees of vigilance of the several towns are unavoidably omitted until next week.)

Resolved, {Article listed several resolutions in support of the anti-masonic cause.}

Resolved, That the following gentlemen compose the Central Corresponding Committee: Elias Ransom, Jr. Esq.[,] Eliakim Hammond, Esq. and William C. House, Esq.

Resolved, That the proceedings of this meeting be signed by the Chairman and Secretary and published in the *Niagara Courier*.

JACOB TOWNSEND, Ch'n.   S. DE VEAUX, Sec'y.

Article no. 149   Subject: Marriage
Ref. October 9, 1828; pg. 3, col. 4

MARRIED, on Sunday evening last, by the Rev. Mr. Curry, Mr. Nathaniel Coe, of Portage, Allegany Co. to Miss Mary White, of this village.

Article no. 150   Subject: Death
Ref. October 9, 1828; pg. 3, col. 4

DIED, September 27th, Mrs. Rhoda Stone, of a short but painful illness, which she bore with Christian fortitude, and expired in the full confidence of a blessed immortality.

Article no. 151   Subject: Advertisement
Ref. October 9, 1828; pg. 3, col. 4

NEW FALL AND WINTER GOODS.

We are this day receiving a general assortment of Goods, which will be sold low, for ready pay.

Also—A good stock of Boots and Shoes, Nails, Window-Glass, &c.—Togeth [sic] with our usual variety.
Hyson Skin Tea, for 6s.
Young Hyson Tea, for 8s.
40 Kegs first quality Powder.
M.H. TUCKER & Co. Oct. 2, 1828.

Article no. 152   Subject: Notice
Ref. October 9, 1828; pg. 3, col. 4

Extract: List of letters remaining in the Post Office at Lewiston, 1 October 1828. [Names listed, below.] Bates Cook, Post Master.

Aimes, Charles
Austin, Nathan
Beatty, Joseph
Bronson, Mr.
Burgess, Isaac
Clark, William
Conway, Michael
Davis, George
Dewey, Freeman
Dunkan, Titus
Edward, David
Ferguson, Harriet
Garlick, Reuben
Graham, Christopher
Griffith, Thomas
Hoag, Samuel, Rev.
Hotchkiss & Woodward, Messrs.
Johnson, William, Lieut., U.C.
Kidd, John, U.C.
Mack, Benjamin
Magrath, James, Rev., U.C.
McCollum, Ebenezer
Mepler, Henry C.
Miller, Benjamin, U.C.
Norton, Alba
Playter, Ely
Pratt, John
Robbs, Hester
Sage, Asahel
Scarborough, John
Anderson, Elizabeth
Barton, Mr.
Bowers, J.R.
Brown, James
Burr, John
Compton, William
Davis, Ebenezer
Deaves, Henry
Doss, David, U.C.
Durand, Henry
Fallen, Marcus
Freeman, Isaac
Grace, Oliver
Grant, Patrick
Harrison, Dennis
Hopkins, Silas
How, John
Kent, Joseph D.P.
Lewis, David
Mackham, Lewis
McCollough, James
McCracken, Robert
Merriam, Joseph
Miller, John P.
P.M. York, U.C.
Porter, Barton & Co., Messrs.
Robbinson, John
Rummerfield, John
Sanders, Hon. Judge
Smith, Israel
Smith, Joshua
Straw, William
Summers, Mary
Titus, John
Tryon, Amos S.
Vannorsel, Garrett
White, Robert
Wilcox, George
Woodward, Mr.
Smith, Sarah
Sullivan, Benjamin W.
Swift, J.F.
Townsend & Barton, Messrs.
Tryon, Mary Ann
Webster, Charles
Whitney, Benjamin, Gen.
Wilkeson, Thomas J.
Yates, Giles

Article no. 153   Subject: Notice
Ref. October 9, 1828; pg. 3, col. 5

Extract: List of letters remaining in the Post Office at Niagara Falls, 1 October 1828. [Names listed, below.] Augustus Porter, Post Master.

Adams, W.W.
Bruin, Herman
Clark, John
Colbertson, Johnson
Devereux, Gen.
Dunscomb, Eliza
Emmons, Alexander
Feaghn, Patrick
Grant, P., Mrs.
Grunway, Edward M.
Helm, Michael
Hodge, George
Hoffman, George B.
Hopkins, Caleb
How, John
Hubbard, Abraham
Hull, Mrs.
Jacobs, Stephen
Leonard, C.H.
McClennen, Samuel
Morris, Caspar W.
Murgatroyd, Isaac G.
Parker, Phillip
Pratt, John
Rice, James
Robinson, Daniel W.
Searle, Charles F.
Slidell, Thomas
Smith, Platt
Stewart, William K.
Thomas, Ambrose
Townsend, Daniel J.
Wellman, Emily
White, Sylvester
Williams, George F.
Wood, William
Worden, Abiah
Britton, John
Burgess, Ebenezer, Rev.
Clark, Sylvester
Cook, J.H.
Diossy, John J.
Durham, Ezra
Emmons, Epaphroditus
Freasher, Joseph
Green, David
Heing, John
Hernandez, S., Consul General
Hoffman, Phillip H.
Hopkinson, Samuel S.
Howell, Mrs.
Hucher, Samuel
Hutley, Joseph
Kissam, Daniel, W., jun.
Levy, Samson
Merry, Cornelius
Morse, Austin
Nova Scotia, Bishop of
Parker, William
Quinn, Thomas
Riggs, Elisha
Rogers, Hannah
Seaver, George
Smith, Isaac
Stevenson, Andrew
Thaxter, Samuel
Thompson, Christopher R.
Tuckerman, Gustavus
White, B.H.
Whitnell, Samuel
Witaker, Richard
Woodward, Darius W.
Wray, John

Article no. 154   Subject: Advertisement
Ref. October 9, 1828; pg. 3, col. 5

A FEW VILLAGE LOTS.

The Subscriber has yet a few Village Lots upon the Frink, Comstock and Mellay Tract, which he continues to sell upon his usual accommodating terms.

S. OLMSTED. Lockport, Oct. 6th, 1828.

Article no. 155   Subject: Advertisement
Ref. October 9, 1828; pg. 3, col. 5

NOTICE.

The Fall Term of the Lewiston Academy will commence on Monday the 15th inst. Mathematical Instruments, and an elegant set of Globes have been prepared for the benefit of the Institution. With these advantages, and an assurance that due attention shall be given to the morals, and intellectual advancement of the Students, we may reasonably anticipate the favourable notice of the public.

The terms of tuition are three dollars per quarter for the Junior and four for the Senior Department.

Board can be obtained for one dollar and fifty cents per week.

By order of the Board of Trustees.

AMOS S. TRYON, Sec' [Sec'y]. Lewiston, Sept. 10, 1828.

Article no. 156   Subject: Advertisement
Ref. October 9, 1828; pg. 3, col. 5

FEATHERS!

Wanted, A quantity of good, live GEESE-FEATHERS. HOUSE & BOUGHTON. October 1, 1828.

Article no. 157   Subject: Notice
Ref. October 9, 1828; pg. 3, col. 5

NOTICE.

All persons indebted to the estate of Asa Bacon deceased, are requested to make immediate payment to Gillet Bacon, who is authorized to settle the estate—and all persons having demands will present them without delay.

BETSEY BACON, Administratrix.
GILLET BACON, Administrator.
Lockport, Oct. 1, 1828.

Article no. 158   Subject: Notice
Ref. October 9, 1828; pg. 3, col. 5

One Cent Reward.

Ran away from the Subscriber on the 26th instant an indented Boy named Daniel Frask, aged ten years, without any coat or shoes; had on a checked woollen shirt, an old pair of woollen pantaloons, vest and hat. This is therefore to forbid all persons harbouring or trusting him on my account, as I shall pay no debts of his contracting after this date.

PERRY GARDNER. Pendleton, Sept. 30th, 1828.

Article no. 159   Subject: Notice
Ref. October 9, 1828; pg. 3, col. 5

BROKE into the enclosure of the subscriber, on or about the twenty-eighth of September last, a BAY HORSE COLT, supposed to be three years old last spring, shod before, with a star in the forehead. The owner is requested to prove property, pay charges, and take him away.

Lockport, October 2, 1828. JOHN W. SMITH.

Article no. 160   Subject: Notice
Ref. October 9, 1828; pg. 3, col. 6

Extract: List of letters remaining in the Post-Office Lockport N.Y. October 1, 1828. Persons calling for any of the above letters are requested to say, they are advertised. [List of names, below.] G.H. Boughton, P.M.

Achenback, Peter	Adams, Sophia
Alger, Samuel	Alvord, Daniel
Anguish, L.	Austin, Jeremiah
Bailey, Joseph	Baker, Elizabeth W.
Baldwin, Mr.	Barber, Abraham
Barnes, A.C.	Barnes, Asenath
Barnes, Collin	Barr, John
Beare, Samuel	Bennet, Almon J.
Bigelow, Amos	Bissel, David
Blaisdel, Samuel	Blood, Russel
Bowman, Brooks	Briggs, Isaac
Brown, Jonathan	Brown, Samuel
Browning, Hannah	Buck, David
Buel, William	Burdick, Abraham
Burner, Bastin	Burns, Patrick
Canfield, Harvey	Carl, Henry
Carrington, Ralph, jun.	Chamberlin, Widow
Chapin, Charlotte	Chappell, Polly
Chatlin, Elizabeth	Clark, D.D.
Collins, Joseph	Collins, Joseph L.
Conkey, Alexander	Converc, Mason
Cook, Judah H.	Cornish, Hiram
Covey, Eldah	Cranson, John
Crossen, David	Dady, Spencer
Dalzell, James	Daws, Hiram R.
Day, Henry	Demmon, Henry
Dexter, Margann	Dexter, William
Dicinger, David	Digee, John
Dillon, Michael	Dillon, William
Donnar, Adam	Doty, William M.
Douglass, Calvin	Draper, Luke
Dunnet, William	Eastman, Timothy
Edson, Abijah	Elliot, John

Fairbanks, Almira
Finch, Noah
Foley, William
Frayne, Edward
Fuller, H.H.
Garley, William
Gibbs, Israel
Grant, Warren W.
Griswold, Lisson
Harrison, Halfred
Harwood, Adeline
Hatter, John
Hawley, Asahel
Hawley, Electa
Henry, Semantha F.
Hildreth, George W.
Holland, John
Huested, Samuel P.
Jinny, Aaron
Jones, Samuel
Kelley, James O.
Kelly, Semanthy
Kimberly, Homer
Layton, Job
Lewis, Henry
Lusk, Samuel D.
M'Nall, Uriah
Mann, Levi B.
Mason, Levi
McAvoy, Thomas
McKnight, Mary
Millard, Hiram
Miller, John F.
Morse, Chauncey
Munger, Asahel
Myars, David
Neal, Joseph
Noag, Samuel
Oliphant, Hiram W.
Orton, John B.
Parks, Hiram
Parmenter, Joseph
Partial, William
Perry, Demas
Pierson, David
Potter, S.M.
Raimant, Thomas
Raney, Wells
Rice, Levi
Richardson, George
Richmond, Brazil
Roberts, Seth

Farrell, Andrew
Fitzpatrick, John
Foster, James O.
Freeman, Daniel
Gardner, Allen
Gary, David
Gilbert, Thomas
Gregory, Ira
Haick, David
Hart, Alpha
Hasset, Patrick
Hawes, Paul
Hawley, Betsey
Heminway, Alanson
Hibbard, Jacob
Hodges, Erastus
Hubbard, Phebe
Ives, William
Johnson, Bennet
Judd, Alfred
Kelly, Phebe
Kent, William C.
Kinnis, Sylvester
Leavenworth, Samuel
Long, Jacob
Lysinger, Thomas
Mahr, Stoffle
Marsh, Caleb
Mather, David
McKeever, John
McLeod, James
Miller, Harvey
Mitchell, Charles F.
Moyer, Samuel
Munro, Samuel
Myers, Martin C.
Needham, Ira
Numan, John
Olnry, Sylvester
Otis, James H.
Parks, Ward
Parsons, Augustus
Peck, Darius
Philips, Peter
Pond, Stephen G.
Prime, Luther
Randall, John
Rea, John
Richards, Ronevel
Richardson, Pardon G.
Robards, Thomas
Robinson, Elisha

Rodgers, Charles G.
Sanders, Israel
Shankland, Robert
Simonds, Harriet
Slayton, Joshua
Smith, Hiram
Smith, Thomas
Southworth, Isaac
Stark, William R.
Stiles, Darwin B.
Stow, Sidney
Terry, Daniel
Tripp, Henry
Tucker, Henry M.
Tuttle, Hiram
Van Camp, Benjamin
Waldo, Chauncey
Walker, John
Watterson, William
Welch, Lucinda
Wheeler, Oliver C.
White, Mary
Williams, Charles
Wilmarth, John
Woodard, –. M.
Woodward, C.C.
Woolcott, Daniel
Wright, George
Young, Uri

Rogers, Liman
Scullion, Thomas
Shepard, Lyman
Simpson, James
Smith, David
Smith, Stephen B.
Soper, Samuel
Staht, William
Stiles, Bradley D.
Stocking, Clarissa
Symonds, William
Thomas, Giles
Trowbridge, Cyrus
Tucker, William
Underwood, Spellman
Van Velzer, —m H.
Walker, James M.
Warner, Thomas B.
Weelbur, Abraham
Weston, Sally Ann
Whippry, George S.
Whitton, Thomas B.
Willis, George B.
Wilson, Robert F.
Woodard, Ralph
Woodward, Corydon C.
Worden, Christopher
York, Simpson

Article no. 161   Subject: Advertisement
Ref. October 9, 1828; pg. 3, col. 6

Country Produce,
Of every kind suited to family consumption, will be very cheerfully received in payment of dues to this paper, at the current market price. Sept. 25.

Article no. 162   Subject: Advertisement
Ref. October 9, 1828; pg. 4, col. 3

Extract: THE MASONIC REVIEW and ANTI-MASONIC MAGAZINE. (Thirty-two octavo pages.) To be published monthly, in an elegant pamphlet form, designed to show the origin, to expose the pretensions, and fully to unfold the true character and tendency of Freemasonry. By Henry Dana Ward, A.M. {Article includes terms of subscription and further description of magazine.} Mr. Ward is known to us as a zealous and able writer upon the subject of Subjective Freemasonry. He is impelled to this task by consideration of the most elevated character; and we earnestly recommend his work to the patronage of all the friends of religious truth and civil liberty.

Article no. 163 Subject: Notice
Ref. October 9, 1828; pg. 4, col. 3

Extract: List of letters remaining in the Post-Office at Royalton, October 1, 1828. [List of names, below.] Geo. Reynale, P.M.

Baldwin, Anson
Bently, Richard
Bowerman, Joshua
Bronson, Amos
Bryan, Lucy
Chase, Benjamin F.
Clement, James
Dart, Freman
Davis, Sophia
Dutton, Amasa, jun.
Foster, James O.
Gates, William
Green, William
Griffen, James
Hart, Tyrus
Haviland, Charles, jun.
Horton, Lewis B.
Hull, Mary
Jackson, Servus
Johnson, David
Kelsey, John
Lindsley, David A.
Loveland, Thomas
Mabee, James
Manchester, Eliza
Michell, Jason
Moore, Walter
Pierce, Jonas
Pratt, Samuel
Riggs, Stephen
Rowly, Myron
Smith, David B.
Sprague, Nelson N.
Stevens, Elean
Stone, Nathan H.
Thayer, Stephen
Turner, Celicia
Wall, Chester
Wells, John F.
Woodcock, Rufus
Wright, Henry
Barmore, Marshel
Blanchard, Ira
Bowman, B.
Bronson, Elnathan B.
Butts, Daniel
Cherry, Elijah
Cutler, George.
Davis, Moses
Drake, William
Fenn, Ethan
Gates, Samuel
Graves, Martha M.
Greenman, Adley
Hart, Tryphena
Harwood, Marville
Holdridge, Felix
Hubbard, Ephraim A.
Hutchins, James L.
Jenvell, Lewis J.
Jones, William
Lee, Thomas
Lockwood, Abraham
Lyon, Amos
Maclary, Thomas
Merchant, John
Moore, Oliver
Orcutt, Erastus
Pratt, Elizabeth
Rice, Jobe
Roberts, William
Sheffield, Alexander
Snyder, Henry C.
Stage, William C.
Stevens, Jacob
Stowell, Nathan
Tobey, Richard W.
Virle, Louisa C.
Wells, John
Wiley, Samuel
Woolworth, Seth T.

Article no. 164 Subject: Notice
Ref. October 9, 1828; pg. 4, col. 4

Extract: List of letters remaining in the Post Office at Youngstown, N.Y. October 1, 1828. [List of names, below.] A.G., Hinman, P.M.

Adair, Daniel O.
Allen, Levi
Arbuthnot, William
Bladen, Jacob
Brown, Thomas
Canfield, Harvey
Crooks, J.
Hadley, Ira
Harvey, Urson
Hyde, Sarah S.
Loyd, John
Lutts, Jacob
McLean, Archibald
Morse, William
Smith, D.M.
Taylor, Ellen
Toner, James
Wilkins, Seymour
Armstrong, B.
Bleyne, Crandle S.
Caine, Sophia
Churchill, James H.
Griffeth, George
Harrington, Uriah
Herrick, Benjamin
Ives, Elisha
Lusk, Rebecca
Mass, Chester H.
Morse, Samuel
Prescott, Eustes
Symonds, Martin
Thompson, Robert
Vroman, John
Williams, John

Article no. 165 Subject: Notice
Ref. October 9, 1828; pg. 4, col. 5

Extract: BY virtue of several executions issued out of the Supreme Court of Judicature of the state of New-York, to me directed and delivered, against the goods and chattels, lands and tenements of David Chapman and Stephen Chapman, I have seized all that certain piece or parcel of land, situate, lying and being in the Village of Manchester, in the town and county of Niagara, (near Niagara Falls,), and described as follows, viz.—{Notice includes description of boundaries.}—containing about three fourths of an acre of land, more or less: Also, a certain other tract of land, in said village of Manchester, described as follows, viz.—{Notice includes description of boundaries.} [bounded westerly on the river:] Also, one other piece of land, lying in the said village of Manchester, bounded and described as follows: {Notice includes description of boundaries.} [deeded by Augustus Porter and Benjamin Barton to John W. Stoughton, 31 January 1816, and on which the old stone fulling mill stands.] On the land above mentioned is an elegant tavern, now occupied by the said David Chapman, and two stone cotton and woollen factories: All which I shall expose for sale at public vendue, at the house of David Chapman, on the premises, 7 November 1828. Dated September 22d, 1828.

JOHN PHILLIPS, Sheriff.

Article no. 166 Subject: Advertisement
Ref. October 23, 1828; pg. 1, col. 4

New Establishment,
In the new Brick Building, three doors east of the Post-Office—where will be found a general assortment of Family Supplies, and Groceries of all kinds, which will be sold cheap for ready pay.

J.A. BENJAMIN. Lockport, Oct. 14, 1828.

Article no. 167	Subject: Advertisement

Ref. October 23, 1828; pg. 1, col. 5

NOW IS THE TIME!

The subscriber offers, at a bargain, a number of Lots, situated in different parts of this Village, at low prices, on accommodating terms, separately or in parcels to suit purchasers.

Since the completion of the Grand Erie Canal, experience has taught us, that money could in no way be so well invested, as in real estate located in the principal towns on its borders.—Scarcely has there been an instance where locations have been made in this village, that purchasers have not received two dollars for one.— From the great number of buildings now erecting, and other improvements, together with the daily arrival of citizens from the east and elsewhere, who are locating themselves here, reasonable expectations are entertained, that a great advance upon real estate will take place the ensuing season.

Apply at my office, opposite L.A. Spalding's.

S. OLMSTED. Lockport, Oct. 8, 1828.

Article no. 168	Subject: Politics

Ref. October 23, 1828; pg. 3, col. 2

Extract: (CIRCULAR.)

Sir: By the resignation of the Hon. Cha's H. Carroll, of his seat in the Senate of this State, the Electors of the 8th Senatorial District have been called upon to select a suitable person to fill the vacancy occasioned by such resignation. ... An Anti-Masonic Convention of Delegates from the counties of Livingston and Monroe was accordingly held at the town of Rush, on the 20th inst. for the purpose of making such nomination, and that meeting resulted in the nomination of James Wadsworth, of Livingston.{Article includes description of Livingston's principles, &c.} We are happy to state that in our part of the District, notwithstanding all the efforts to misrepresent, distract and divide, our cause appears highly prosperous, and affords the surest promise of success. Rochester, Oct. 22nd, 1828. By order of the Convention.

JOHN MERCHANT, Ch'n.

TABOR WARD, Sec'y.

[Editor's note:] The call for a Convention at Batavia, to select a candidate for the Senate in this district to supply the place of Judge Carroll, has been countermanded; it being considered best to leave the selection of a candidate to the people of Livingston. How well that duty has been performed, will be apparent from the choice they have made: the name of Wadsworth is a host in itself.

Article no. 169	Subject: Social Welfare

Ref. October 23, 1828; pg. 3, col. 3

COUNTY POOR HOUSE.

At the late meeting of the Board of Supervisors in this village, a resolution was passed, authorising the raising of the necessary funds for the purchase of a farm, and the erection thereon of a Poor House for this county, the ensuing year. This is a most judicious measure. The poor-rates for several years past, have constituted a large part of the taxes levied on the people; and during the past season, the support of paupers, owing the general sickness prevalent thro'-out the county, has been onerous in the extreme: indeed, we speak from a knowledge of the fact, that the additional expense to which the county has this year been put, for want of a poor house, would have almost been sufficient to meet all the expenditures necessary for the erection of a suitable building. We are pleased, therefore, that the Supervisors have determined to make the necessary arrangements in that respect, without delay.

Five commissioners, to wit: Messrs. G.H. Boughton, Henry W. Clark, Asher Freeman, Dexter P. Sprague, and William Doty—have been appointed, to make a selection of a suitable site for the contemplated establishment; and any information which might be given them on the subject, will no doubt be thankfully received. The farm is not to exceed one hundred acres, and must be conveniently situated.

Article no. 170	Subject: Politics

Ref. October 23, 1828; pg. 3, col. 3

At a meeting of the Anti-Masonic citizens of the town of Lockport, convened pursuant to public notice, at the house of Samuel Jennings, on Wednesday, 22d inst., for the purpose of nominating a candidate for the office of Justice of the Peace for said town, to supply the place of Henry Norton, Esq., whose present term of service will expire with the current year—Mr. Seth Parsons was called to the chair, and A.T. Prentice appointed Secretary: whereupon it was unanimously Resolved, That whereas the present incumbent, Henry Norton, Jr. having faithfully and satisfactorily discharged the duties of said office for the term he has served, he be recommended as a suitable person to be re-elected.

A resolution that the proceedings be signed by the Chairman and Secretary, and published, was then passed, and the meeting adjourned.

SETH PARSONS, Chm'n.

A.T. PRENTICE, Sec'y.

Article no. 171 Subject: Education
Ref. October 23, 1828; pg. 3, col. 4

Ontario Female Seminary.—The first term of this institution under its present Principal, ended on Friday of last week, with a cursory examination before the Board of Trustees. From the necessary brevity of the exercises, there was not the same opportunity of judging of the progress of the pupils, as a more minute and extended examination would have afforded; but we have rarely witnessed one, in which equal promptitude and accuracy in answering the respective questions were evinced. The course of instruction pursued, appeared to have been very properly adapted to exercise the intelligence of the pupils, and to induce a habit of reflection and reasoning upon the subjects to which their attention had been directed. We mention this as a peculiarity, creditable to the judgment and skill of the instructers [sic]. The mechanical method pursued in most schools, of learning by rote a multiplicity of principles and facts, without applying them to practice, or turning them to any useful purpose, is very little calculated to promote the legitimate ends of education.

The present character and prospects of this institution, are a subject of just pride and felicitation to the village of Canandaigua, and to the western section of the state. We have before expressed the belief, and we now repeat it, with a confidence strengthened by the experience of the past term, that this seminary is distined [sic] to distinguished usefulness and prosperity. The completion of the building lately added to the school edifice, renders the whole, in point of commodiousness and elegance, second to none in the U. States.

A course of lectures and experiments on chemistry, is shortly to be commenced in the Philosophical Institute of Canandaigua, to which by a standing provision of its constitution, the pupils of the Seminary and Academy are gratuitously admitted. Measures have been taken for procuring in time the necessary apparatus, a part of which has already arrived. By an advertisement in this paper it will be seen, that the Seminary is to re-open on the 15th of October.—*Ontario Repository.*

Article no. 172 Subject: Politics
Ref. October 23, 1828; pg. 3, col. 5

Extract: THE ELECTION.
National Nominations ... State Nominations ...
Anti-Masonic District and County Nominations ...
[Listed, below.]

- Adams, John Quincy; nominated for President.
- Boughton, George H.; state of New York; for Senator.
- Catlin, Henry; Niagara County, New York; for County Clerk.
- Cook, Theron B.; Niagara County, New York; for one of four Coroner posts.
- Cooke, Lothrop; Niagara County, New York; for one of four Coroner posts.
- Crary, John; state of New York; for Lieut. Governor of the state of New-York.
- Garnsey, John; state of New York; for Assembly.
- Granger, Francis; state of New York; for Lieut. Governor of the state of New-York.
- Holmes, Daniel; Niagara County, New York; for one of four Coroner posts.
- Norton, Ebenezer F.; state of New York; for Congress, 30th District.
- Phillips, John; Niagara County, New York; for Sheriff.
- Rush, Richard; for Vice-President of the United States.
- Saxton, Asher; Niagara County, New York; for one of four Coroner posts.
- Southwick, Solomon; state of New York; for Governor of the state of New-York.
- Thompson, Smith; state of New York; for Governor of the state of New-York.
- Wadsworth, James; state of New York; for Senator, 8th District.
- Walden, Ebenezer; for Elector of the United States.

Article no. 173 Subject: Politics
Ref. October 23, 1828; pg. 3, col. 5

To the Electors of the County of Niagara.

I offer myself as a Candidate for the Office of Clerk of this County at the ensuing election. Having been in the Office for three years past, and done most of the business of it, as a Deputy, I have of course acquired a practical knowledge of its duties; and (if elected,) you will have my best exertions to discharge them with punctuality and correctness.

HENRY K. HOPKINS. Oct. 15th, 1828.

Article no. 174 Subject: Politics
Ref. October 23, 1828; pg. 3, col. 5

Anti-Masonic.
To the Free and Independent Electors
of the County of Niagara:

In compliance with the wishes of a respectable number of my friends, I have consented to offer myself as a candidate for the Office of County Clerk, at the ensuing election. Relying on the impartial determination of my fellow-citizens, who must spurn at the dictation of those who have usurped the right of directing and controlling the deliberations of our late County Convention, I submit the matter to their just decision, with the assurance that if elected, I shall aim to discharge the duties of that Office to the best of my knowledge and ability.

CARLOSS B. WOODWARD. Lockport, Oct. 21, 1828.

Article no. 175 Subject: Notice
Ref. October 23, 1828; pg. 3, col. 6

NOTICE.

All persons indebted to the subscriber for tuition, are requested to make immediate payment.
HEMAN FERRISS. Lockport, Oct. 23d, 1828.

Article no. 176 Subject: Advertisement
Ref. October 23, 1828; pg. 3, col. 6

FOR SALE.

The subscriber has for sale a new Patent Lever Gold Watch. Lockport, Oct. 23, 1828. J. CATLIN.

Article no. 177 Subject: Advertisement
Ref. October 23, 1828; pg. 3, col. 6

NOTICE.

The Subscriber having purchased of Lewis Goddard, the Right, Tools, &c. for making Pumps, is now ready to attend to all calls in that line of business.
NICHOLAS BRATT. Lockport, Oct. 16, 1828.

Article no. 178 Subject: Notice
Ref. October 23, 1828; pg. 3, col. 6

SHERIFF'S SALE.

By virtue of an execution issued out of the Supreme Court of Judicature of the state of New-York, and to me directed and delivered, against the goods and chattels, lands and tenements of Daniel Van Horn, Ezra Gleason, and Christopher L. Taylor, I have seized and taken all their goods and chattels, lands and tenements, to wit: all the right, title, interest, property, possession, claim and demand of the said Daniel Van Horn, Ezra Gleason, and Christopher L. Taylor, or any or either of them, of, in and to the following piece or parcel of land, situate, lying and being in the town of Hartland, in the county of Niagara, in the state of New-York, being part or parcel of a certain township which on a map or survey of divers tracts or townships of land of the Holland Land Company, made for the said Holland Land Company by Joseph Ellicott, surveyor, is distinguished by townseip [sic] number fifteen in the fifth range of said townships, and which said tract of land on a certain other map or survey of said township into sections and lots made for the said Holland Land Company by the said Joseph Ellicott, is distinguished by the north part of lot number 8, in the 9th section in said township, containing sixty-nine acres, be the same more or less. All of which I shall expose for sale as the Law directs, on the 6th day of December next at the house of John Goodeno, now occupied as a tavern, in the town of Hartland, in the county of Niagara, at 11 o'clock, A.M. Dated Hartland Oct. 23, 1828.
JOHN PHILLIPS, Sheriff.

Article no. 179 Subject: Politics
Ref. October 23, 1828; pg. 4, col. 1

Extract: ANTI-MASONIC COUNTY CONVENTION.

At an Anti-Masonic County Convention of Delegates from the various towns of the county of Niagara, held at the house of Samuel Jennings, innkeeper, in the village of Lockport, in said county, on Wednesday the 8th October inst., at 2 o'clock P.M., the following Delegates appeared and took their seats: [Listed, below.] The convention was called to order by Elias Ransom, Jun. Esq. Jacob Townsend was called to the chair, and Samuel De Veaux, appointed Secretary. The following resolutions were then adopted: {Article includes outline of resolutions.}

[Transcriber's note: See key for numerically coded references, after the list of index entries.]

- Alvord, Daniel; Lockport, New York (1) (2)
- Ash, Nathan; Porter, New York (3)
- Bacon, James; Lockport, New York (2)
- Baker, Charles; Wilson, New York (4) (5)
- Bills, Thomas; Hartland, New York (6) (24)
- Boughton, George H.; Niagara, New York. The Convention resolved to support Boughton at the ensuing election as a candidate for the Senate.
- Bradner, William; Niagara, New York (22)
- Brown, John, jun.; Wilson, New York (5)
- Catlin, Henry; Niagara, New York. The Convention resolved to support Catlin at the ensuing election for the office of Clerk of the county.
- Chaplin, Daniel; Hartland, New York (6) (24)
- Clapsaddle, John; Porter, New York (8)
- Clark, Henry W.; Niagara, New York (9)
- Collar, Joshua D.; Wilson, New York (5)
- Colville, Randel; Newfane, New York (10)
- Cook, Lothrop; Niagara, New York (11) (12)
- Cook, Theron B.; Hartland, New York (11) (13)
- Crary, John; state of New York. The Convention resolved to support Crary at the ensuing election as the candidate for Lieutenant Governor [of the state of New York].
- Crozier, William; Cambria, New York (14)
- Davis, James; Wilson, New York (4)
- De Veaux, Samuel; Niagara, New York; appointed Secretary to the Convention. (9)
- Dickerson, Alexander; Lewiston, New York (12)
- Doty, William; Porter, New York (8)
- Earl, William; Cambria, New York (15)
- Fenn, Decius S.; Royalton, New York (16)
- Fenn, Ethan; Royalton, New York (17)
- Fields, Eldad; Niagara, New York (7) (22)
- Freeman, Asher; Royalton, New York (16)
- Garsey, John; Niagara, New York. The Convention resolved to support Garsey at the ensuing election as a candidate for member of Assembly.
- Gray, John; Lewiston, New York (18)

- Hammond, Eliakim; Cambria, New York (14) (15) (20)
- Hayes, Stephen; Newfane, New York (19)
- Hess, John; Newfane, New York (10)
- Holmes, Daniel; Wilson, New York (4)
- Holmes, Daniel; Niagara, New York (11)
- House, William C.; Niagara County, New York (20)
- Houstater, Jacob; Cambria, New York (14)
- Hurd, Eli; Royalton, New York (17)
- Johnston, Asahel; Hartland, New York (13)
- Kenyon, Allen; Hartland, New York (6)
- Kinyon, Allen; Hartland, New York (13) (24)
- Kline, Matthias; Lewiston, New York (12)
- McNeil, Hiram; Cambria, New York (14)
- Millikin, Asa; Pendleton, New York (21)
- Minor, Alexander; Wilson, New York (5)
- Moss, Solomon; Porter, New York (3)
- Newman, Almiron; Newfane, New York (19)
- Newman, Elisha; Newfane, New York (10)
- Newman, Ira; Niagara, New York (7) (22)
- Norton, Ebenezer F.; Erie County, New York. The Convention resolved to support Norton at the ensuing election as a member of Congress.
- Oliver, Daniel; Cambria, New York (15)
- Orton, Myron; Cambria, New York (14)
- Parsons, Aaron; Niagara, New York (7) (22)
- Parsons, Seth; Lockport, New York (2)
- Peck, George; Hartland, New York (6) (24)
- Phillips, John; Niagara, New York. The Convention resolved to support Phillips at the ensuing election for the office of Sheriff.
- Potter, Darius; Hartland, New York (6) (24)
- Prentice, Walter W.; Lockport, New York (2)
- Ransom, Elias, jun., Esq.; Lockport, New York; called the Convention to order. (1) (20)
- Reynale, George; Royalton, New York (16) (17)
- Rogers, Erastus; Pendleton, New York (21) (23)
- Ross, Samuel L.; Royalton, New York (17)
- Saxton, Asher; Niagara, New York (11)
- Schyler, John; Pendleton, New York (23)
- Sheldon, Simon S.; Wilson, New York (5)
- Simmons, Elijah; Hartland, New York (24)
- Smith, Albe P.; Niagara, New York (7) (22)
- Smith, Thomas F.; Royalton, New York (17)
- Southwick, Solomon; state of New York. The Convention resolved to support Southwick at the ensuing election as the candidate for Governor [of the state of New York].
- Taylor, Richard J.; Lewiston, New York (12)
- Tompkins, Ira; Newfane, New York (10)
- Tower, Peter; Porter, New York (3)
- Townsend, Jacob; Lewiston, New York; Chairman. (18)
- Tryon, Josiah; Lewiston, New York (12) (18)
- Valentine, James; Royalton, New York (17)
- Van Horne, James; Newfane, New York (19)
- Vanslike, Garret; Pendleton, New York (21)
- Walden, Ebenezer, Hon.; Erie County, New York. The Anti-Masonic Central Committee (composed of W.C. House, E. Ransom, jun., and E. Hammond) recommended Walden, knowing him as a consistent and thorough-going Anti-Mason, for the post of Elector of President and Vice-President at the ensuing General Election in November.
- Walker, Leonard H.; Porter, New York (3) (8)
- Williams, John; Lockport, New York (1) (2)
- Yerrington, Lorin; Niagara, New York (9)

Key:
(1) Elias Ransom, Jr., John Williams and Daniel Alvord represented the village of Lockport.
(2) Seth Parsons, John Williams, Walter W. Prentice, Daniel Alvord and James Bacon were to compose the committee of vigilance for the village of Lockport, to be authorized to call meetings at any time they may think proper, in promoting the anti-masonic cause.
(3) Peter Tower, Leonard H. Walker, Nathan Ash and Solomon Moss were to compose the committee of vigilance for the village of Porter, etc.
(4) Charles Baker, James Davis and Daniel Holmes represented the village of Wilson.
(5) Charles Baker, Joshua D. Collar, John Brown, Jr., Alexander Minor and Simon S. Sheldon were to compose the committee of vigilance for the village of Wilson, etc.
(6) Elijah Simmons, Allen Kenyon, Daniel Chaplin, George Peck, Darius Potter and Thomas Bills were to compose the committee of vigilance for the village of Hartland, etc.
(7) William Bradner, Albe P. Smith, Aaron Parsons, Ira Newman and Eldad Fields were to compose the committee of vigilance for the town of Niagara, etc.
(8) John Clapsaddle, William Doty and Leonard H. Walker represented the village of Porter.
(9) Lorin Yerrington, Samuel De Veaux and Henry W. Clark represented the town of Niagara.
(10) Ira Tompkins, John Hess, Randel Colville and Elisha Newman were to compose the committee of vigilance for the village of New-Fane, etc.
(11) The Convention resolved to support Daniel Holmes, Asher Saxton, Theron B. Cook and Lothrop Cook at the ensuing election for the office of Coroner.
(12) Josiah Tryon, Alexander Dickerson, Lothrop Cooke, Richard J. Taylor and Matthias Kline were

to compose the committee of vigilance for the town of Lewiston, etc.

(13) Theron B. Cook, Asahel Johnston and Allen Kinyon represented the village of Hartland.

(14) Myron Orton, Jacob Houstater, Eliakim Hammond, Hiram McNeil and William Crozier were to compose the committee of vigilance for the village of Cambria, etc.

(15) Daniel Oliver, Eliakim Hammond and William Earl represented the village of Cambria.

(16) Asher Freeman, George Reynale and Decius S. Fenn represented the village of Royalton.

(17) George Reynale, Eli Hurd, Ethan Fenn, Thomas F. Smith, Samuel L. Ross and James Valentine were to compose the committee of vigilance for the village of Royalton, etc.

(18) Jacob Townsend, John Gray and Josiah Tryon represented the village of Lewiston.

(19) Almiron Newman, Stephen Hayes and James Van Horn represented the village of New-Fane.

(20) The Convention resolved, that Elias Ransom, Jr. Esq., Eliakim Hammond, Esq., and William C. House, Esq. would compose the Central Corresponding Committee.

(21) Asa Millikin, Garret Vanslike and Erastus Rogers were to compose the committee of vigilance for the village of Pendleton, etc.

(22) William Bradner, Albe P. Smith, Aaron Parsons, Ira Newman and Eldad Fields were to compose the committee of vigilance for the town of Niagara, etc.

(23) John Schyler and Erastus Rogers represented the village of Pendleton.

(24) Elijah Simmons, Allen Kenyon, Daniel Chaplin, George Peck, Darius Potter and Thomas Bills were to compose the committee of vigilance for the village of Hartland, etc.

Article no. 180 Subject: Notice
Ref. October 23, 1828; pg. 4, col. 2

NOTICE.

All persons indebted to the estate of Jairus Rose, late of the town of Cambria, deceased, are requested to make immediate payment to the subscriber, and save further trouble and cost.—Also, all persons having demands against said estate are requested to present them for settlement. GEORGE P. ROSE, Executor.

The like proceedings are requested on the part of the subscriber, in his own case.

GEORGE P. ROSE. Oct. 11, 1828.

Article no. 181 Subject: Notice
Ref. October 23, 1828; pg. 4, col. 3

CAUTION.

Whereas the subscribers gave four notes of hand for $50 each—two to be paid in cash, and two in stock, to a person by the name of Isaac Briggs, dated on or about the 6th of June 1828, and payable in December or January next. This is therefore to caution all persons from purchasing said notes, as the alleged value for which they were given, having never been received, we are determined not to pay the same.

FRANCIS SAUNDERS, IRA S. SAUNDERS.

Lewiston, Sept. 8, 1828.

Article no. 182 Subject: Advertisement
Ref. November 15, 1831; pg. 1, col. 1

Printed and published every Tuesday, by
M. CADWALLADER.
Office in the brick block, Main-street—over the store of S. Parsons & Co.
Terms—Village subscribers, $2.50; mail subscribers and those calling at the office, $2, per year.

Article no. 183 Subject: Politics
Ref. November 15, 1831; pg. 1, col. 1

Extract: Correspondence between the Hon. Richard Rush and the Committee of the National Anti-Masonic Convention.

Butternuts, Otsego County, (N.Y.) October 5, 1831.

Sir:—{Article includes letter addressed to the Hon. Richard Rush, written by John C. Morris, Harmar Denny and Joshua V. Gibbins, directed by the following:} In the Anti-Masonic Convention, Baltimore 28th Sept. 1831. Resolved unanimously, That a committee of three members be appointed to express by written communication to the Honourable Richard Rush, of Pennsylvania, the profound sense of this Convention of the patriotism, principle, and firmness which dictated his eloquent exposition of the evils of Freemasonry, and their high appreciation of the beneficial results which it cannot fail to produce. Mr. Morris, of New-York, Mr. Denny, of Pennsylvania, and Mr. Gibbins, of Delaware, were appointed [to] said Committee.

[Followed by:] Mr. Rush's Reply. York, (Pa.) Oct. 15, 1831. Gentlemen: I received yesterday your letter of 5th inst. conveying to me a copy of the resolution of the Anti-Masonic Convention at Baltimore passed on the 28th of last month approving of the sentiments I have expressed in relation to Freemasonry; and, I beg to assure you, that I am gratefully sensible to the honour of a vote of approbation by a body so distinguished; and that I fully appreciate the very kind terms in which you have been pleased to communicate it to me. {Article includes remainder of letter.} I renew the expression of my gratitude and thanks for so valued a mark of its favour. I remain, Gentlemen, With great respect, Your most obedient, and obliged servant, Richard Rush. [Length, 1 column.]

Article no. 184   Subject: Court
Ref. November 15, 1831; pg. 1, col. 3

Extract: From the *Eastport Sentinel*, Oct. 26.
TRIAL—CONVICTION—FINE & IMPRISONMENT OF AMERICAN SETTLERS OF MADAWASKA!

We have received the *St. Johns [sic] Courier*, of the 23d, which contains an account of the Trial and Conviction at the Supreme Court, at Fredericton, of Barnabas Hannawell, Jesse Whetlock and Daniel Savage, for certain "seditious acts, (as they are called by the Provincials) at the Madawaska settlement," which 'seditious acts,' our readers have before been apprized, consisted in choosing town officers in the newly incorporated Town of Madawaska. The trial took place on the 15th inst. The defendants appeared without Counsel. One of them, Hannawell, in his defence, said, "that having received the warrant, they were obliged under the law of the State of Maine to act, they would have been liable to punishment under their laws if they had declined. That in the situation of the country there was a difficulty on both sides, and of two evils they thought they had chosen the least, as they were led to suppose from what the two officers, Messrs. Maclouch and Coombee, had said, they would not be interfered with so long as they confined themselves to the west side of the river."

The Jury, after a short consultation, returned a verdict of Guilty, when the defendants were asked whether they had any thing to offer the Court, answered in the negative. His Honour, Mr. Justice Chipman, then addressed them, and observed:

"That it was sufficient merely to state the charge of which they had been found guilty to show its aggravated character without adding a word of comment. ... The defendants appeared to be persons not wanting in understanding and discretion, and must have perceived the difference between the proceedings of the American Agents (Messrs. Dean and Kavannah) alluded to, and their own doings, ... {Article includes remainder of the judge's opinion, concluding with:}

"That each of the Defendants do pay a fine to the King of fifty pounds, and be imprisoned in the Common Gaol of the County for three calendar months, and stand committed until the said fines are paid."

Thus it is seen that American citizens acting under the law of the State are Fined and Imprisoned by a foreign power! We wait to see whether our Governor has energy for an occasion which calls upon him to Act, in some way or other, in the defence of our laws and the rights and liberties of our people.

The above imprisoned American citizens, with Daniel Bean, John Baker, and twenty-seven other persons, are also charged on another indictment, presented against them by the Grand Jury, which charges them with the intention "to stir up and procure sedition in the Province," &c. &c. It was deemed expedient, says the *Courier*, by the Crown officers, to suffer proceedings to stand over until the meeting of the Supreme Court, in February next.

The Government of N. Brunswick have proceeded too far in the Madawaska affair. It would have been sufficient for them, and would have answered every purpose, to have forbidden the choice of officers, &c. which they did do. Why then forcibly arrest, fine and imprison American citizens? Do they wish to provoke hostilities on our part? Our advice is, that they forthwith release the prisoners, and fully and amply indemnify them for all injury they may have sustained.

Article no. 185   Subject: Agriculture
Ref. November 15, 1831; pg. 1, col. 5

From the *Quebec Gazette*, Oct. 26.

We are sorry to hear that several of the cargoes of wheat shipped from this country for the united kingdom have come to a bad market. Much of it arrived in a damaged state, and the prospects and results of the harvest at home, have lowered the prices. The loss will be considerable, and it has tended to diminish confidence in mercantile transactions here. Most of the business in the wheat line in this country was, however, done on commission, and the effect will only be felt, in cases where houses at home may fail, which we are informed has been the case in some instances.

A certain degree of embarrassment is felt in the commercial world in England, probably resulting from speculation on the state of public affairs in Europe, and their actual unsettled state.

Article no. 186   Subject: Transportation
Ref. November 15, 1831; pg. 1, col. 5

Extract: Rail Roads. Since the Syracuse Convention, several meetings have been held in various parts of the state on the subject of rail-road communication, and a variety of routes have been indicated, according to the interests of different sections. {Article includes description of proposal.} [Rail-roads mentioned: Ithaca and Owego [sic], and the Pennsylvania line. Place names mentioned: Boston, Buffalo, Chautauque lake, Fredonia, Geneva, Ithaca, Lewiston, New-York, North River, Schenectady, Welland canal, and Westfield.] Reprinted from the *Buffalo Republican* newspaper.

Article no. 187   Subject: Death
Ref. November 15, 1831; pg. 1, col. 5

Funeral of Major General Barton.—Our flags from the shipping in the harbour, and at the several military posts, were yesterday displayed at half-mast, in honour of the memory of this veteran general of the American revolution, whose funeral was solemnized at 3 o'clock P.M. At 3 o'clock the procession moved from his late residence in South Main-street, under the escort of the independent company of cadets. The artillery, volunteers, and light infantry, followed in rear of the corpse. On the coffin was placed the sword given by congress to general Barton, for his gallant capture of general Prescott. Minute guns were fired from the moment the procession moved, until the aged veteran was deposited in his grave.

Article no. 188   Subject: History
Ref. November 15, 1831; pg. 1, col. 6

Mr. R.R. Waldron has deposited in the Portsmouth Atheneum [sic], the "Strong Box" taken during the Indian War, from Ralle, the Jesuit, at Norridgewock, in 1621, by Col. Westbrook.

Article no. 189   Subject: Politics
Ref. November 15, 1831; pg. 2, col. 3

Extract: WHIG TICKET.
Anti-Masonic Republican Nomination.
For President, William Wirt.
For Vice-President, Amos Ellmaker.

The Election. We have not yet received returns of the election to any great extent. So far as we have received them, however, there is no cause for sorrow. {Editorial opinion continues, concluding with this prediction:} When the whole returns come in, it will be seen that poor Freemasonry, and her mate, the Regency, are in a poor way! [Transcriber's note: Place names mentioned include: Albany, Cayuga, Columbia, Greene, Oneida, Onondaga, Ontario, Orleans, Rensselaer, Schenectady, Schoharie, Seneca, Tioga, Wayne, Westchester, and Yates counties.]

Article no. 190   Subject: Politics
Ref. November 15, 1831; pg. 2, col. 3

NIAGARA COUNTY. The number of votes polled in this county this year, was only 1125—of which the antimasonic candidates received 1119.

Article no. 191   Subject: Politics
Ref. November 15, 1831; pg. 2, col. 3

Extract: The *Balance* [newspaper] takes exceptions to our remarks in reference to Hiram Gardner, Esq., and calls them "abuse." Had we written any thing that was one fifteenth part as villanous [sic] and abusive as their article in reference to the Justice of the Peace who issued his warrant to apprehend the land-pirates who were attempting to rob a peaceable citizen of his property, there might have been cause of complaint. {Article includes additional editorial opinion.} [Transcriber's note: This article appears in the Editorial columns. A similar editorial article appears in column 4 of the same page.]

Article no. 192   Subject: Politics
Ref. November 15, 1831; pg. 2, col. 4

MADAWASKA.—The Governor of the state of Maine has called a special meeting of the Executive Council, for the purpose of advising with them on the Madawaska troubles.—Important consequences depend on their measures. A writer in the *Portland Advertiser* denies a suggestion in the *Washington Globe*, that the Governor of Maine had any knowledge "that there was a distinct understanding, that until the question was finally settled, each of the parties should remain in the exercise of the same jurisdiction over such parts of the territory as was then held by them respectively."

This case has become the more urgent since the conviction, sentence and imprisonment, by a court of New-Brunswick, of three American citizens, "for conspiring to subvert His Majesty's authority" in those parts. [Reprinted from the] *Craftsman*.

Article no. 193   Subject: Death
Ref. November 15, 1831; pg. 2, col. 5

From the *Westchester Herald*.

Another Revolutionary Patriot gone.—We have to lament the death of another distinguished patriot of the Revolution. Gen. Philip Van Cortlandt, of ths [sic] county, died at his residence in the town of Cortlandt, on Sunday, the 5th instant, at 8 o'clock in the evening, aged 82 years. He was at the time of his decease, the senior surviving officer in this country of the army of the Revolution. During the revolutionary war he was the companion of Washington and Lafayette. He had the command of a regiment in the Continental army in the line of the State of New York, and served his country in that capacity honestly and faithfully, enduring every hardship and privation, until the close of the war. He was at the taking of Burgoyne at Saratoga, and distinguished himself as a gallant officer at the battle of Beman's Heights, previous to the surrunder [sic] of Burgoyne. He was one of the members from this county of the State Convention, held at Poughkeepsie, in 17888 [sic], for the adoption of the Constitution of the U. States, and his vote was recorded in favour of that sacred instrument, which was carried in this State by a majority of only three. He was afterwards elected by his fellow citizens as a member of Congress of the United States, and served his country in that capacity for several years in succession with much ability. He was remarkable for his personal dignity,—and combined two traits of character seldom united in the person, loftiness of manner with urbanity of disposition. No man was held superior in estimation either on account of amiableness of manners, or benevolence of heart.

Article no. 194 Subject: Marriage
Ref. November 15, 1831; pg. 2, col. 6

MARRIED—in Cambria, on the 16th inst. by the Rev. Mr. Taggart, of this village, Mr. Otis Brooks, to Miss Elizabeth Smith, both of the former place.

Article no. 195 Subject: Advertisement
Ref. November 15, 1831; pg. 2, col. 6

NEW SUPPLIES!
Latest Fall and Winter Fashions.

G.S. Place has just received from New-York his Fall and Winter's supply of Fashionable Clothing, &c., to which he calls the attention of his numerous customers, whom he flatters himself can now supply with every article needed in his line on much more favourable terms than heretofore afforded in this place.

Having also receieved [sic] the latest city fashions, he is prepared to cut and make all manner of garments in a fashionable and most superior style.

He has also made considerable additions to his stock—among which are superior qualities of

Black, blue, brown, &c. Cloths,
"   "   "   " Cassimeres,
Sattinets, and Beverteens,
Silk and other Vestings, &c. &c.

which will be made up to order at the shortest notice.

He invites the public to an examination of his articles. Every thing needed to guard against the frosts of winter are to be found among them. Nov. 15, 1831.

Article no. 196 Subject: Advertisement
Ref. November 15, 1831; pg. 2, col. 6

Milenery [sic] and Mantuamaking.

Mrs. SEARS and Miss CALKINS respectfully inform the Ladies of Lockport and its vicinity, that they have taken a shop two doors east of House & Boughton's store, where they will promptly attend to all calls in their line of business. Having received patterns of the latest fashions, they are well prepared to please the taste of every customer.

Mrs. Sears tenders her thanks to the public for past favours, and solicits a continuance of their patronage.

Lockport, November 15th, 1831.

Article no. 197 Subject: Notice
Ref. November 15, 1831; pg. 2, col. 6

TWENTY-FIVE CENTS REWARD!

Ran away, on the 4th of November inst., an indented apprentice, named Erastus Van Tassel. All persons are forbid harbouring or trusting said boy—and whoever will return him to me, shall receive the above reward, and nothing more.

JACOB TOWNSEND. Lewiston, Nov. 15th, 1831.

Article no. 198 Subject: Advertisement
Ref. November 15, 1831; pg. 2, col. 6

SHOES.

8 Trunks, containing Ladies' Morocco and Stuff walking Shoes and Pumps—Ladies' Stuff Boots—black and coloured Gaiter Boots—children's Morocco, Stuff and Bolivar Boots—Women's calf Boots and Shoes—Men's thick Shoes, Brogans, and Morocco Pumps—Boy's Brogans, &c. Just received and for sale by

HOUSE & BOUGHTON. Oct. 31.

Article no. 199 Subject: Advertisement
Ref. November 15, 1831; pg. 2, col. 6

Old and well-known Establishment!
A.T. PRENTICE,
Clock and Watchmaker and Jeweller.

Respectfully informs his old customers and the public generally, that he still continues to give his personal attendance at his old stand on Main-street, in the village of Lockport,—where he is at all times ready to wait on those who may favour him with orders in his line—assuring them also, that their work will be done in a Workmanlike manner, and promptly. He informs them, also, that his stated price for cleaning a watch is Three Shillings, for glasses 1s. 6d. and all other work in proportion.

He also offers for sale, Curtis & Dunning's Time-pieces, at $18, and warranted. He also continues to keep a well assorted lot of Fashionable Jewellery.—Also, Watch Chains, Seals and Keys, and other Trinkets, which will be disposed of at prices suitable to the state of the times.

He also offers to the public, Silverwork of superior manufacture, and at reasonable rates.

He would particularly mention for the information of the public, also, that he will at all times execute any kinds of Engraving usually done at similar establishments. In conclusion, he respectfully solicits a continuance of the liberal patronage which he has heretofore received at the hands of his fellow-citizens. Lockport, Nov. 8th, 1831.

Article no. 200   Subject: Advertisement
Ref. November 15, 1831; pg. 2, col. 6

CORN BROOMS.

300 Corn Brooms, just received and for sale by the Subscribers. HOUSE & BOUGNHTO [sic]. October 31. [Transcriber's note: This advertisement was followed by several more, similarly short advertisements for this vendor, appearing in the same column, for: Timothy seed; Cheap circassians; and, Camblets and plaids.]

Article no. 201   Subject: Advertisement
Ref. November 15, 1831; pg. 2, col. 6

WOOD FOR SALE!

L.A. SPALDING will deliver good Wood to those who may wish to purchase. Lockport, 10 month 29, 1831.

Article no. 202   Subject: Advertisement
Ref. November 15, 1831; pg. 3, col. 1

LEONARD'S OFFICE.
Drawn Nos. of Extra Class No. 32.
55, 46, 39, 49, 17, 35, 29, 14, 7.
$40,000 for $10!
Draws this Week!
No Blanks.
Class, No. 11, for 1831.

prize of	$40,000:	1 prizes of	$3,000
::	$10,000:	10 ::	$1,000
::	$5,000:	10 ::	$500
::	$4,000:	30 ::	$100

Tickets $10—Shares in proportion. Purchasers can be supplied with packages of the schemes.

N.B. Persons holding Prize Tickets can have Cash at sight by presenting them at the above. Nov. 15.

Article no. 203   Subject: Notice
Ref. November 15, 1831; pg. 3, col. 1

Extract: LIST OF LANDS SOLD FOR TAXES, IN 1830.
Comptroller's Office, Albany,
October 13, 1831.

Notice is hereby given, that the following lots, pieces or parcels of land, situate in the county of Niagara, were sold for arrears of taxes by the Comptroller, at a sale of lands, for arrears of taxes, which sale closed on the fifth day of May, 1830, and [illegible] remain unredeemed, and that the sum carried [illegible] against each piece, lot or parcel of land, will be required to redeem the same at the expiratioen [sic] of the [illegible] for the redemption thereof, which will be on the [fifth?] day of May, 1832. [Transcriber's note: Words marked "illegible" were blurred in the left-hand margin.]

Persons named in the article include:
- Coleman, T.; boundary cited in description of land in village of Kempsville;
- Hill, John; boundary cited in description of land in part of Holland Company's Purchase;
- Horton, D.; redeemed parcel in part of Holland Company's Purchase;
- Mudget A.; village of Kempsville;
- Northrup, F.; boundary cited in description of land in part of Holland Company's Purchase; and,
- Sturges, T.N.; boundary cited in description of land in part of Holland Company's Purchase.

Place names mentioned: Holland Company's Purchase, Kempsville village, Lewiston village, Lockport village, Mile Reservation, or Niagara Tract, and Pendleton Village.

Article no. 204   Subject: Advertisement
Ref. November 15, 1831; pg. 3, col. 2

20 PIECES black, blue, brown, olive, drab, and mixed Cloths and Cassimeres.

15 pieces dark, and light blue and mixed sattinets.
::   ::   blue and crimson Pelisse Cloths.
20   ::   Flannels and Baizes, assorted colours.
3000 yards Sheetings.
4000   ::   Shirtings.
200   ::   Ticking.
10 pieces Fustian and Bang-up Cords.
40 pair Rose and Point Blankets.
20   ::   Horse [Blankets].
Just received and for sale by
HOUSE & BOUGHTON. Oct. 31.

Article no. 205   Subject: Education
Ref. November 15, 1831; pg. 3, col. 2

SCHOOL.

R. Littlefield proposes to open a Select School, on Monday next, in the upper room of Thomas Smith's building, in which will be taught, in the Classical Department, the Latin, and Greek Languages, Algebra, Geometry, Trigonometry, Surveying, and Navigation; also Rhetoric, Logic, History, &c. The common English Department will comprise English Grammar, Arithmetic, Reading, Writing and Spelling. Declamation and Composition in both departments if required.

Classical Department, $5,00 per quarter.
English do. $3,00 per quarter.
Lockport, Oct. 24th, 1831.

Article no. 206   Subject: Advertisement
Ref. November 15, 1831; pg. 3, col. 2

AXES.

100 Cast Steel ground Axes, a superior quality, for sale (price $1,25) by   WILLIAM HUMPHREY,
Sign of the Padlock, Lower Lockport.

Article no. 207   Subject: Advertisement
Ref. November 15, 1831; pg. 3, col. 2

TO FARMERS AND OTHERS!
Nursery.

The Subscriber, residing in Hartland, near the Ridge Road, and about 12 miles from Lockport, informs farmers and others, desirous of improving their orchards, that he has a large collection of first rate

Ingrafted Fruit Trees,

consisting of Apples, Plums, Pears, &c. His collection of young Apple trees is very large, and of the most superior kinds known. He will dispose of them at the rate of $12.50 per hundred—which is about half the rate usually charged.

As this is about the season for transplanting, the attention of the public is particularly called to his Nursery.

MICHAEL ROBSON. November 1, 1831.

Article no. 208   Subject: Advertisement
Ref. November 15, 1831; pg. 3, col. 2

FASHIONABLE TAILORING.

The subscriber having just returned from the city of New-York, is enabled to present to the citizens of Lockport, and its vicinity, the

Latest Fashions

which have arrived from London and Paris—and is confident in the belief that he can do justice to all who may favour him with their patronage.

The subscriber warrants that any work in his line of business will be done at his establishment in a manner equally as well as at any shop in the city of New-York. He intends punctually to fill his orders, and to the entire satisfaction of his customers.

JAMES P. RIDNER. Lockport, Aug. 30, 1831.

N.B. Cutting done at short notice—and warranted to fit if correctly made up.

Article no. 209   Subject: Advertisement
Ref. November 15, 1831; pg. 3, col. 2

READY MADE CLOTHING.

A General assortment of Ready-Made Clothing, such as Round Jackets, Vests, Men's and Boy's Caps, &c., for sale by

SETH PARSONS & Co. Sept. 27.

Article no. 210   Subject: Advertisement
Ref. November 15, 1831; pg. 3, col. 2

1832.

The Anti-Masonic, Temperance, Western, and Pocket Almanacs, by the gross, dozen or single copy, for sale at the book store of

Sept. 27.   N. LEONARD.

Article no. 211   Subject: Advertisement
Ref. November 15, 1831; pg. 3, col. 2

HARDWARE STORE,
Lockport, (Lower Town,)
At the Sign of the Padlock.

WILLIAM HUMPHREY late of the firm of J.R. Stafford & Co. respectfully informs the inhabitants of this and the adjoining Counties, that he has opened an entire New Stock of fresh and choice goods, all of which are of the latest importations. Among them are

Machinists', Blacksmiths', Carpenters', Masons', Coopers', Shoemakers', and Tailors' Tools.

A general assortment of
Cabinet and Saddlery Ware.

—Also—

Iron, Steel, Nails, Nail Rods, Hoop & Band Iron, Tin plate, Wire, Mill cranks, Spindles and gudgeons, Knives and forks, Pen and pocket knives, Razors and straps, Tea and table spoons, Locks, Hinges, Butts and screws, Thumb and Norfolk latches, Tea trays, Candlesticks, Brass' Andirons, Shovels and tongs, Scissors and shears, &c. &c. &c.

Stoves, of improved patterns. Stove pipe, boilers, &c. Caldron Kettles. Hollow Ware. Pots, Kettles, Bake-pans, Spiders, Cart and Wagon boxes, Mill, X Cut, and Tennon Saws.

Together with every other article in the Hardware line usually called for.

Also manufactured and kept constantly on hand
Tin and Sheet Iron Ware.

All the above will be sold cheap for cash, or approved credit. October 10, 1831.

Article no. 212   Subject: Advertisement
Ref. November 15, 1831; pg. 3, col. 2

FUR CAPS AND COLLARS.

Just received, a large supply of superior Fur and other Caps, of all fashions. Also, a large lot of superior Fur Collars. For sale at fair prices.

S.C. LOCKWOOD. Oct. 11th, 1831.

Article no. 213 Subject: Advertisement
Ref. November 15, 1831; pg. 3, col. 2

HARNESS LEATHER.

15000 Lbs. of superior Harness Leather for sale at the Green Store, or at the Lockport Tannery, by
 Sept. 13. GEO. W. ROGERS & Co.

Article no. 214 Subject: Advertisement
Ref. November 15, 1831; pg. 3, col. 2

An Argument to the Purse.

We have taken the Brick Store recently occupied by W. Parsons & Co., where we have on hand
 An Extensive Assortment of
 Dry Goods, Groceries, Hardware, &c.

Which we wish to dispose of for ready pay alone, upon the principle of "mutual consideration, or one thing for another."

We make no promises but what we intend shall be fully realized. We therefore say nothing about "reduced prices," "cheaper than ever," or having "purchased at auction for cash," or that we will sell below cost—but we will only say, that our arrangements are such as will enable us at all times to exchange goods for cash or country produce at "lower rates" than heretofore offered in this place. We will also pay cash for most articles usually offered in this market.

We invite all who wish to purchase for cash, or exchange other articles for goods, to call—with the assurance that they shall not be disappointed.

L. FELLOWS & Co. Lockport, Sept. 20.

Article no. 215 Subject: Advertisement
Ref. November 15, 1831; pg. 3, col. 3

To Farmers and Others.
DOMESTIC SPINNER.

The subscriber respectfully informs farmers and others, that he has purchased the right for Niagara county, of making and vending
 Penny's Improved Domestic Spinner,
and that he is now ready to dispose of individual rights to use this valuable Machine to all who may wish to avail themselves of its advantages.

This machine is to be employed in Spinning Wool, and is intended for families and small manufacturing establishments and will be found worthy of general patronage.

The subscriber now has one of these machines in good order for working, at his residence in Pendleton, and all who might be inclined to purchase, were they satisfied of its utility, can therefore come and examine for themselves—and by proving it be satisfied that it really is an improvement, and an important labour-saving machine that no wool-grower should be without.

The machines will be disposed of at very reasonable rates, and on accommodating terms.

S.P. CLARKE. Pendleton, June 28th, 1831.

Article no. 216 Subject: Advertisement
Ref. November 15, 1831; pg. 3, col. 3

DRUMS.

A lot of good and well finished Drums, just received, and for sale at manufacturer's prices.

W.W. PRENTICE. July 5.

Article no. 217 Subject: Advertisement
Ref. November 15, 1831; pg. 3, col. 3

Extract: ROGERS & BROWN have just received a fresh supply of Groceries—viz. [List includes brandy, gin, rum, port, &c.; Old Hyson, Young Hyson, &c. teas; Havana and St. Croix sugar, lump and loaf sugar, raisins, prunes, figs, coffee, spices, dye woods and paints, linseed and lamp oil; shad, mackerel and cod fish.] The above articles may be found in connection with a large stock of Dry Goods, Crockery and Hardware, at the Stone Building, formerly occupied by Mr. T. Smith—and many good bargains await those who will call. [Transcriber's note: Another advertisement appears in the same column for the same vendor, offering pork for sale.]

Article no. 218 Subject: Advertisement
Ref. November 15, 1831; pg. 3, col. 3

Extract: NEW ARRIVAL.

The subscriber has received in addition to his former Stock, a general assortment of School, Miscellaneous and Blank books, and is prepared to furnish Merchants, Teachers and others, by the quantity, on as good terms as can be found west of Albany. The following are among his School Books ... Miscellaneous Books ... Blank Books ... Stationary [sic] ... {Advertisement includes lists of each of these kinds of books or stationery.} Also, Blank Mortgages, Deeds and Leases; Justices and Attorney's Blanks, neatly printed, kept constantly for sale—also, a choice lot of Musical Instruments, of various kinds, and of superior quality, purchased of the manufacturers themselves, and for sale at their prices. Persons wishing to purchase School Books, or any other of the abovementioned articles, will find it to their advantage to call at the Bookstore opposite Main-street bridge.

N. LEONARD. Lockport, May 16, 1831.

Article no. 219 Subject: Advertisement
Ref. November 15, 1831; pg. 3, col. 3

Village Lots!

The subscriber, as Agent for Hawley & Ralston, offers for sale a variety of

Village Lots,

situated in the vicinity of the Court House and Public Square, being well located for dwellings, on elevated, airy and healthy ground, with a southern and eastern exposure, affording a pleasant prospect of the Village and the surrounding country. They will be sold on reasonable terms and a liberal credit.

For further particulars inquire of Edward J. Chase, at the office of the subscriber, on Canal-street, opposite Main-street Bridge—or of

H. GARDNER. Lockport, 20th Oct. 1830.

Article no. 220 Subject: Advertisement
Ref. November 15, 1831; pg. 3, col. 3

Upper Leather & Calf-skins.
For sale by the subscribers, at the Green Store,
45 doz. of good slaughter Upper Leather,
30 do. first chop Calf-skins.
Sept. 13. GEO. W. ROGERS & Co.

Article no. 221 Subject: Advertisement
Ref. November 15, 1831; pg. 3, col. 4

NEW AND VERY SUPERIOR
CLOTHING.
(Spring and Summer Fashions.)

The subscriber has just received from the city of New-York, and is now opening, in the building lately occupied by A.R. Benedict as a dry good store, on Main-street, nearly opposite Smith and Southworth's Drug store, his Spring supply of Ready Made Clothing, &c.—consisting of

Fine and common black, blue, brown and mixt &c., broadcloth Coats;
  do. do. do. Cassimere Pantaloons;
  do. do. do. Satinet do.;
Cassimere, toilinet, circassian, Mersailles, silk and all other kinds of Vests, &c., &c., &c.

All of superior qualities and the lastest New-York fashions.

Together with

A large supply of fashionable Spring and Summer Clothign [sic], made in the best style. Also—a good supply of most articles usually found in clothing warehouses, such as suspenders, stocks, &c.

He has also on hand a selected assortment of Cloths and Cassimeres, Vestings, &c., which he will make to order in superior style, on short notice.

The subscriber would request all persons desirous of fitting themselves out in good style, to give him a call, and examine his ware and prices. No one shall go away dissatisfied with either.

G.S. PLACE. May 17, 1831.

Article no. 222 Subject: Advertisement
Ref. November 15, 1831; pg. 3, col. 4

Extract: NEW GOODS! At Reduced Prices.

HOUSE & BOUGHTON are receiving large additions to their stock of Goods, which now comprises a very general assortment of Staple and Fancy Goods, suited for the market and season, to which they invite the attention of the public. [List of goods includes Gros de Naps, Italian Lustrings, Sinchews, &c.; ginghams, printed muslins, cambrics and calicoes; capes, collars, pelarines and dress handkerchiefs; cloths, cassimeres, kerseymeres, &c.; ready-made clothing; hardware, crockery and glass-ware; a general assortment of Groceries; cut and wrought nails, &c.] June 14.

Article no. 223 Subject: Advertisement
Ref. November 15, 1831; pg. 3, col. 4

Extract: NEW SPRING AND SUMMER GOODS.

Rogers & Brown have now received their Spring supply of Dry goods, &c. which they offer to their old customers at unusually low prices. Their stock comprises an extensive and carefully selected assortment of the most fashionable patterns, and of superior qualities—and they confidently invite their friends to call and examine for themselves. The following are a few of their articles [List includes: broadcloths, cassimeres, pelisse cloths, flannels, &c.; Sarsnet and sinchew silks, changeable Gro de Naples, black and blue-black Italian lustrings, &c.; calicoes, ginghams, linens, muslins, handkerchiefs; capes, collars, veils; waddings, trimmings, millinets, linings, ribbons; ladies' Leghorn hats, Dunstable straw hats, &c.; shawls, cravats, combs, hosiery; gloves and mitts; wicking, tick, diaper, canvass, shirtings, cambrics, vestings, buttons, cotton, thread; carpet binding, bobbin, &c.; hardware, groceries, dye stuffs and paints.] The above Goods were purchased with great care, and principally at auction, with cash; and their customers and the public may rest assured that they will be sold as low or lower than at any other establishment. May 24.

Article no. 224 Subject: Advertisement
Ref. November 15, 1831; pg. 3, col. 4

BOLIVAR HATS.
1 Case first quality Bolivar Hats;—Also, Misses' Gimp Cottages,—for sale unusually low, by
SETH PARSONS & Co.

Article no. 225   Subject: Notice
Ref. November 15, 1831; pg. 3, col. 4

NOTICE is hereby given that an application will be made to the Legislature of the state of New-York at its next session for an act to incorporate a company for manufacturing purposes, to be established at the village of Niagara Falls in the county of Niagara, and for a canal from above the dam at Tonewanta to the said village, with a capital of one hundred thousand dollars, with the privilege of increasing ...

[Transcriber's note: The remainder of the article was clipped from the original newspaper record].

Article no. 226   Subject: Advertisement
Ref. November 15, 1831; pg. 3, col. 5

COOKE & STOW.
Attorneys at Law.
Lewiston, Niagara Co., N.Y.
June, 1831.

Article no. 227   Subject: Advertisement
Ref. November 15, 1831; pg. 3, col. 5

GENTLEMEN OF FASHION,
Look at This!

Just received at the Stone Building, opposite Hughes' Hotel, a choice lot of Cloths, Blk. silk Velvet Vestings, Cassimeres, Nankeens, Beverteens, Elegant white Marseilles, fancy silk and cotton Vestings, Velvet Cords, Lastings; Super. Bombazines, for Vests, &c.

Some of the above Cloths are very elegant.

Also—Stocks, Collars, Suspenders, Cravats, all kinds of choice Trimmings, different descriptions of Goods for Summer wearing Apparel, &c.

The subscriber does not pretend that he is going to sell wonderful cheap things—nor that he is going to undersell any of the numerous establishments of his kind of business—(consisting of almost every merchant in Lockport)—for that is not agreeable to his motto, "live and let live;" but he assures his customers, and the public generally, that they shall have good and fashionable clothing, made upon honour, for fair prices—and made to order, with as much dispatch as they can be executed by any of the Establishments above hinted at. Gentlemen wishing to be fitted out with suits at his shop—for no man shall go out of his shop dissatisfied—i.e. if he is a reasonable man.

J. TRYON. Lockport[,] May 4, 1831.

Article no. 228   Subject: Advertisement
Ref. November 15, 1831; pg. 3, col. 5

HOUSE & BOUGHTON have on hand a large supply of fresh Groceries, which they will sell to innkeepers, in small quantities, at reduced prices. Their stock of Teas having been purchased from this spring's importations, are warranted fresh, and of the first quality—
Cognac Brandy,
St. Croix & Jamaica Rum,
Holland & Country Gin,
Madeira,
Port,
Sicily &
Malaga Wines,

Lump and brown Sugar, Coffee, Raisins, Lemons, Citron, and Spices of all kinds. June 16, 1831.

Article no. 229   Subject: Advertisement
Ref. November 15, 1831; pg. 3, col. 5

LEATHER.

GEO. W. ROGERS & Co. offer for sale, at the Green Store,
15,000 lbs. first chop Spanish Sole Leather,
6,500 "   " Slaughter do.
400 Sides " Upper Leather,
30 Doz. Calf Skins,
at moderate prices for cash. Jan. 5, 1831.

Cash paid for Hides, at the Lockport Tannery, or at the green store, by GEO. ROGERS & Co. Jan. 5, 1831.

Article no. 230   Subject: Advertisement
Ref. November 15, 1831; pg. 3, col. 5

WRAPPING and CAP PAPER by the ream, for sale by N. LEONARD. May 17.

Article no. 231   Subject: Notice
Ref. November 15, 1831; pg. 3, col. 5

CAUTION!

Whereas my wife Phoebe has eloped from me without just cause—I therefore hereby forewarn all persons against harbouring or trusting her after this date, as I will pay no debts of her contracting of any kind. Dated Somerset, October 29, 1831. MOSES NORTH.

Article no. 232   Subject: Notice
Ref. November 15, 1831; pg. 3, col. 5

ELOPEMENT!

Whereas Mary my wife has left my bed and board without any just provocation, and refuses to return and live with me, this is to forbid all persons harbouring or trusting her on my account as I will pay no debts of her contrating [sic] after this date. Oct. 27, 1831. ELI SLY.

Article no. 233   Subject: Advertisement
Ref. November 15, 1831; pg. 3, col. 5

WHISKEY & WHITE FISH.
20 Bbls first rate rectified Whiskey,
10 do. White Fish—for sale by
Feb 17. ROGERS & BROWN.

Article no. 234 Subject: Advertisement
Ref. November 15, 1831; pg. 3, col. 5

Extract: Edward Giddins'
Anti-Masonic Almanac for 1832.

In press and will be published the present week, by William Williams, No. 60 Genesee-street, Utica. Sold also by [Listed, below.] This number of the Anti-Masonic almanac is much enlarged from any of the former numbers, as will appear from the table of contents below; but without increasing the price from that of last year. This has been effected by the increased demand for the same in this and other states which has warranted the stereotyping of it, and thereby enabling the publisher to supply them on better terms than they otherwise could be sold. Orders will be promptly executed. Price $60 the thousand; $7 the hundred, $1 the dozen; retail price 12 1-2 cents. Contents: {Advertisement includes extensive listing of contents.}

Agents for the sale of Edward Giddins' Anti-Masonic Almanac for 1832:

- Beckwith, C.C.; Providence, Rhode Island
- Bryan, S.C. & Alex.; Augusta, Georgia
- Bunce, John L.; Haverhill, New Hampshire
- Clarke, John; Philadelphia, Pennsylvania
- Collins & Hannay, Messrs.; New York, New York
- Dukehart, Valerius; Baltimore, Maryland
- Eggleston, Nathaniel; Hartford, Connecticut,
- Ellis & Shotwell, Messrs.; Macon, Georgia
- Faxton, Mr.; Buffalo, New York
- Giddins, Edward; Lockport, New York
- Grigg, John; Philadelphia, Pennsylvania
- Harrison, D.W.; Charleston, South Carolina
- M'Elrath & Bangs, Messrs.; New York, New York
- Marsh, John; Boston, Massachusetts; doing business as John Marsh & Co.
- Marshall & Dean, Messrs.; Rochester, New York
- Packard, D.P.; Albany, New York
- Paddock, L.; Watertown, New York
- Percival, James; Geneseo, New York
- Prentiss, Cyrus; Ravenna, Ohio
- Skinner & Dewey, Messrs.; New York, New York
- Sleight, H.C.; New York, New York
- Steele & Faxton, Messrs.; Buffalo, New York
- Wells, Stephen; Detroit, Michigan

Article no. 235 Subject: Advertisement
Ref. November 15, 1831; pg. 3, col. 5

SAW-LOGS.

Wanted immediately—A quantity of White Wood, Chestnut, Oak, and Hemlock Saw-Logs. Apply to
L.A. SPALDING. 6th mo. 27, 1831.

Article no. 236 Subject: Advertisement
Ref. November 15, 1831; pg. 3, col. 6

LATEST FASHIONS.

The subscriber still continues to manufacture and to keep on hand at his well known and old established stand in in [sic] this village, a large supply of

Hats,

of the latest and most approved fashions, and of superior workmanship and materials. He invites a continuance of the liberal share of patronage formerly given him—and assures his old customers, that they will be as fairly dealt with as heretofore: and those who have not yet purchased at his shop, are requested to make a trial, as he is certain of rendering them every satisfaction.

For sale as usual, a fair supply of Caps, of all kinds—Buffalo Robes, &c.

Casd [sic] paid for Hatting and Shipping Furs, as heretofore.

N.B. The subscriber particularly wishes the public to note and bear in mind, that he is a practical hatter, and has made his calling the sole study of his business life.

S.C. LOCKWOOD. Lockport, Aug. 23d, 1831.

Article no. 237 Subject: Advertisement
Ref. November 15, 1831; pg. 3, col. 6

Rochester Slaughtering Establishment.

The subscribers are now erecting and will have in complete order, by the 1st of 10th month (Oct.) next, a slaughter-house and other necessary buildings, where can be slaughtered and packed from 50 to 75 head of cattle daily.

To those who may be disposed to barrel their beef, either for an Eastern or Canada market, this place unites more advantages than any other point between Buffalo and Albany. Our terms are reasonable and will be made known on application to us. Barrels and salt, both coarse and fine, will be provided, and cash paid for hides and tallow.

We will pay cash on delivery for 1000 head of fat cattle, over 3 years old, delivered at our yards in Rochester, from and after the 1st of 10th mo. (Oct.) next.

REFERENCES.

Hart, Griffith & Co., 22 South-st., New-York
Morgan and Winslow, 33 West-st., New-York
A.M. Schermerhorn, Pres. Monroe bl., Rochester
Jonathan Child, Rochester
Griffith, Brothers & Son, Rochester
J. Seymour, cashier bank, Rochester
Pliny Sexton, Palmyra
Henry Jessup, Palmyra
Thomas Beals, Canandaigua
James Wadsworth, Geneseo

William T. Cuyler, Geneseo
Sheldon Thompson, Buffalo
George Palmer, Buffalo
Lyman A. Spalding, Lockport
John Pound, Lockport
THORN & FINK. Rochester, 22d of 7th mo. 1831.

Article no. 238 Subject: Advertisement
Ref. November 15, 1831; pg. 3, col. 6

NEW SUMMER & FALL GOODS.

We have just received from New-York, in addition to our spring purchases, a large supply of
Summer and Fall Goods,
which with our former stock comprises a very general assortment of Staple and Fancy Articles. We invite our customers and the public to call and examine them.
SETH PARSONS & Co. July 18.
[Transcriber's note: Farther down the same column, are two more advertisements for this merchant, one for sales of fish; and the other for sales of iron, nails, &c.]

Article no. 239 Subject: Advertisement
Ref. November 15, 1831; pg. 3, col. 6

CASH FOR HIDES AND SHEEP-SKINS!

The subscriber will pay cash for any quantity of Hides and Sheep-skins, delivered at his shop on Main-street, one door east of the store formerly occupied by L.A. Spalding:
Where may be found a good assortment of all kinds of
Leather
cheap for ready pay.
THEODORE STONE. Lockport, 19th July, 1831.

Article no. 240 Subject: Advertisement
Ref. November 15, 1831; pg. 3, col. 6

W.W. PRENTICE.
Clock & Watchmaker, Jeweller, &c.

Continues to carry on his business with his usual attention, at his old and well known stand on
Canal-street,
adjoining House & Boughton's mercantile establishment; where he Repairs and Cleans Watches, Clocks, &c., with promptness and skill.

He will continue to keep on hand a choice lot of Jewellery, &c.—but begs leave to inform his friends, the public generally, that he intends to devote almost his sole attention to the cleaning and repairing of all kinds of time-pieces—in which line, he trusts to merit a continuance of the liberal patronage heretofore awarded him.
Lockport, Dec. 30, 1830.

Article no. 241 Subject: Advertisement
Ref. November 15, 1831; pg. 3, col. 6

PLOUGHS.
200 Ploughs, warranted sound, made at Lockport Furnace, expressly for Farmers' use, for sale by
YERINGTON & STICKNEY. March 31.

N.B. Ploughs Repaired, and Machinery Castings made and Turned to order on short notice, at the above Furnace.

Article no. 242 Subject: Advertisement
Ref. November 15, 1831; pg. 3, col. 6

LOCKPORT
CABINET WAREHOUSE.

S.W. PRENTICE having now permanently established himself in his new
Cabinet Shop,
On Main-Street, Lockport, near Spalding's store, is prepared to furnish any articles in his line of business on as reasonable terms and of as good a quality as can be obtained at any other establishment in the country. Such Ware as is not usually kept on hand, will be made to order on short notice. Lumber and most kind of country produce will be received in payment for Furniture.
Lockport, August 19, 1831.

Article no. 243 Subject: Advertisement
Ref. November 15, 1831; pg. 3, col. 6

TIME-PIECES!

A Number of Curtis & Dunning's superior Warranted Time-Pieces.—just received and for sale by
W.W. PRENTICE.
Canal-street, near Main-street Bridge, Lockport.

Article no. 244 Subject: Advertisement
Ref. November 15, 1831; pg. 3, col. 6

CARPETING.

A Few pieces of Carpeting, Hearth Rugs, Carpet Binding, Bed Lace, and Fringe for Rugs, for sale by
HOUSE & BOUGHTON. May 3.

Article no. 245 Subject: Advertisement
Ref. November 15, 1831; pg. 3, col. 6

CLYDE GLASS.
50 Boxes 7 by 9
50 do. 8 by 10
10 do. 10 by 12
 5 do. 10 by 14
Clyde Glass—for sale by
Dec. 16. ROGERS & BROWN.

Article no. 246 Subject: Advertisement
Ref. November 15, 1831; pg. 3, col. 6

BLANKS:

Attorneys' and Justices' Blanks; also Pathmasters' Blanks.

Bonds, Mortgage Deeds, and Leases;

Neatly printed, and for sale by

April 8. N. LEONARD.

Article no. 247 Subject: Advertisement
Ref. November 15, 1831; pg. 3, col. 6

FLOUR.

A constant supply of fresh ground flour, kept at Spalding's Mill.

Article no. 248 Subject: Advertisement
Ref. November 15, 1831; pg. 3, col. 6

WILLIAM FOX,
Barber and Hair-Dresser.

Continues his business as usual at his old stand on Main-street. Thankful for past favours, he solicits a continuance of them, assuring his friends and the public, that every attention will be paid to give general satisfaction.

Lockport, May 27, 1830.

Article no. 249 Subject: Advertisement
Ref. November 15, 1831; pg. 4, col. 4

PORK & HAMS.

The subscribers have on hand, and for sale—

100 [lbs.] Pork—3000 lbs. Hams.

Feb. 17. ROGERS & BROWN.

Article no. 250 Subject: Notice
Ref. November 15, 1831; pg. 4, col. 4

Extract: MORTGAGE SALE.

Whereas, default has been made in the payment of a certain sum of money, secured by indenture of mortgage, bearing date 8 October 1829, executed by Lorenzo A. Kelsey and Andrew Estes, to Hezekiah H. Smith and Gideon L. Kelsey, and recorded in the Clerk's office of Niagara county, in book of Mortgages number 3, (three,) on pages 122 and 123—upon which said Indenture of Mortgage there is now due and payable to John Daly, to whom said mortgage was duly assigned, at the time of the first publication of this notice, the sum of $1,040.57: Now, therefore, notice is hereby given, that by virtue of a power of sale contained in said Mortgage, and by force of the statute in such case made and provided, the premises described in said mortgage, to wit: All that certain piece or parcel of land, situate, lying and being in Youngstown, known and distinguished as being lot No. 4, in the first range of lots, bounded {Notice includes description of boundaries.}—will be sold at public auction, at the inn now kept by John J. Ryckman, known as the Lewiston Hotel, 7 April 1832. Dated October 10th, 1831.

JOHN DALY, Assignee. COOKE & STOW, Att'ys.

Article no. 251 Subject: Transportation
Ref. November 15, 1831; pg. 4, col. 4

RAILROAD—From Buffalo to the Cayuga Lake—Notice is hereby given, that an application will be made to the legislature of this state, at its next annual session, to incorporate a company to construct a Railroad from Buffalo, in the county of Erie, to the Cayuga Lake or the outlet thereof, for the transportation of passengers, goods, wares and merchandizes, with a capital of $3,000,000.

September 26, 1831.

[Transcriber's note: Two other, similar notices appear in this column, one for a railroad from Schenectady, on the Hudson River, to Buffalo; and the other, from Albany to Buffalo. Place names mentioned include: Albany, Auburn, Batavia, Buffalo, Canandaigua, Geneva, Hudson river, Rochester, Schenectady, and Syracuse.]

Article no. 252 Subject: Advertisement
Ref. November 15, 1831; pg. 4, col. 4

Extract: H. SLAYTON's Rheumatic and Canker Plaster.

This Plaster is a compound of most kinds of Adhesive Salve now in use, with the addition of powerful remedies for Canker and Scrofulous Eruptions. {Advertisement includes further description of the Plaster, followed by Recommendations, or testimonials.}

Sold at wholesale and retail by the Proprietor, in Royalton; Smith & Southworth, Lockport; T.F. Stewart, Hartland; James Northam, Middleport; Dr. Thomas, Medina; T. Andrews, Rochester; S.O. Almy, Le Roy; J.B. Elliott, Brockport—and most other Druggists in this section of the state.

Article no. 253 Subject: Advertisement
Ref. November 15, 1831; pg. 4, col. 5

Extract: Leather, Boots and SHOES,
Wholesale and Retail.

The subscribers are now receiving at the Green Store, a general assortment of Leather, Boots and Shoes, Shoemakers' Tools, &c., of every description. The following are a few of the leading articles: [Listed, including several items under the Leather, and Boots and Shoes headings; also, shoe thread, shoe knives, awl blades and hafts, &c., 500 pairs of Boots and Shoes of their own manufacture, of every description, warranted in every respect to be first rate articles.] The subscribers will sell all the above mentioned articles with a variety of others not enumerated, at much lower prices than they have ever before been offered in the county of Niagara, for ready pay.

G.W. ROGERS & Co. Lockport, May 20, 1830.

N.B. Cash paid for Hemlock Bark—also for Hides and Calf Skins, at the Lockport Tannery.

Article no. 254	Subject: Advertisement
Ref. November 15, 1831; pg. 4, col. 5	

AETNA INSURANCE COMPANY,
of Hartford, Conn.
Capital 200,000 Dollars,
(With liberty to increase the same to
half a million of Dollars,)

Offer to ensure Dwelling-Houses, Stores, Mills, Manufactories, Distilleries, Barns, Ships and Vessels in port or on the stocks, Goods, and every other species of insurable personal property, against Loss or Damage by Fire, at as low rates of premium as any similar institution in good standing.

The Aetna Insurance Company was incorporated in 1819, and the reputation it has acquired for promptness and liberality in the adjustment and payment of losses, requires no additional pledge to entitle it to a liberal share of public patronage. Persons wishing to be insured, can apply to

LOTHROP COOKE, Lewiston, N.Y.

Who is appointed agent, with full power to receive proposals, and issue Policies, without the delay necessarily attendant on an application to the Office. June, 1830.

Article no. 255	Subject: Advertisement
Ref. November 15, 1831; pg. 4, col. 5	

BUFFALO FIRE AND MARINE ENSURANCE COMPANY.—Capital One hundred thousand dollars. This Company having obtained a charter of the legislature of this state for the purpose of effecting Ensurance against Fire, and on the inland transportation of Goods, upon the Rivers, Canals and Lakes of this and the adjoining states and territories; and in compliance with the provisions of its charter, having paid the required amount of capital stock, are now ready to receive proposals for all kinds of Fire and Marine Ensurance which may be offered to them, on liberal terms. They pledge themselves to the public, that their business shall be conducted on the most fair and equitable principles; and all losses which they may sustain will be promptly adjusted.

CHARLES TOWNSEND, Pres't.
L.F. ALLEN, Sec'y.
Apply to LYMAN A. SPALDING, Agent, Lockport, N.Y. June 24, 1830.

Article no. 256	Subject: Advertisement
Ref. November 15, 1831; pg. 4, col. 5	

AGENCY.

L.A. SPALDING offers his services to the public generally, for the collection of money in any part of the United States. He will also forward money to any place designated, either in the United States, England, Ireland, or Scotland, and ensure its safe carriage. His charges will be moderate.

For all sums of money, not less than twenty dollars nor more than five hundred dollars, which may be placed in his hands, he will allow interest at the rate of six per cent. per annum, provided it remains not less than sixty days.— Larger sums than five hundred dollars, will be received on such terms as may be agreed upon. Persons having money to loan on bond and mortgage can be informed of safe investments.

Lockport, Niagara county, N.Y. 7th month, 1830.

Article no. 257	Subject: Advertisement
Ref. November 15, 1831; pg. 4, col. 5	

TURNING.

The subscriber takes this method to inform the public, that he has two good Turning Lathes in complete operation, and is ready at all times to do any kind of

Wood Turning,

in the best manner, at his shop, near Spalding's Flouring Mill, in the village of Lockport.

SHELDON B. HAND. Oct, 29, 1830.

Article no. 258	Subject: Advertisement
Ref. November 15, 1831; pg. 4, col. 5	

SOLE LEATHER.

25000 Lbs. Spanish and Slaughter Sole Leather for sale by GEO. W. ROGERS & Co. Sept. 13.

Article no. 259	Subject: Notice
Ref. November 15, 1831; pg. 4, col. 5	

REDEMPTION OF LANDS SOLD FOR TAXES.
State of New York, Comptroller's Office.

Notice is hereby given, pursuant to Sec. 76 Title 3, of Chap. 13 of the first part of the Revised Statutes, that unless the lands sold for taxes, at the general tax sale, held at the capitol in the city of Albany, in the months of April and May, 1830, shall be redeemed, by the payment into the treasury of the state, on or before the fifth day of May next, after the date hereof of the amount for which each parcel of the said lands was sold, and the interest thereon, at the rate of ten per centum per annum, from the date of the sale, to the date of the payment, the lands so sold, and remaining unredeemed, will be conveyed to the purchasers thereof. Dated Albany, 12th Oct. 1831.

SILAS WRIGHT, Jr. Comptroller.

Article no. 260   Subject: Notice
Ref. November 15, 1831; pg. 4, col. 5

RAIL-ROAD.

Application will be made to the Legislature of this state, at its next annual session, to incorporate a company to construct a Rail-Road from the village of Buffalo, in the county of Erie, by way of Niagara Falls, to the village of Lewiston, in the county of Niagara, with a capital of $200,000, for the transportation of passengers, goods, wares and merchandise.—Oct. 26, 1831.

Augustus Porter, David M. Day, Samuel De Veaux, Peter B. Porter, Jr., Reuben B. Heacock, Wm. Hotchkiss, Pierre A Barker.

Article no. 261   Subject: Advertisement
Ref. November 15, 1831; pg. 4, col. 6

DOCT. C. VAN BRUNT

respectfully informs the inhabitants of Mountain Ridge, and its vicinity, that he will attend to the practice of
Physic & Surgery,
[in] their neighbourhood, and respectfully solicits a share of public patronage. Mountain Ridge, Dec. 9, 1830.

Article no. 262   Subject: Advertisement
Ref. November 15, 1831; pg. 4, col. 6

VALUABLE VILLAGE PROPERTY.

The subscriber is desirous of disposing of all his property in the village of Lockport, consisting of one lot and buildings on Main-street, adjoining the Washington House. The buildings are large and well fitted up for the accommodation of private families, or for business:

Likewise, Business Lots on Buffalo-street some of which are near the intersection of Buffalo and Main-streets:—Dwelling Lots on Walnut, East Front, and High streets—together with a tract of eight acres on the south side of and adjoining High-street.

The above property will be disposed of in lots to suit the purchaser, and on very favourable terms. For further particulars inquire of Alfred Holmes.

H.S. PLATT. October 20, 1830 [sic].

Article no. 263   Subject: Advertisement
Ref. November 15, 1831; pg. 4, col. 6

Extract: A word to the wise is sufficient.
20 years' experience in various climates—
12 years in extensive hospitals.
Salus Populi Suprema Lex.

DR. GEORGE COOKE Continues, as usual to be consulted at his offices. Strangers are respectfully apprised, Dr. Cooke after being legally bred to the medical profession in the city of London, has been a practical member of said faculty of physic for many years, and latterly from the city of New-York. His practice, from being general, he confines to a particular branch of medicine, which engages his profound attention. His experience is very great—his success astonishing. He publicly cautions the unfortunate against the abuse of Mercury. ... Those persons who may have contracted disease, or suspect latent poison, are invited to make application to Dr. Cooke, at his establishment, the Lock Dispensary, an institution of unrivalled celebrity, exclusively devoted to the treatment and prevention of a certain class of diseases. ... All cases are guaranteed.—No dietting [sic] required, nor suspension from business in ordinary cases. ... Dr. Cooke's real respectability, skill and integrity, offer, in all cases, a sure guarantee. No letters will be taken in unless post paid. All city letters must be handed in. To individuals who would prefer the advantages of a more private consultation, Dr. Cooke respectfully offers his personal attention, at his residence, next adjoining the Lock Dispensary, where he will invariably be found at home, to receive the confidence of those, who may, from time to time, require his services, and in all cases as a standard rule, the most honourable secrecy will be impartially observed. Counselling Official Departments, No. 2 Green st. and No. 2 Store-lane, Albany. Don't mistake the name and the numbers.

Article no. 264   Subject: Advertisement
Ref. November 15, 1831; pg. 4, col. 6

Extract: Valuable Family Medicines,
for sale by
SMITH & SOUTHWORTH, Lockport.

De [la] Monterat's Columbian Vegetable Specific. For the cure of Consumptions, Asthma, Pleurisy, Spitting of Blood and Palmonary [sic] Affections of every kind. {Advertisement includes further description of product, accompanied by testimonials, followed by:} Doctor Chapman's Anti-Dyspectic or Sour Stomach Pills—An Infallible Cure for Indigestion. These pills have been highly approved of by those who have used them for the above named disease, and are prescribed by several physicians of eminence in this and other cities. ... The proprietor deems it unncessary to publish any certificates, as by their own merits alone they can and will be sustained.

Article no. 265   Subject: Weather
Ref. December 6, 1831; pg. 2, col. 1

The *Albany Daily Advertiser* of yesterday says, that on Sunday, snow fell in that city to the depth of two or three inches, and sleigh bells were ringing. "A few miles to the east, there is said to be good sleighing."

Article no. 266 Subject: Religion
Ref. December 6, 1831; pg. 2, col. 2

The number of Sunday Schools in this country is 7254; teachers 62,218; pupils 451,075.

Article no. 267 Subject: Religion
Ref. December 6, 1831; pg. 2, col. 3

THANKSGIVING.

On Thursday next, a sermon will be delivered at the Presbyterian Meeting House, in this village, designed to be in accordance with the spirit of our governor's proclamation; all are invited to attend services, to commence at the usual hour; Elder Taggart, of the baptist church is expected to preach the sermon.

Lockport[,] 4th Dec. 1831.

Article no. 268 Subject: Notice
Ref. December 6, 1831; pg. 2, col. 3

Niagara County Clerk's Office
December 2d, 1831.

All persons having Deeds, Mortgages, or Miscellaneous papers, at the clerks [sic] office, of Niagara county; the recording of which remaining unpaid for; are hereby requested to call and pay for such Recording, at or before the close of the present year.

And to such; whose papers have remained in the clerk's office, of said county, from one to three years, the Recording unpaid for, are hereby particularly requested, to call and pay for the Recording of their respective papers, at the time above specified for payment. Or suits will be instituted, against each and every delinquent, and without further notice.

HENRY CATLIN, Clerk of said county.

Article no. 269 Subject: Notice
Ref. December 6, 1831; pg. 2, col. 3

SHERIFF'S SALE.

By virtue of a writ of fieri facias, issued out of the supreme court of judicature, and to me directed and delivered against the goods and chattels, lands and tenements of Charles Brown, in the county of Niagara, I shall expose for sale at public auction, on the 19th day of January next, at 10 o'clock A.M. at the house now occupied by Samuel Jennings, in the village of Lockport, called the Hotel. All the right, title, interest, claim and demand of the said Charles Brown, or into and out of lot number four on the south side of Niagara-street, in the village of Lockport, on the west side of the Erie Canal, said lot lying in the corner of said Niagara and Transit streets. The interest of said Brown in said lot being a leashold [sic] interest of twenty-four feet taken off from the west end of said lot No. 4, together with the buildings thereon erected. Dated 5th December 1831. H. McNEIL, Sheriff.

Article no. 270 Subject: Advertisement
Ref. December 6, 1831; pg. 2, col. 3

SATTINETTS AND HOMEMADE CLOTHS.

ROGERS & BROWN have on hand 30 pcs. Sattinetts and 20 [pcs.] Homemade cloths at less than last years [sic] prices. Dec. 6.

[Transcriber's note: This advertisement is followed, in the same column, by several more for the same vendor, for the sale of: coloured Italian lustrings; Merino shawls; Leghorn hats; and, broadcloths.]

Article no. 271 Subject: Advertisement
Ref. December 6, 1831; pg. 2, col. 3

WANTED.

Any quantity of Saw Logs, of different kinds of timber, delivered at our saw-mill during the winter for which we will pay the highest price. PARSONS GOODING & Co.

Article no. 272 Subject: Notice
Ref. December 6, 1831; pg. 2, col. 4

In the matter of the sale of the real estate of Alanson Hemenway deceased. Notice is hereby given, that on the 22d day of January next, at two o'clock in the afternoon of that day, will be sold at public auction, at the Washington House, occupied by Samuel B. Thompson, in the town of Lockport, in pursuance of an order of the Surrogate of the county of Niagara, all the estate, right, title, interest, property and claim of Alanson Hemenway, late of the town of Lockport, aforesaid deceased, and all the estate, right, title, property and claim of the heirs of the said deceased in and to the following described piece and parcel of land, and the contract hereinafter mentioned, to wit: being part and parcel of farm lot number eleven, in the fourteenth township, and seventh range of townships of the Holland Land Company so called, and is bounded as follows: North and south by the lines of said lot, East by a line parallel with the east line of said lot, and sixteen chains and ninety-seven links, distant therefrom, and west by a line parallel with said East line of said lot, and twenty-nine chains and seventy-seven links distant therefrom, containing seventy-five acres of land more or less.—The interest in said land so to be sold being held under and by virtue of a contract for the sale of said land, executed by Wilkem Willink, and others on the 29th of September, 1830.

Electa C. Hemenway, Bordman H. Bosworth,
Admintrators for Alanson Hemenway, deceased.
December 6th, 1831.

Article no. 273   Subject: Marriage
Ref. December 6, 1831; pg. 2, col. 4

MARRIED—in Cambria, on the 4th inst., by the Rev. Mr. Halsey, Mr. William Gould, to Miss Nancy Thompson, both of Cambria.

Article no. 274   Subject: Marriage
Ref. December 6, 1831; pg. 2, col. 4

MARRIED—in Cambria, by [the Rev. Mr. Halsey], Mr. John Burchard, of Lima, Livingston county, to Miss Adeline Thompson, of Cambria.

Article no. 275   Subject: Marriage
Ref. December 6, 1831; pg. 2, col. 4

MARRIED—in this village, on the 4th inst., by the Rev. Mr. Taggart, Edwin L. Faxton, to Miss Thirza Norton, all of this village.

Article no. 276   Subject: Marriage
Ref. December 6, 1831; pg. 2, col. 4

MARRIED—on the [4th inst.] by [the Rev. Mr. Taggart], Benjamin Covill to Mrs. Amanda Johnson, of this village.

Article no. 277   Subject: Notice
Ref. December 6, 1831; pg. 2, col. 4

Extract: OFFICIAL CANVASS.
Niagara County ss.

We the board of county canvassers of the votes taken at the general election, held in the county of Niagara, on the seventh, eighth and ninth days of November, in the year 1831, having received the statements of the votes taken in each town of the said county, do certify, that the whole number of votes given in the county of Niagara, at such election, for the office of Senator of the eighth senatorial district, was 1125. Of the votes thus given for the office of Senator: John Birdsall, 1119; John Schuyler, 1; Ira Saunders, 1; John Dickinson, 1; Uncle Tom, 1; Parkhurst Whitney, 1. We, the board of county canvassers certify the above statement to be correct. Dated at Lockport, 15 November 1831. JAMES VAN HORN, Chairman. HENRY CATLIN, Secretary.

Article no. 278   Subject: Notice
Ref. December 6, 1831; pg. 2, col. 4

Extract: OFFICIAL CANVASS.
Niagara County ss.

We the board of county canvassers of the votes taken at the general election held in the county of Niagara on the seventh, eighth and ninth days of November, in the year 1831, having received the statements of the votes taken in each town of the said county, do certify, that the whole number of votes given in the county of Niagara, at such election, for the office of member of Assembly, was 1121. Of the votes thus given for the office of member of Assembly: Henry Norton, 1101; Timothy Page, 1; Rufus Fanning, 1; Henry Fenner, 1; Almon H. Millard, 1. We, the board of county canvassers, certify the above statement to be correct. Dated at Lockport, 15 November 1831. JAMES VAN HORN, Chairman. HENRY CATLIN, Secretary.

Article no. 279   Subject: Notice
Ref. December 6, 1831; pg. 2, col. 4

Extract: OFFICIAL CANVASS.
Niagara County ss.

We the board of county canvassers of the votes taken at the general election held in the county of Niagara on the seventh, eighth and ninth days of November, in the year 1831, having received the statements of the votes taken in each town of the said county, do certify, that the whole number of votes given in the county of Niagara, at such election, for the office of clerk, was 1103. Of the votes thus given for the office of clerk, Henry Catlin received 1103 votes. We, the board of county canvassers certify the above statement to be correct. Dated at Lockport, 15 November 1831. JAMES VAN HORN, Chairman. HENRY CATLIN, Secretary.

Article no. 280   Subject: Notice
Ref. December 6, 1831; pg. 2, col. 4

Extract: OFFICIAL CANVASS.
Niagara County ss.

We the board of county canvassers of the votes taken at the general election held in the county of Niagara on the seventh, eighth and ninth days of November, in the year 1831, having received the statements of the votes taken in each town of the said county, do certify, that the whole number of votes given in the county of Niagara, at such election, for the office of Coroners, was 4399. Of the votes thus given for the office of Coroners: Aaron Parsons, 1100; Thomas N. Lee, 1100; Daniel Kelly, 1099; Seth Parsons, 1196. We, the board of county canvassers, certify the above statement to be correct. The board therefore determine and declare, that Aaron Parsons, Thomas N. Lee, Daniel Kelly and Seth Parsons, by the greatest number of votes, are duly elected coroners. Dated at Lockport, 15 November 1831. JAMES VAN HORN, Chairman. HENRY CATLIN, Secretary.

| Article no. 281 | Subject: Notice |
Ref. December 6, 1831; pg. 2, col. 5

PROCLAMATION,

By Enos T. Throop, Governor of the state of New-York:

Being conscious that a periodical oblation of our hearts to Almighty God is acceptable to him, and a pleasing duty; and that it is highly becoming in nations, recipients of his favour, as well as individuals; I do in humble reverence, and in conformity to usage, recommend to the people of this state, the observance of Thursday the eighth day of December next, as a day of Prayer and Thanksgiving. Let us, with united hearts, on that day, renew to Him our acknowledgments of gratitude, for those peculiar national institutions by which he has distinguished us among the nations of the earth, and whereby all our civil, religious and personal rights are secured; and for having established schools among us, and other means of public institution, whereby our capacity for enjoyment is enlarged, and we are enabled better to understand and defend our civil and social privileges: and among the innumerable favours which we have received from his bountiful providence, during the past year, let us particularly thank Him, for healthful and fruitful seasons, for the growing spirit of laudable enterprise and diversified industry, and for his remarkable interposition in staying the desolating moral pestilence of intemperate drinking.

[L. S.] In witness whereof, I have hereunto set my hand, and affixed the privy seal of the state, this twentieth day of October, in the year of our Lord one thousand eight hundred and thirty-one. E.T. THROOP.

| Article no. 282 | Subject: Notice |
Ref. December 6, 1831; pg. 2, col. 5

Extract: MORTGAGE SALE,

By virtue of a power contained in a certain mortgage, executed by David A. Thompson to Jesse P. Haines, Nathan Comstock and Isaac W. Smith, bearing date 13 May 1829, and recorded in Niagara county clerk's office 14 May 1829, in book of Mortgages No. 2, on pages 421 and 422, and which has been duly assigned to the subscribers, and on which there is now claimed to be due and owing to the assignees the sum of $1498, will be sold at public vendue to the highest bidder, at the house or inn now occupied by Samuel Jennings, in Lockport, 8 May 1832, the premises described in the said mortgage, which are as follows, to wit:—All that certain tract or parcel of land situate in the village of Lockport, in the county of Niagara and State of New-York, being parts of lots number ten and twelve, in the fourteenth township and sixth range of the Holland purchase (so called,) and bounded and described as follows:—{Notice includes description of boundaries} containing two acres and forty-five hundredths of an acre of land, be the same more or less.

Dated November 22d, 1831. HOUSE & BOUGHTON.

| Article no. 283 | Subject: Advertisement |
Ref. December 6, 1831; pg. 2, col. 5

Extract: GREAT BARGAINS!

ROGERS & BROWN are now opening a large assortment of Goods, purchased at least 20 per cent. lower than any offered the present season. They confidently invite their friends and the public to call, with the full assurance of their being able to buy at far less prices than has been known in this place heretofore. The following comprise a part of their assortment: Dry Goods—[List includes broadcloths, Invisible Green for Gentlemen's frock coats, millers' cloths, cassimeres, Petershams, sattinets, camlet and tartan plaids, silk, vestings, Bombazets, calicoes, gingham, &c.]; Silk Goods—[List includes Italian lustrings, Gro de Naps, Levantines, sinchews and sarsnets, Florences, ribbons, taffetas, veils, braids, buttons, cravats, lace, diaper, hosiery, gloves and mitts, umbrellas, looking-glasses, tickings, &c.]; Groceries—[List includes rum, cognac, brandy, gin, wines, whiskey, lump sugar, St. Croix and New-Orleans sugar, coffee, tobacco, pepper, spices, chocolate, dye-woods, paints and oil, lamp oil, &c.]; Crockery, and Hardware. The above goods were mostly bought at auction, at the late low prices, and must offer a great inducement to those who wish to purchase.

| Article no. 284 | Subject: Notice |
Ref. December 6, 1831; pg. 2, col. 6

Extract: MORTGAGE SALE.

Default having been made in the payment of a certain sum of money, secured by indenture of mortgage, bearing date 18 June 1830, executed by James F. Mason to Amasa Chaffy, and recorded in Niagara county clerk's office, in book of Mortgages No. 3, (number three,) on pages 113, 114, and 115, on which there is now claimed to be due the sum of $849.52—now therefore, notice is hereby given that by virtue of a power contained in said mortgage, and by force of the statute in such case made and provided, the several pieces and parcels of land contained in the said mortgage, and described therein as follows, to wit: "all that certain piece or parcel of land situated and being in the village of Lockport, in the county of Niagara, and being part and parcel of farm lot number twelve in the fourteenth township, and sixth range, of the Holland purchase (so called,) and being parts and parcels of village lots number eleven and thirteen, on the north side of Main-street, in said village, and is bounded as follows, {Notice includes description of boundaries}—Also the one half part in common and undivided of all that certain other piece or parcel of land being parcel of the farm lot aforesaid, [mapped for Jared Comstock, and others, by Jesse P. Haines, surveyor,] known and distinguished as village lot number fourteen, on the south side of Main-street, in the village of Lockport, on the east side of the Erie Canal {Notice includes further description of land,}—and also the one half part in common and undivided of all that certain other piece or parcel of land being village lot number six, on the south side of Niagara street, in said village of Lockport, bounded as follows {Notice includes description of boundaries}; the said two last mentioned lots being numbered according to a map or survey of a part of the village of Lockport, made for one William M. Bond. And also, the one half part in common, and undivided of all that certain other piece or parcel of land being village lot number fifteen, on the north side of (late) Walnut, now Genesee street, in said village {Notice includes further description of land}"—will be severally sold at public auction, at the Inn now kept by Samuel Jennings, in Lockport, 19 May 1832. Dated 28th Nov. 1831. AMASA CHAFFE [sic], Mortgagee. By E. RANSOM, Jr. Att'y.

Article no. 285   Subject: Advertisement
Ref. December 6, 1831; pg. 2, col. 6

HARD TIMES—GOODS CHEAP!!

The subscribers have received a large supply of Fall and Winter Goods. Without particularizing they would say to their friends and the public, that their goods are purchased as low, (vide "20 per cent.") and will be sold as cheap as at any other establishment in the country—without exception.

They have in their late purchases
        Dry Goods, in great variety—
        Hardware—Crockery—Groceries—

A large lot of Iron and Nails, which will be sold very low.

The above goods are offered with confidence in the fact that those who call and examine them, will purchase materially to their advantage. They will pay Cash for Wheat, Pork, Oats, and Butter, and would respectfully, solicit a continuance of the patronage of a generous public.

SETH PARSONS & Co. Lockport, Nov. 26th, 1831.

Article no. 286   Subject: Advertisement
Ref. December 6, 1831; pg. 2, col. 6

ARRIVED THIS DAY, NOV. 28th 1831.
3 Pieces Crimson Merino Circassian,
3 do. Assorted colours do.
2 do. Orange and light blue common do.
1 do. Blue Goats Hair Camblet
1 do. Brown do. do. do.
1 do. Indigo Blue, common do.
and for sale by HOUSE & BOUGHTON. Nov. 28, 1831.

Article no. 287   Subject: Advertisement
Ref. December 6, 1831; pg. 2, col. 6

SHAWLS.

An elegant assortment of Merino, Cashmere, Thibet, Border Rich, Valencia, Adelaide, Prussian, Brauganza, Cassimere and Cotton Shawls, for sale by HOUSE & BOUGHTON. Nov. 28.

Article no. 288   Subject: Advertisement
Ref. December 6, 1831; pg. 2, col. 6

SCHOOL BOOKS.

Just received by N. Leonard, a complete assortment of School Books of the latest Editions, containing many improvements which are well worthy the attention of parents and teachers who are requested to call and examine.

Lockport, Nov. 29.

Article no. 289   Subject: Advertisement
Ref. December 6, 1831; pg. 2, col. 6

FAMILY BIBLES.

A choice lot of the above article just received and for sale at low prices by N. LEONARD. Nov. 29.

Article no. 290   Subject: Notice
Ref. December 6, 1831; pg. 2, col. 6

TWO DOLLARS REWARD.
STRAY COW.

Strayed from the subscriber in August last, a red Cow with a Line Back, some white about her legs, and a roan coloured head and back, whoever will give information so that the owner may get her again, shall have the above reward and all reasonable charges paid.

JOSEPH RUSHMORE. Lockport, Nov. 29th 1831.

Article no. 291   Subject: Advertisement
Ref. December 6, 1831; pg. 2, col. 6

NEW GOODS!
G.S. PLACE, Merchant Tailor.

Has just returned from New-York, with his fall and winter goods, and is manufacturing and keeps constantly on hand, from 500 to 1000 garments of ready made clothing all of a superiour [sic] quality, and of the latest New-York fashions, for sale by
        G.S. PLACE.

Gentlemen, that have close [sic] to cut, or cut and make, can be accommodated on reasonable terms, at the shortest notice, by
        G.S. Place, Merchant Tailor. Lockport, Nov. 29th 1831.

Article no. 292 Subject: Advertisement
Ref. December 6, 1831; pg. 2, col. 6

BROADCLOTHS AND CASSIMERES.

Just received 14 pieces of Broadcloths and Cassimeres, of various colours suitable for Coats, Surtout Coats, Pantaloons &c., which will be made to order in the Latest fall and winter fashions. By

G.S. PLACE, Merchant Tailor.
N.B. Cutting done for farmers and others as usual.
Lockport, Nov. 29.

Article no. 293 Subject: Advertisement
Ref. December 6, 1831; pg. 2, col. 6

CAMBLETS.

4 Pieces Goats Hair, and imitation Camblet, which will be made to order by

G.S. PLACE, Merchant Tailor.
Lockport, Nov. 29th, 1831.

Article no. 294 Subject: Advertisement
Ref. December 6, 1831; pg. 3, col. 1

Lockport Classical School,
by J.B. CHASE, A.B.

The attention of parents and guardians of this village, is respectfully invited to the above named school; in which are taught all the branches of education usually studied in High Schools and Academies in this country. The Principal thinks, from his long experience in the business of teaching, and his devotion to the cause of education, that he will not fail of giving satisfaction to all who may patronize him. Those who would wish for information relative to the school are referred to the following gentlemen—Dr. Southworth, Mr. L. Fellows, J.M. Parks, Esq., T. Chapin, Esq., Mr. J. Bacon, Mr. Giddins, Mr. Trowbridge, and Mr. Ralston, all of whom have had an opportunity of ascertaining, in some degree, the character of the school. A competent assistant will be employed, and every exertion shall be made to render the school deserving of patronage, and a pleasant and profitable resort for children and youth.

Next quarter will commence on the 31st inst. in the new building opposite Mr. Whitcher's store.

Tuition from Two to Four Dollars per quarter.
Lockport, Oct. 17, 1831.

Article no. 295 Subject: Advertisement
Ref. December 6, 1831; pg. 3, col. 1

TIMOTHY SEED.

The highest price paid for 100 bushels Timothy Seed, by

HOUSE & BOUGHTON. October 31.

[Transcriber's note: This advertisement was followed by another for this vendor, in the same column, for "Cheap Circassians."]

Article no. 296 Subject: Court
Ref. December 6, 1831; pg. 3, col. 1

Niagara County Clerk's Office, Lockport,
November 22d, 1831.

NOTICE is hereby given, that the names of persons to serve as Grand and Petit Jurors, at the next court of common pleas and general sessions of the peace, to be held in and for the county of Niagara, on the first Tuesday of January next, A.D. 1832, will be drawn on Monday the 28th of November instant, at ten o'clock in the forenoon of that day, at the clerk's office of said county, pursuant to law.

HENRY CATLIN, Clerk of Niagara county.

Article no. 297 Subject: Transportation
Ref. December 6, 1831; pg. 3, col. 1

Extract: NOTICE is hereby given, that the subscribers and their associates [listed, below], intend to apply to the Legislature of this state, at the next annual session, to incorporate a company to construct a Rail-Road from Schenectady to Buffalo, to pass through the towns of Utica and Salina, with a capital of $5,000,000; with a power to increase the same to $10,000,000, for the transportation of persons and their baggage, and under such restrictions as that the same tolls shall be paid into the canal fund, for the carriage of all property other than baggage, as would be paid for the same property on the canal, and such further regulations as the Legislature may deem proper.

Dated Syracuse, October 12th, 1831. Committee of the Syracuse Convention.

Adams, William H.
Benton, N.S.
Boughton, George H.
Burnet, Moses D.
Cambrelling, Churchill C.
Clark, Lot
Corning, Erastus
Darling, William
Earll, Nehemiah H.
Feeter, George H.
Gardner, Hiram
Grandin, Philip
Hubbell, Walter
Ingersoll, Justus
Johnson, Elisha
Mann, Charles A.
Nickerson, Orson
Barnes, Wheeler
Birdsall, Samuel
Bronson, Parliament
Butler, Charles
Childs, Perry G.
Coe, Bela O.
Cuyler, Joseph
De Graff, John L.
Fay, John
Frisbie, Hiram
Garrow, Nathaniel
Haight, Fletcher M.
Hunt, James B.
James, William
M'Neil, Daniel
Morgan, T.S.
Rose, Robert S.

Rosevelt, N.I.
Schermerhorn, A.M.
Sherwood, John M.
Stebbins, Charles
Stow, William S.
Walton, Jon'a.
Wilkeson, Samuel
Yates, A.I.
Yates, John B.
Sackett, Garry V.
Seymour, Henry
Smith, Israel
Stoughtenburg, T.A.
Stryker, James
Warren, Stephen
Wilkinson, John
Yates, G.F.

Article no. 298   Subject: Advertisement
Ref. December 6, 1831; pg. 3, col. 1

NEW BOOKS.

N. LEONARD is now receiving from N. York an extensive assortment of School, Miscellaneous and Blank Books, of good qualities of paper, printing and binding, and will be sold at low prices. "Call and see." Nov. 22.

Article no. 299   Subject: Advertisement
Ref. December 6, 1831; pg. 3, col. 1

WOOD FOR SALE!

L.A. SPALDING will deliver good Wood to those who may wish to purchase. Lockport, 10 month 20, 1831.

Article no. 300   Subject: Manufacture
Ref. February 21, 1832; pg. 2, col. 2

Cotton Manufactures in the State of New-York.—The following statement was furnished to the *American Advocate* by Mr. Williams, editor of the *N.Y. Annual Register*, and one of the Committee appointed by the late Tariff Convention to ascertain the facts here presented:

There are in the State of New-York, 112 Cotton Manufactories.

Amount of capital invested, $4,485,500
Value of goods manufactured annually, $3,530,250
Pounds of cotton used annually, 7,961,670 lbs.
Equal to 26,533 bales of 300 lbs. each.
Number of spindles in use, 157,316
Number of persons employed and sustained by said establishments, 15,971.

Article no. 301   Subject: Fire
Ref. February 21, 1832; pg. 2, col. 2

Church Burnt.—We are informed that St. Peters [sic] Episcopal Church, at Auburn, was destroyed by fire on Sunday. A fine organ was also burnt, and a large and well toned bell was destroyed.

Article no. 302   Subject: Editorial
Ref. February 21, 1832; pg. 2, col. 3

Extract: BANK COMMISSIONER.

Mr. Lewis Eaton, Senator of the Second district, but a resident of the Eighth, and late President of the Branch Bank in the lower town, has been elected, we learn, Bank Commissioner, in the room of Mr. Rees. You need not stare at this, reader, for it is literally true! The bargain has been confirmed! ... Lewis Eaton is a right clever fellow—and more than that, he is just such a man as the Albany Stockjobbers would wish to see a member of the Bank Triumvirate. ... The Regency must be hard run for timber, that's certain!—or else, it is more convenient that a hanger-on of the party, who turns out not to be quite so important a personage as some folks heretofore imagined he was, should be done for out of the bank fund, rather than out of the private funds of the Albany aristocracy. [Transcriber's note: This article appears in the Editorial columns.]

Article no. 303   Subject: Politics
Ref. February 21, 1832; pg. 2, col. 6

Extract: STATE OFFICERS.—On Monday of last week, the state officers, and one regent of the university, in the place of B.F. Butler, resigned, were elected by the legislature. The vote stood—[Listed, below.] Mr. Tracy, an anti-mason, was absent from the senate, and nearly one third of the anti-masons in the other house were also absent, on account of sickness or other causes no less imperious.—*Utica Elucidator*.

Format—Post sought: Name of candidate (No. of votes cast in senate, No. of votes cast in assembly).

For comptroller: Silas Wright, Jun. (23, 86), John C. Spencer (7, 22).
For attorney general: Greene C. Bronson (23, 85), Samuel M. Hopkins (7, 21).
For regent of the university, one in the place of B.F. Butler, resigned: John L. Veile (23, 82), Samuel A. Foot (7, 21).
For surveyor general: Simeon De Witt (2, 86), James Geddes (7, 17).
For secretary of state: Azariah C. Flagg (23, 86), Gideon Hawley (7, 22).
For treasurer: Abraham Keyser (23, 84), William Mayell (7, 22).
For commissary general: Alexander M. Muir (23, 84), Peter Sken Smith (6, 22), William H. Spencer (1, 0).

Article no. 304   Subject: Marriage
Ref. February 21, 1832; pg. 2, col. 6

MARRIED—On Sunday the 12th inst., by William Crosier, Esq., Mr. Benjamin D. Compton, of Lewiston, to Miss Jane Depue, of Cambria.

Article no. 305   Subject: Politics
Ref. February 21, 1832; pg. 3, col. 1

ANTI-MASONIC STATE CONVENTION.

The Republican Electors of the State of New-York, opposed to Secret Societies, are requested to assemble in their respective Counties, and appoint a number of Delegates corresponding with their Representation in the House of Assembly, to meet in State Convention, at Utica, on Thursday the 21st day of June next, for the purpose of nominating suitable candidates for Governor and Lieutenant-Governor of the State, and of nominating Electors of President and Vice-President of the United States.

Samuel Works, Harvey Ely, Fred'k Whittlesey,
Frederick A. Backus, Thurlow Weed, Bates Cooke,
Timothy Fitch.

Feb. 9, 1832.   State Central Committee.

Article no. 306   Subject: Advertisement
Ref. February 21, 1832; pg. 3, col. 1

CABINET WARE, &C.
W.W. STANARD

Informs his friends and the public that he continues to carry on the

Cabinetmaking Business,

in all its various branches, at his well-known stand, No. 76 Main-street—west of the Canal, and one door east of the Mansion House—where he will be pleased to receive the orders of his customers and fill them promptly.

Secretaries, Sideboards, Dining and Tea Tables, Work Stands, &c., &c., of all the various patterns and prices, constantly for sale, or made to order.

All persons needing articles in the above line, will do well to "remember 76!"   Feb. 14th 1832.

Article no. 307   Subject: Advertisement
Ref. February 21, 1832; pg. 3, col. 1

TEMPLE OF FASHION.

The last Report of the present Fashions have just been received by the subscriber from Regent-street, London, through the medium of his New York friends. It will be unnecessary for him to boast of his capacity in Cutting, or the excellence and number of his workmen. His friends have tried him, and he leaves it to them to say, whether he has not passed the ordeal, and came out unscathed by trial. He is to be found at his old stand, immediately over Eaton & Brown's Store, in the Lower Town, where he will be happy to satisfy his numerous patrons, and in a manner, by which he will not suffer in comparison, with those, who boast much of the superiority of their workmanship.

JAMES P. RIDNER. Lockport, Feb. 7, 1832.

Article no. 308   Subject: Advertisement
Ref. February 21, 1832; pg. 3, col. 2

Goods! cheap Goods!

The Subscriber begs leave to inform the public that he has purchased the stock in trade of Mr. G. Timmerman, in the town of Royalton, on the Batavia road, and intends to do business at the same stand.

Intending to make considerable additions in a short time to his present well selected variety, he hopes to receive a liberal share of public patronage—assuring his customers that he will at all times serve them on as good terms as can be had elsewhere, for ready pay.

JACOB TURNER.

N.B. Mr. Timmerman now has charge, and will have for some time to come, of the establishment. His well known character is a warrant that those who may favour the establishment with their custom, will meet with liberal and fair usage. Feb. 7, 1832.

Article no. 309   Subject: Advertisement
Ref. February 21, 1832; pg. 3, col. 2

BUTTER AND WHITEFISH.

G. BACON has just received a quantity of Butter, which he offers for sale by the firkin. Also, a few barrels of White-Fish, which he will sell by the barrel or pound.

Lockport, January 9th, 1832.

Article no. 310   Subject: Advertisement
Ref. February 21, 1832; pg. 3, col. 2

Latest London Fashions!

G.S. PLACE has just received, through his attentive New-York friends, patterns of the latest London Fashions for garments of all kinds, and is accordingly prepared to fit out his customers in real fashionable style.

As he has on hand a large assortment of superior Cloths, Cassimeres, &c. and has in his employ a number of good workmen, he can furnish all orders in his line at short notice, and in the best style of workmanship. "A word to the wise is sufficient."

Article no. 311   Subject: Notice
Ref. February 21, 1832; pg. 3, col. 2

To those indebted to, or holding contracts from, the Holland Land Company. Certificates of deposit to my credit in the Lockport Bank, will be received as cash at the offices of the Holland Land Company, at this place and Buffalo, in payment of any debts due the Company at either of those offices.

DAVID E. EVANS, Agent. Batavia, Jan. 2d, 1832.

Article no. 312   Subject: Advertisement
Ref. February 21, 1832; pg. 3, col. 2

New and Cheap Goods!

Just opened and for sale by E. FOLSOM, in the store one door west from H. Gardner's Law Office, Canal-street, an entire new stock of

Dry Goods,

comprising a general assortment suited to the season. Also, an assortment of

Ready Made Clothing:

all of which will be sold cheap for Cash.
Cash paid for Tallow, Lard and Beeswax.
Lockport, January 16th, 1832.

Article no. 313   Subject: Advertisement
Ref. February 21, 1832; pg. 3, col. 2

FARMERS' MILLS!

On the Eighteen-Mile Creek, a little north of the village of Lockport.

The subscribers have at length completed their Mills, and they are now in operation and in fine order for

Grist Grinding.

As their Mills are built expressly for Custom Work, they would respectfully solicit a liberal share of public patronage—for they will spare no pains to deserve well of the public, and to do justly by all who may favour them with their custom.

At their Saw-Mill they will purchase Logs, saw upon shares, or by the thousand, as shall best suit their customers.

They will endeavour that no person shall go away dissatisfied, who has grain to grind or logs to saw at their Mills.

Please try the Farmers' Mills!
PARSONS, GOODING & Co. Lockport, Jan. 2, 1832.

Article no. 314   Subject: Health & Medicine
Ref. February 21, 1832; pg. 3, col. 2

LOCK HOSPITAL.—The very great attention necessary to be bestowed on that class of Disease, for the care of which the founder of this Institution has realized some celebrity, has induced Dr. Cooke to establish, in addition to his present numerous offices at the Albany Lock Dispensary, an Hospital, for the reception of such Patients from the country or city who may require more than the ordinary means for their recovery, being the only one of the kind in the United States. The system on which this Hospital is conducted is the same as that of the celebrated Lock Hospitals of London and Dublin, excepting that of being a private instead of a public institution. Persons desirous of placing themselves under the immediate care of Dr. Cooke, may apply to him at the Hospital, where, in consideration of proper remuneration for his services, they will receive that consistent mode of treatment, which is almost invariably attended with success. Terms of admission obtained at the Hospital. Hours of consultation at the dispensary as usual. No. 2, Store Lane, Albany. Jan. 6.

Article no. 315   Subject: Advertisement
Ref. February 21, 1832; pg. 3, col. 2

Flour and Meal.

SETH PARSONS & CO. keep Flour and Meal constantly for sale at their store on Main-street. Jan. 3, 1832.

Article no. 316   Subject: Advertisement
Ref. February 21, 1832; pg. 3, col. 3

HARDWARE STORE.
Farmers and Mechanics, Attention!
JAMES R. STAFFORD has on hand, at his store,
Sign of the Mill-Saw and Bell,
Lockport, (Upper Village.)
50 tons Swedes and Russia Iron;
10 doz. Cast-steel Axes, warranted good:
—Also—
Cabinet-Makers', Carpenters' and Joiners'
Tools—of every description:

And every other article in the Hardware line kept expressly for the accommodation of Farmers and Mechanics. He also carries on the

Copper, Tin and Sheet Iron Manufacturing,

in all its various branches. All work in which line will be done with neatness and despatch, and no pains spared to accommodate those who may favour him with their patronage.

N.B. Just received—A quantity of Rifle Barrels and Locks, and other articles, for the accommodation of Gunsmiths. Lockport, Dec. 20, 1831.

Article no. 317   Subject: Advertisement
Ref. February 21, 1832; pg. 3, col. 4

CASH TO LOAN.

L.A. SPALDING offers his services to negociate loans of money upon reasonable terms. He will also allow interest on money deposited with him, for any time over thirty days. Lockport, 12th mo. 12th, 1831.

Article no. 318   Subject: Notice
Ref. February 21, 1832; pg. 3, col. 4

ADMINISTRATOR'S NOTICE.

Pursuant to an order of Hiram Gardner, Esq. Surrogate of the County of Niagara, notice is hereby given to all persons who have claims against Daniel Washburn, late of the town of Lockport, in said county, deceased, to

exhibit the same, with the vouchers thereof, to Seth Parsons, administrator of the Estate of the said Daniel Washburn, at his office in the store of Seth Parsons & Co., in the town of Lockport, in said county, at or before the 9th day of June, next.—And all persons indebted to said estate, are hereby required to settle the same without delay.—Dated the 9th day of January, 1832.
SETH PARSONS, Administrator.

Article no. 319　　Subject: Advertisement
Ref. February 21, 1832; pg. 3, col. 4

CASH FOR SAW LOGS.

Wanted 1000 Saw Logs—of Pine, Oak, Whitewood, Hemlock, Chesnut [sic] and Black Walnut, timber, a part to be delivered immediately, upon the opening of the Canal in the spring and the residue during the season. Security will be required for the fulfilment of the contract.
L.A. SPALDING.

Article no. 320　　Subject: Advertisement
Ref. February 21, 1832; pg. 3, col. 4

100,000 Feet Pine Lumber, from 3-4 inch to 2 1-2 inch thick, just received and for sale by
　　L.A. SPALDING. 5th Month 31, 1831.

Article no. 321　　Subject: Advertisement
Ref. February 21, 1832; pg. 4, col. 3

Farm for Sale!

The subscribers offer for sale an Article of a valuable Farm, containing about 150 acres—60 acres improved—with a fine young orchard, a comfortable dwelling House and Barn,—lying within 3 miles of this village. Any person wishing to purchase, will do well to call and examine the premises.
ROGERS & BROWN. Lockport, Jan. 16th, 1832.

Article no. 322　　Subject: Notice
Ref. February 21, 1832; pg. 4, col. 3

SIX CENTS REWARD!

Ran or was inveigled away from the subscriber, on the 9th inst., a bound boy called Calvin Brown, aged 10 years. All persons are forbid harbouring or trusting said boy. The above Reward, but no charges, will be paid to the person returning him.
ALANSON ARNOLD. Royalton, Feb. 9, 1832.

Article no. 323　　Subject: Notice
Ref. February 21, 1832; pg. 4, col. 3

Extract: SHERIFF'S SALE.

By virtue of a writ of fieri facias, issued out of the supreme court of judicature of the state of New-York, and to me directed and delivered, against the goods and chattles [sic], lands and tenements, of Charles Brown, in the county of Niagara. [First public auction date was set for 9 February 1832 and the accompanying notice dated 27th December, 1831. After one postponement, this notice was posted:] The sale of the above property is further postponed until the 9th day of March next, then to take place at the same hour and place above mentioned [i.e., the house now occupied by Samuel Jennings, in the village of Lockport, called the Hotel]. Dated Feb. 10, 1832. HIRAM McNEIL, Sheriff.

Article no. 324　　Subject: Advertisement
Ref. February 21, 1832; pg. 4, col. 4

MUSICAL INSTRUMENTS.

N. Leonard has for sale a good assortment of Violins, Flutes, Clarionets, Flageolets, and Fifes of the first quality and low prices.

Article no. 325　　Subject: Notice
Ref. February 21, 1832; pg. 4, col. 4

SHERIFF'S SALE.

By virtue of a writ of fieri facias, issued out of the Supreme Court of judicature of the people of the State of New-York, and to me directed and delivered, against the goods and chattels, lands and tenements, real estate and chattels real, of Ferris Angevine, I have seized and taken that certain piece and parcel of land, situate in the town of Niagara, County of Niagara, known as lot number fifty-nine, containing one hundred acres, together with all the right, title, claim, interest and demand of the said Ferris Angevine in the same; which I shall expose to sale at public auction, at the house of Parkhurst Whitney, in the said town, on the 29th day of February next, at one o'clock in the afternoon of that day.
Dated January 3d, 1832.
HIRAM McNEIL, Sheriff.
By RUFUS MANNING, Dep'y Sheriff.

Article no. 326　　Subject: Notice
Ref. February 21, 1832; pg. 4, col. 4

NOTICE is hereby given, that the Trustees of the village of Lockport will apply to the Legislature of the State of New York, at its present session, for an alteration of the act incorporating the village of Lockport.
January 14, 1832.

Article no. 327　　Subject: Notice
Ref. February 21, 1832; pg. 4, col. 5

Extract: MORTGAGE SALE.

By virtue of a power contained in a certain mortgage, executed by David A. Thompson to Jesse P. Haines,

Nathan Comstock and Isaac W. Smith, bearing date 13 May 1829, and recorded in Niagara county clerk's office 14 May 1829, in book of Mortgages No. 2, on pages 421 and 422, and which has been duly assigned to the subscribers, and on which there is now claimed to be owing to the assignees the sum of $1513.50, will be sold at public vendue to the highest bidder, at the house or inn now occupied by Samuel Jennings, in Lockport, 22 June 1832, the premises described in the said mortgage, which are as follows, to wit: All that certain tract or parcel of land situate in the village of Lockport, in the county of Niagara and State of New-York, being parts of lots number ten and twelve, in the fourteenth township and sixth range of the Holland Purchase (so called,) and bounded and described as follows:—{Notice includes description of boundaries,} containing two acres and forty-five hundredths of an acre of land, be the same more or less.

Dated January 3d, 1832.
HOUSE & BOUGHTON.

Article no. 328 Subject: Health & Medicine
Ref. June 26, 1832; pg. 1, col. 1

Extract: CHOLERA. Below will be found the Report of the Edinburgh Board of Health [Saratoga County], in reference to this disease. Although our section of country may not be visited by this dreadful scourge—and although we are far from wishing to create unnecessary alarm—still we think it would be prudent for every family to provide themselves with the remedies therein recommended. They will cost but a trifle—and therefore the loss will be small, should our citizens be so favoured by Providence as to be exempted from the ravages of this fell disease. Prevention is, in all things, far better than cure—and is much the cheapest. {Following this preamble, appeared the Report of the Edinburgh Board of Health, on the mode of preventing and treating the Cholera.} [Length, 1-1/2 columns.]

Article no. 329 Subject: Slavery
Ref. June 26, 1832; pg. 1, col. 5

Extract: From the *Daily Albany Argus*,
AMERICAN COLONIZATION SOCIETY.

To the Clergy of all religious denominations in the state of New-York, and to their respective congregations.

The approach of our national anniversary, with which, by the kindness of a benevolent and Christian public, the interests of the American Colonization Society have been peculiarly associated, induces us to address you. Presuming that you are friendly to our cause, we cannot doubt your willingness to have the subject brought renewedly to your consideration; &c. [The remainder of the address mentions: the massacre at Southampton in Virginia; the "manifest evils ... resulting from a coloured population;" emancipation of slaves as soon as the means can be provided for their conveyance to the colony [in Africa]; reconvey these people, who came here Pagans, to the land of their fathers as Christians.] Under a deep sense of the importance of an enterprize so pure and benevolent in its object—so broad and lasting in its effects,—combining the dearest interests of two continents in its operation, and stretching into eternity in its consequences, we feel emboldened to make this further appeal to the liberality, patriotism and christian charity of our fellow-citizens to sustain it. The amount of your collections may be remitted to Richard Yates, esq., Treasurer of the N.Y. State Colonization Society, Albany;—to Moses Allen, esq., New York—or they may be paid over to L.H. Clark, esq., the agent of the American Colonization Society for this state. In behalf of the N.Y. State Col. Society John Savage, President. H. Bleecker, J.T. Norton, B.F. Butler, Gerrit Smith, John Willard, C.R. Webster, Managers. Richard Yates, Treasurer. R.V. De Witt, Secretary.

Article no. 330 Subject: Crime
Ref. June 26, 1832; pg. 2, col. 2

Brutal Outrage.—On Sunday last a most disgraceful, and we fear tragic scene was enacted in the lower part of this city [Buffalo], near the canal. The particulars we have not learned; but only that a band of labourers employed in digging a canal across the low grounds, beneath the Terrace, were the actors. They were seen by a person who did not dare approach them, assembled around one, not of their number, beating him, as he lay prostrate, with great fury. When they left him he remained motionless. This was near dark, and the man has not been since found. Several citizens were attracted to the scene by the tumult, all of whom were severely beaten. The offenders are Connaught Irishmen. Five of them, we learn, are secured in prison, to await an investigation of the affair. We looked in a moment at the office while they were under examination, and more untamed, lawless looking beings in human shape, certainly never before fell under our observation. We could well imagine, if such were Connaught men, that the station of peace officers there, is no sinecure. We hope and trust that when our city government is fully organized, (for we are literally in the chrysalis state, just now,) we shall be spared the narrations of scenes like this, as occurring within our bounds.—*Buffalo Jour.*

Article no. 331   Subject: Politics
Ref. June 26, 1832; pg. 2, col. 2

From the *Ontario Phoenix*.

A Sign.—During the present session of the Circuit of this county, the Grand Jury took the following vote for President and Vice-President:

President—Wm. Wirt 13
    Henry Clay 4
    Andrew Jackson 1
Vice-President—Amos Ellmaker 9
    John Sergeant 4
    Martin Van Buren 1

Article no. 332   Subject: Health & Medicine
Ref. June 26, 1832; pg. 2, col. 3

THE CHOLERA. In our last, we mentioned a rumour of a vessel, having Cholera on board, which was said to be quarantined at Niagara, U.C. In order to ascertain the truth of this rumour—as also that of an additional one which had reached us, that there had been cases at Youngstown, in this county—we addressed a note to the Hon A.G. Hinman, of the latter place, requesting the truth and particulars in reference to these reports—to which note we received the annexed reply—which we deem proper to lay before the public. It will be perceived from Judge H.'s note, that the reports in circulation relative to the extensive spread of the disease at York, U.C., are very much exaggerated. Besides, it is by no means certain that either the person who died aboard the vessel at Niagara, or the sentinel who afterwards was taken sick, were affected by the Asiatic Cholera—though it is possible they may. But whatever the disease may have been, we think some measures should be adopted by the authorities on the frontier, to prevent the landing on our shores of any person from the British Provinces who may be labouring under this plague. We suggest this, not because we believe in the contagiousness of the disease; but simply because there are many—perhaps a majority of this community—who do, and to whose honest convictions and natural apprehensions some attention should be paid. If, notwithstanding the adoption of all warrantable and possible precautions to the contrary, the disease should visit us, there will be no ground for the attaching of blame to any person.

    Youngstown, Saturday evening, 28th June.

Dear Sir—I have just received yours of yesterday, and can now only say in reply, that on Tuesday of this week, a schooner arrived at Niagara, from the foot of the Lake, with a passenger (not an emigrant) on board, who had been taken sick a few hours previous. He was visited by several Physicians, and his case thought to be Cholera. The vessel anchored a few rods from the shore, and a sentinel was placed there to prevent any landing from the vessel. The next morning (Wednesday) the man died; and on Thursday morning the soldier was attacked with the same disease—he is, however, likely to recover. I regret that it is not in my power, at this time, to give you a more particular account of these cases. That they were the malignant cholera, is generally admitted. These are the only cases that have occurred at Niagara—none at this place. Letters received to-day at Niagara, from York, state that 8 new cases have occurred at that place—two previous. In great haste, yours, &c.

A.G. HINMAN.

We have received further verbal information from York, 48 hours later than that contained in Judge H.'s letter—up to which time, the number of Cholera cases at York were reported at 18.

Article no. 333   Subject: Health & Medicine
Ref. June 26, 1832; pg. 2, col. 3

FURTHER INFORMATION! A letter from a gentleman at Lewiston, received by us this morning, says—"There was a death on board the steamboat Niagara, at Fort George, to-day, (Monday,) under circumstances which leave little doubt of its being occasioned by the Real Cholera. The mate of the boat is since taken with the same disease."

Should any thing transpire on this frontier, in reference to this disease, which would seem to require a public notice, previous to our next regular publication, we shall take prompt measures to lay it before our readers.

Article no. 334   Subject: Health & Medicine
Ref. June 26, 1832; pg. 2, col. 3

Our advices from the east in reference to the above disease are not very full or satisfactory. It still continues its ravages, however, at Quebec and Montreal—but by no means with that fatality which we at first were led to believe. The accounts from Canada have, in this respect, been very unnecessarily exaggerated. By the report of the Montreal Board of Health, it appears there had been, up to the 15th June, twelve hundred and four cases of the disease, including those that were slightly affected, of whom 234 had died. This does not show a mortality by any means so great as has usually been reported on the authority of letter writers and travellers.

In summing up the cases in this state and Vermont, we find there have been, up to the 20th inst., at Plattsburgh, 7 caes—of whom 5 died and 2 remain. At Mechanicsville, 1 case—an emigrant from Montreal. The4 [sic] cases at Fort Miller have been pronounced to be the common cholera. Two cases at Whitehall—one, a drunkard from aboard a steamboat. At Burlington, Vt., there had been but one case, certain, of Cholera—three other suspicious cases, terminating fatally, were supposed to have been occasioned by other diseases.

A letter from Sackets-Harbour, June 18th, published in the *Albany Evening Journal*, states, that great alarm is spread all along that section of country, as the emigrants from Quebec and Montreal were crowding in the thousands up the St. Lawrence. There had been, up to the date of the letter, 3 cases at Prescott, U.C., and fears were entertained that it would break out at Ogdensburgh, as many emigrants had landed there.

Take all the accounts together, however, and it is evident that the alarm and dismay has been greater than the actual progress of the disease would seem to us to warrant. Still, no relaxation should be suffered in the work of purification—though there may be a very judicious abatement in the excited feelings of the people. The Cholera is a disease that should be faced calmly.

P.S. The last advices from Montreal state that the Cholera is abating there. [Transcriber's note: This article appears in the Editorial columns.]

Article no. 335 Subject: Health & Medicine
Ref. June 26, 1832; pg. 2, col. 4

PROCEEDINGS AT LEWISTON. It will be seen by the proceedings which we give below, that the citizens of Lewiston, have, with a praiseworthy promptness, resolved to adopt efficient measures to prevent the introduction,—so far as human efforts are competent to the task,—of the Cholera into our country through the agency of the foreign emigrants from Quebec and Montreal, who are crowding in hundreds towards the upper parts of Lake Ontario. If energetically seconded by every inhabitant of the frontier, it is possible that the disease may, through their exertions, be kept from this section of the country. There is no principle of justice or humanity which requires that persons who are labouring under a malignant distemper, should be allowed to debark upon our shores, and to infect the atmosphere, as it were, with the virus of a terrible pestilence: we trust, therefore, that no mistaken notions of kindness, nor any mercenary feelings, may prompt any person to violate the sanitary resolutions adopted by the citizens of Lewiston. [Transcriber's note: This article appears in the Editorial columns.]

Article no. 336 Subject: Health & Medicine
Ref. June 26, 1832; pg. 2, col. 4

CIRCULAR.

At a meeting of the inhabitants of the Village of Lewiston, convened at the Frontier House, on the 25th day of June 1832, for the purpose of taking into consideration the most efficient means of preventing the introduction of the Asiatic Cholera into our country, Major Benjamin Barton was called to the chair, and Horatio J. Stow appointed Secretary. A Committee was then appointed, who submitted the following Preamble and Resolutions, which were unanimously adopted:

Whereas this meeting has the most unquestionable evidence that the Asiatic Cholera has broken out and is already raging to an alarming extent in some parts of Canada—and whereas, it is satisfactorily ascertained that the disease was introduced into that country by emigrants from Europe—and whereas, many of these emigrants have heretofore and still continue to come to the United States, thereby exposing us all to that most direful malady—therefore,

Resolved, That so long as the Asiatic Cholera shall prevail in the provinces of Upper or Lower Canada, no person coming from either of said Provinces, shall be permitted to land at any other landing places or wharves or shores, than at the regular ferries at Lewiston and Youngstown.

Resolved, That no foreign Emigrants, during the prevalence of the Asiatic Cholera in either of the Canadas, be permitted to land within the towns of Lewiston and Porter. Resolved, That John Gray, Ansel M. Hurd, William Hotchkiss, and Samuel Manly, be a Committee of Vigilance to see that the above Resolutions be carried into effect, and that said Committee be authorized to employ a sufficient guard for that purpose.

Resolved, That no Steamboat, or other vessel or boat, other than ferry boats, be permitted to land or discharge either passengers or cargo within the towns of Lewiston and Porter, during the prevalence of the Cholera in the Canadas, without a permit from the Committee of Vigilance, or from a Health Officer whom they may appoint.

Resolved, That the keepers of the several ferries, and owners of boats, in the towns of Lewiston and Porter, be requested to co-operate with us in carrying into effect the foregoing Resolutions.

Resolved, That all persons violating, or attempting to violate, the above Resolutions, shall be dealt with according to law.

Resolved, That, acting under the strongest impulse of our nature—sanctioned by the first law laid down by the Great Creator, that of self-preservation—we pledge ourselves to the public, under all responsibilities, and at every hazard, to prevent the further introduction of Emigrants.

BENJAMIN BARTON, Chairman.
H.J. STOW, Secretary.

Article no. 337 Subject: Politics
Ref. June 26, 1832; pg. 2, col. 4

Extract: STATE CONVENTION.

We have received, through the *Albany Evening Journal*, and a slip from the office of the *Utica Elucidator*, a brief statement of the proceedings of the Anti-Masonic State Convention, which met in the latter city on the 21st inst. One hundred delegates were present from 49 counties. [Selection of officers, listed below.] After the appointment of the Committees to report an Electoral Ticket and an Address, the Convention proceeded to ballot for candidates for Governor and Lieutenant-Governor. On counting the ballots, it appeared that Francis Granger, of Ontario, was the unanimous choice of the Convention as a candidate for the office of governor, and Samuel Stevens, of N.Y., for that of lieut.-governor. The Committees for the formation of an Electoral Ticket, reported the following, which was also unanimously adopted: [Names of Committee members, listed below.] Mr. Spencer then reported an able and eloquent Address, which was unanimously adopted—the present State Central Committee was reappointed—and the Convention adjourned,—having been in session but one day. We shall give the proceedings entire, as soon as received.

[Transcriber's note: See key for numbered codes, after list of names.]

- Baker, Chauncey; Jefferson, New York (1)
- Bois, Joseph; Washington, New York (1)
- Boughton, G.H.; Niagara County, New York (1)
- Burr, Calvin; Tompkins, New York (1)
- Cook, Robert; Cayuga, New York (1)
- Cotheal, Henry; New York, New York (1)
- Cushman, Jabez N.; Rensselaer, New York. (2)
- Dalliba, James A.; Essex, New York (1)
- Defreest, Martin; Rensselaer, New York (1)
- Dubois, Cort; Dutchess, New York (1)
- Dubois, Nathaniel; Orange, New York (1)
- Dunham, Shubael; Genesee, New York (1)
- Dunlap, Josiah; Steuben, New York (1)
- Gay, George A.; Ulster, New York (1)
- Gebhard, John; Schoharie, New York (1)
- Granger, Francis; Ontario County, New York; was the unanimous choice for the office of governor, as balloted at the Convention.
- Hathaway, Charles; Delaware, New York (1)
- Hawks, James; Otsego, New York (1)
- Hawley, Gideon; Albany, New York (1)
- Howell, Nathaniel W.; Ontario County, New York (1)
- Huntington, George; Oneida, New York (1)
- Hutchinson, Hollom; Livingston, New York (1)
- Kent, James; New York, New York (1), and Senatorial Elector.
- Lacey, Samuel; Monroe, New York (1)
- Livingston, Robert; St. Lawrence, New York (1)
- Lord, Eleazeer; New York, New York (1)
- Lyman, Samuel P.; Oneida, New York (2)
- M'Kinstry, Justus; Columbia, New York (1)
- M'Martin, Duncan; Montgomery, New York (1)
- Mather, Hiram F.; Onondaga, New York (1)
- Miller, John; Cortland, New York (1)
- Mixer, Nathan; Chautauque, New York (1)
- Morris, John Cox; Otsego, New York (3)
- Per Lee, Edmund G.; Chenango, New York (1)
- Potter, Ellis; New York, New York (1)
- Rose, Robert S.; Seneca, New York (1)
- Shoemaker, Robert; Herkimer, New York (1)
- Smith, Asa B.; Wayne, New York (1)
- Smith, Gerrit; Madison, New York (1)
- Spencer, John C.; Ontario County, New York (1), and Senatorial Elector.
- Stevens, Samuel; New York, New York; was the unanimous choice for the office of lieutenant governor, as balloted at the Convention.
- Townsend, Robert, jun.; New York, New York (3)
- Tracy, A.H., Hon.; Erie County, New York; chosen President of the Convention.
- Tucker, Joseph; New York, New York (1)
- Turk, James; Westchester, New York (1)
- Tuttle, William; Greene, New York (1)
- Waring, Gilbert; Saratoga, New York (1)
- Wilbur, Orrin; Lewis, New York (1)
- Wood, Silas; Suffolk, New York (1)

Key:

(1) Member of the Committee for the formation of an Electoral Ticket, as adopted at the Convention.
(2) Samuel P. Lyman, of Oneida, and Jabez N. Cushman, of Rensselaer, were chosen Secretaries of the Anti-Masonic State Convention.
(3) John Cox Morris, of Otsego, and Robert Townsend, Jr., of N.Y. were chosen Vice-Presidents of the Convention.

Article no. 338 Subject: Health & Medicine
Ref. June 26, 1832; pg. 2, col. 6

After our paper had gone to press this day, we received the following proceedings of a meeting held in this village, in reference to the Cholera. As they interest our citizens generally, we have delayed our sheet in part, in order to give them publicity.

LOCKPORT MEETING.

At a meeting of the inhabitants of the village of Lockport, in the county of Niagara, held in said village, on the 26th June, inst., for the purpose of taking into consideration the present danger of the introduction of the disease called the Asiatic Cholera among us, and the means of preventing the same, the following resolutions were passed:

Resolved, That immediate information of the provisions of the recent law passed by the Legislature of this state, for the purpose of preventing the introduction of said disease therein, should be given to the officers and inhabitants of the several towns in said county, bordering upon Lake Ontario.

Resolved, That the inhabitants, and particularly the supervisors, justices of the peace, and overseers of the poor, of said towns, be earnestly requested to inform themselves of the provisions of said law, and to take immediate and prompt measures to carry them into effect.

Resolved, That the Boards of Health of the village and town of Lockport, be earnestly requested to take prompt measures to carry the provisions of said law into immediate effect, to distribute information throughout the county of the powers and duties of the several officers and inhabitants under the same, and to take all necessary and prompt measures to prevent the introduction of said disease among us.

Resolved, That the members of this meeting will by all necessary ways and means in their power aid the health officers in carrying into effect the provisions of said law, and any regulations they may adopt under the same; and that it be recommended to the inhabitants of the county generally, to afford prompt and all necessary and efficient aid and support to the health officers of the several towns and villages, in any measures they may adopt for the purpose of guarding against the introduction of said disease.

SETH PARSONS, Chairman.

L.F. BOWEN, Secretary.

Article no. 339 Subject: Marriage
Ref. June 26, 1832; pg. 2, col. 6

MARRIED—On the 20th inst., at Royalton, Niagara Co., by the Rev. Mr. O'Flyng [surname not fully legible], Henry K. Hopkins, Esq., of Lockport, Attorney at Law, to Miss Julietta E. Buell, daughter of Mr. Daniel W. Buell, of the former place.

Article no. 340 Subject: Advertisement
Ref. June 26, 1832; pg. 2, col. 6

NEW BOOKS for sale by N. LEONARD:
The works of the Rev. Robert Hall,
Sparks' Life of Gouverneur Morris;
Adventures on the Columbia River, by Ross Cox
Keith's Evidence of Prophecy;
Bryant's Poems: The Swallow Barn;
Conversations with an Ambitious Student;
The False Step and the Sisters;
Romance and Reality; British Spy;
Life of Sir Walter Raleigh;
Mackintosh's Ethical Philosophy.
June 26.

Article no. 341 Subject: Advertisement
Ref. June 26, 1832; pg. 2, col. 6

PORK.—Mess, Prime and 1-Hog Pork, by the bbl. for sale by [L. FELLOWS & Co. March 6.]

Article no. 342 Subject: Advertisement
Ref. June 26, 1832; pg. 3, col. 1

Extract: NEW GOODS! Greater Bargains than ever!
ROGERS & BROWN Have opened their Spring Stock of Goods, and find them cheaper than ever! They offer the following, (with many others not enumerated,) at such prices will induce all to buy that are in want: [List includes broadcloths, cassimeres, sattinets, calicoes, Irish linen, lawn laces and Bishop's lawn, diaper, ticking, lasting, burlap, duck, &c.; vestings, cravats, muslin, hose, silk and linen gloves, parasols, Leghorn and Dunstable hats, bobbinet lace and lace edging, sheeting, wicking, batting, wadding, suspenders, room and window Paper, letter and cap Paper, Quills, cotton yarn, pins & needles, thread of all descriptions. Silk Goods, including: Gros de Naps, Indies, Swiss, Berlins and Masques, sinchews and sarsenets, lustrings, Levantines, gauze, camblets, Florences, crape, handkerchiefs, shawls, veils, ribbons for hat trimmings, taffetas, sewing silk & twist, vestings, cravats. Groceries, including: teas, rum, brandy, gin, wines, sugar, molasses, coffees, pepper, pimento, ginger, cassia, chocolate, rice, cloves, nutmegs, raisins (Bloom, muscatel and Smyrna), prunes, lemon syrup, Stoughton's bitters; herring, codfish and mackerel; Macaboy, Scotch and Rappee snuff; smoking and chewing tobacco, bar lead and shot, blasting powder; indigo, borax, red and white chalk, annato; liquorice ball, Lee's Pills, allum, madder; sweet, castor and olive Oil; blue vitriol, salts, oils, &c. Crockery and Glassware, Hardware, and Looking-Glasses.] The above Goods were mostly purchased this spring, and offer great inducements to those who wish to buy. June 26.

Article no. 343   Subject: Advertisement
Ref. June 26, 1832; pg. 3, col. 1

NOTICE.

The subscriber respectfully informs his customers, and the public generally, that he has discontinued business for the present, and has disposed of his stock in trade to Mr. William Ward, by whom the business will be carried on, at the old stand, for the future.

In returning his thanks to his old friends and customers for the liberal support they have awarded him, the undersigned would beg leave to recommend his successor to their patronage, as one who will do ample justice to all who may favour him with their custom.

S.C. LOCKWOOD. Lockport, April, 8 1832. [sic]

Article no. 344   Subject: Advertisement
Ref. June 26, 1832; pg. 3, col. 1

HAT AND CAP STORE.

The subscriber begs leave to inform the citizens of Lockport, and its vicinity, that having purchased the stock in trade of Mr. S.C. Lockwood, he is now prepared to furnish all articles in his line, of the latest fashions and best workmanship, at prices commensurate with the state of the times. A liberal share of patronage at the hands of his fellow-citizens, is respectfully solicited.

Hatting and Shipping Furs purchased as usual.

WILLIAM WARD. June 19th, 1832.

Article no. 345   Subject: Advertisement
Ref. June 26, 1832; pg. 3, col. 1

BROADCLOTHS.

A First rate assortment of Broadcloths, for sale much lower, than ever before sold in this place. Please call and examine. SETH PARSONS & Co. Lockport, June 2, 1832.

Article no. 346   Subject: Advertisement
Ref. June 26, 1832; pg. 3, col. 2

FOR SALE—

A second-hand Gig, on good terms. Apply to

L.A. SPALDING.

Article no. 347   Subject: Advertisement
Ref. June 26, 1832; pg. 3, col. 2

NEW Publications!—Eugene Aram, forming Nos. 19 and 20 of Novelist's Library: Count Robert of Paris; Bravo; Life of Sir Isaac Newton; and Palestine, or the Holy Land, forming Nos. 26 and 27 of Family Library, just received at the Book Store of

N. LEONARD. March 6, 1832.

Article no. 348   Subject: Advertisement
Ref. June 26, 1832; pg. 3, col. 2

Extract: Lockport Drug Store.
Doctors Southworth and Reynale

Respectfully inform the inhabitants of Lockport, and its vicinity, that they have established themselves as Apothecaries, in the building lately occupied by Southworth and Smith, on Main-Street, (nearly opposite the Brick Block,) where they intend to keep constantly on hand a complete assortment of Drugs, Medicines, Dye Stuffs, Paints, Oils and Varnish, to which they particularly invite the attention of Physicians, Clothiers, &c. They also keep on hand a general assortment of Patent Medicines, among which may be found the following valuable articles: [List includes: Ware's Vegetable Bilious Pills, Relfe's Anti-Bilious Pills, Relfe's Aromatic Female Pills, Relfe's Asthmatic Pills, Relfe's Vegetable Specific, Hunter's Pills, Turlington's Balsam of Life, Pectoral Oil, Dr. Jebb's Liniment, Finche's celebrated Ointment, Deal's German Eye Water, Dole's German Eye Water, Albion corn Plaster, Finche's Vegetable Bitters, Wilber's Vegetable Itch Ointment, Dr. Pierson's Welsh Cough Drops, Ware's Anti-Anetus, Poladelphis or India Extract, British Antiseptic Dentrifice, Vegetable Lithontriptic and Specific Solvent Powders, Dr. Waterhouse's Antiphlogistic and Strengthening Plaster, T. Smith's Adhesive Plaster, La Mott's Cough Drops, Genuine Elixir Pectorale, Anderson's Cough Drops, Godfrey's Cordial, Bateman's Drops, British Oil, Swaim's Panacea, Dr. Roberts' Welsh Medicamentum {The advertisement includes the conditions indicated for the products listed to this point,}

[Essential oils ranging from oil of peppermint to wormwood and vitriol, Soda and Seidlitz Powders, Aromatic and Cephalic Snuff, Rowland's Macassar Oil, Percussion Powder and Naples Soap, perfumeries, rose water, Antique a la Tubereuse, and:]

The Patent Nipple: (This article we, S&R, do confidently recommend to the public as the safest and best remedy ever used for excoriated or sore nipples.) They have also on hand a good assortment of Confectionary of all kinds—together with many other articles not above enumerated.

N.B. Doctors S. & R. still intend to devote their time and talents to the practice of Physic and Surgery; and feel confident that their long experience in the above professions will entitle them to a liberal share of public patronage. Lockport, Feb. 28th, 1832.

Article no. 349 Subject: Advertisement
Ref. June 26, 1832; pg. 3, col. 3

Summer Clothing, &c.

G.S. PLACE has just received and is now opening, a superior lot of Summer Clothing, which will be sold at more favourable prices than has ever been known in this place. May 22.

[Transcriber's note: This advertisement was followed by another from the same vendor for "Broadcloths, &c."]

Article no. 350 Subject: Advertisement
Ref. June 26, 1832; pg. 3, col. 3

LUMBER.

150000 Feet of Pine Lumber, just received from Canada, by the subscriber at his Lumber Yard.—Having prepared a first rate board kiln, dry lumber may be had at any time on short notice.

All kinds of lumber kept on hand or furnished to order, and a few pieces of pine timber for evetroughs also for sale.

L.A. SPALDING. Lockport, 6 mo. 6, 1832.

[Transcriber's note: This advert was followed by another from the same vendor for "100000 brick for sale."]

Article no. 351 Subject: Advertisement
Ref. June 26, 1832; pg. 3, col. 3

Leghorn Hats.

A Prime Case of Leghorn Hats, just arrived from New-York—and will be sold unusually low, by the subscribers
SETH PARSONS & Co. Lockport, June 2, 1832.

[Transcriber's note: Three more advertisements appear for the same vendor, farther down in the same column; one for New and Cheap Goods suited to the season; the second, for flour and meal; and, the third for fish.]

Article no. 352 Subject: Advertisement
Ref. June 26, 1832; pg. 3, col. 3

BOOKS!—NEW BOOKS!

LEONARD has just received his spring supply of Books. Call, see and purchase! June 12.

Article no. 353 Subject: Advertisement
Ref. June 26, 1832; pg. 3, col. 3

CASH STORE!

New Goods Selling Off Cheap for Ready Pay Only.

M.H. TUCKER & Co. at the Post-Office, are now receiving a general assortment of seasonable Goods, which they offer to the Public at prices that cannot fail to satisfy those who have cash to pay for them. Hereafter they will not credit out goods, but sell for Cash, and at a little above the New-York wholesale prices.

Lockport, June 12th, 1832.

Article no. 354 Subject: Advertisement
Ref. June 26, 1832; pg. 3, col. 3

The subscribers having entered into partnership as Physicans and Surgeons, respectfully offer their professional services to the public.

J.K. SKINNER, M.D.
J.A. DENISON, Jr., M.D.
Lockport, Lower Town, June 3d, 1832.

Article no. 355 Subject: Advertisement
Ref. June 26, 1832; pg. 3, col. 3

Millinery and Mantuamaking!

MISS GILSON respectfully begs leave to inform the ladies of Middleport, and its vicinity, that she has opened a shop of the above business, in that village, where she will be happy to receive orders in her line. She has recently received patterns of the

Latest Spring Fashions,

and will be able to execute her work according to the most modern and approved taste. She has and intends constantly to keep on hand an assortment of

Hats, Plain Bonnets, &c.

adapted to the spring and summer seasons, and made according to the New-York fashions.

Miss G. assures the ladies who favour her with their orders, that she will endeavour to please them in the fulfilment. Middleport, May 29th, 1832.

Article no. 356 Subject: Advertisement
Ref. June 26, 1832; pg. 3, col. 3

A Chance for Good Bargains!

The subscriber, having removed to Michigan, wishes to dispose of his valuable property in the flourishing village of Lockport.

A part of this property consists of one lot and buildings on Main-street, adjoining the Washington house. The buildings are large and well fitted up—and well situated as residences for private families, being in close proximity to the business part of the village.

Also, several business lots on Buffalo-street—some of which are near the intersection of Buffalo and Main-streets, and opposite the new and commodious tavern house on the corner of Canal and Main-streets. Also, Dwelling Lots on Walnut, Cottage and High streets,—together with a tract of eight acres on the south side of and adjoining High-street.

One of the lots, on the corner of Cottage and High-streets, containing two acres, well picketed in, is most eligibly situated for a dwelling, being on an elevated spot that commands a full view of the village and adjacent country, and also, with the help of a glass, of Lake Ontario.

The above property will be disposed off [sic] in lots to suit purchasers, and on very favourable terms. For further particulars, inquire of Alfred Holmes, Esq., agent, in the village of Lockport.

H.S. PLATT. Lockport, May 15th, 1832.

Article no. 357	Subject: Advertisement
Ref. June 26, 1832; pg. 3, col. 3	

NON-IMPRISONMENT ACT.

The "Act to abolish Imprisonment for Debt, and to punish Fraudulent Debtors," for sale by N. LEONARD.

Article no. 358	Subject: Advertisement
Ref. June 26, 1832; pg. 3, col. 4	

Spring Fashions!

The subscriber has received from New-York his charts of the latest London Fashions; and all those desirous of having garments made up in the latest style, would do well to call at his New Establishment, in T. Smith's Stone Building, Main-street. Don't delay!

G.S. PLACE, Merchant tailor. May 22.

Article no. 359	Subject: Advertisement
Ref. June 26, 1832; pg. 3, col. 4	

BROWN in his Shop!

The subscriber would inform his old friends and customers, that he can be found constantly at his shop on Niagara-Street, corner of Transit, where he will execute all kinds of

Smith-Work,

and particularly Edge Tools with promptness and in a workmanlike manner. As he intends in future to be in his shop himself, he feels confident of giving satisfaction to his customers—and he would therefore be happy to receive a liberal share of orders in his line.

CHARLES BROWN. Lockport, April 23, 1832.

Article no. 360	Subject: Advertisement
Ref. June 26, 1832; pg. 3, col. 4	

NEW GOODS!

JAMES R. STAFFORD is now receiving his spring supply of

Hardware.

Having during the winter disposed of his old stock of Cabinet Ware, he can now offer in that line, the best assortment ever before offered here.

Carpenters' and Joiners' Tools, at reduced prices, and prime articles.

Cast-Steel Axes, (no sham!) at 8s., 10s, 12s., 14s and 16s.

Every article in the Hardware line may be found at his establishment, on Main-street, near the west corner of the street leading to Spalding's mill.

Stoves of all kinds kept as usual. Copper, Sheet Iron, and Tin Ware always on hand or made to order.

Further particulars next week.

Wanted—Three lads as apprentices to the Cooper, Sheet-Iron and Tin Manufacturing business. None need apply except those who can bring first rate recommendations. Also, 3 or 4 steady men, to peddle Tin Ware. May 15.

Article no. 361	Subject: Advertisement
Ref. June 26, 1832; pg. 3, col. 4	

GRIND STONES.

The subscribers have a quantity of the above article on hand, which they offer for sale at reduced prices.

ROGERS & BROWN. Lockport, May 8.

Article no. 362	Subject: Advertisement
Ref. June 26, 1832; pg. 3, col. 4	

Houses, lots and farms for sale.
By L.A. Spalding.

The undersigned has a number of choice Village Lots, suitable for dwellings, in various parts of this village, which he offers for sale.

Some of the lots are situated on East-Main, Walnut, Market, Chesnut, Washburn, Lock, Church, Allen, Ontario, Caledonia, Green, and Grand-streets, and one lot on Buffalo-street, adjoining Gillet Bacon's Grocery and Provision Store on the east. One Lot on Walnut street has a comfortable dwelling house thereon, a small barn, and is under fence—now occupied by Benjamin Carpenter.

The lots on the corner of Chesnut and Washburn streets are under fine improvement—have a good dwelling thereon, a great variety of choice fruit trees and shrubbery, and a good garden—now occupied by S. Allen.

The lot at the Corner of Caledonia and Gooding streets has a first rate Cooper Shop thereon, calculated for ten hands, and is within a short distance of two large flouring mills—now occupied by William Doughten.

All of the aforesaid property will be sold on accommodating terms.

Also a Farm, adjoining the village of Pendleton, of 216 acres.

Another of 75 acres, adjoining this village, presently occupied by Jedeiah Darling—and several others left in charge to sell.

L.A. SPALDING. Lockport, 5 mo. 1 1832.

Article no. 363	Subject: Notice

Ref. June 26, 1832; pg. 3, col. 4

Extract: SHERIFF'S SALE.

By virtue of an execution issued out of the clerk's office, in the county of Niagara, and state of New-York, and to me directed and delivered, against the goods and chattles [sic], lands and tenements, of Jeremiah Burr, I have seized and taken all that certain tract, piece or parcel of land situate, lying and being in the village of Lockport, in the county of Niagara, being part or parcel of farm lot Number Twelve, in the Fourteenth Township and Sixth Range of the Holland Land Company's Lands (so called,) and which [on a map made for the proprietors by Jesse P. Haines, surveyor, and filed in the office of the clerk of the County of Niagara] is known and distinguished as village lot number five on the north side of Niagara-street, in the said village of Lockport {Notice includes further description of land;} and all the right, title, claim, interest and demand of the said Jeremiah Burr, of, in, and to said above described premises, I shall expose to sail [sic], as the law directs, at public vendue, at the house now kept by Samuel B. Thompson, and known as the Washington House, in Lockport, 26 June 1832. Dated Lockport, June 12th, 1832. H. McNEIL, Sheriff.

Article no. 364	Subject: Advertisement

Ref. June 26, 1832; pg. 4, col. 2

STORAGE AND FORWARDING.

The subscribers receive goods at their Warehouse (at the foot of the locks,) to store or forward to any part of the Union. They also advance liberally in cash on any property left with them for sale, either in this or the New-York market.

ROGERS & BROWN. Lockport, May 8.

Article no. 365	Subject: Notice

Ref. June 26, 1832; pg. 4, col. 2

Extract: SHERIFF'S SALE.

By virtue of a writ of fieri facias, issued out of the Supreme Court of Judicature of the State of New-York, and to me directed and delivered, against the goods and chattles [sic], lands and tenements, of Otis Hathaway, Seymour Scovell and John Gooding, I have seized and taken all the right, title, and interest of the said Otis in and to those certain tracts or pieces of land, hereinafter described: [(1) one being part of farm lot no. 10, in the 14th section, 14th township, and 6th range of the Holland Purchase (so called,) in the village of Lockport, mapped by Jesse P. Haines, surveyor, and adjoins land deeded by Nathan Comstock and his wife to Henry S. Platt and Job Batty; (2) one being part of lot no. 8, in the aforesaid section, township and range, in Lockport, bounding a tract of land deeded to Joseph H. Patterson by Jared Comstock and wife, 8 February 1827] And also, all the right, title and interest of Seymour Scovell in and to the following pieces and parcels of land, viz: [(3) one in Lockport, and being part of farm lot no. 59, in the 14th township and 7th range, and known and distinguished on the map of a part of the village of Lockport as village lot no. 5, and the east half of village lot no. 7, on the north side of Niagara-street, upon which is situated the house formerly known as the Niagara Hotel; (4) one being part of farm lot no. 70, in the 14th township and 7th range, containing 106 acres of land; (5) those certain pieces and parcels of land, situate in the lower village of Lockport, on Market-street, Exchange and Garden-streets, comprising village lots nos. 1-5, containing 120 rods of land, and upon which is situated the Lockport House; (6) a piece of land, being part of lot no. 11, in the 14th township and 6th range, conveyed to John Gooding by Ambrose Beach, by deed bearing date 4 February 1828, and recorded in Niagara county clerk's office, in Book of Deeds No. 4, on pages 21 and 22, 13 September 1828, containing one acres and 16 hundredths of land.] And also all the right, title and interest of the said John Gooding in and to the following pieces and parcels of land: [(7 & 8) two pieces of land in Lockport, parts of Farm lot no. 12, in the 14th township and 6th range, lying in the village of Lockport, each of which, in part, bound L.A. Spalding's land and also Davis Hurd's land; (9) a piece of land, being part of farm lot no. 59, in the 14th township and 7th range, bounded, in part, by a piece of land conveyed by Eseck Brown and wife to Wm. M. Bond, 10 October 1821; (10) a piece of land, being part of farm lot no. 10, in the 14th township and 6th range, that bounds, in part, the Erie canal, containing about 47 hundredths of an acre of land; (11) another piece of land, being part of farm lot no. 12, that was mapped for Jared Comstock and others by Jesse P. Haines, Surveyor, and containing 5 acres and 9 tenths of an acre of land, more or less; (12) another piece of land, being part of farm lot no. 12, part of which was formerly owned by Elias Ransom, Jr., and also lands deeded by L.A. Spalding to James F. Mason, 10 November 1826, and recorded in the clerk's office of Niagara county, in Liber 2 of Deeds, at pages 466, &c., and containing seven and three-fourths of acres of land, more or less; (13) another piece of land in Lockport, part of lot no. 12 aforesaid, and bounded, in part, by land owned by George Levalley, and including land deeded by Lyman A. Spalding to James F. Mason, and bounded, in part, by land deeded by John Gooding to L.A. Spalding before 1 July 1828, and bounded, in part, by land formerly owned by Hiram B.

Hopkins; (14) another piece of land, in the village of Lockport; (15) another piece of land, situate in the village of Lockport, and known and distinguished as and being village lots no. 20 and 22, containing 1 and a half acres in the whole; and, (16) another piece of land, being part of farm lot no. 11, 14th township and 6th range, containing 60 acres, more or less.] And each of which several above described pieces and parcels of land I shall expose to sale at public auction, at the tavern or inn now kept by Samuel Jennings, in the village of Lockport, on Thursday, the 2d day of August next, at 10 o'clock in the forenoon of that day. Dated June 19th, 1832.

JOHN PHILLIPS, Late Sheriff.

[Transcriber's note: Descriptions of parcels of land have been abridged; in particular, boundary data have been omitted. Length of article, 1-3/4 columns.]

Article no. 366   Subject: Notice
Ref. June 26, 1832; pg. 4, col. 4

Extract: MORTGAGE SALE.

Default having been made in the payment of a certain sum of money, secured by indenture of mortgage bearing date 18 June 1830, executed by James F. Mason to Amasa Chaffy, and recorded in Niagara county clerk's office, in book of Mortgages No. 3, (number three) on pages 113, 114, and 115, on which there is now claimed to be due the sum of $852.67—now therefore, notice is hereby given that by virtue of a power contained in said mortgage, and by force of the statute in such case made and provided the several pieces and parcels of land contained in the said mortgage and described therein as follows: {Notice includes description of land in the village of Lockport} [mapped by Jesse P. Haines for Jared Comstock and others; two lots mapped for William M. Bond] will be severally sold at public auction, at the Inn now kept by Samuel Jennings, in the village of Lockport, on the ninth day of June next, at one o'clock in the afternoon of that day. Dated 19th Dec. 1831.

AMASA CHAFFE [sic], Mortgagee.
By E. RANSOM, Jr. Att'y.

The sale of the above property is postponed until Monday the 3d day of September next—then to take place at 1 o'clock, P.M. at the place abovementioned. Dated June 9th, 1832. Amasa Chaffe, Mortgagee. By E. Ransom, Jr., his Att'y.

Article no. 367   Subject: Notice
Ref. June 26, 1832; pg. 4, col. 5

Extract: IN CHANCERY—
Before the Vice-Chancellor of the Eighth Circuit—
Jonathan Child, complainant, vs. Otis Hathaway, Jared Comstock and Hiram Wright, defendants

In pursuance of a decretal order of the Court of Chancery made in the above cause will be sold under the direction of the subscriber, at public auction, at the Washington House, in the village of Lockport, and county of Niagara, on Friday 29 June 1832, all that piece or parcel of land situate and lying in the village of Lockport, in said county of Niagara, being part and parcel of farm lot number twelve, in the fourteenth section of township number fourteen, in the sixth range of townships of the Holland Purchase, (so called,) and bounded and particularly described as follows: {Notice includes description of boundaries} [mapped for Hathaway by Jesse P. Haines, surveyor; bounded, in part, by lands deeded by Jared Comstock, Nathan Comstock and Darius Comstock to Davis Hurd, 3 June 1825]—and also all that certain other piece or parcel of land situate and lying in said village of Lockport, being part of said farm lot number twelve, known and particularly described as part of village lot number twenty-five, on the west side of the North street [mapped by Jesse Haines for Jared Comstock and others] {Notice includes description of boundaries}— together with all and singular the hereditaments and appurtenances thereunto belonging or in any wise pertaining.—Dated Lockport 3d May, 1832.

H. GARDNER, Master in Chancery.

Article no. 368   Subject: Notice
Ref. June 26, 1832; pg. 4, col. 6

ADMINISTRATOR'S NOTICE.

Notice is hereby given, to all persons who have claims against Patrick Fannerty, late of the town of Cambria, in the county of Niagara, deceased, to exhibit the same, with the vouchers and evidences thereof, to Thomas Comstock, one of his Administrators, at the dwelling house of the said Administrator, in the said town of Cambria, on or before the 12th day of October next.

Dated the 7th day of April, 1832.

Article no. 369   Subject: Notice
Ref. October 30, 1832; pg. 1, col. 2

Extract: WHEREAS John A. Benjamin of the village of Lockport, by indenture of mortgage, bearing date 8 January 1829, for the purpose of securing the payment of $300 and interest annually, in the manner in said mortgage particularly specified—did mortgage to John Gooding, of the same place, that certain piece or parcel of land, described in said mortgage as follows—"All that certain tract or parcel of land, situate in the village of Lockport, in the county of Niagara, and being part and parcel of farm lot number twelve, in the fourteenth section of township number fourteen, in the sixth range of townships of the Holland purchase (so called,) and being village lots number thirteen, on Gooding-street, and fourteen on West Front-street, and bounded as follows:—{Notice includes description of boundaries}—containing thirty-nine square rods of land, be the same more or less:" which said indenture of mortgage has been duly recorded in the Clerk's office of Niagara county, in Book of Mortgages No. 2, on pages 557, &c., and which said indenture of mortgage, has been duly assigned to Portous R. Root, and the assignment thereof has been duly recorded in the aforesaid Clerk's office—and where as [sic] default has been made in the payment of the money secured by the said mortgage, and there is claimed to be due thereon on the day of the first publication of this notice, for principal and interest, the sum of $376.65.— Now therefore, notice is hereby given, that by virtue of a power of sale in said mortgage contained, and in pursuance of the statute in such case made and provided, the mortgaged premises above described will be sold at public auction, at the Eagle Tavern, kept by J.W. Witbeck, in Lockport, 21 February 1833.

HENRY K. HOPKINS, Attorney for Assignee.

Article no. 370   Subject: Notice
Ref. October 30, 1832; pg. 1, col. 3

STATE OF NEW YORK.
Secretary's Office.
Albany, July 10, 1832.

Sir—I hereby give you notice, that at the next general election in this state, to be holden on the 5th, 6th and 7th days of November next, a governor and lieutenant governor are to be elected.

And also, that a Senator is to be chosen in the Eighth Senate District, in the place of Philo C. Fuller, whose term of service will expire on the last day of December next.

A.C. FLAGG, Secretary of State.

To the Sheriff of the county of Niagara.

N.B. The inspectors of Election in the several towns in your county will give notice of the election of a Representative to Congress from the 33d Congressional District; and that 42 electors of President and Vice President are to be chosen at the general election. Also, for the choice of members of Assembly, and for filling any vacancies in county offices that may exist.

A general election is to be held in the county of Niagara, on the 5th, 6th and 7th days of November next, at which time will be chosen a Governor, Lieutenant Governor, Senator, Representative in Congress, 42 Electors of President and Vice President, and one member of Assembly, as mentioned in the notice of the Secretary of State, of which the above is a copy. Dated Sheriff's Office, Lockport, July 24th, A.D. 1832.

H. McNEIL, Sheriff of Niagara county.

Article no. 371   Subject: Notice
Ref. October 30, 1832; pg. 1, col. 3

Extract: MORTAGE SALE.

Default having been made in the payment of a certain sum of money, secured by indenture of mortgage, bearing date 14 January 1832, executed by William M. Sechler to George Reynale, and recorded in Niagara county clerk's office, in book of Mortgages No. 3, on pages 441 and 442, and on which there is now claimed to be due the sum of $79.25—now, therefore, notice is hereby given, that by virtue of a power contained in said mortgage, and the statute in such case made and provided, the said piece or parcel of land contained in said mortgage and described therein as follows, to wit: "All that certain piece or parcel of land, situate, lying and being in the town of Royalton, in said county of Niagara, being part and parcel of a certain township, which [on a map made for the Holland Land Company by Joseph Ellicott, Surveyor] is distinguished by township Number fourteen in the 5th range of said township—and which said tract of land [on another map made by Ellicott] is distinguished by lot number seven in the twelvth [sic] section of said township, bounded as follows {Notice includes description of boundaries}—containing one half acre of land"—will be sold at public auction at the Eagle Tavern, kept by J.W. Witbeck, in the village of Lockport, 5 February 1833. GEORGE REYNALE, mortgagee. J. CENTER, Attorney.

Article no. 372   Subject: Notice
Ref. October 30, 1832; pg. 1, col. 3

Extract: SHERIFF'S SALE.

By virtue of a writ of fieri facias issued out of the Supreme Court of Judicature of the state of New-York, and to me directed and delivered, against the goods and chattels, lands and tenements of Asa Millikin and Orrin Fisk, I have seized and taken the two following pieces of land, viz—All that certain piece or parcel of land situate in the town of Pendleton, in the county of Niagara, and state of New-York, as follows, to wit, Lot number thirty, three rods in from Washington-street, and ten rods deep, containing thirty rods of ground, more or less {Notice includes further description of land:} one parcel of ground in said village of Pendleton as follows—south east part of lot number seven, on Washington-street {Notice includes further description of land,} containing sixteen hundred feet of ground, be the same more or less, reference to be had [for both lots] to the map of said village on file in the county clerk's office at Lockport, county and state aforesaid: all of which I shall expose to sale, as the law directs, at the Eagle Tavern, kept by J.W. Witbeck, in the village of Lockport, 10 November 1832. Dated at Lockport, the 25th September, 1832.

HIRAM McNEIL, Sheriff.

Article no. 373	Subject: Notice

Ref. October 30, 1832; pg. 1, col. 3

ADMINISTRATOR'S SALE. By order of Hiram Gardner, Esq., Surrogate of the County of Niagara, on the 10th day of September inst.; I the subscriber, administrator of the goods, chattles [sic] and credits of Daniel Washburn, late of the town of Lockport, deceased, shall sell at public auction 12 November 1832, at the house of J.W. Witbeck, in the town of Lockport and county of Niagara aforesaid, all the estate, right, title, interest, property and claim of the said deceased, and of his heirs, under and by virtue of a certain contract or articles of agreement bearing date 14 September 1825, executed by William Willink and others of one part, and the said deceased of the other part; and also all the right, title, interest, property and claim of the said deceased, and his heirs, under and by virtue of any other contract or agreement, or title, or of or for any other cause, in and to the equal undivided half of the following piece of land, to wit: being lot number seventy nine of township thirteen, range six, of the Holland Land Company (so called,) bounded and described as follows—north by the north line of said lot thirty-nine chains twenty-four links; east by the east line forty-nine chains; south by the south line forty chains; west by the west line forty chains; containing one hundred and sixty acres, be the same more or less. Dated Lockport, September 11, A.D. 1832.

SETH PARSONS, Administrator.

Article no. 374	Subject: Notice

Ref. October 30, 1832; pg. 1, col. 3

Extract: MORTGAGE SALE.

By virtue of a power of sale contained in a mortgage executed by James Lendrum to Boardman H. Bosworth, bearing date 22 March 1830, and assigned by Bosworth to Lyman A. Spalding, recorded in the clerk's office of Niagara county, in book number 3 of mortgages, on pages 599 and 600; on which said mortgage there is claimed to be due at the first publication of this notice, $52.71, the premises in said mortgage described, to wit, "All that certain tract or parcel of land situate in the village of Lockport, in the county of Niagara, and state of New-York, being part of lot number twelve, fourteenth section, and township number fourteen, in the sixth range, and known and distinguished on a map [made by Jesse P. Haines, surveyor] as village lots numbers thirty-three and thirty-five, on the south side of Grand-street {Notice includes further description of land} will be sold at public auction or vendue, at the Eagle Tavern, kept by J.W. Witbeck, in Lockport, 28 March 1833.

Dated Lockport, October 9th, 1832. LYMAN A. SPALDING, Assignee. H.K. HOPKINS, Attorney.

Article no. 375	Subject: Notice

Ref. October 30, 1832; pg. 1, col. 4

SURROGATE'S NOTICE.

The people of the state of New-York, by the grace of God free and independent: To all whom these presents shall come or may concern, and especially to the next of kin of Katharine Hustler, late of the town of Lewiston, in the county of Niagara, deceased, send Greeting.

You, and each of you, are hereby cited and required, personally to be and appear before Hiram Gardner, Esquire, Surrogate of our said county of Niagara, at his office in Lockport on the 24th day of October, at one o'clock, in the afternoon of that day, then and there to oppose or support as you may see fit, the probate of a certain instrument in writing, purporting to be the last will and testament of the said Katharine Hustler, which has been lef [left] with our said Surrogate, by Robert Fleming, Bates Cook and Willard Smith, who claim to be executors thereof, and which will be at the time and place aforesaid, offered for probate. In testimony whereof, we have caused the seal of office of our said Surrogate, to be hereunto affixed.

Witness Hiram Gardner, Esq., Surrogate of our said County, at Lockport, this 3d day of October, A.D. 1832.

H. GARDNER, Surrogate.

Article no. 376	Subject: Notice

Ref. October 30, 1832; pg. 1, col. 4

SURROGATE'S NOTICE.

The people of the state of New-York, by the grace of God free and independent: To all whom these presents shall come or may concern, and especially to the next of kin of Martha Kelsey, late of the town of Lewiston, in the county of Niagara, deceased, send Greeting.

You, and each of you, are hereby cited and required, personally to be and appear before Hiram Gardner, Esquire, Surrogate of our said county of Niagara, at his office in Lockport on the 24th day of October next, at one o'clock, in the afternoon of that day, then and there to oppose or support as you may see fit, the probate of a certain instrument in writing, purporting to be the last will and testament, of the said Martha Kelsey, which had been left with our said Surrogate, by Bates Cook, Jacob Townsend and James Murray, who claim to be executors thereof, and which will be at the time and place aforesaid, offered for probate.

In testimony whereof, we have caused the seal of office of our said Surrogate, to be hereunto affixed.

Witness H. Gardner, Esq., Surrogate of our said County, at Lockport, this 3d day of October, A.D. 1832.

H. GARDNER, Surrogate.

Article no. 377 Subject: Notice
Ref. October 30, 1832; pg. 1, col. 4

PURSUANT to an order of Hiram Gardner, Surrogate of the county of Niagara, notice is hereby given, to all persons who have claims against Joash Taylor, late of the town of Cambria, in said County, deceased, to exhibit the same, with the vouchers therefor, to Miles N. Taylor, one of the administrators of the goods and chattels of the said deceased, at the dwelling of the said administrator, in the town of Cambria, in said County, at or before the 22d day of February next. Dated Aug. 18th, 1832.

MILES N. TAYLOR, Administrator.

Article no. 378 Subject: Notice
Ref. October 30, 1832; pg. 1, col. 4

Extract: List of Letters remaining in the post-office at Pendleton, Sept. 30, 1832. [Names listed, below.] S.P. CLARKE, P.M.

Beckwith, J., Widow	Corn, Adin
Crandell, Joseph	Darling, William
Dayharh, Jacob	Dixon, Susan
Edmiston, Andrew	Holmes, John
Kishlar, James	Lewis, Ambrose
Madison, Levi	Milliken, Charles A.
Odle, Peter	Pickard, Coonrod
Shipman, William	Thayre, Nathan
Van Volkenburgh, Lambert	Vanslyke, Garret
Vanslyke, George	Vanslyke, John
Warner, Alfred	Wilson, John
Wingert, Elizabeth	Winn, John

Article no. 379 Subject: Agriculture
Ref. October 30, 1832; pg. 1, col. 4

N.B.!!—The attention of a part of the inhabitants in this vicinity to the following, may prove a very great benefit to the subscriber and those interested:

The subscriber wishes to inform his customers generally, without any exception, that he wants the balances of their accounts. It is now after harvest, and it has been satisfactorily demonstrated to farmers generally, that the fall season is the best time to get a price for wheat, and the sooner after the harvest the better. After the market opens every individual, by thrashing a day or two, may settle off his store debts, and thereby relieve himself from those to whom he is indebted, and the community generally. It will not answer this fall to put off payment till after seeding, as has usually been the practice; the pressure of the times will not admit of it. I have not, for my part, collected much in the fore part of the season, for this reason, that there was no money in the country, nor any means of raising any. The evil must now be remedied.

Such as neglect this call must expect to have their memories jogged by a different process.

JACOB COMPTON. Mountain Ridge, Aug. 14, 1832.

Article no. 380 Subject: Advertisement
Ref. October 30, 1832; pg. 1, col. 4

Daniel Greenvault,
Plain and Fancy Sash-Maker, and Glazier,

Has established the above business, on Main-street, in the village of Lockport, nearly opposite Mr. F. Gibb's store, where he will keep constantly on hand a supply of

Plain Sash,

manufactured of good and well seasoned stuff, and in a workmanlike manner.

Fancy Sash,

made of wood with accuracy and beauty.

All orders in his line thankfully received and promptly attended to.

N.B. Sash made by hand at factory prices. July 31.

Article no. 381 Subject: Advertisement
Ref. October 30, 1832; pg. 1, col. 4

E. White and Wm. Hagar,

RESPECTFULLY inform the Printers of the United States, to whom they have long been individually known as established Letter Founders, that they have now formed a co-partnership in said business, and hope by their united skill, and extensive experience, to be able to give full satisfaction to all who may favour them with orders.

The introduction of machinery, in place of the tedious and unhealthy process of casting type by hand, long a dissideratum by the European and American Founders, was, by American ingenuity, and a heavy expenditure of time and money on the part of our senior partner, first successfully accomplished. Extensive use of the machine cast letter, has fully tested and established its superiority in every particular, over that cast by the old process.

The letter foundry business will hereafter be carried on by the parties before named, under the firm of WHITE, HAGAR & Co. Their specimen exhibits a complete series from Diamond to 14 lines Pica.—The book and news type being of the most modern light faced style.

White, Hagar & Co. are agents for the sale of the Smith and Rust Printing Presses, which they can furnish to their customers at the manufacturer's prices. Chases, Cases, Composing Sticks, Ink, and every article used in the Printing business, kept for sale, and furnished on short notice. Old type taken in exchange for new, at 9 sts. [illegible] per pound. June 2, 1832.

Article no. 382   Subject: Education
Ref. October 30, 1832; pg. 1, col. 5

LEWISTON ACADEMY.

The Term will commence on the 24th inst. During vacation such improvements have been made and are being made, as will give Students advantages and accommodations not before enjoyed here. The third story of the Academy has been finished, and will now accommodate, with pleasant and convenient rooms for study, a large number of students. A new building, gravel walks, and other additions and improvements are being made.

Lectures will commence with and continue through the term. A lecture on Chemistry every week—on Philosophy once in two weeks.

The Trustees feel confident that this institution now affords advantages both in accommodations and instruction which can be had in few other institutions. The cholera has ceased and the village is very healthy. Board $1.50 per week.

BENJAMIN BARTON, NATHANIEL LEONARD, ROBERT FLEMING, NATHAN BAKER.
Lewiston, Sept. 17th, 1832.

Article no. 383   Subject: Advertisement
Ref. October 30, 1832; pg. 1, col. 5

REMOVAL.

Wm. FOX, Barber & Hairdresser,

Has removed his Establishment to his new building, on Main-street, immediately opposite the Eagle Tavern, where he will be happy to wait upon his old customers and friends as heretofore.

Razors honed and set as usual.
Lockport, Sept. 8, 1832.

Article no. 384   Subject: Advertisement
Ref. October 30, 1832; pg. 1, col. 5

ROGERS & BROWN

Will start for New York as early as the 10th of October next. All those having engagements with them will act accordingly, and receive their thanks. Sept. 17.

Article no. 385   Subject: Advertisement
Ref. October 30, 1832; pg. 1, col. 5

CIRCULAR.

New-York, 15th Aug. 1832.

The subscribers have on hand, and are constantly receiving by arrivals from Liverpool, a full stock of Goods suitable for the approaching season, and invite their customers and buyers generally to purchase. Their stock consists of

British and American Dry Goods,
together with a general assortment of
French, Italian and India Silks, Leghorn Hats, &c., &c.
Their best attention will be given to the execution of orders.

CUSHMAN & FALCONER, No. 188 Pearl-street.

Article no. 386   Subject: Advertisement
Ref. October 30, 1832; pg. 1, col. 5

CASH FOR WHEAT
At the Farmers' Mills.
C.F. MITCHELL

Having purchased an interest in the Mills recently erected by Parsons, Gooding & Co. the superintendence thereof devolves on him. To those who have done business with him while having charge of the Mill belonging to E. Bissell, Esq., of this village, little need be said: to those who have not, he would simply say, that the best thing they can do for themselves or perhaps for him either, is to bring their grists to grind and their Wheat to sell. And to all, notice is particularly given, that if they either bring their grain to grind or to sell they shall be fully accommodated.

The Mill is now in complete order; and all grists will not only be ground Well, but Promptly.

Farmers desiring good work, will find it exactly at the
FARMERS' MILLS,
a little north of the Canal, in this village.
The highest price, in Cash, paid at all times for Wheat.
C.F. MITCHELL & Co. Lockport, July 27, 1832.

Article no. 387   Subject: Notice
Ref. October 30, 1832; pg. 1, col. 5

ONCE MORE!

We would ask our friends to pay us what is our due, that we may discharge our debts. All who comply with this intimation, will receive our thanks; and those who are indebted to us, and neglect this notice, may expect to be waited upon by some person, in the name of the People of the State of New-York, for we are in earnest, we must have pay.

SETH PARSONS & CO. Lockport, Sept. 4, 1832.

Article no. 388   Subject: Notice
Ref. October 30, 1832; pg. 1, col. 5

All persons indebted to the subscriber, either by note or account, if not paid immediately, will have to settle with Daniel Alvord, Justice of the Peace—this is the last warning.

JAMES R. STAFFORD. Lockport, August 10, 1832.

Article no. 389 Subject: Advertisement
Ref. October 30, 1832; pg. 1, col. 5

HARNESS LEATHER.

15000 Lbs. of superior Harness Leather for sale at the Green Store, or at the Lockport Tannery, by
GEO. W. ROGERS & CO.

Article no. 390 Subject: Advertisement
Ref. October 30, 1832; pg. 1, col. 5

PINE SHINGLES.

125M. first rate Western Shingles, for sale by
(July 24.) ROGERS & BROWN.

Article no. 391 Subject: Advertisement
Ref. October 30, 1832; pg. 1, col. 5

RED CEDAR POSTS for sale by
L.A. SPALDING. Lockport, 7 mo. 28, 1832.

Article no. 392 Subject: Advertisement
Ref. October 30, 1832; pg. 1, col. 5

HORSES FOR SALE.

A very smart poney [sic]—a great traveller, and also a good family horse—for sale on good terms, and reasonable credit, with security: Also, too [sic] young Mares, both supposed to be with foal, for sale on like terms. Apply to L.A. SPALDING. Lockport, 7 mo. 28, 1832.

Article no. 393 Subject: Advertisement
Ref. October 30, 1832; pg. 1, col. 5

VALUABLE BOOKS FOR CHILDREN.

Peter Parley's Book of Curiosities, natural and artificial; Do. History of Ancient and Modern Greece; Do. Early History of the Southern States; Do. Life of Christopher Columbus, with illustrations; Do. Life of George Washington, Do.; Do. First Book of History; Do. Tales about Europe, Asia, Africa, America, Seas, &c.; Do. Geography; Do. Sun, Moon and Stars.

The above works are for sale at the Bookstore of
N. LEONARD.

Article no. 394 Subject: Notice
Ref. October 30, 1832; pg. 1, col. 5

Notice.

The subscriber, having disposed of his stock of Hardware, makes the last call upon those indebted to him, as he intends leaving the place in a short time. Those notes and accounts which remain unpaid, will be placed in the hands of an attorney for immediate collection.

The Tin, Copper, Sheet-Iron, Stove & Hollow-Ware Business will be carried on in all its various branches by E.W. Lewis, under the firm of J.R. Stafford & Co.

JAS. B. STAFFORD. Sept. 18, 1832.

N.B. Call and see if we will do as well as our neighbours.

Article no. 395 Subject: Advertisement
Ref. October 30, 1832; pg. 1, col. 6

New Clothing Store.

The subscriber begs leave to apprise the public that he has opened a

CLOTHING STORE,

on Main-street, opposite the store of S. Parsons & Co., in the village of Lockport, where he will be pleased to furnish those who may favour him with their custom, with all articles in his line, of a superior quality and workmanship, and at as reasonable rates as they can be had at any other establishment in the village.

A share of public patronage is requested.

July 3. G.H. ALLEN, Agent.

Article no. 396 Subject: Politics
Ref. October 30, 1832; pg. 2, col. 1

Citizens of Niagara county, in the following selection of names you are presented with the true WHIG TICKET. Let every freeman, therefore, who stands up for his country, and his country only, be at his post promptly on the days of Election, ready to do all those things which may be required of him as an independent man.

———

Anti-Masonic Republican Ticket.
For President,
 William Wirt.
For Vice-President,
 Amos Ellmaker.
For Governor,
 Francis Granger.
For Lieut.-Governor,
 Samuel Stevens.
For Representative in Congress,
 Gideon Hard.
For Senator,
 John Griffen.
For Member of Assembly,
 Henry Norton.
Electors—(of President and Vice-President,)
At large,
 James Kent, of New-York,
 John C. Spencer, of Ontario,
First District.
 Silas Wood,
 Henry Cotheal,
 Joseph Tucker,
 Eleazer Lord,
 Ellis Potter.
Second District.
 Court Dubois,
 George A. Gay,

Nathaniel Dubois,
Charles Hathaway,
James Turk.
Third District.
Martin De Freest,
Justus M'Kinstry,
Gideon Hawley,
William Tuttle,
John Gebhard,
Fourth District.
Joseph Bois,
Robert Livingston,
Gilbert Waring,
Duncan M'Martin, Jr.
John L. Curtenius.
Fifth District.
George Huntington,
Orrin Wilburn,
Chauncey Baker,
Nicholas Shoemaker,
Gerrit Smith.
Sixth District.
James Hawks,
Edmund G. Per Lee,
John Miller,
Calvin Burr,
Josiah Dunlap.
Seventh District.
Robert Cook,
Hiram F. Mather,
Robert S. Rose,
Asa B. Smith,
Nathaniel W. Howell.
Eighth District.
Nathan Mixer,
Shubael Dunham,
Hololm Hutchinson,
Samuel Lacy,
George H. Boughton.

Article no. 397   Subject: Notice
Ref. October 30, 1832; pg. 2, col. 1

Anti-Masonic Committee Room.
The Room immediately over the store of Messrs. S. Parsons & Co. has been engaged as an Anti-Masonic Committee Room.

Article no. 398   Subject: Politics
Ref. October 30, 1832; pg. 2, col. 1

Extract: FELLOW-CITIZENS—On the three first days of next week, will be decided, for two years to come, the character of the administration of the government of this state, and in a measure, that of the national government, for the succeeding four years. In view of these important events, it becomes the peculiar obligation of the American freeman seriously to ponder the measure of duty which falls to his share. ... At the approaching election various principles in the policy of our government are to be settled. Foremost in the rank of these, we place that contended for by a vast majority of the people of Western New-York—to wit, that in a government dependent upon popular opinion for its existence, Secret Associations, under whatever plausible pretext they may be formed, are eminently dangerous; and that the safety and happiness of the people, the peace of the land, and the honour and dignity of the nation, altogether and inseparably depend upon the maintenance, in all its purity, of our Constitution, and the Supremacy of the Laws. To this end, therefore, do we urge every freeman, every American citizen, so to cast his vote, that this important principle may be firmly established—that it may be converted, as it were, into a component part of our political theory, that shall stand the test of all future efforts to subvert it. As a means, Antimasons, of settling this important feature in our political affairs, you have offered to your acceptance candidates for office every way worthy of your support—they are men without guile, and above deceit—and in yielding them your confidence, you may do it with a certainty that it will not be misplaced. Let then every man of you, who feels the spirit of a freeman animate him, take his post at the polls, and not depart thence until victory crowns the cause he advocates. [Transcriber's note: This article appears in the Editorial section, for 1+ more columns.]

Article no. 399   Subject: Politics
Ref. October 30, 1832; pg. 2, col. 2

Extract: A BROKEN REED! The masonics place all their reliance for success on Western New-York! They have flooded the country with forgeries so numerous, and misrepresentations so gross, but nevertheless calculated to deceive the unwary Antimason, unless he called to mind the real character of freemasonry—such, in short, as it has been exhibited in this country—that they have almost prevailed on themselves to believe that they will do something handsome! ... Antimasons drive ahead the work which they have so nobly begun, Western New-York will show majorities for Democratic Antimasonry, at the coming election, such as were never known in the whole history of politics. Let our eastern friends therefore buckle on their armour in confidence for the fight. The "Young Lion of the West" will ring such a peal in the ears of the people's oppressors, that they shall shake in their very shoes. [Transcriber's note: This article appears in the Editorial columns.]

Article no. 400 Subject: Politics
Ref. October 30, 1832; pg. 2, col. 3

Extract: CANAL TOLLS. Let every farmer when he goes to the polls bear in mind, that in casting his vote, he either votes on or off about six cents per bushel on the price of his wheat. This we can demonstrate in a few words. The tolls now levied on a bushel of wheat, in taking it to Albany, is about 12 cents. This is higher that [sic] it need be, by six cents. Why then, asks a reader perhaps, do our rulers continue it? We will answer. In the first place, Canal Funds are those upon which for years they have been living—have been growing rich—have been amasing [sic] the most princely fortunes. They now have about two millions in their hands—and it is this large amount of the people's money which has enabled them to buy up bank stock, and control their appointment of that political monster, the Bank Triumvirate—a body which, if not controlled by the people, will drive them like slaves before them with rods of scorpions! ... In conclusion, fellow-citizens, let us impress on your minds, what is our firm belief that if our present corrupt rulers are spurned from office, there is a reasonable prospect that the tolls will be reduced as low as the requisites of the canal will permit. If confidence is longer reposed in those who now control the government, the fear is the tolls may be increased. The longer they enjoy the emoluments of office, the more insatiable do they become, and they will not stop at any measures to gratify their desires. [Transcriber's note: This article appears in the Editorial columns. Length, 1 column.]

Article no. 401 Subject: Politics
Ref. October 30, 1832; pg. 2, col. 5

FORGERIES AND FALSE AFFIDAVITS. The masonic affidavit makers are at work, as was anticipated. One Jesse Sexton of Oneida county, has been suborned to make oath that George Huntington, one of our Electors, had told him, that he never was an antimason, and that if elected he should vote for Clay and Sergeant! Mr. Huntington has given the lie direct to this affidavit maker, and declares that he never held any such conversation with Sexton, or any other man. What shall be said of a party which seeks to carry its point by perjury?

Mr. Edwin Croswell also a short time since declared that Chancellor Kent had written to Mr. White, delegate in Congress from Florida, informing him that the Electors nominated by the Antimasons, would vote for Clay, if they were elected. But Croswell would not pay any attention to this. He had, as he thought, named an individual as the correspondent of Mr. K. who was too far off to contradict the tale himself, 'until after the election.' But the base wretch was caught in his own trap. Mr. White was detained by illness in Virginia, and seeing Croswell's assertion, he promptly met it, by declaring under his proper signature, that he was a total stranger to Chancellor Kent, and had never received a letter, such as Croswell alluded to, from him or any other candidate on the electoral ticket. Thus that lie was "chased home."

Similar stories have been propagated about almost every elector on our ticket, and as promptly contradicted; and yet the poor miserable scoundrels who conduct the masonic journals have not had the grace to acknowledge their faults. Indeed, we confidently look for the production, at a period when too late to be contradicted, of shoals of false affidavits, intended to deceive Antimasonic voters. But the people must be on their guard. They know the character of the party with which they are contending, and can judge for themselves of the truth or falsehood of any thing they may get up. They must remember that freemasonry is a liar from the beginning, and the Regency worse. [Transcriber's note: This article appears in the Editorial columns.]

Article no. 402 Subject: Politics
Ref. October 30, 1832; pg. 2, col. 6

Lot Clark & Co., of the *Balance*, say that "if the Antimasons will pay the [$]30,000 of which Myron Holley wronged the state, they will off-set the fifty cents which Judge Marcy wronged it of." It is grossly untrue that Mr. Holley ever wronged the state of a single cent. And of this we have in evidence the deliberate and voluntary act of a legislature composed of the political friends of the very party now in power, who allowed Mr. H. every dollar of the amount for which he was said to be a defaulter. Instead of Mr. H. owing the state any thing, it is our deliberate opinion, that the state owes him. But the scurvy wretches of the *Balance* would do well to say as little about offsets as possible. The $30,000 which that worthy friend of Messrs. Wright, Young & Co., Pierce, of Cayuga marsh memory, cheated the state—and the $50,000 lost, through Wright's gross neglect, in the Middle District Bank—to say nothing of the thousands which are annually bestowed on their noisy electioneerers, or wasted on the canals and elsewhere—stand as charges against the mismanagement, or worse, of the Regency, which they will be unable to offset in any other way than by paying them out of the Spoils which they have taken from the vanquished people.
[Transcriber's note: This article appears in the Editorial columns.]

Article no. 403 Subject: Editorial
Ref. October 30, 1832; pg. 2, col. 6

Col. Charles Molyneux was nominated by the Masonic Convention assembled here on Teusday [sic] last, as a candidate for Assembly. Setting aside Col. M's masonry, we always thought he was a pretty clever fellow, and we cannot conceive what bad thing he has been doing of late, that should have induced the Regency thus to "use him up," by conferring their honours upon him! But it is all a family affair. And as Col. M. is more likely to be engaged in preparing mint juleps to cheer the hearts of the masonics, after they shall be defeated in November, than in making laws for the People, we are disposed to let the matter drop.

Article no. 404 Subject: Politics
Ref. October 30, 1832; pg. 2, col. 6

Extract: It was not our intention to have again alluded to the bill of Marcy for work done to his pantaloons. What we have already said, we deemed sufficient to portray his character for rapacity, and to convince the public that they should at least be cautious in trusting a man of his avaricious disposition with the control of the public funds—it being hard to distinguish, so far as principle is concerned, between wrongfully taking fifty cents or fifty thousand dollars. The friends of the spoil taking Senator having seen fit, however, to deny the truth of the published bill, and to pronounce it, in some instances, a coinage of the editor of this print, we have deemed it necessary, in self-defence, this week to publish the bill entire, with the County Clerk's certificate of its being a correct copy of that on file in his office. Take note, then, reader, of the following

"Spoils.
State of New York, to William L. Marcy, Dr.
For expenses of holding Special Court at Lockport, in June, 1830." {Article includes itemization of expenses.} [Total expenses, $70 73 1-2, of which $15.65 were captioned, Estimated expenses of return. This account of expenses was followed by a transcription of the deposition made by William L. Marcy, stating, in part:] that he did not immediately or directly return after the adjournment of the court, but went into Canada and around by Buffalo, and he is therefore unable to specify the items for the expenses of his return from court, but he is confident that if he had returned directly, he should have expended as much as he did in going to the court, and therefore thinks the estimate made in the account is just and fair.
Sworn and subscribed this 31st March, 1831, before me SILAS WRIGHT, Jr. Comptroller, Comptroller's Office, Albany. {Article includes an accounting for the line item, "Phillips' bill for board, &c." for $35.62, which was certified as follows:}
Niagara County, ss.
I, Henry Catlin, Clerk of Niagara County aforesaid, do hereby certify, that the foregoing document, purporting to be a bill of the expenses of William L. Marcy, while holding a Special Circuit Court in the village of Lockport, is a true copy of that now on file in my office. In testimony whereof, I have hereunto set my hand, and affixed the seal of my office, at Lockport, this 30th day of October, 1832. HENRY CATLIN, Clerk, Nia. Co.
[Transcriber's note: This article appears in the Editorial columns.]

Article no. 405 Subject: Death
Ref. October 30, 1832; pg. 3, col. 3

DIED—In this village, on Thursday last, of the hooping-cough, Emma Hickox, daughter of George H. Boughton, Esq., in the 5th year of her age.

Article no. 406 Subject: Notice
Ref. October 30, 1832; pg. 3, col. 3

NOTICE.
The subscriber, contemplating new arrangements in business, requests all who have unsettled accounts with him, to call and arrange the same without delay, and oblige their old friend,
I.W. SMITH.
N.B. Having so far recovered from my severe and protracted indisposition, as to be able to attend to Professional duties, I would inform my old friends, that at all reasonable hours I will be ready to wait on them. Office in No. 1, Spalding's Building, Main-street—and for the present in L.A. Spalding's office.
I.W.S. Lockport, 10 mo. 30th, 1832.

Article no. 407 Subject: Advertisement
Ref. October 30, 1832; pg. 3, col. 3

ALMANACS FOR 1833.
Just received by N. Leonard, the Western Christian and German Almanacs, for sale by the gross, dozen or single.

Article no. 408 Subject: Advertisement
Ref. October 30, 1832; pg. 3, col. 3

More new Books at the Lockport Bookstore.
Westward Ho! in two volumes, by J.K. Paulding, author of the Dutchman's Fireside; Heidenmaur, by Cooper, two vols.; Arlington, by the author of "Granby," in two vols.; Life of Celebrated Travellers, forming Nos. 38, 39, 40, Life of Frederick the Great, forming Nos. 41, 42, of the Family Library; Tokens for 1833, Pearl for 1833.

Article no. 409	Subject: Notice
Ref. October 30, 1832; pg. 3, col. 3	

SHERIFF'S SALE.

By virtue of an execution issued out of the Clerk's office of the county of Niagara, and to me directed and delivered, against the goods and chattels, lands and tenements, of George S. Whippey, I have seized and taken all that certain piece or parcel of land, situate, lying, and being in the village of Lockport, known and distinguished on a certain map or survey of a part of said village, made for the proprietors by Jesse P. Haines, Surveyor, and filed in the office of the Clerk of the county of Niagara, as village lot number 31, on the north side of Walnut-street in said village, being one chain wide, and about two chains thirty-seven and a half links long, according to said map, reference being thereto had—containing about one fourth of an acre, be the same more or less—and all the right, title, claim, interest and demand of the [said] George S. Whippey, of, to, in or against which said above described piece or parcel of land, together with the appurtenances thereunto in any manner appertaining or belonging, I shall expose to sale at public vendue as the law directs, at the house now kept by J.W. Witbeck, known as the Eagle Tavern, in Lockport, on Thursday the 13th day of December next, at ten o'clock in the forenoon of that day. Dated Lockport, Oct. 30, 1832. H. McNEIL, Sheriff.

Article no. 410	Subject: Notice
Ref. October 30, 1832; pg. 3, col. 3	

List of Letters remaining in the Post-Office, at Royalton Centre, Sept. 30th, 1832. [Names listed, below.] J. TIMERMAN, P.M.

Axtell, Charles
Fisk, Orin
Gillet, Eliphal
Knox, John R.
Reynolds, Joshua
Thirstenan, Zera
Zachariah, George
Cochran, Oliver
Garnsey, John
Hutchins, Samuel
Merrit, Freeman
Scott, William
Underwood, Spelman

Article no. 411	Subject: Advertisement
Ref. October 30, 1832; pg. 3, col. 3	

WANTED—

A good Milch Cow. Inquire of the subscriber, at the Farmers' Mills, C.F. MITCHELL.

Article no. 412	Subject: Notice
Ref. October 30, 1832; pg. 3, col. 3	

STRAY COW.

Has been missing between two and three months, a small, dark brown, or black cow, about five years old, with some whtie [sic] on her forehead, and a scar on her back, (other marks not recollected.) Whoever will leave information at this office, where she may be found, shall be reasonably rewarded. October 9th, 1832.

Article no. 413	Subject: Notice
Ref. October 30, 1832; pg. 3, col. 3	

To my Customers!

OBLIGE me by settling your accounts by the 20th instant, or I must oblige you.

Oct. 1, 1832. VOLNEY SPALDING.

New Goods—Just received, a fresh supply.

V. SPALDING.

Article no. 414	Subject: Advertisement
Ref. October 30, 1832; pg. 3, col. 3	

Extract: Albany Eagle Air Furnace
and
Machine Shop,
MANY & WARD, proprietors,
(Formerly Corning, Norton & Co.)

Manufacture to order Iron Castings for Gearing Mills, malt mills, mashing machines, steam engines, &c. &c. Their collection of patterns is very great, embracing almost every calculation required. A constant supply of Potash Kettles, cauldrons, bark mills, paper mill screws and press plates, stoves, hollow ware, forge hammers, waggon boxes, sash weights, Edwards scale beams, Bull's platform scales, sleigh shoes, portable furnaces, hall scrapers, hawser irons, mandrills for coppersmiths, &c. &c., may be found on hand at all times. M. & W. having made several additions of Plough Patterns to their former assortment, now publish, for the benefit of their country customers, a new and perfect list of the Plough Castings manufactured by them: {Advertisement lists brands and models.} Also, the celebrated Side-Hill Plough; together with Shares of various other kinds. Country founders can be supplied with Pig-Iron, Fire Brick, Coal, Amboy Sand, and Clay. Boring, Turning, and Finishing, in all their various branches, executed with neatness and despatch. Also, Screws cut to order. Wm. V. Many will furnish plans and calculations for Mills, &c. Patterns made to order. Cotton machinists may obtain castings at this Furnace made of Scotch Iron.

All orders will receive prompt attention, and Castings forwarded to any part of the U. States or Canada. Orders may be addressed to MANY & WARD, 84 Beaver-street, Albany, or to the care of Messrs. Erastus Corning & Co., of whom, also, every information may be obtained. Albany, Sept, 18, 1832.

Article no. 415 Subject: Notice
Ref. October 30, 1832; pg. 3, col. 4

NOTICE.

The subscribers received on the 21st of May last, from boat *Ohio*, Capt. O. Allen, Troy & Erie line, a Chest, painted blue, of the common size, without address. It was said to belong to a lady of Batavia, Genesee county. The owner is requested to call, pay charges, and take it away.

Sept. 18. ROGERS & BROWN.

Article no. 416 Subject: Advertisement
Ref. October 30, 1832; pg. 3, col. 4

Extract: Something New!

The subscriber would inform his old friends and customers, that he has, within a few days, opened a large and well selected assortment of Watches, Jewellery, &c. at his old and noted stand on Main-street, where he will be happy to see all those with whom he has heretofore dealt, so much to the satisfaction of both buyer and seller. His stock is a complete one; and every person can depend upon finding the article that just suits him! Among the articles which he offers he would particularize the following: [List includes: silver and gold watches; German mantel time pieces, Curtis & Dunning's superior time pieces; seals, keys and rings; ear-rings, breast pins, finger rings, shirt studs, waist buckles; bead bags and guard chains; pencils and leads, backgammon boards, spectacles, table and tea spoons, silver thimbles, pen and knives, razors and scissors, ivory haft and silver mounted dirks, snuff and tobacco boxes, shirt buttons, ivory pocket combs, shaving soap, superior violin strings]—Together with a large assortment of all minor articles usually kept in an Establishment of the kind. Silver Table, Tea, Salt and Mustard Spoons kept constantly for sale, or made to order at short notice. Watches, Clocks, &c., repaired as usual.

A.T. PRENTICE. Lockport, Sept. 11, 1832.

Article no. 417 Subject: Advertisement
Ref. October 30, 1832; pg. 3, col. 5

Irving's new book, the Alhambra; Adventures of a Younger Son; Pitcairn's Island and Otaheite; Lives and Voyages of Early Navigators; Life of the Dutchess [sic] D'Abrantes; Life of Stephen Girard; Dr. Lardner's Cabinet Biography of Eminent British Statesmen—for sale by

July 3. N. LEONARD.

Article no. 418 Subject: Notice
Ref. October 30, 1832; pg. 3, col. 5

CAUTION.

Domestic difficulties compels me to take this method of forbidding all persons trusting or harbouring, in any wise dealing with my wife, as I will pay no debts of her contracting after this date: Also, forbidding, under penalty of the law, all borrowing, lending, trading or trafficking whatever directly or indirectly, with any member of my family, my son Andrew J. excepted.

Dated Hartland, August 30, 1832. JOHN SEEVER.

Article no. 419 Subject: Advertisement
Ref. October 30, 1832; pg. 3, col. 5

GLASS & PAINT STORE.

The subscriber has on hand, and intends to keep, a good supply of

Glass and Paints,

which he offers low for cash. Also English Glass of all sizes, from 7 by 9, to 22 by 28: likewise a good supply of Sash, made by hand, at factory prices.

DANIEL GREENVAULT.

Main-st. nearly opposite E. Gibbs' store.

Lockport, July 31.

Article no. 420 Subject: Advertisement
Ref. October 30, 1832; pg. 3, col. 6

CAMBLETS, PLAIDS, &c.

1 Piece super Brown Merino Camblet,
1 do. do. Blue Goat Hair do.
1 do. do. Brown imitation do.
10 do. common do.
10 do. Plaid Camblets and Tartans. Queen's and Caroline's Stripes and Plaids, blue and common Moreens, &c. for sale low by

Oct. 29. HOUSE & BOUGHTON.

Article no. 421 Subject: Advertisement
Ref. October 30, 1832; pg. 3, col. 6

CHEAP GOODS.

HOUSE & BOUGHTON have just received a fresh supply of Goods, to which they invite the attention of the Public, and assure them they are offered on such terms, as to make it an object to call and supply themselves. They will not be undersold by any establishment in the village. In addition to their stock of Dry Goods, which is heavy, they keep Hardware, Crockery, and Groceries, which renders their assortment general and complete. October 24.

Article no. 422 Subject: Politics
Ref. October 30, 1832; pg. 4, col. 1

Extract: Anti-Masonic Whig Nominations: [Listed, below.]
NIAGARA COUNTY CONVENTION.

At a Convention of Delegates, representing the Democratic Anti-Masons of the several towns of Niagara County, assembled at the Court House in Lockport, on Wednesday, 10th October, Asher Freeman, Esq., of Royalton, was called to the Chair, and A.H. Moss, of Porter, appointed Secretary. The Convention being thus organized, thirty-two Delegates, representing ten towns, took their seats. It was then on motion resolved, That a committee be appointed to draft Resolutions expressive of the feelings of this Convention, and an Address to the freemen of the County—{Article includes the Address.} [The Convention further resolved that a Committee, to consist of one from each town, be appointed to report the name of a suitable person to represent the County in the Legislature of this state—Listed, below.] {Article includes outline of resolutions, to make political statements, and to put forth national, state and county nominations, followed by an Address to the Freemen of Niagara County.} [The Address included the names of citizens appointed to the Central and Vigilant Committees of the towns and villages of Niagara County; names listed, below.]

[Transcriber's note: Refer to the key for the coded numerals, after the list of names.]

Allen, T. (2)
Anquish, Lewis (2)
Austen, Freeman, jun. (6)
Bailey, J.S (7)
Baker, Charles (8)
Baker, Stephen (12)
Barris, Isaac (8)
Benedict, George R. (18)
Bickford, Samuel, jun. (12)
Bosworth, B.H. (4)
Bridsall, Jonathan (12)
Bronson, A. (18)
Brown, John (5)
Bugbee, George (18)
Burr, Calvin (10)
Bush, S. (4)
Campbell, Ezekiel (14)
Canfield, D. (5)
Carpenter, Benjamin (3)
Carrington, Asa (18)
Chaffee, Warren (14)
Alvord, E. (4)
Ash, Caleb (6)
Baer, Ira (6)
Bailey, Jon. (2)
Baker, Chauncey (10)
Barnes, Stephen (14)
Beamer, James (16)
Benedict, Ira (14)
Boles, Joseph (10)
Boughton, George H. (10)
Bristoll, L. (19)
Bronson, C. (4)
Buchanan, John (4)
Bullen, Joseph (20)
Bush, John (21)
Cadwallader, M. (19)
Canfield, D. (5) (6)
Carpenter, B. (4)
Carpenter, W. (18)
Castle, Ezra (11)
Chapin, T.H. (4)
Chapin, Thomas (1)
Clark, H.W. (1)
Cleaveland, A.H. (6)
Colby, William L. (14)
Compton, J. (19)
Comstock, H. (4)
Cooke, Bates (19)
Craig, John (17)
Cuddeback, J.S. (25)
Curtiss, Gilbert (6)
Davis, Nathaniel (9)
De Veaux, S. (1)
Dewey, M. (2)
Doty, William (6)
Dubois, Court (10)
Dunham, Shubael (10)
Ellmaker, Amos; supported for Vice-President
Forbes, James (21)
Freeman, P. (18)
Gates, H. (4)
Gebhard, John (10)
Gould, John (26)
Granger, Francis; New York; supported for Governor
Griswold, Jesse (4)
Hard, Gideon; supported for Congress
Hartley, Jesse (22)
Hathaway, Charles (10)
Hawks, James (10)
Hawley, R. (7)
Hayes, S. (24)
Herington, D. (20)
Hinman, H. (18)
Holmes, D. (7)
Howell, Nathaniel T. (10)
Hurd, A.M. (15)
Jeffrey, William (9)
Keyes, H. (22)
Kite, William, jun. (6)
Kitredge, Ezra (12)
Knowles, William (8)
Landers, Harry (21)
Lee, J. (23)
Leonard, C. (3) (4)
Lord, Eleazer (10)
Mather, Hiram F. (10)
McClue, R.W. (25)
Chaplin, Daniel (12)
Clarke, S.P. (23)
Cleaveland, J. (6)
Cole, D. (9)
Compton, Jacob (16)
Cook, Robert (10)
Cotheal, Henry (10)
Crapsey, D.W. (17)
Curtenius, John L. (10)
Davis, James (19)
De Freest, Martin (10)
Demaree, C. (23)
Dickerson, A. (7)
Downer, R. (20)
Dubois, Nathaniel (10)
Dunlap, Josiah (10)
Fenn, E. (7) (18)

Freeman, Asher, Esq.; Chair
Galusha, D. (21)
Gay, George A. (10)
Gould, David (14)
Gould, John, jun. (4)
Griffen, John; supported for Senator

Hammond, E. (13)
Harrison, Dennis (15)

Hatch, J. (23)
Hathaway, Silvester R. (14)
Hawley, Gideon (10)
Hawley, Robert (4)
Herington, Clark K. (12)
Herington, James (12)
Hitchcock, John (14)
Houstater, Jacob (14)
Huntington, George (10)
Hutchinson, Hollom (10)
Kent, James (10)
Kinyon, Allen (11) (12)
Kitredge, A. (7)
Knoll, Jeremiah (6)
Lacey, Samuel (10)
Lawrence, Asa (18)
Leland, O. (18)
Livingston, Robert (10)
Manly, Samuel (16)
McArthur, G. (6)
McCormick, James (6)

McKinstry, Justus (10)
McLaughlin, J., jun. (6)
McMartin, Duncan, jun. (10)
Merritt, S.S. (25)
Miller, John (10)
Mixer, Nathan (10)
Morris, Joseph (6)
Moss, A.H. (7)
Mudge, John, jun. (11)
Newman, A. (24)
Norton, Henry (28)
Orton, Myron (13)
Outwater, J. (25)
Paige, T. (18)
Parsons, Aaron (2)
Per Lee, Edmund G. (10)
Pool, Thomas (16)
Pratt, A.M. (12)
Ransom, E., jun. (26)
Reynale, George (26)
Richards, R. (23)
Robinson, Riley (9)
Rumery, E. (21)
Seeley, E. (12)
Smith, A. (25)
Smith, G.M. (25)
Smith, Griffin (6)
Smith, Jacob, jun. (4)
Spalding, L.A. (4)
Stahl, E. (3) (4)
Stevens, Samuel; supported for Lieut.-Governor
Stone, J.P. (18)
Stow, H.J. (15)
Taylor, M.N. (14)
Thacher, H. (23)
Thompson, George (9)
Tower, P. (6)
Tucker, Joseph (10)
Tuttle, William (10)
Van Horn, C. (25)
Van Horn, James (24)
Vroman, Sydney (6)
Walker, L.H. (5) (6)
Ware, S.L. (2)
Waterman, J.B. (12)
West, Ira (9)
Wilbur, Orrin (10)

McKnight, John (2)
McLeland, R.J. (18)
McNall, J. (18)
Millard, O.L. (4)
Mitchell, C.F. (4) (19)
Morgan, William (27)
Mosely, H.H. (23)
Moss, C.H. (6)
Newcomb, A.W. (18)
Norcross, Willard (4)
Oliver, Alexander (9)
Ostrander, P. (18)
Owen, Joseph A. (18)
Pardy, Alvah (2)
Pease, Adam (21)
Phillips, Joseph (4)
Potter, Ellis (10)
Pratt, H. (21)
Raymond, E.W. (4)
Reynolds, Reuben (16)
Robinson, John, jun. (16)
Rose, Robert S. (10)
Scott, William (7)
Shoemaker, Nicholas (10)
Smith, Asa B. (10)
Smith, Gerrit (10)
Smith, H.B. (18)
Smith, T.F. (17) (18)
Spencer, John C. (10)
Stahl, William (4)
Stewart, T.F. (12)
Stone, Payson (18)
Sutherland, Joel (16)
Teachout, Abraham (12)
Thomas, Eben (18)
Tower, Otis (9)
Towsley, William (14)
Turk, James (10)
Van Buren, Martin (29)
Van Horn, J., jun. (25)
Van Volkenburgh, C. (22)
Wakeman, Stephen, jun. (4)
Ward, N.M. (7)
Waring, Gilbert (10)
Webber, Thomas (13)
Wichterman, G.D. (4)
Williams, Ira O. (18)

Williams, John (4)
Wirt, William; supported for President
Worden, Samuel (2)
Works, Samuel (4)

Winchip, W.L. (18)
Wood, Silas (10)
Worden, Semy (2) (19)
Yerington, L. (4)

Key: Appointed to a committee, as indicated, or other:
(1) the Central Committee for the village of Niagara.
(2) the Vigilant Committee for the village of Niagara.
(3) the Central Committee for the village of Lockport.
(4) the Vigilant Committee for the village of Lockport.
(5) the Central Committee for the village of Porter.
(6) the Vigilant Committee for the village of Porter.
(7) a Committee to report the name of a suitable person to represent Niagara County in the Legislature of this state.
(8) the Central Committee for the village of Wilson.
(9) the Vigilant Committee for the village of Wilson.
(10) one of forty-two Electors of President and Vice-President.
(11) the Central Committee for the village of Hartland.
(12) the Vigilant Committee for the village of Hartland.
(13) the Central Committee for the village of Cambria.
(14) the Vigilant Committee for the village of Cambria.
(15) the Central Committee for the village of Lewiston.
(16) the Vigilant Committee for the village of Lewiston.
(17) the Central Committee for the village of Royalton.
(18) the Vigilant Committee for the village of Royalton.
(19) a Committee to draft Resolutions expressive of this Convention of Delegates.
(20) the Central Committee for the village of Somerset.
(21) the Vigilant Committee for the village of Somerset.
(22) the Central Committee for the village of Pendleton.
(23) the Vigilant Committee for the village of Pendleton.
(24) the Central Committee for the village of New-Fane.
(25) the Vigilant Committee for the village of New-Fane.
(26) the County Central Committee.
(27) of Batavia, New York; cited in the Address to the Freemen of Niagara County at the Convention. In September 1926, William Morgan was suddenly seized and forcibly transported to Canandaigua; thence after a short confinement, he was again taken and conveyed to Fort Niagara, where he was murdered.
(28) Supported as a suitable Candidate for Assembly, to represent the County in the State Legislature.
(29) The Convention resolved, That Martin Van Buren has entailed upon our state a venal system of politics, &c.

Article no. 423   Subject: Advertisement
Ref. December 18, 1832; pg. 1, col. 2

A GREAT BARGAIN!

For sale, an excellent Farm, one and three-fourths of a mile westerly from this village, on the new and nearest road to Niagara Falls, containing one hundred acres of land, on which are a good log house, barn, well, orchard, &c. &c., with about 30 acres under good fence.

The price is 20 dollars per acre—but as the owner resides in Michigan, he has concluded to sell it for the most generous offer near his price.

Purchasers are invited to call upon the subscriber upon the premises.

Also, the Farm where Dea. Ambrose Grow now resides, containing 60 acres, 2 framed and one log house, and a large framed Barn, and good corners for business. For further particulars call as above.

REUBEN WINCHELL, Lockport, Nov. 3rd, 1832.

Article no. 424   Subject: Transportation
Ref. December 18, 1832; pg. 1, col. 2

NOTICE is hereby given, that an application will be made to the Legislature of the state of New-York, at its next session, for an act of incorporation to authorise a company to make a navigable canal from the Tonawanta creek, above the dam near its mouth, to the Falls of Niagara, on the most eligible route—and also, to establish manufactories at said Falls,—with a capital of half a million of dollars. Niagara Falls, Nov. 6, 1832.

Article no. 425   Subject: Temperance
Ref. December 18, 1832; pg. 1, col. 3

The address of E.I. Chase, Esq., before the Lockport Temperance Society, at its annual meeting on the 11th inst., is on file, and will be given in our next.

Article no. 426   Subject: Temperance
Ref. December 18, 1832; pg. 1, col. 3

(*Communicated.*)

TEMPERANCE.—The inhabitants of Pendleton convened, agreeably to previous notice, on the 4th instant, and after hearing an address from the Corresponding Secretary of the County Society, they organized, and formed a Town Society, denominated The Pendleton Temperance Society, auxiliary to the Niagara County Society.

Elder LEMAN ANDREWS, President.
LYMAN E. THAYER, Esq., Secretary.

A few inhabitants, with a becoming spirit, and a desire to promote the happiness of their fellow-citizens, had previously attempted to sustain a Society in that town—but, as in almost every instance, when the subject of Temperance is first introduced into a place, they encountered many obstacles and met with considerable opposition, and their attempt to serve the cause of humanity, was almost, if not entirely, prostrated. The present Society being organized auxiliary to the County Society, and a number of the first men of the town having ardently entered into the work of reform, will, we are confident, receive the cordial support of every friend of temperance in that town.

Article no. 427   Subject: Land and Property
Ref. December 18, 1832; pg. 2, col. 3

The farm and country seat at Newtown, owned by the late Gov. Clinton, (with about thirty one acres of land,) was, on Saturday, sold at auction by Messrs. Blecker & Son for $1,450.

Article no. 428   Subject: Notice
Ref. December 18, 1832; pg. 2, col. 4

To the Patrons of the *Courier.*

The publisher [M. Cadwallader] of this paper contemplating a change in his business on the first day of January ensuing, hereby informs his patrons and friends, that their accounts will be made up to the 25th day of December instant, and payment will be required as soon thereafter as an agent can present them. This step has become absolutely necessary, in order to enable the publisher to continue his business, and cannot longer be deferred. Dec. 18.

Article no. 429   Subject: Notice
Ref. December 18, 1832; pg. 2, col. 4

We beg the indulgence of our readers for the barrenness that may be exhibited in the editorial department of our present and a few succeeding numbers.

Article no. 430   Subject: Editorial
Ref. December 18, 1832; pg. 2, col. 4

Antimasonic Almanac for 1833. This periodical has been on our editorial desk for several weeks, and an apology is certainly due to the auther [sic] for not noticing it at an earlier day. From the many excellent numbers which preceded this, we had supposed that the business of almanac making had been brought to its height—but in the present number Mr. Giddins appears to have improved upon himself, giving us in reality a book, filled with matter interesting to every class of our citizens. Many improvements have also been made in the astronomical calculations of this periodical, which greatly enhance its value as a calendar, but our time will not admit of our noticing them particularly. Several thousands of this work ought to be immediately purchased, and distributed in regions where antimasonry is unknown. We know of no mode in which the good seed could be more cheaply sown.

Article no. 431	Subject: Agriculture
Ref. December 18, 1832; pg. 2, col. 4	

New-York Farmer and American Gardener's Magazine. This is the title of a monthly publication of thirty-two large quarto pages, which will be commenced after the first of January next, in the city of N. York, by Mr. D.K. Minor, at $3 per year. From an examination of the specimen number before us, we think it well worthy of the patronage of those engaged in agricultural pursuits—and feeling an interest in encouraging every thing that may tend to advance the business and prosperity of the farmer, we will in our next publish the prospectus of the publisher, and cheerfully receive and forward the names of those who may wish to patronize it. The specimen number can be seen at our office.

Article no. 432	Subject: Manufacture
Ref. December 18, 1832; pg. 3, col. 1	

Woodworth's Planing Machine.—At the Steam Foundry of Beals, Wilkeson & Co. we have witnessed the operation of a machine for planing, tonguing and grooving floor plank, ceiling, &c. It will finish 18 feet of plank per minute, bringing them to an exact thickness and width, thereby diminishing the labour of laying them at least one half. The shavings produced will more than supply the engine, and accomplish the work of 35 men, during the working hours, at an expense of about one sixth the usual rate, unquestionable [sic] ranks it among "labour saving machines," and makes it a desirable object in large or growing towns. The plank [sic] are reduced to thickness by three knives placed upon a cylinder, revolving about 2300 times per minute, thereby producing a perfectly smoth [sic] surface, the tonguing and grooving by knives placed on cylinders similar to the facing cutter. Made and sold by S.B. Schenck, Attleboro, Mass., now in this city.—*Buffalo Jour.*

Article no. 433	Subject: Politics
Ref. December 18, 1832; pg. 3, col. 2	

Extract: It having been pretty widely rumoured that our friend Reynale had fallen into the hands of the Philistines, and been stripped by them of sundry "cool thousands" in the way of bets, ... he has deemed it necessary, in order to correct the many idle tales that are afloat, to publish the card which follows. ...

A CARD.—Mr. Editor: I take this method to correct false reports, and to give a general answer to all inquiries, respecting my bets on the late elections. My whole bets did not amount to $800. They were made on counties and the general election in this state, and on governor and electors in Pennsylvania.—I was the winner on this state, and the loser on Pennsylvania. My whole loss was less than $500.—It was fairly lost and paid, and the winners are welcome to it—particularly as it was all paid out of my Jackson fund!

GEO. REYNALE. Lockport, 18th Dec.

Article no. 434	Subject: Temperance
Ref. December 18, 1832; pg. 3, col. 2	

NOTICE.

The annual meeting of the Youths' Temperance Society of this village, will be held at the Brick Church, on Tuesday, the 25th day of Dec. inst[.] at 6 o'clock, P.M. It is desired that all who have "ears to hear," will attend, and heartily co-operate in the annihilation of a vice which has attached to this nation the appellation of "drunkards." An address will be delivered.

By order of the Board of Managers.

Wm. L. PARSONS, Sec'y. Lockport, Dec. 15, 1832.

Article no. 435	Subject: Temperance
Ref. December 18, 1832; pg. 3, col. 2	

Extract: Office N.Y. St. T.S. Albany, Dec. 2, 1832.

The period is fast approaching when it has been usual for the several auxiliary Temperance Societies in the state of N.Y. to send in their annual reports; and communications have already been received at this office, inquiring when they would be wanted this year. ... The committee cannot but express their most ardent desire that every society should shake off the bands of sloth, and address itself to work. The favourable season has arrived, the woes of intemperance are not removed; the eyes of our country, of the world, are upon us, and our responsibilities involve all that is held dear by man, that is cherished by the patriot, and that is venerated by the christian. By order of the Ex. Com., E.C. Delavan, Chairman.

Article no. 436	Subject: Notice
Ref. December 18, 1832; pg. 3, col. 2	

NOTICE

Is hereby given, that the debts due to Morris H. Tucker, either by note, bond, or book account, have all been assigned to Edward Bissell and Sidney Smith. Payment must therefore by made to them, or their agents, at the stores lately occupied by said Tucker, and to no other person.

Goods are now sold at the said store at first cost, either for cash or approved paper. Those indebted by book account are desired to call and settle. Payment of all notes due is requested as soon as is convenient.

EDWARD BISSELL, SIDNEY SMITH. Dec. 18.

Article no. 437   Subject: Advertisement
Ref. December 18, 1832; pg. 3, col. 2

IRON,
An extensive assortment, for sale by
SETH PARSONS & Co. Dec. 18.

Article no. 438   Subject: Advertisement
Ref. December 18, 1832; pg. 3, col. 2

SHOES and BOOTS,
In great variety, for Ladies, Gentlemen and Children, for sale by SETH PARSONS & Co. Dec. 18.

Article no. 439   Subject: Advertisement
Ref. December 18, 1832; pg. 3, col. 2

Millinery and Mantuamaking!
MISS GIBSON respectfully begs leave to inform the ladies of Middleport, and the adjacent country, that she continues the above business in said village, where she will be happy to receive orders in her line. She has recently received patterns and plates of the
Latest Fashions,
and will be able to execute her work according to the most modern and approved taste. She has and intends to keep on hand a general assortment of Straw and Silk Hats and Plain Bonnets—Also, Gro-de-nap Silks, Plumes and Trimmings of all kinds, too numerous to mention.

Miss G. returns her grateful acknowledgments for past patronage, assures the Ladies who favour her with their orders, that she will endeavour to please them in the fulfilment. Middleport, Dec. 18th, 1832.

Article no. 440   Subject: Advertisement
Ref. December 18, 1832; pg. 3, col. 2

CHEAP!—CHEAP!
Fall and Winter Clothing.
G.S. PLACE has just returned from N. York, and is now manufacturing his Fall and Winter Clothing; such as
Coats, Pea-Coats, Vests,
Over Coats, Cloaks, Pantaloons, &c.
of the best quality of Goods, and warranted well made, in the latest fashions.

Clothes cut and made are warranted to fit. Cutting done for Farmers and others as usual. Lockport, Dec. 4, 1832.

Article no. 441   Subject: Advertisement
Ref. December 18, 1832; pg. 3, col. 3

Auction!
The subscriber, contemplating new arrangements in business, will sell at auction (unless previously disposed of at private sale) on the 15th day of January next, at 2 o'clock, P.M., a first rate Saddle Horse, (a real racker,) a new Saddle, with plated stirrups of the break off kind, and pad and oil cloth cover; a Bridle, with English steel wire bits, Halter; two double Horse-Blankets, with circingles with pads; one set plated Gig Harness; one do. for common use; a new Sleigh, fitted for one horse or two, a capital article; a one-horse Wagon; Whips; Spurs—and all the needfuls for a first-rate pill-peddling establishment. The whole will be disposed of on a credit, if desired, of from 6 to 9 months, providing good security be given.

I.W. SMITH. Lockport, 12 mo. 18th, 1832.

P.S. At the same time will be sold a complete set of Garden Tools, consisting of garden stone Rollers, two sizes, with iron gudgeons; three iron Bars, assorted sizes, with and without claws; Sledges, Hammers, Spades, Shovels, Pickaxes, Pruning Hooks, Budding Knives, transplanting Trowels, Mattocks, Hoes, broad and narrow — in short, all the paraphernalia of gardening. I.W.S.

Article no. 442   Subject: Advertisement
Ref. December 18, 1832; pg. 3, col. 3

E.I. CHASE,
Attorney at Law and Solicitor in Chancery.
Office over F. Bissell's Store. Nov. 13.

Article no. 443   Subject: Advertisement
Ref. December 18, 1832; pg. 3, col. 3

Extract: New Store! New Goods! Cheaper than ever!
GEO. LEVERETT & Co. respectfully inform the inhabitants of Lockport and its vicinity, that they are now receiving and opening a very general assortment of Fall and Winter goods, which they offer (at about cost and transportation) for the ready pay. All wishing to purchase cheap, will please call and look for themselves. Their stock consists in part of [List includes broadcloths, cassimeres, satinets, sheetings, shirtings, ticking, flannels, wicking, batting, wadding, yarn, calicoes, circassians, &c. Groceries include teas, sugars, coffee, pepper, spices, chocolate, raisins, rice, indigo, ginger, snuff, port, wines, molasses, lamp oil.] Also A general assortment of Crockery, Glass-ware, &c.:—all which they offer for sale in the brick block of buildings, a few doors east of the Lockport House, (Lower Town.) N.B. All kinds of country produce taken in exchange for Goods.

Article no. 444   Subject: Advertisement
Ref. December 18, 1832; pg. 3, col. 3

BLANKETS.—Rose, English, Duffel Point and Horse Blankets, for sale by HOUSE & BOUGHTON. Nov. 27.

Article no. 445 Subject: Advertisement
Ref. December 18, 1832; pg. 3, col. 3

CARPETS.
2 Pcs. Superior Ingrain Carpeting.
2 pcs. Cotton do.;
1 pce. Venetian Stair do.
12 Hearth Rugs, some rich and splendid patterns;
6 gro. Carpet Binding;
Manilla, Alicant and Rope hall and door Mats, &c.
Just received and for sale by
    HOUSE & BOUGHTON. Nov. 27.

Article no. 446 Subject: Advertisement
Ref. December 18, 1832; pg. 3, col. 3

Giddins' Almanac for 1833—Just received and for sale at this office, by the gross or otherwise. Nov. 13.

Article no. 447 Subject: Advertisement
Ref. December 18, 1832; pg. 3, col. 3

Extract: Shoes.
HOUSE & BOUGHTON keep a general assortment of coarse and fine Shoes, which they offer for sale at reduced prices. Among them are [various quantities listed for each of morocco stitched and seal walking Shoes, spring-heel undressed morocco Pumps, morocco Boots, leather Boots, walking shoes, Brogans, stuff spring-heel walking shoes, heeled Pumps, Bolivar Slips and Boots, Gaiter Boots, Over-shoes, and thick shoes and boots, for Women, Misses, Children, Men and Boys.]

Article no. 449 Subject: Advertisement
Ref. December 18, 1832; pg. 3, col. 3

Almanacs for 1833.
The Antimasonic, Western, Christian, Comic, German, Day's Pocket, and Porter's Health Almanacs, for 1833, just received, and for sale by the gross, dozen or single copy, at the Lockport Bookstore. Nov. 13.

Article no. 450 Subject: Advertisement
Ref. December 18, 1832; pg. 3, col. 3

CODFISH.
2000 Lbs. Codfish, for sale by
July 24. ROGERS & BROWN.
[Transcriber's note: This advertisement was followed by another from the same vendor, in the same column: Connecticut Mess Shad for sale.]

Article no. 451 Subject: Advertisement
Ref. December 18, 1832; pg. 3, col. 4

Wanted Immediately—
Journeymen Tailors. Apply to
G.S. PLACE. Dec. 11.

Article no. 452 Subject: Notice
Ref. December 18, 1832; pg. 3, col. 4

Canal Bank of Lockport.
Notice is hereby given, that application will be made to the Legislature of this state, at its next session, for a bank to be called the Canal Bank of Lockport, to be located in the upper village of Lockport, with a capital of one hundred thousand dollars. Dec. 11.

Article no. 453 Subject: Advertisement
Ref. December 18, 1832; pg. 3, col. 4

Hardware.
WM. HUMPHREY, at the sign of the Padlock, Lockport, (Lower Town,) is now receiving his fall stock of
Fancy Hardware, Saddlery, and Cutlery:
Also, English, American, Swedes and Rusia [sic] Bar-Iron;
Swedes, American, German and Sanderson, Brothers & Co.'s Blistered and Cost Steel;
English Hoop Iron; American Band do.
Nail, Spike, and Braziers' Rods;
Plated Sleigh and Cutter Shoes;
Wrought and Cut Nails; Bar and Sheet Lead;
Spades and Shovels; Mill and Cross-cut Saws;
Brass Andirons and Shovels and Tongs;
Rrass [sic] and Wire Fire Fenders;
Tea, Dinner and Sleigh Bells;
Carpenters' and Joiners' Bench Tools;
Saws, Squares, Adzes, Hand and Broad Axes;
Log, Trace and Halter Chains;
Davis & Co.'s, Simmons' and Mitchell's Cast-steel Axes. Also, an assortment of Box, Oven, Hall and Cooking Stoves, Stove Pipe, &c., &c.
All which he is ready to dispose of upon the most favourable terms to the purchasers. November 20.

Article no. 454 Subject: Notice
Ref. December 18, 1832; pg. 3, col. 4

CAUTION.—Whereas the subscribers a few days since gave two notes of hand to one David Baney—one for $7, payable on the first day of January next, and the other for $8, payable on the first day of April next: this is therefore to caution all persons against taking an assignment of said notes, as no value has been given for them, and we are determined not to pay them. Dated November 29th, 1832.
WILLIAM EAGER, LINAS WILCOX.

Article no. 455 Subject: Advertisement
Ref. December 18, 1832; pg. 3, col. 4

Parsons & Phelps.
Booksellers and Stationers,
No. 24 Exchange-street, Rochester,

Have on hand a large assortment of School, Classical, Theological, Medical and Miscellaneous Books—also, a large assortment of Stationary [sic], including

Letter and Foolscap Paper,
Wrapping do.
Slates, Pencils, &c.
Russia and Holland Quills, &c., &c.

All of which will be sold on the most reasonable terms.

Merchants, Library Companies, School Teachers, and all others who purchase by the quantity, supplied at liberal disgust [sic!]. Orders promptly attended to. Nov. 13.

Article no. 456 Subject: Advertisement
Ref. December 18, 1832; pg. 3, col. 4

New Goods.

HOUSE & BOUGHTON are now opening a larger assortment of

Fall and Winter Goods,

than has heretofore been offered in the village. They invite their old customers, and all others, to examine their stock before purchasing, as they feel confident they can accommodate them with almost every article usually called for, and at such prices as cannot fail to be satisfactory. They are not confined to one branch, but keep a general assortment of

Dry Goods, Crockery, Hardware and Groceries.

H. & B. particularly invite the attention of the public to their assortment of Cloths and Cassimeres, &c.—Calicoes and Prints from 9 to 25 cents per yard; Brown Shirtings from 6 to 9 cents; Brown Sheetings from 10 to 14 cents, and other goods in proportion. Nov. 15, 1832.

Article no. 457 Subject: Advertisement
Ref. December 18, 1832; pg. 3, col. 4

S. JENNINGS

Has again opened a Tavern at his old stand in the Village of Lockport, where he will be thankful for a share of public patronage. Lockport, Nov. 20, 1832.

Article no. 458 Subject: Advertisement
Ref. December 18, 1832; pg. 3, col. 4

Dress Hdkfs. and Hat Ribbons.
An elegant assortment for sale unusually low by
HOUSE & BOUGHTON. Nov. 15.

Article no. 459 Subject: Advertisement
Ref. December 18, 1832; pg. 3, col. 4

Fur Caps, Collars, &c.
Men's, sea otter, acorn, flat and opera Caps;
Boys' do. do. do. do.
Men's and boy's hair seal
Superior sea otter Gloves;
Sea otter and natural seal Collars;
Just received and for sale by
HOUSE & BOUGHTON. Nov. 15.

Article no. 460 Subject: Advertisement
Ref. December 18, 1832; pg. 3, col. 4

Wanted,

A Partner—who can furnish from 500 to $1000, either in cash, or suitable groceries, for a profitable Summer and Winter Establishment, in the best situation for a Soda Fountain, Restauranteur, &c., on an extensive scale, in the Western District. The most unquestionable references will be given.

Apply at the office of the *Niagara Courier*, or address W.S., through the post-office. Lockport, Nov. 12, 1832.

Article no. 461 Subject: Notice
Ref. December 18, 1832; pg. 3, col. 4

CAUTION. On the 12th January, 1830, Joseph Aikin signed a quit claim deed in favour of Truman C. Dewey, for a part of Lot No. 34, township 14, in 8th range, 96 acres, lying between Mr. Playter's farm and that of Mr. D. Smith in Lewiston, and deposited the same with me for safe keeping, to be delivered to said Dewey, on certain conditions, which have not been complied with. The paper, during my absence the past winter, in some way came to the hands of Wm. L. Colby, without my knowledge or consent, or that of any person in charge of my office, where the imperfect deed was left by me. This notice is given to guard all persons against any imposition which may be attempted under cover of that paper.

BATES COOKE. Lewiston, 20th Nov. 1832.

Article no. 462 Subject: Notice
Ref. December 18, 1832; pg. 3, col. 4

To the Public.

The above caution of Bates Cooke, Esq., in relation to the Deed mentioned therein, requires explanation, and in some respects contradiction, because it is in some respects untrue, and Mr. Cooke must have known it. In May, 1830, my sister purchased the farm mentioned in Mr. Cooke's caution of Mr. Dewey, and took his deed for the same. Some time in the fall of 1831, according to my best recollection, I called on Mr. Cooke for the purpose of seeing a deed of the same farm, from the Holland Land Company, to Jabez Van Allen, one from Van Allen to Joseph Aiken, and one from Aiken to Truman C. Dewey, the man from whom my sister purchased, which deeds it appears had been left with Mr. Cooke for safe keeping—none of them had been recorded. He showed the deeds to me, remarking at the same time, that they ought not to remain in this situation, but should be recorded. I asked Mr. Cooke if there was any claim or incumbrance on the deeds. He said there was none. Mr. Dewey had always said the same, which I have no doubt was true. My sister, of course, wanted these deeds recorded, to show a complete claim of title from the Holland Land Company, consequently some time last winter I called at Mr. Cooke's office for the deeds, and a young man who appeared to officiate as clerk in the office, without any hesitation delivered them to me. To these facts I am willing to testify. But Mr. Dewey has left the country. Whether he owes Mr. Cooke or not I am unable to say. If so, whether Mr. Cooke intends to take advantage of Dewey's absence to affrighten me to pay him Dewey's debts, by insinuating in a public newspaper what he dare not state directly, that I purloined the deed from Aiken to Dewey from his office, or whether he thinks that the influence of his name appended to such a false insinuation, and to threatening letters, is sufficient to affrighten me into a compliance with his terms, I am unable to say: at any rate, I shall make considerable resistance before I shall consent to be deprived of my property in this way even by a member of congress.

Dec. 3d, 1832. Wm. L. COLBY.

Article no. 463 Subject: Advertisement
Ref. December 18, 1832; pg. 3, col. 5

CODFISH.—10 quintals first quality Codfish, for sale by
Nov. 27.   HOUSE & BOUGHTON.

[Transcriber's note: This advertisement was followed by three more for the same vendor, in the same column, for: groceries; refined sugar; and, circassians and camblets.]

Article no. 464 Subject: Advertisement
Ref. December 18, 1832; pg. 3, col. 5

NEW WORKS

Received by N. Leonard.—Abercrombie on the Intellectual Powers, and the Investigation of Truth; Landers' expedition to the Niger, and discovery of its terminaton; Turner's Sacred History of the World; The works of the Rev. E. Beckersteth; Thoughts in affliction; The Refuge, containing the Righteous Man's Habitation in the time of Plague and Pestilence; Tales of Early Ages; Life in Russia, Spain and Portugal; Narganset Chief, or the adventures of a wanderer; Memoir of Celebrated Female Sovereigns; The Young Man's own Book; A Manual of Politeness, Intellectual Improvement and moral deportment. [Transcriber's note: This advertisement was followed by another from the same vendor, in the same column, for: "Books! Books!"]

Article no. 465 Subject: Education
Ref. December 18, 1832; pg. 3, col. 5

Select Classical School.
J.B. CHASE

Will recommence his School on the 19th instant, and hopes to receive the patronage of his friends. He has determined to locate himself permanently in Lockport, as a teacher, and has accordingly purchased the building known as the Exchange Coffee-House, which will be fitted up for   School Purposes.

It must be conceded by all, that this building, both in point of location and convenience, is far preferable to any other in this village. The assembly room will be converted into a school room, and the small upper rooms can be appropriated to the use of such of the larger students as may prefer retirement while preparing their lessons.

In order the better to discharge the important duties of his station, he will procure, as soon as may be, an extensive apparatus, so as to enable him to deliver lectures on the different branches of Philosophy, and illustrate them by ocular demonstrations.

His terms of tuition will be as follows, viz.

For the common branches, such as Reading, Writing, Geography, Arithmetic and Grammar, ... $3 00

For Philosophy in its various branches, ... 3 50

For Book-Keeping and Mathematics, ... 4 00

For the Latin and Greek Languages, ... 4 50

A reasonable deduction will be made to such as may choose to pay tuition in advance.

Suitable assistants, as circumstances may require, will be employed; so that scholars may, not only, not lose their time and money under his care, but acquire such practical knowledge as shall enable them to discharge the duties of life with credit to themselves and honour to their friends.

Lockport, Nov. 7, 1832.

Article no. 466 Subject: Advertisement
Ref. December 18, 1832; pg. 3, col. 5

FOR SALE OR TO RENT—

The Pot and Pearl Ashery situated on Transit-street, and formerly occupied by Hayward & Rawson. Terms reasonable. Apply to E. RAWSON. Sept. 17.

Article no. 467 Subject: Advertisement
Ref. December 18, 1832; pg. 3, col. 5

S.G. SCOTT.
Barber and Fashionable Hair Cutter.

Has opened a shop on Main-street, opposite F. Northam's Store. S.G.S. flatters himself, that from his practice in New-York city, to merit a share of public patronage. N.B. Razors honed in a first rate manner.

Lockport, Nov. 6, 1832.

Article no. 468	Subject: Notice
Ref. December 18, 1832; pg. 3, col. 5	

Caution.

The Public are cautioned against discounting or purchasing a certain note for Three Hundred Dollars, made by J.D. Cooper, dated the 15th October, 1832, payable at the Lockport Bank, six months after date. The said note was lost or stolen in the city of New-York, about the 1st of November. A capy [sic] of said note can be seen by applying to ROGERS & BROWN. Dec. 5.

Article no. 469	Subject: Advertisement
Ref. December 18, 1832; pg. 3, col. 6	

COOKE & STOW.
Attorneys at Law.
Lewiston, Niagara Co., N.Y.
June, 1832.

Article no. 470	Subject: Advertisement
Ref. December 18, 1832; pg. 3, col. 6	

NEW AND CHEAP GOODS.

The subscribers are receiving from New-York a first rate assortment of

Goods

suited to the season; and having purchased them at the present unusually low prices, they are prepared to sell them lower than they have ever been sold in this place.

Their assortment is general, and well selected: and they would solicit those who purchase Goods for cash, to call and examine their assortment: and they hereby are assured that they shall have goods at least as low as at any store in Lockport.

SETH PARSONS & Co.
Lockport, May 29th [or 20th], 1832.

Article no. 471	Subject: Advertisement
Ref. December 18, 1832; pg. 3, col. 6	

FOWLING PIECES.

A Few first rate English Fowling Pieces, part Percussion Locks, for sale by
[HOUSE & BOUGHTON. Oct. 30.]
[Transcriber's note: This advertisement was followed by another for the same vendor, in the same column, for: "Cloths and Cassimeres, &c."]

Article no. 472	Subject: Notice
Ref. December 18, 1832; pg. 4, col. 2	

Extract: SHERIFF'S SALE.

By virtue of a writ of Fieri Facias, issued out of the Supreme Court of Judicature of the state of New-York, and to me directed and delivered, against the goods and chattels, lands and tenements, of Daniel Washburn (now deceased) and Otis Hathaway, I have seized and taken all those several pieces or parcels of land, situate and lying in the village of Lockport, in the county of Niagara, hereinafter mentioned and described, viz: All that certain piece or parcel of land situate in said village of Lockport, being part or parcel of farm lot No. 12, in the 14th section of Township No. 14, in the 6th range of townships, and which may be known and described as the middle part of a certain village lot in said village, known and distinguished [on a map made for Jared Comstock and others] by Jesse P. Haines, Surveyor, and filed in the office of the Clerk of the county of Niagara, as village lot No. 2, on the south side of Main-street, and on the westerly side of the canal in said village, and bounded as follows—{Notice includes description of boundaries.} [bounds, in part, a lot deeded by Hathaway to Jonathan Chase, 2 July 1829, and also a lot deeded by Hathaway to Halstead H. Parker, 21 November 1829,] which last mentioned deed is recorded in Niagara County Records, Book of Deeds No. 5, on page 112; {Notice includes further description of land.} And also that certain other piece or parcel of land in said village, being part and parcel of farm lot No. 10, in the 14th section of township No. 14, in the 6th range, and known and distinguished on the engraved map of said village, made by Jesse P. Haines, Surveyor, and filed in the office of the clerk of the county of Niagara, as village lot number two hundred and twenty-eight, on the southerly side of Market-street in said village—reference being had to said map:—And also village lot number two hundred and seventy-seven, on the north side of said Market-street, according to said engraved map—reference being thereto had: And also all that certain piece or parcel of land in said village, being part of said farm lot number ten, and bounded as follows: {Notice includes description of boundaries.} And also village lot number one and three, on the north side of Union-street, in said village, according to said engraved map; And also village lots number four, eight, and ten, on the south side of Chesnut-street, in said village, according to said engraved map: And also village lot number eighteen, on the west side of East Fifth-street, according to said engraved map: And also village lot number eight, on the west side of a street without name, running from Union-street to Market-street, at the west end of Mechanic-street, according to said map: And also that certain piece or parcel of land, situate in said village, being part of farm lot number eight, in the fourteenth section of township number fourteen, in the sixth range, bounded as follows {Notice includes description of boundaries.} [bounds in part:] a certain tract of land conveyed to one Joseph Patterson by Jared Comstock and wife, by deed dated [8 February 1827], which deed is recorded in Niagara County Records, Book of Deeds No. 3, on pages 314 and 315; {Notice includes further description of boundaries.} Which several pieces and parcels of land, and all the right, title, interest, claim and demand of the said Otis Hathaway of, in and to the same, with the appurtenances thereto belonging, I shall expose to sale, at public Auction or Vendue, as the law directs, at the house kept by J.W. Witbeck, known as the Eagle Tavern, in Lockport, 12 January 1833.

JOHN PHILLIPS, late Sheriff.

Article no. 473	Subject: Notice
Ref. December 18, 1832; pg. 4, col. 5	

SHERIFF'S SALE.

By virtue of a writ of fieri facias, issued out of the supreme court of judicature of the state of New-York, and to me directed and delivered, against the goods and chattels, lands and tenements, of Anson Smith, I have seized and taken the following piece or parcel of land, viz.—All that piece or parcel of land, situate and lying in the village of Lockport, in the county of Niagara, known and described as the east three fourths of a certain village lot in said village, known and described on a certain supplementary map or survey of a part of said village of Lockport, made for the proprietors by Jesse P. Haines, surveyor, as village lot Number Five, on the north side of Main-street, in the block next east of the Friend's Meeting-house, in said village, reference being had to said map—the said land hereby conveyed, being the whole of said village lot number Five, according to said map, except a strip of one rod wide from off the west side thereof—All of which I shall expose to sale as the law directs, at the tavern or inn called the Eagle Tavern, now kept by J.W. Witbeck, in the village of Lockport, on Saturday, the 29th day of December, 1832, at 10 o'clock in the forenoon of that day. Dated at Lockport, the 13th day of November, A.D. 1832.

HIRAM McNEIL, Sheriff.

Article no. 474	Subject: Education
Ref. January 23, 1833; pg. 1, col. 6	

Extract: COMMON SCHOOLS OF NEW-YORK.

The annual report required of the Secretary of State, as Superintendent of Common Schools, was made to the Assembly on Monday. The following extracts from this document exhibit a most gratifying view of the progress and results of the system of common school instruction in this State:—[Outline of the document: There are 55 organized counties, and 811 towns and wards in the State, and returns have been received from the clerks of all the counties. There are 9,600 school districts organized in the State; 8,941 of these districts have made their annual reports. The Trustees are required to furnish a census of the children over five and under sixteen years of age, who reside in their respective districts on the last day of December each year; and also the number of children taught in each district during the year ending on that day: in the districts from which reports have been received, there were, on 31 December 1831, 508,878 children over five and under sixteen years of age; 494,959 scholars taught in the same districts during the year, in the common schools of the State; and, 8,941 district schools have been kept open for the reception of pupils an average period of eight out of twelve months. 267 new districts have been formed during 1831. School moneys [sic] received by the Commissioners of the several towns, and paid to the Trustees of the several districts, amount to $305,582.78, $100,000 of which were paid from the State Treasury, $188,384.53 raised by a tax on the property of the inhabitants of the several towns in the State, and $17,198.25 derived from local funds possessed by some towns. The amount paid for teachers' wages, over and above the public money appointed by the Commissioners, is $358,320.17. This sum, when added to the public money, gives a total of $663,902.95 paid for teachers' wages; except about $60,000 in the city of New-York, which is raised by a special tax, and applied to the erection of school houses. Further statistics about the productive capital raised, the perpetuity of and increases to the school fund, balance of school fund capital uninvested, amount of bonds and mortgages.] Those who founded our common school system, never contemplated that the public funds would at any time yield a revenue adequate to the support of such an extensive establishment, &c. The voluntary contribution of the inhabitants of the school districts, form so important a portion of the means which are necessary to give effect to the school system, &c. {Article includes further statistics from the returns.} These returns show, that where the State, or the school fund, pays one dollar for teachers' wages, the inhabitant of the town by a tax upon his property, pays $1.28 cents, ($60,000 deducted for New York) and by voluntary contribution in the school district where he resides, $3.58 cents for the same object, and the proportion of 17 cents is derived from the local school fund. {Further statistics about the grand total of expenses, $1,125,162.45,} expended annually for the support of the common schools of the State. {Followed by summary remarks about the sources of funds;} and the residue, neatly sixth-elevenths, (being $605,799,) is paid voluntarily by the parents and guardians of the scholars, for the balance of their school bills, (after applying the public money,) and for school books.

Article no. 475	Subject: Crime
Ref. January 23, 1833; pg. 2, col. 2

Auburn Prison.—The annual report of the inspectors of this prison, was made to the Senate yesterday. The total amount of the earnings of the convicts for the year; [sic] is stated at $41,833.47; and for the expenditures of the general support of the prison at $38,305.31, leaving a balance in favour of the prison of $3,528.16. In addition to this balance, credited with the expense of keeping, feeding and clothing about 100 convicts who have been employed since the first of June last in the erection of the new cells in the south wing, whose labour has not been taken into the account of profit to the prison; and also the erection of a workshop 100 feet by 40. The number of convicts in the prison at the commencement of the year, was 646; received during the year, 192; discharged by expiration of sentence 115, by pardon 27, one by order of the supreme court, and 27 by death; leaving at the prison on the 1st inst. 683. Of the number received during the year, 60 were from the prison at Sing-Sing. The 200 cells directed by an act of the last session to be erected in the south wing of the prison, are completed and were occupied by convicts on the 1st inst.—*Argus*.

Article no. 476	Subject: Transportation
Ref. January 23, 1833; pg. 2, col. 4

Extract: The expenses on the canals of this state, last year, amounted to nearly seven hundred thousand dollars—and some [of] our eastern brethren of the quill wonder how it could happen that they were so great. To us the wonder is, when we look at the course adopted by the canal commissioners, they were no more! ... Indeed, so exclusively for political effect is the business of the canal transacted, that we are credibly informed the very dirt heavers must buy their flour and meat and other necessaries from a certain highly favoured brawling "hickory pole" grocer, no matter what his prices may be, or make up their minds to take a discharge! These are matters which call loudly for inquiry into and reform; but—"when the sky falls we shall catch larks!"
[Transcriber's note: This article appears in the Editorial columns. Length, almost 1 column.]

Article no. 477	Subject: Government
Ref. January 23, 1833; pg. 2, col. 5

Azariah C. Flagg, late Secretary of State, has been promoted to the rank of Comptroller of this state, in place of Silas Wright, Jr., promoted to the U.S. Senate—and John A. Dix, late Adjutant General, has been promoted to the vacant Secretaryship. Thus the wooden bowls are crawling up very rapidly from little to big, "according to the usages of the republican party"—which means, rotation from one office to another, according to quality and price!

The caucus has not yet settled who is to be Adjutant General in place of Mr. Dix. Only one can have it, though many want it. "A was an apple pie: B bit it, C cut it," &c., runs the nursery tale—and so is it with the Adjutant Generalship, among the nine hundred and ninety-nine patriots who are fishing for it. He who has the most pliant conscience will get it—but as there is so large a field to select from, it will require a considerable degree of political nicety to decide this important point!
[Transcriber's note: This article appears in the Editorial columns. Length, almost 1 column.]

Article no. 478	Subject: Editorial
Ref. January 23, 1833; pg. 2, col. 5

Enos T. Throop, late governor of the great state of New-York, "an empire within itself," has certainly been "hoisted down" to the post of Naval Officer of the port of New-York, the Senate of the U.S. having confirmed his nomination! Whon [sic] Enos looks up to the elevated point where he was once perched, he must certainly wonder how he got there! But, said the worm to the eagle, "I crawled!"

Article no. 479	Subject: Agriculture
Ref. January 23, 1833; pg. 2, col. 5

Congress is now busily engaged in debating the propitiatory tariff bill, to the exclusion of almost all other business. Let this bill pass, and if wheat is not as low as fifty cents per bushel, within a year, in the county of Niagara, our farmers will be indebted for their good fortune to some other cause than the good will of our Jackson rulers. [Transcriber's note: This article appears in the Editorial columns. Length, almost 1 column.]

Article no. 480	Subject: Temperance
Ref. January 23, 1833; pg. 2, col. 5

Extract: COUNTY TEMPERANCE SOCIETY.

The annual meeting of the Niagara county Temperance Society, was held at the Brick Meeting House, in this village, on the 18th of December last, when a report was made by the corresponding Secretary, and a very able address delivered by Gen. A.H. Porter, after which the following officers were chosen for the ensuing year:— [Listed, below.]

On motion, it was Resolved, That Henry Norton, Esq. member of Assembly from this county, be a delegate from this Society, to the New-York State Society, at their annual meeting. {Article includes further resolutions about next meeting, &c.}

- Bancroft, Wiley; chosen one of the Directors of the society.
- Belden, Charles; chosen one of the Vice-Presidents.
- Daniels, William P.; chosen one of the Vice-Presidents.
- Dayton, Nathan; chosen one of the Directors.
- Gooding, John; chosen one of the Directors.
- Hinman, A.G.; chosen one of the Vice-Presidents.
- Hitchcock, S.F.; chosen one of the Vice-Presidents.
- M'Collum, Joel, Hon.; chosen President of the County Temperance Society.
- Norton, Henry, Esq.; member of Assembly from this county; nominated to be a delegate from this Society, to the New-York State Society, at their annual meeting.
- Parsons, Seth; chosen one of the Directors.
- Porter, A.H.; chosen one of the Vice-Presidents; delivered a very able address.
- Southworth, Isaac; chosen one of the Directors.
- Spalding, L.A.; chosen one of the Vice-Presidents.
- Tucker, M.H.; Corresponding Secretary; recorded the minutes of the Annual meeting.
- Works, Samuel; chosen one of the Directors.

Article no. 481   Subject: Religion
Ref. January 23, 1833; pg. 3, col. 1

NOTICE.—A meeting of the subscribers to the Free Church, will be held in the Hall of the Exchange Buildings, in this village, on the 29th inst., at 6 o'clock, P.M., for the appointment of a Building Committee, and the transaction of such other business in relation to said Church, as by the meeting may be deemed necessary.
JOHN GOODING, WILLIS PECK. Jan. 22.

Article no. 482   Subject: Advertisement
Ref. January 23, 1833; pg. 3, col. 1

TO PRINTERS—A RARE OFFER.
The health of the undersigned is so poor, that his physician has decided he must relinquish his business. He therefore offers the establishment of The Gem, for sale—together with the Job Office attached. The Gem is now in its fifth year, and enjoys an extensive and profitable patronage; as does also his Job Office, both of which are situated in the best location in the village of Rochester, N.Y. To any one who can pay one half of the money down, and give good paper for the remainder on time, this presents one of the best opportunities in Printing, in western New-York. Letters, post-paid, will be attended to—but it were much better, and I should prefer it, if person[s] wishing to purchase, could call personally upon the proprietor, and examine for themselves.
Address, EDWIN SCRANTOM,
Jan. 1, 1833. Rochester, N.Y.

Article no. 483   Subject: Marriage
Ref. January 23, 1833; pg. 3, col. 2

MARRIED—On Thursday evening last, in this village, by the Rev. Mr. Myers, Robert H. Stevens, Esq., to Miss Sarah Smith.

Article no. 484   Subject: Advertisement
Ref. January 23, 1833; pg. 3, col. 2

BOOKS lately received by N. LEONARD:
Langhorn's Plutarch, complete in one vol.;
Josephus, in one and two vols.;
Newton's works, 2 vols.;
Chalmer's works, 1 vol.;
Channing's Discourses and Review;
McIntosh's Ethical Philosophy;
The Writings of Jefferson and Gou. [sic] Morris;
Stewart's Commentary on the Romans;
Burton's Anatomy of Melancholy;
Jones' Church History;
Percy Anecdotes;
Renwick's Elements of Mechanicks.
Lockport, Jan. 23, 1833.

Article no. 485   Subject: Advertisement
Ref. January 23, 1833; pg. 3, col. 2

Extract: LEONARD'S OFFICE.
{Advertisement includes announcement of winning lottery ticket numbers.} Leonard expects to shell out a few more of the good prizes in the above scheme. Call and prepare yourselves for cold weather. Purchasers can be supplied with packages in all the schemes. N.B. Persons holding Prize Tickets can have the Cash at sight by presenting them at the above office. Jan. 23.

Article no. 486   Subject: Notice
Ref. January 23, 1833; pg. 3, col. 2

PICKED up in the street, a few days ago, a Silk Pocket Handkerchief. The owner can have it, by calling at this office. Jan. 23.

Article no. 487   Subject: Social Welfare
Ref. January 23, 1833; pg. 3, col. 2

NOTICE is hereby given, that application will be made to the legislature of the state of New-York in its present session, by the Board of Supervisors of the county of Niagara, for the passage of a law authorizing the building of a poor-house for the use of said county—also, for the passage of a law authorizing the said Supervisors to borrow a sum not exceeding six thousand dollars, to build the said poor-house—and also, for the passage of a law, authorizing the said Board to raise the said money so to be expended, by a tax upon the said county, at such time or times as they may elect to do so.—Jan. 23d, 1833.

Article no. 488	Subject: Advertisement
Ref. January 23, 1833; pg. 3, col. 2	

GOODS at Auction.

The stock of Goods recently belonging to M.H. TUCKER, will be sold at

Auction,

on Monday, February 4th. The sale to commence at 10 o'clock, at the Store heretofore occupied by him in Lockport, Upper Town,

For sums under $25, cash;

For sums above $25 and under $50, at 60 days credit;

For sums above $50 and under $100, three month credit;

For sums over $100 at six months credit;

In all cases approved endorsed Notes, and for sums over $50, Notes payable at the Lockport Bank.

The said stock of Goods will be sold at Cost, at the stores heretofore occupied by him in Upper and Lower Lockport, until the first of February next. Those who wish to avail themselves of the opportunity ef [sic] procuring Cheap Goods, will do well to call at either of the above mentioned places and make their purchases.

EDWARD BISSELL, SIDNEY SMITH, Assignees.

Lockport, Jan. 16, 1833.

Article no. 489	Subject: Notice
Ref. January 23, 1833; pg. 3, col. 2	

STRAY CATTLE.

Came into the inclosure of the subscriber, about the first of December last, two yearling Cattle: one a light red Steer, with a little white on the forehead—the other a reddish brindled Heifer, a little white in the forehead and on both hind legs. The owner is desired to prove his property, pay the charges, and take them away.

IRA GREGORY. Cambria, Jan. 16, 1833.

Article no. 490	Subject: Advertisement
Ref. January 23, 1833; pg. 3, col. 2	

NOTICE.

Lockport, Jan. 9, 1833.

By the caption you see a NOTICE I give,
That in Lockport myself and family live;
And further, that we by industrious strife,
Are engaged to amend our condition in life.
For means, we like others, concur with our taste,
Our time we hope therefore will not run to waste;
So various, indeed, are our branches of trade,
That, on my part, Trunks, Traps and Valises are made.
I also the Ladies of Lockport would tell,
That I make Bandboxes that look very well;
And they are aware, the convenience of such
To the female, cannot be applauded too much.
I now would invite the public attention,
To that you will see I did not above mention—
That we make Stocks and Collars, of all sizes and fashion,
For old men and young, in town, state or nation:
We also would tell all who new clothes would get,
That we can make cloth into garments that fit—
We mean, if they're cut right before they're brot here;
For the make or the finish you need not to fear.
Now a compliment for you my pen I'll employ,
Its effect on your minds I hope to enjoy;
Your custom and cash we wish and solicit,
And invite from each one at least one short visit.
The place where to find us it's proper to state,
And I'll tell in a moment—have patience to wait—
'Tis opposite the office where Uncle Sam's man
Hands letters to all those who call, if he can.
Now your very respectful servant and friend
I'll remain, if I can, until my days end—
Until you with feelings of grief, or of joy,
Will say to yourselves, Oh! where is—LE ROY.

Article no. 491	Subject: Politics
Ref. March 20, 1833; pg. 1, col. 1	

Extract: COLONEL STONE'S LETTER.

We find the following letter from the pen of Col. Stone, upon the subject of freemasonry, travelling the rounds of the Free Press. To whom this letter was addressed, we know not. It is a good one, however, and should be generally read.

New-York, April 2, 1832.

Sir,—It is a subject of no ordinary satisfaction to me, and will doubtless afford still greater relief to yourself, to find that somewhat desultory communication, has at length been brought to a point at which it can be said in the words of the wise preacher of old, "let us bear the conclusion of the whole matter." At the close of the rapid survey of speculative Freemasonry in which the preceding essays were commenced, a variety of reasons were given why in my humble opinion, the institution ought to be totally abandoned, on its own merits, independently of any charges of mal-conduct that might have been preferred against it. ... I am constrained to say, that in full view of the facts which have been disclosed in the preceding irregular narrative, the institution of Freemasonry ought to be abolished for its demerits—and that for the following reasons:—{Article includes discussion of reasons.}

WM. L. STONE. [Length: 1-1/2 columns.]

Article no. 492 Subject: Court
Ref. March 20, 1833; pg. 1, col. 2

Extract: From the *Chenango Telegraph*.

CHARLES MEDBURY, Esq.—In compliance with our promise, we this week give a sketch of the trial and conviction of this gentleman, at the late General Sessions for this county. The indictment is probably the first of the nature ever found in the county; and as the offence, and the principles settled by the verdict, are somewhat new, we deem it proper to notice it at more length, that the community might know what their rights, and justices what their duties, are. The indictment, as before stated, was for wilfully refusing to hear a complaint made before him, as a justice, against a person charged with a crime, and refusing to examine the complainant on oath. {Article includes description of case and witnesses called.} [Medbury kept an office in New-Berlin. Names mentioned: Burwell, Reeve Dilley, Mr. Hancox, Mr. Hyde, Squire Pike, Anthony Roberts, Pardon Simmons.] The jury after deliberation found the defendant guilty. The verdict settles the fact, that a justice of the peace cannot shuffle off a complaint made to him by a respectable citizen, with impunity; but that it is his duty to examine the complainant on oath and then decide whether it is proper to issue process—not to decide peremptorily and without examination. [Length, 2/3 column.]

Article no. 493 Subject: Temperance
Ref. March 20, 1833; pg. 1, col. 6

Cost of Vice in New-York.—The following article on this subject, we copy from the *Genius of Temperance*.

"It appears, that the expenditures for the almshouse, bridewell and penitentiary, charities, coroner's fees and expenses, courts, police and watch, (to say nothing of the sum disposed of by the board of health, which is $102,575.87,) amount to $278,758.91,—nearly the whole of which is paid for the support of City Vices! one of the prominent sources of which is the vending of strong drink! But this is paid for—and the public, of course, must not complain! Yes—Paid for! 'How much are we paid?' do you ask? Why–why–a considerable part of $22,178! And this is to satisfy the patient public—this is to refund the $275,000 drawn by the tax gatherer from the people's pockets—this is to cover the multiplied enormities growing out of this system of blood!—this is to remunerate for the untold and inexpressible griefs, and distresses, and woundings of the family and domestic circles! The 'beauties of the licenses laws!'—how much more beautiful do they appear, as they are unfolded to the gaze of the public!["]

Article no. 494 Subject: Agriculture
Ref. March 20, 1833; pg. 2, col. 1

Extract: From the *Rochester Inquirer*.
To the Farmers of Western New York.

Having, as I trust, in a former number conclusively refuted the exploded dogma that duties on goods, such as are manufactured by our own citizens, is a "tax," but that on the contrary, that every article which has been efficiently protected, has invariably been furnished to the consumer, at very greatly reduced prices, I proceed to examine further the effects of the retaliating, and prohibitory duties imposed by Great Britain on all the productions of the grain-growing states, and to show that they have greatly reduced our export to that country (excepting such articles as cotton, rice, &c.) to a degree of degrading insignificance, and causing the most intense distress to the farming interest, and depressing and suffering to all classes of our citizens. {Article includes the Essay.} This condensed view of the subject, will enable the farmer to form some adequate idea of the incalculable importance of a permanent home market for the products of our own industry, and for this object it is presented. The Constitution says that "Congress shall have power to regulate commerce with foreign nations," and by fostering and protecting our own skill and industry, in the establishment of manufactories for furnishing ourselves with 30 millions of fabrics annually, otherwise imported from foreign nations which persevere in excluding all the products of the northern states from their dominions, such a market has already been secured in the manufacturing states. ... Shall we, then, support foreign industry, by consuming foreign fabrics? or, in the language of Thomas Jefferson, "place the manufacturer by the side of the farmer, that they may wrest the weapon of distress from the foreign hand, which has so long wantonly wielded it?" Jefferson added, "that he who now was against domestic manufactures, must be for reducing us to a state of dependence on that nation. I am proud to say that I am not one of them." It is difficult to repress the rising of an honest indignation, which must swell the bosom of every man who has a drop of American blood in him, when he contemplates the following fact—it is indeed humiliating, yet it is instructing: {Article includes statistics of exports and imports in 1825 and 1826.} Farmers and mechanics, be not deceived [by] the sycophants of "party." Be yours a loftier patriotism—a more elevated purpose. Your numerical power, renders you the peculiar guardians of these sacred rights.—Cherish and sustain them, as the pledges of your independence. Upon you their preservation or destruction depends.

COLBERT. [Length, 1+ columns.]

Article no. 495   Subject: Transportation
Ref. March 20, 1833; pg. 2, col. 2

Extract: RATES OF TOLL. At a Meeting of the Canal Board, at the Comptroller's office in the city of Albany, on the 9th of March, 1833, the following rates of Toll were established, in lieu of all rates heretofore established by this Board. {List includes tolls for items subsumed under the following categories: Provisions; Iron, Minerals, Oars [sic], &c.; Furs, Peltries, Skins, &c.; Furniture, &c.; Stone, Slate, &c.; Lumber, Wood, &c.; Agricultural Productions, &c.; Articles not enumerated; and, Boats and Passengers.} [Length, 1-1/2 columns.]

Article no. 496   Subject: Education
Ref. March 20, 1833; pg. 2, col. 3

Extract: Literature Fund.—The Regents of the University of this State, have made a distribution of $10,000 of the income of this fund for the last year, among the several Incorporated Academies entitled to the same. The sum of $1,250 is distributed in each Senatorial district. The following is the amount awarded to the several institutions within the 7th and 8th districts: {Amounts were listed for the following districts and schools: Seventh District: Auburn, Cayuga, Canandaigua, Onondaga, Ontario Female Seminary, Ovid, Pompey, Yates county Academy and Female Seminary; and, Eighth District: Buffalo L. and S. Academy, Fredonia, Gaines, Leweston [sic], Middlebury, Monroe, Rochester High School, Springville.}

Article no. 497   Subject: Agriculture
Ref. March 20, 1833; pg. 2, col. 4

TOLLS.

By reference to another column, it will be seen that the rates of toll on the Erie Canal have been materially lessened. The difference on a bushel of wheat, from this place to Albany, is about 3 1-2 cents—and on a barrel of flour about 14 cents.

For this reduction, our farmers are much indebted to the exertions of the HON. ALBERT H. TRACY, of Buffalo, Senator from this district. [Transcriber's note: This article appears in the Editorial columns.]

Article no. 498   Subject: Court
Ref. March 20, 1833; pg. 2, col. 4

COUNTY JUDGES. The governor and Senate have confirmed the nominations for judges of Niagara Co., made by the Sub-Regency of Lockport. Only the whole Bench are freemasons of a high order! [Transcriber's note: This article appears in the Editorial columns.]

Article no. 499   Subject: Politics
Ref. March 20, 1833; pg. 2, col. 4

Extract: TOWN MEETINGS.

We are pleased to perceive that our antimasonic friends in other counties in this state, are "up and doing," and seem determined to show, in the results of the spring elections, that our cause has "died away" after the old fashion! ... We mentioned, a week or two ago, that in Broome county three towns had been heard from, in all which Democratic Antimasonry was gloriously triumphant. Since then, two more towns have been heard from: to wit: Town of Vesta—Antimasonic ticket elected by ninety majority! ... Town of Barker—the good cause triumphant by forty majority. Good! thus far all the towns in Broome are antimasonic to the core. There are four more yet to hear from. From Oswego county the news is cheering. We write it down as follows: {Article includes description of Antimasonic vs. Masonic balances of power in Towns of Scriba, New-Haven, Hannibal, Richland, and Oswego.} Madison county. In this county, the masonic presses have been for some time boasting, that "the prospects of Antimasonry were blasted for ever." {Article includes description of Antimasonic vs. Masonic political balance in Casenovia, Fenner, De Ruyter, Georgetown, and Lebanon, followed by similar paragraphs for Oneida and Lawrence counties.}
[Transcriber's note: This article appears in the Editorial columns.]

Article no. 500   Subject: Transportation
Ref. March 20, 1833; pg. 2, col. 4

Jonas Earll once swore that he knew nothing about his business as a Canal Commissioner. The Legislature, we perceive, are about appointing an additional acting Commissioner. Had they not better, while their hand is in, appoint an efficient one in place of Earll? [Transcriber's note: This article appears in the Editorial columns.]

Article no. 501   Subject: Temperance
Ref. March 20, 1833; pg. 2, col. 4

Death from Intemperance! Seth Parsons, Esq., coroner, was on Wednesday morning last called to view the body of a man, called John Mason, which was found in the street lifeless. The verdict of the jury was, "chilled to death in state of intoxication." Thus has another victim been added to the thousands which have gone before of that fell destroyer, Intemperance.

Mason is said to have relations in the town of Lewiston.

Article no. 502 Subject: Death
Ref. March 20, 1833; pg. 2, col. 5

From the *Albany Journal.*
DEATH OF GENERAL WADSWORTH.

General William Wadsworth, died at his residence, at Geneseo, Livingston county, on the 6th inst. General W. was one of the Pioneers by whose industry and enterprise, Western New York has been converted from a "waving forest" into Cities, Villages, Grottos and Gardens. He was a man of ardent temperament, warm affections, and generous impulses. We regret that we cannot now avail ourselves of such data of General W's. life, as would enable us to pay an appropriate tribute to the memory of a friend for whom we have long cherished the highest regard. It will be recollected that General Wadsworth, whose Division was called into service to protect the frontier, volunteered to cross the Niagara, ascended the Heights of Queenston, in company with the Spartan Van Rensselaer, and gallantly participated in the dangers and honours of that sanguinary conflict.

The following letter, from a friend, furnishes, briefly, the particulars attending General W's. disease:—

Geneseo, March 7, 1833.

Our old friend General Wadsworth, has closed his earthly labours. He died yesterday afternoon. His attack (which, strange as it may seem considering his active habits, was of the Gout,) commenced about three weeks since; and was from the beginning the more alarming, from the disease not as usual seating itself, but continuing to change its position; it finally settled in his head, and, although not exceedingly painful, has conquered one of the most vigorous constitutions in the world."

Article no. 503 Subject: Religion
Ref. March 20, 1833; pg. 2, col. 5

Mr. Southwick's Lectures on the Bible.—On the evening of Sunday last, Mr. Southwick delivered his first Lecture upon the Bible, to a large and respectable audience, who were, as far as we have the means of judging, highly pleased with the able and instructive manner in which he treated his subject. His second Lecture will be delivered on Wednesday evening next, and we earnestly recommend to all who admire genius or talent, to be present, if within their power. We believe, and are not singular in the opinion, that no one who attends these the [sic] Lectures will regret it.—*Wash. Co. Post.*

Article no. 504 Subject: Religion
Ref. March 20, 1833; pg. 2, col. 5

Church Burnt.—On the morning of the 28th ult. the Associate Reformed Church of Caledonia, of which the Rev. D. McLaren is Pastor, was destroyed by fire. It had recently undergone a thorough repair, and has cost eight or $9000. The loss will be severely felt by the congregation.—*Geneva Gazette.*

Article no. 505 Subject: Accident
Ref. March 20, 1833; pg. 2, col. 6

Fatal Accident.—We learn that a young Dutch woman, employed in Bear's Tavern, two miles north of this City, while engaged in carrying a heavy stick of fire wood on her shoulder, yesterday, she slipped and fell upon the floor, when the wood struck the side of her head, causing almost instantaneous death.—*Buffalo Pat.* Feb. 26.

Article no. 506 Subject: Temperance
Ref. March 20, 1833; pg. 2, col. 6

Generous Liberality.—The Hon. Stephen Rensselear [sic], has paid for 5000 copies of the *Temperance Almanac*, to be distributed in Albany city and county.

Article no. 507 Subject: Notice
Ref. March 20, 1833; pg. 2, col. 6

From the *Rochester Observer.*

Wilberforce Colony U.C.—From information derived from gentlemen in this village, whose character and information on the subject entitle them to public credence, we stated last week, our full confidence that Mr. Steward is a duly authorized manager of this colony; we now copy from *Western Recorder*, the following

CAUTION TO THE PUBLIC.

The public are cautioned against one Israel Lewis, who has formerly been emploved [sic] as agent of the Wilberforce settlement in Upper Canada. The said Lewis has obtained in this city, at different times, upwards of fifteen hundred dollars, for the above named settlement; of which money he has paid over short of one hundred dollars, and gives no account of the funds collected by him. Editors of other papers are requested to give the above an insertion.

ARTHUR TAPPAN. New-York, Feb. 16, 1833.

Article no. 508 Subject: Agriculture
Ref. March 20, 1833; pg. 2, col. 6

Notice to Farmers.

The undersigned Standing Committee, appointed at a Convention held in Monroe, respectfully recommend to the inhabitants of Livingston, Genesee, Erie, Niagara, Ontario, Orleans[,] Wayne, and Monroe, who are opposed to the Milling and Forwarding Coalitions, which obstruct the fair and regular course of business, that a Convention, consisting of two or more Delegates from each town of the above counties, be held at Stanley's Tavern in Le Roy, on the 26th day of March next, at 10 o'clock, A.M., to adopt such measures as shall be deemed advisable.

All printers in the above counties, friendly to the objects of this notice, are requested to give it publicity in their papers.

ISAAC LACEY, SAMUEL P. GOULD,
SIMEON M. COE, JOEL WHEELER,
OLIVER CULVER, Committee. February 23, 1833.

Article no. 509   Subject: Temperance
Ref. March 20, 1833; pg. 2, col. 6

TEMPERANCE NOTICE.

The Board of Managers, of the Niagara County Temperance Society, are requested to meet at the office of Lyman A. Spalding Thursday evening next, 21st inst., at half past 6 o'clock.

A general attendance is requested.

March 16th, 1833. M.H. TUCKER Sec'ry.

Article no. 510   Subject: Advertisement
Ref. March 20, 1833; pg. 2, col. 6

COAL WANTED.

2000 Bushels charcoal wanted, at the subscriber's Lumber yard.

L.A. SPALDING. Lockport, 3d mo. 7, 1833.

Article no. 511   Subject: Advertisement
Ref. March 20, 1833; pg. 2, col. 6

FRUIT TREES.

The subscriber wishes to inform the public, that he has on hand a good assortment of

Fruit Trees,

(particularly apples,) which he offers for sale on the most reasonable terms.

MICHAEL ROBSON.

Johnson Creek, 3d mo. 12th 1833.

Article no. 512   Subject: Advertisement
Ref. March 20, 1833; pg. 2, col. 6

Highly Important to Farmers.

The subscriber has purchased the entire

WARREN's

Improved Threshing Machine,

for the counties of Orleans and Niagara, which surpasses anything of the kind hitherto introduced.

Those wishing to purchase either rights or machines will find it for their interest to examine the article before purchasing any other[.] For further particulars they will please call upon Messrs. Clark Fairman & Co. of Medina, or Mr. Samuel Works, of Lockport: and at both of these places they will find the machines on opening of navigation.

LEVI BEEBEE. March 20th, 1833.

Article no. 513   Subject: Advertisement
Ref. March 20, 1833; pg. 2, col. 6

Valuable Farm for Sale.

The subscriber offers for sale, her well known Farm, situated about a mile and a half east of the village of Lockport, a short distance south of the Batavia road. This farm contains 200 acres—80 of which are under good improvement. The buildings consist of two comfortable

Dwellings,

and a good Frame Barn, 30 by 40 feet.—There is a small creek running through the farm, nearly in the center, which contains water most of the year. There is also a good orchard, of the best selected and grafted trees, of almost every variety of fruit. The land is of a superior quality.

The stock on the farm will also be sold, consisting of 25 head of cattle, 3 horses, and a number of hogs.

The above property will be sold at private sale. Inquire of the subscriber on the premises.

SARAH PERRY. March 20, 1833.

Article no. 514   Subject: Advertisement
Ref. March 20, 1833; pg. 2, col. 6

Seed and Plant Store, &c.

The subscriber begs leave to inform the Ladies and Gentlemen of Lockport, and its vicinity, that, on or about the first of May next, he will open for sale, at the old store of House and Boughton, a very rare selection of

Flower Seeds and Green House Plants,

all imported last fall, and warranted to be of the best quality and varieties.

JOHN B. SMITH. Lockport, March 13th, 1833.

Article no. 515   Subject: Advertisement
Ref. March 20, 1833; pg. 3, col. 1

REDUCED PRICES.

Earthenware, China, Glass, and Looking-Glasses.

THOMAS J. BARROW & Co., Importers, No. 88 Water-st., New-York, are now receiving their spring patterns of

Earthernware, China, &c.

by last arrivals from Liverpool. Their stock comprises every variety in the line, and is surpassed by none in extent or quality. They have made such arrangements in England for the purchase of their goods, as enable them to hold out the strongest inducements to merchants dealing in the line, particularly those buying for cash or city acceptances, who will find it greatly to their interests to call, as they are determined to sell at the very lowest prices which it is possible for the article to be put.

New-York, March 7th, 1833.

Article no. 516 Subject: Notice
Ref. March 20, 1833; pg. 3, col. 1

NOTICE—The subscriber hereby forbids all persons harbouring or trusting any person on his account, without a written order under his hand, as he will pay no debts contracted without such authority by any one of his family. Dated at Royalton, the 11th day of March, 1833.
DAVID CHASE.

Article no. 517 Subject: Notice
Ref. February 21, 1832; pg. 4, col. 3

SIX CENTS REWARD!

Ran or was inveigled away from the subscriber, on the 9th inst., a bound boy called Calvin Brown, aged 10 years. All persons are forbid harbouring or trusting said boy. The above Reward, but no charges, will be paid to the person returning him.
ALANSON ARNOLD. Royalton, Feb. 9, 1832.

Article no. 518 Subject: Social Welfare
Ref. March 20, 1833; pg. 3, col. 1

NOTICE.

The Superintendents of the Poor in the county of Niagara, will receive sealed proposals, until Monday, 25th day of the present month, for a Physician and Surgeon to attend at the Poor-House, in said county, for one year, commencing on the 13th of May next—the Physician to furnish all necessary medicines and medical aid, to all the paupers at the Poor-House, for the keeper and his family, and also for all the paupers within the corporate bounds of the village of Lockport. He must attend once in each week, on a certain day, and as much oftener as may be necessary. The Superintendents will attend in the room over the store of Mr. F. Bissell, on Main-street, at 9 o'clock, A.M., on the 25th inst. for the purpose of closing the contract, and transacting such other business as may come before them.
By order of the Superintendents. March 13th.
G. BACON, Clerk.

Article no. 519 Subject: Advertisement
Ref. March 20, 1833; pg. 3, col. 1

BEDSTEAD FACTORY,
AND TURNING.

The subscriber has commenced the business of
TURNING WOOD
of all kinds, to suit customers, as also the Manufacturing of Bedsteads, of various descriptions.

His Saw-mill is in good order, and sawing done on usual terms—either for a share, or 2s. 6d. per hundred: but if payment is made on or before the 1st day of May next, 2s. per hundred will be received in full for the sawing.

TO RENT.

The subscriber will rent his whole establishment, consisting of a small farm, house, barn, saw-mill and machinery for turning, &c. The building for the machinery is 22 by 40 feet, and will contain two turning lathes, and two circular saws, with a sufficient water power. The whole, or a part will be rented for one or more years, and possession given on the first day of May next.
LYMAN LISCOMB. Royalton, Feb. 28th, 1833.

Article no. 520 Subject: Advertisement
Ref. March 20, 1833; pg. 3, col. 1

SCHOOL BOOKS
For sale by N. LEONARD:

Webster's, Marshall's, Cobb's and Sears' Spelling Books,

Walker's, Webster's, Johnson's, and Cobb's Walker, Dictionaries.

Kirkham's, Murray's, Ingersoll's, Greenleaf's, Cardell's, and Hamlin's Grammars;

Daboll's, Smith's, Colburn's, Ryan's, Emerson's, Willet's, and Ostrander's Arithmetics:—

Olney's, Woodbridge's, Malte Brun's, Hart's, Willard's, Morse and Willet's, Geographies and Atlasses [sic];

Murray's Sequel, Introduction, Key, and Exercises.

English Readers; Historical Readers; Hales' and Goodrich's History U. States;

American First Class Book;

Columbian and National Orators;

French, Latin and Greek Dictionaries,

Grammars and Readers;

Writing and Ciphering Books, &c. &c.

Lockport, March 6th, 1833.

Article no. 521 Subject: Advertisement
Ref. March 20, 1833; pg. 3, col. 1

SCHOOL REWARDS.

N. LEONARD, has for sale a large assortment of Toy Books, Printed and Engraved Tickets, &c.
Lockport, March 6th, 1833.

Article no. 522 Subject: Notice
Ref. March 20, 1833; pg. 3, col. 1

PROCLAMATION.

By Hiram McNeil, Esquire, Sheriff of Niagara County.

By virtue of a writ of venire facias or precept to me directed and delivered.—Notice is hereby given, that a Circuit Court and Court of Oyer and Terminer and General Jail Delivery, will be held at the Court House in the town of Lockport, in and for the county of Niagara, on the first Monday in April next, at ten o'clock in the forenoon of that day; and all persons who will prosecute against persons confined in the said county, are requested to be then and there present to prosecute as may be just; and all persons bound to appear at the said court by recognizance or otherwise, are required to appear thereat; and all Justices of the Peace, and Coroners, and other officers, who have taken any recognizance for the appearance of any person at the said court, or who have taken any inquisition or the examination of any prisoner or witness, are requested to return such recognizances, inquisitions, and examinations to the said court, at the opening thereof—and to be then and there present, with their rolls, records, indictments, and other remembrances, to do the things which to their offices appertain.

HIRAM McNEIL, Sheriff.
Sheriff's Office, Lockport, March 6, 1833.

Article no. 523　　　Subject: Advertisement
Ref. March 20, 1833; pg. 3, col. 1

Clover Seed.

The subscribers have purchased, and will receive, about the 1st of March, 75 Bushels of Pennsylvania Clover Seed, a first rate article. Those wishing to purchase, will do well to delay until they can see it.

ROGERS & BROWN. Feb. 11, 1833.

Article no. 524　　　Subject: Advertisement
Ref. March 20, 1833; pg. 3, col. 1

BROADCLOTHS, &c.

ROGERS & BROWN offer for sale

75 pieces of different coloured Broadcloths, at lower prices than ever before offered in the market, say, from $1.25 to $9 per yard;

20 pcs. of Cassimere, from 7s. to 20s. per yard;

125 do.　Satinets, from　4s. to 8s.　do. do.

Jan. 2, 1833.

Article no. 525　　　Subject: Advertisement
Ref. March 20, 1833; pg. 3, col. 2

Royal Sharpe, M.D.

Respectfully informs the inhabitants of the village of Lockport and its vicinity, that he has recently taken the room on Main-street, No. 3, upstairs, Spalding's buildings—directly over Lyman A. Spalding's office, where prompt attendance, at all hours, may be had to all calls in Physic and Surgery.

Having had the benefit of three public courses in Medical instruction, and several years' experience in practice, he confidently solicits a share of public patronage.

Lockport, Feb. 20, 1833.

Article no. 526　　　Subject: Advertisement
Ref. March 20, 1833; pg. 3, col. 2

BROWN SHIRTINGS.
For sale by the subscribers by the bale
3,500 Yds. of Utica Shirtings,
2,500 do. of Rhode-Island do.
Feb. 11, 1833. ROGERS & BROWN.

Article no. 527　　　Subject: Advertisement
Ref. March 20, 1833; pg. 3, col. 2

WHISKEY.

ROGERS & BROWN offer for sale, 25 Barrels of Buffalo Whiskey—which is old and good. Feb. 11, 1833.

Article no. 528　　　Subject: Advertisement
Ref. March 20, 1833; pg. 3, col. 2

NEW FIRM.

The undersigned having purchased the stock in trade of the late firm of J.R. Stafford & Co., will, under the firm of Cooper & Gilbert, continue the

Tin, Copper, Sheet-Iron, Stove & Hollow-Ware

business, in all its various branches, at the old stand on Main-street.

They have now on hand a good assortment of Tin Ware—also, a lot of Stoves, of all kinds—Cooking Utensils, of every description—a good lot of Stove Pipe, &c., &c.—and they will invite the former customers of the establishment, and all others needing articles in their line, to give them a call.

All kinds of Job Work executed at short notice and in a workmanlike manner.

All kinds of Country Produce will be received in exchange for articles in their line.

N.B. Farmers dealt with on liberal and advantageous terms.

CHARLES COOPER, JONATHAN GILBERT.
Lockport, Jan. 30th, 1833.

WANTED—Six or eight Pedlars. None but men of respectability, who can give security, need apply. C. & G.

Article no. 529　　　Subject: Advertisement
Ref. March 20, 1833; pg. 3, col. 2

KEMPVILLE HOTEL.

The undersigned, having taken the Public House situated in the village of Kempville, (mouth of the 18-mile Creek,) in Niagara county, known as the

Kempville Hotel,

beg leave to inform their fellow-citizens who may have occasions to visit that section of the county, that they have made all suitable and necessary arrangements to administer to the wants of travellers in good and comfortable style—and solicit a share of the patronage of their friends and fellow-citizens, trusting that nothing shall be lacking on their part, to give general satisfaction to their customers.

MOSES SPENCER. Kempville, Jan. 30th, 1833.

Article no. 530 Subject: Education
Ref. March 20, 1833; pg. 3, col. 2

Extract: School of Science.

The subscriber proposes opening a School in the village of Lockport, so soon as a sufficient number of students can be procured to justify the undertaking, where instruction will be given in the various departments of Mathematical and Physical Science.

In order to accommodate the terms, as near as practicable, to the intricacy of the branches taught, or to the labour of giving instruction therein, they will be divided into four sections, as follows: {Advertisement includes descriptions of Arithmetic, Logarithms &c., Geometry &c., and Descriptive & Practical Astronomy &c. sections, with subsections itemized under each.}

The mode of instruction, as far as practicable, will be oral, combined with that introduced by the celebrated Pestalozzi; and consequently the number of students will be limited to twelve.

Access can be had to a select scientific library of upwards of 250 volumes. Mathematical and astronomical instruments, a celestial globe and philosophical apparatus, for elucidation, will be provided as fast as the success of the school will warrant.

Hours of attendance.—Between the autumnal and vernal equinox, the hours of attendance will be from 9 to 12 A.M., and from 1 to 4 P.M., on Mondays, Tuesdays, Thursdays and Fridays; between the vernal and autumnal equinox, from 9 to 12 A.M., and from 2 to 5 P.M., of the same days.

Terms.—For instruction in any or all of the branches in the first section, 3 dollars for each calendar month; second section, 4 dollars; third section, 5 dollars; fourth section, 6 dollars; and in all cases paid monthly in advance.

An evening school to accommodate such as cannot conveniently attend by day, at half the above prices.

EDWARD GIDDINS. Lockport, 25th December, 1832.

Article no. 531 Subject: Advertisement
Ref. March 20, 1833; pg. 3, col. 2

HAT AND CAP STORE.

The subscriber begs leave to inform the citizens of Lockport, and its vicinity, that having purchased the stock in trade of Mr. S.C. Lockwood, he is now prepared to furnish all articles in his line, of the latest fashions and best workmanship, at prices commensurate with the state of the times.

A liberal share of patronage at the hands of his fellow-citizens, is respectfully solicited. Hatting and Shipping Furs purchased as usual.

WILLIAM WARD. June 19th, 1832.

Article no. 532 Subject: Advertisement
Ref. March 20, 1833; pg. 3, col. 2

Staves Wanted.

SETH PARSONS & Co. will pay cash, and the highest price, for Rough Hogshead and Pipe Staves, on delivery. They will also contract for Staves to be delivered in the Spring. Feb. 5, 1833.

Article no. 533 Subject: Notice
Ref. March 20, 1833; pg. 3, col. 4

ASSIGNEE NOTICE.

BOND & FAVOR having recently assigned to the subscriber their effects for the benefit of their creditors, all persons indebted to said firm are requested to make immediate payment to the subscriber, at the store recently occupied by Bond & Favor.

The stock of Goods on hand will be sold at Cost for ready pay. Great Bargains are offered.

L.A. SPALDING, Assignee. Lockport, 2d mo. 18, 1833.

Article no. 534 Subject: Advertisement
Ref. March 20, 1833; pg. 3, col. 4

REFINED SUGAR.

1 Tierce Louisiana Refined Sugar, a fine article for table use, for sale by HOUSE & BOUGHTON. Nov. 27.

Article no. 535 Subject: Advertisement
Ref. March 20, 1833; pg. 3, col. 4

Salt!

300 BBLS. Onondaga salt, for sale at the lowest market price, by ROGERS & BROWN. Jan. 9, 1833.

Article no. 536 Subject: Notice
Ref. March 20, 1833; pg. 3, col. 4

Extra Notice.

The subscribers once more give notice to those who are and have for a long time been indebted to them, that payment must be made soon, or they will be under the necessity of enforcing collection in a legal way. They hope this notice will be sufficient.

SETH PARSONS & Co. Lockport, Jan. 9, 1833.

Article no. 537 Subject: Advertisement
Ref. March 20, 1833; pg. 3, col. 4

BLANKETS.—Rose, English, Duffel Point and Horse Blankets, for sale by HOUSE & BOUGHTON. Nov. 27.

Article no. 538 Subject: Notice
Ref. March 20, 1833; pg. 3, col. 4

SAVE COST!!

All persons indebted to James R. Stafford are hereby notified that his demands are left with E.I. Chase, Attorney, for immediate collection. Unless all demands are settled very soon Mr. Chase is directed to sue.

Lockport, Feb. 18, 1833.

Article no. 539 Subject: Advertisement
Ref. March 20, 1833; pg. 3, col. 5

Extract: AMERICAN RAILROAD JOURNAL AND ADVOCATE OF INTERNAL IMPROVEMENTS, Volume 2d.—This Journal was commenced on the 3d of January, 1832, {Advertisement includes description of purpose and contents.} Price of binding, 50 cents, 75 cents, or $1, according to quantity. Published at No. 35 Wall-street, New-York, by D.K. MINOR.

Subscriptions available at the office of the *Niagara Courier* [M. Cadwallader, proprietor].

Article no. 540 Subject: Advertisement
Ref. March 20, 1833; pg. 3, col. 5

Extract: NEW-YORK FARMER AND AMERICAN GARDENER'S MAGAZINE. Whole number, Vol. 6. New Series. Volume First. No. 1, for January, 1833, is just published. {Advert includes description of purpose and subject matter.} Terms, Three Dollars per annum, in advance, and will not be sent without, as, at its present prices it will not pay a commission for collecting, nor bear the loss arising from want of punctuality on the part of the subscribers. D.K. MINOR, Proprietor, 35 Wall-street, New-York. Subscriptions available at the office of the *Niagara Courier* [M. Cadwallader, proprietor].

Article no. 541 Subject: Advertisement
Ref. March 20, 1833; pg. 3, col. 5

Extract: NEW-YORK AMERICAN, Daily, Volume 13—an evening paper, which gives the latest news of the day, both foreign and domestic, up to the hour of departure of the mails, south and north. {Advertisement includes further description of content.} Terms, Ten dollars per annum, in advance. Published at No. 35 Wall-street, N.Y., by D.K. MINOR.

Article no. 542 Subject: Advertisement
Ref. March 20, 1833; pg. 3, col. 5

Extract: NEW-YORK AMERICAN, Semi-weekly, Volume 13, is printed on a large imperial sheet of superior paper, and will contain the latest news, both foreign and domestic, with copious collections from literary and scientific journals, both European and American; {Advertisement includes further description of content.} Terms, Four dollars per annum, in advance—or five dollars, if not paid in advance. Published at No. 35 Wall-street, N.Y., by D.K. MINOR.

Article no. 543 Subject: Advertisement
Ref. March 20, 1833; pg. 3, col. 5

Extract: NEW-YORK AMERICAN, Tri-weekly, Volume 2d.—The Tri-Weekly American contains the same that is given in the Daily paper, and differs from it only in being published every other, instead [of] every day. {Advertisement includes further description of convenience and content.} Terms, Five dollars per year, in advance. Published at No. 35 Wall-street, New-York, by D.K. MINOR.

Article no. 544 Subject: Advertisement
Ref. March 20, 1833; pg. 3, col. 5

THE GENESEE FARMER
AND GARDENER'S JOURNAL.
A weekly Agricultural Paper, published in Rochester, (N.Y.)
by LUTHER TUCKER & Co.

The Farmer is printed in quarto form, suitable for binding, on fine paper and fair type, making an annual volume, with Title Page and Index, of 424 pages, at the low price of $2,50 per annum, or $2,00 if paid in advance. No subscription will be received for a less term than six months, and all subscribers must commence with the volume, Jan. 1, or the half volume, July 1. The third volume was commenced, Jan. 5, 1833. The first and second volumes can be supplied to new subscribers. Subscriptions received by N. Leonard, Lockport.

Article no. 545 Subject: Advertisement
Ref. March 20, 1833; pg. 3, col. 5

CODFISH.
2000 Lbs. Codfish, for sale by
ROGERS & BROWN. Jan. 24.

Article no. 546 Subject: Advertisement
Ref. March 20, 1833; pg. 3, col. 5

Broadcloths, &c.

The subscriber is now opening a splendid lot of Broadcloths, &c., and is prepared to execute all orders in his line, with promptness, and in the most fashionable style. G.S. PLACE, Merchant tailor.

Article no. 547	Subject: Advertisement
Ref. March 20, 1833; pg. 3, col. 5	

Antimasonic Almanacs—
A small lot just received and for sale at this office [the *Niagara Courier*]. Feb. 12.

Article no. 548	Subject: History
Ref. March 20, 1833; pg. 4, col. 1	

Extract: From the *New-York Commercial Advertiser*.
The Indians of the Far West.
Mandan Village, Upper Missouri, August 12, 1832.

Dear Sir—I would gladly shrink from the undertaking which I am about to commence, did I not feel bound by the promise in my last letter, to give you a description of an annual religious ceremony, which I witnessed, a short time since, in this village, in company of two other gentlemen, who were with me in continual attendance for four days, that we might lose nothing of this strange exhibition. With my enthusiasm for the Indian character, I took great interest in witnessing every form and feature of these rites, and consequently was too much engaged to think of my meals. {Article includes remainder of essay, concluding with:} I have made four paintings which will embrace the whole of these scenes, and I intend to publish to the world, with the certificates of the two gentlemen who were with me, "that I have nothing extenuated, nor ought set down in malice." The strange and interesting traditions of this people, with regard to their origin, &c. and their reasons and arguments for observing this annual ceremony in all its forms and cruelties, will be a subject for a future epistle. Adieu, yours, &c.
GEO. CATLIN. [Length: 3 columns.]

Article no. 549	Subject: Notice
Ref. March 20, 1833; pg. 4, col. 6	

TO EXONERATE FROM IMPRISONMENT.
Pursuant to the Revised Statutes, part second, chap. 5, Title 1, Article 5, relating to "voluntary assignments by an insolvent for the purpose of exonerating his person from imprisonment."
GEORGE MACAN, notice first published 13th Feb. 1833, to appear before the Hon. Hiram Gardner, Supreme Court Commissioner, at his office in Lockport, in the county of Niagara, on the first day of May, 1833, at 2 o'clock in the afternoon.

Article no. 550	Subject: Notice
Ref. March 20, 1833; pg. 4, col. 6	

Extract: SHERIFF'S SALE.
By virtue of an Execution issued out of the court of Common Pleas for the county of Niagara, and state of New-York, and to me directed and delivered, against the goods and chattels, lands and tenements, of Otis Hathaway, of my bailiwick, I have seized and taken all that certain piece or parcel of land, lying and being in the village of Lockport, in the county of Niagara, being part and parcel of farm lot No. 12, in the 14th section of township number 14, in the 6th range, known and distinguished as follows: Being part and parcel of a certain village lot, distinguished and laid down on a certain map ... made for the proprietors by Jesse P. Haines, Surveyor, and filed in the office of the Clerk of the county of Niagara, as village lot No. 2, on the south side of Main-street, and on the westerly side of the Erie Canal, bounded as follows: {Notice includes description of boundaries,} [bounded, in part, by land owned by Norton Porter;] which said piece or parcel of land, and all the right, title, claim and demand of Otis Hathaway, of, in and to the same, together with all the appurtenances thereunto belonging, I shall expose to sale at public vendue, as the law directs, at the House now kept by J.W. Witbeck, known as the Eagle Tavern, in Lockport, 5 April 1833.
H. McNEIL, Sheriff. Dated Feb. 13th, 1833.

Article no. 551	Subject: Politics
Ref. April 17, 1833; pg. 1, col. 5	

The *Albany Argus* abuses and denounces Antimasonry in set terms. Since the death of the *Craftsman*, the *Argus* has been the regularly authorised mouthpiece and adjunct of disgraced and murderous Freemasonry. The following extract from that profligate print has all the malignity and bitterness that characterised the abuse and persecution heaped upon us in the early days of our cause. It renews before us the same spirit that Masons exhibited against those patriotic individuals who first went forward to the investigation of the Morgan murder, at the peril of their lives.—Antimasons can no longer doubt (if they ever had any doubts,) on which side of this question Van Buren stands. Let him and the Regency share the fate of their Idols and its Jachin and Boaz. Thus speaks the *Argus:—Roch. Inq.* [Anti-antimasonry article follows in the original.]

Article no. 552	Subject: Temperance
Ref. April 17, 1833; pg. 1, col. 5	

Progress of Temperance. The benefits resulting from the efforts making to suppress intemperance, have reached every State of the Union. By appealing to the understandings of men—to their pride—their ambition—their self-respect and regard for their families—by the force of example, and respect for reputation, a change has been effected, which no excise, tax upon licenses, or any other indirect legislation could possibly effect. Public opinion, after all, is the greatest and most effectual lawmaker in the U. States, and its decree against the use of ardent spirits, unless reversed by the indiscreet zeal of some of its friends, will, ere long, be consummated. As an exemplification of the truth of these remarks, a letter has been recently received in this city from a merchant in Alabama, who has given a detail of facts, showing the diminished consumption of ardent spirits in that State, which have fallen under his own observation. He states that in 1824 and 1825, he usually retailed about one hundred barrels of whiskey, besides a large quantity of rum and brandy. From the latter period, as the Temperance Societies have multiplied, so that in 1831 he sold only one barrel of whiskey and one pipe of brandy. He further states, that as his sales of spirits have declined, those of sugar and coffee have advanced—that the people have become more able and willing to pay their debts—and that the shelf in their cabins, instead of being decorated with jugs and bottles, is now stored with books—and smiling happy faces are to be seen, where, very lately, could be found only sallow and squalid misery. Facts like these are more powerful than argument. They carry conviction with them, and make at once the best practical commentary upon themselves.—*N. Y. Com. Adv.*

Article no. 553   Subject: Court
Ref. April 17, 1833; pg. 1, col. 6

Trial of Steeprock. Our engagements last week prevented us from preparing an account of the trial of this Indian for the murder of his wife in July last. Not having been present during the examination of the witnesses, and consequently being unable to state with precision the facts in this case, we copy the following from the *Times and Press* of last week.—*Batavia Adv.*

The Circuit Court and Court of Oyer and Terminer for this county, closed its setting on Saturday last. The only case that excited any considerable interest, was the trial of John Steeprock, for the killing of his wife, in July last.

It appeared in evidence that on the 19th or 20th of July last, Steeprock was seen by another Indian, on the west bank of the Tonnewanda feeder wending his way towards the Indian village—that soon after he passed the witness, his wife was seen in full chase, after him—soon after the witness heard a scream, and after the lapse of a few seconds, another scream—and then, to use the expressive language of the Indian witness, was heard the voice of Steeprock "in full anger." It appeared from the evidence of another witness, a white man, that returning from the Indian village, he saw Steeprock, near the road on the bank of the feeder, sitting beside the dead body of his wife, fanning her face with his handkerchief, and that Steeprock was crying—on being interrogated as [to] the cause of her death, he answered, "Cholera." Soon after this, a number of persons arrived at the place, and on examination several bruises were discovered on the person of the deceased—one on the side of the head, another on the breast, and a third under the short rib. Upon this, Steeprock was charged with having murdered her—he acknowledged that he had killed her, but that it was in self defence.—The facts in relation to the killing were from the confessions of Steeprock himself, no one having witnessed the rencontre between them. It appears that they had been out soliciting provisions, and had accumulated a basket full of meat, potatoes, &c. and were returning home, Mrs. Steeprock, somewhat under the influence of liquor. While at Cheeney's tavern, which is about two miles from the Indian village, Steeprock for fear his wife would pawn the basket and contents, for liquor, took the basket, unknown to his wife, and started on. She overtook him about half way to the village, and immediately commenced an assault upon him, first making the accusation that he had stolen her meat, &c. Here it should be remarked that Steeprock's wife was an uncommon stout woman, and had the reputation of being the greatest fighter in the tribe. She made a furious attack upon him, and he repulsed her—again and again she renewed the attack, and he as often repulsed her, and being somewhat incensed at her conduct, he undoubtedly made use of more force that he was aware of—at all events as Steeprock expressed himself, the "breath went out of the body—she breathed no more." The jury returned a verdict of Not Guilty.

Article no. 554   Subject: Court
Ref. April 17, 1833; pg. 2, col. 1

Extract: Slander Suit.—A case of slander was tried last week in Troy, in which Miss Achsah L. Clark was plaintiff, and John O. Martling, defendant. The trial lasted two whole days, and resulted in a verdict of $1200 damages. {Article includes description of trial and evidence.} [Other names mentioned: Mr. Elijah Wild, Miss Eliza Clark, Mr. Buel, Judge Vanderpool; Mr. Hunt, counsel for the plaintiff. Length, ½ column.]

Article no. 555   Subject: Children
Ref. April 17, 1833; pg. 2, col. 1

From the *Albany Daily Advertiser*.
A singular adventure.

A little boy, aged about 3 years, son of Col. Hogan, keeper of the jail, was missing on Saturday, 6th inst. for about 7 hours, and search was made for him in every direction, but in vain. A little child about his own age, who could not speak plain, was continually saying to its mother, 'Boy in hole,' 'Boy in hole,' and pointed to a hole in the end of the arch over Eagle-st. at its junction with Beaver street. His importunities at length attracted attention, and it being known that Mr. H's child was missing, a man descended by a rope fastened under his arms, to the bottom of the creek, a distance of twenty feet, with a lantern. He there found a boy's cap, but he searched no further, and was drawn up.—The cap was identified as that of Mr. H's boy. Sheriff Gallup went to the place and offered a reward to any person who could descend and search for the child. None could be found, when the Sheriff himself pulled off his coat and was making preparations to go down; when a coloured man was induced to descend, with a lantern.—After proceeding about 300 feet in the creek as it goes down Beaver street, and which is covered by an arch about 4 feet high, he found the little fellow sitting in the mud and filth, and resting against the wall of the arch, almost exhausted. He brought him to the hole, and he was hoisted out and presented to his, till then, afflicted, but now overjoyed parents. It appears that after falling in the hole, he had wandered thus far, and had become so fatigued that he could not make his way back to the hole, or probably he became bewildered and deprived of the power of exercising his thinking faculties. He was in the place from 10 in the morning till 5 in the afternoon.

Article no. 556   Subject: Religion
Ref. April 17, 1833; pg. 2, col. 4

NOTICE.—On Wednesday the 24th instant, Mr. Cochrane will deliver, in the basement story of the first Presbyterian Church in this village, a Lecture, introductory to a course, on the Philosophy of Moral Science. The doors will be open at early candle-light, and the admission free.

Lockport, April 17th, 1833.

Article no. 557   Subject: Notice
Ref. April 17, 1833; pg. 2, col. 4

We must crave the indulgence of our patrons should our editorial department, occasionally, present rather a meagre appearance. We have much manual labour at times to perform, to make the two ends of the year come snugly together without doing injustice to our neighbours. At such seasons, the labours of the editor must give way to those of the printer.

Article no. 558   Subject: Notice
Ref. April 17, 1833; pg. 2, col. 4

The Canal Commissioners have given notice that the canal will be ready for navigation on the 22d inst. Had not their incompetent agents here been so busily engaged, all winter and spring, in wasting the public money, navigation might have commenced a week ago. After expending ten or fifteen thousand dollars before the late freshet, an expenditure of at least half that sum, since that event, has been necessary, to put the canal in as good condition as it was before our scientific repairers touched it. [Transcriber's note: This article appears in the Editorial columns.]

Article no. 559   Subject: Editorial
Ref. April 17, 1833; pg. 2, col. 4

We are extremely sorry that we have not time to waste at present in using up the small game of the *Balance*. It is a matter of doubt, however, whether the milk of human kindness would not so mollify our heart, even did leisure serve us, as to forbid our treading any further upon the poor bruised worms in the matter of the town meetings. If they can take comfort in chuckling over the circumstance of their party coming out second best, it were the very ne plus ultra of cruelty to dash the cup from their lips! But apropos! a sum in the political rule of three for them: If they crow so loudly over a 'Waterloo defeat,' what would be the measure of their exultation did victory such as ours fall to their lot?—Goodness! all creation would hardly be large enough for them to sound their notes in.

Article no. 560   Subject: Government
Ref. April 17, 1833; pg. 2, col. 4

The Editor of the *Argus* is delighted with the passage of a bill increasing the Salaries of the Chancellor and Judges. This is quite natural. The Office-holding fraternity are mutually interested in lifting salaries. The Judges now receive about $7 per day, and our Republican State Paper urges an increase to between eight and nine dollars a day. The Treasury is empty, and must be replenished from the fruits of honest industry, to be again lavished upon luxurious and pampered Office-holders. The People toil and sweat through the year, to enable Office-holders to dress in "purple and fine linen, and fare sumptuously every day." But it avails little, or nothing, to point out these abuses. There is not enough of the spirit of other and better days, left among us, to rebuke and correct them. The People, the once watchful, independent and chivalric supporters of genuine Republicanism, are tamely hewing the wood and drawing the water of overgrown, overgorged, aristrocratical Office-holders. The Republic is running to idleness and luxury. The many are yielding up all power to the few. But "Ephraim is joined to his Idols—let him alone.["]—*Albany Journal*. [Transcriber's note: This article appears in the Editorial columns.]

Article no. 561 Subject: Crime
Ref. April 17, 1833; pg. 2, col. 5

From the *N.Y. Daily Advertiser.*

Warning to Strangers.—This afternoon a countryman went on board of a North River steam boat to go up home. He had occasion to purchase something by which he exposed his money, which was observed by a youngster called Herrick, who commenced a conversation with him, and proposed to take a little walk before the boat should start. They walked off a short distance, when they observed a young man called Smith Cooper, ahead of them, drop a tobacca box, which was picked up by Herrick and a lottery ticket taken out, and Cooper called to him and asked whether he had lost any thing; C. stopped, and on feeling his pocket stated his loss. Herrick said that there was not any ticket in it, upon which C. offered to bet him $25, that there was, H. said that he would bet, but his money was all on board, and urged the countryman to make the bet and persuaded him to take out his money. The box in the meantime was thrown down, picked up and opened, and a ticket found in it, which had been introduced by one of the parties unobserved by the countryman, upon which H. took the money out of the countrymon's [sic] hand, and handed it to C., saying "there you have won it, let us go," and both started. The countryman, not willing to lose his money, gave chase to C. and overtook him, and had him committed on the charge, and obtained his money. H. made off another way and escaped.

Article no. 562 Subject: Court
Ref. April 17, 1833; pg. 2, col. 5

Liabilities of Partners. Judge Hoffman of New-York, has decided, that partnership property cannot be taken for individual debts. The interest may be claimed, but the property cannot be seized. The possession and disposal of property mast [sic] remain with the firm.

Article no. 563 Subject: Crime
Ref. April 17, 1833; pg. 2, col. 5

Slight [sic] of Hand. Two merchants were robbed a few days since on board of the steamboat between Poughkeepsie and New York; one of $300, and the other of $2700.

Article no. 564 Subject: Agriculture
Ref. April 17, 1833; pg. 2, col. 5

Superior. The Ox Superior, which was recently exhibited in our streets, has been slaughtered by Messrs. Valentine & Jenkins, No. 46 Fulton market. Some of the best cuts having brought one dollar per pound. The animal was raised by Richard Townsend & Son, of L. Island, was six years old, had consumed about 700 bushels of Indian meal in the last three years, and weighed alive 2874 pounds. Its height at the fore shoulder was 5 feet 10 inches—girth 10, 3—length to forehead 9, and to the nose 10 feet. The weight of the slaughtered carcass was 1890 pounds—and the beef pronounced the finest ever offered in our market.—*N.Y. Advocate.*

Article no. 565 Subject: Agriculture
Ref. April 17, 1833; pg. 2, col. 6

English Reciprocity. 5000 bushels of wheat have been sent back from Liverpool to New-York, because they could not be sold there, in consequence of the heavy duties. Our farmers are told, however, by a certain class of politicians, that we must admit English productions into our ports without any duty.

Article no. 566 Subject: Agriculture
Ref. April 17, 1833; pg. 2, col. 6

As "seed time" is fast approaching, and as Madame Moon, out of pure perverseness, is oftentimes "out of season" for the interests of farmers, we have, for their especial benefit, selected the following clever directions for cheating her! Gardeners, also, might take a hint from them. Gemini! how pale the crabbed old jade will turn, when she comes to find out how neatly she has been tricked.

HOW TO CHEAT THE MOON.

Some farmers are very careful to sow their spring crops and gardens at a proper time of the moon, and thus frequently anticipate, or pass over the best season of the year. By attending to the following directions, they will escape all the inconvenience arising from the influence of the moon. Select some fair day, as near the usual time of sowing as possible—arise very early in the morning, and sow your seed boldly: Cover all up carefully before night, making the land appear smooth and even. When the moon comes on the next evening she will not be able to determine whether the field has been sown or not, and will therefore bestow no influence upon it, either bad or good. It is important that the land be thoroughly dried, so that it can be made to appear natural.

Whenever wheat turns to cheat, it is done by the influence of the moon. By attending to the above directions, and sowing clean seed, that evil may also be avoided.—*Genesee Farmer.*

Article no. 567 Subject: Advertisement
Ref. April 17, 1833; pg. 2, col. 6

New Establishment,
Of Drugs, Medicines, Paints, Oils,
Dye-stuffs, Perfumery, &c. &c.

G.W. MERCHANT respectfully informs the inhabitants of Lockport and the public generally, that he has opened a store in the Exchange Buildings, Lockport (lower town,) where he intends keeping a general assortment of Goods of the first quality; (most of which he has selected with his own hands;) and will sell as low as can be bought elsewhere. Among his articles are the following: Tincture of Bark, prepared with Brandy, and a general assortment of other compounds carefully prepared by himself, for the use of families; Marseilles Table Oil, Mushroom Ketchup, Tomato do.; Capers; Gorgona Anchovies, West India and American Pepper-Sauce; Maccaroni and Vermicilla; Citron; Preserved Ginger; Loaf Sugar, Nuts; Box, Sultana Raisins; Eng. Currants; Mace; Nutmegs, and other spices; Camphor; Opium; Arrowroot; Pearl Barley; Sage; Prussian Blue; Chrome Green; do. Yellow; Rose pink, drop lake; Vermillion; Tapioca; Confectionary; Sugar dust; Quinine; Croton Oil; Piperine; Morphine; Iodine; Chloride of Soda and Lime; Otto [Attar] of Roses; Gold and silver Leaf; Gold, silver, and copper Bronze; Holden's and Kidder's superior Indelible Ink—warranted; Rocky Mountain Bear's Oil, to promote the growth and beauty of the Hair: together with many other articles.

G.W.M. anticipates that by a strict personal attention to business, he will be favoured with a share of public patronage.

Particular attention will be paid to Physician's [sic] prescriptions and family orders. Medicines personally delivered at any hour of the night.

Lockport, April 17, 1833.

Article no. 568 Subject: Advertisement
Ref. April 17, 1833; pg. 2, col. 6

Yellow Locust Trees

Can be had by applying immediately to L.A. SPALDING. Ten trees for one dollar, or 1s. for a single one. Every yard should be ornamented with this beautiful shade tree. They grow rapidly, and are valuable in many respects. 4th mo. 17, 1833.

Article no. 569 Subject: Advertisement
Ref. April 17, 1833; pg. 2, col. 6

A first rate yoke of Oxen for sale by the subscriber in Camra.—Also, a pair of three years old Steers. Inquire of Amos Benedict, Samuel Cuykendall, or the subscriber.
April 17, 1833. IRA BENEDICT.

Article no. 570 Subject: Advertisement
Ref. April 17, 1833; pg. 2, col. 6

LEMON SYRUP,
Of very superior quality, for sale to wholesale and retail by G.W. MERCHANT. Chemist and Apothecary. Lower Lockport, April 17, 1833.

Article no. 571 Subject: Advertisement
Ref. April 17, 1833; pg. 2, col. 6

To the Public.
A most important and invaluable discovery.
Transparent Cement.

The proprietor of this invaluable article after much time and money spent in fruitless experiments, has at last succeeded in producing an article which he offers to the public with the fullest confidence of its great importance as an indispensible article in family economy. This is warranted to mend effectually all articles of Glass ware, Window Glass, &c. &c.; likewise China, earthen ware, Polished Steel, &c. without the cement being in the least degree visible. With the view of placing it within the reach of every family, the proprietor has determined to sell it at the extreme low price of 25 cents. Plain and ample directions accompany each vial. A liberal discount will be made to those who purchase by the quantity.

Prepared and sold wholesale and retail, by G.W. Merchant, Chemist and Apothecary, Lower Lockport, Niagara county, N.Y. and most of the Stores throughout the country. April 17, 1833.

Article no. 572 Subject: Advertisement
Ref. April 17, 1833; pg. 3, col. 3

GRIND STONES.

The subscribers have a quantity of the above article on hand, which they offer for sale at reduced prices.
ROGERS & BROWN. Lockport, May 8.

Article no. 573 Subject: Notice
Ref. April 17, 1833; pg. 3, col. 4

List of letters remaining in the Post Office at Pendleton, April 1st, 1833. [Names listed, below.] S.P. CLARKE, P.M.

Allcot, Helam
Bartlett, Philander
Blowers, William
Cole, William
Hartley, Jesse
Howe, Edward
Moore, John
Sincler, Hosea B.
Thayre, Nathan
Wart, Christian
Wilson, Reuben
Andrus, Elder
Becker, Christian
Clark, George P.
Edmerson, Andrew
Henderson, James
Levenworth, David
Roberts, William
Taylor, Peter
Thompson, Nathaniel
Wilson, John
Wingart, Elizabeth

Article no. 574 Subject: Notice
Ref. April 17, 1833; pg. 3, col. 5

NOTICE.
I hereby forbid all persons to trust or harbour my apprentice boy, by name of Chester W. Gillet, aged 18

years, on my account, he having left my service without leave, as he has frequently done. Dated Lewiston, March 28th, 1833. MATHIAS KLINE.

Article no. 575   Subject: Notice
Ref. April 17, 1833; pg. 3, col. 6

NOTICE.

Pursuant to the requirements of the last will and testament of William Herrington, deceased, the undersigned Executors in said will named, will expose to sale at public auction or vendue, on the premises, on the 18th day of May next, at one o'clock in the afternoon, all the real estate of the said William Herrington, being the farm lately occupied by him, lying in the town of Hartland, in the county of Niagara, containing one hundred and seventy acres of excellent land, comprising lot number 4, in the 9th section of the 15th township, in the 5th range, and the middle one third of lot number one, in the 10th section, 15th township, and 5th range, of the Holland Company's Land (so called.)—The said farm is eligibly situated on the Ridge Road, has about 90 acres under first rate improvement, a good brick dwelling-house, 26 feet by 38, three good frame barns, spacious and good sheds, and other out houses, all in good repair. There is on the farm two wells of excellent water, and it is otherwise well watered; also a large and excellent orchard, of various kinds of fruit. Terms made known on the day of sale.

DAVID HERRINGTON, JAMES HERRINGTON, JONATHAN HERRINGTON, Executors.
Hartland, 28th March, 1833.

Article no. 576   Subject: Advertisement
Ref. April 17, 1833; pg. 4, col. 1

Farm for sale.

The subscriber offers for sale the Farm on which he now lives, situated a short distance east of this village, on Main-street, or Batavia road, and within the Corporation. This Farm is beautifully situated, having a fair prospect of the village and Lake Ontario. It contains 111 acres—of which 80 are cleared and under good improvement and well fenced. The soil is of good quality, well watered, and excellent for wheat and grass. There are now on said premises, two new framed Dwelling Houses, and a Barn, 30 by 40 feet, an Orchard consisting of 200 apple trees, of improved fruit, with peaches, plums, cherries of various kinds, &c. Also, an extensive Brick Yard, with conveniences for making any quantity of brick.

Also—Another Lot, east of the village, on the south side of Main-street, containing one acre.

Also—A lot, two miles east of the village, on the Batavia road, and near the Cold Springs, containing five and a half acres of land, all well fenced. There is on this lot an extensive bed of good sand, which renders it very valuable.

A good title will be given for the above mentioned property, and a liberal credit for a part of the purchase money. For terms apply to the subscriber on the premises.

PETER AIKINS. Lockport, April 16th, 1833.

Article no. 577   Subject: Advertisement
Ref. April 17, 1833; pg. 4, col. 1

DYE STUFFS, PAINTS, &c.—The subscriber has on hand a large stock of the above articles of the first quality, which he offers for cash at wholesale, at a small advance from the N. York wholesale prices.

Consumers of the above articles would act wise to save the expense of a journey to N. York.

G.W. MERCHANT, Lower Lockport. April 17, 1833.

Article no. 578   Subject: Notice
Ref. April 17, 1833; pg. 4, col. 1

SHERIFF'S SALE.

By virtue of an execution issued out of the clerk's office, in the county of Niagara, and state of New-York, and to me directed and delivered, against the goods and chattles [sic], lands and tenements, of Jeremiah Burr, I have seized and taken all that certain tract, piece or parcel of land situate, lying and being in the village of Lockport, in the county of Niagara, being part or parcel of farm lot Number Twelve, in the Fourteenth Township and Sixth Range of the Holland Land Company's Lands (so called,) and which on a map or survey of a part of said lot number twelve into village lots, made for the proprietors by Jesse P. Haines, surveyor, and filed in the office of the clerk of the County of Niagara, is known and distinguished as village lot number five on the north side of Niagara street, in the said village of Lockport, being one chain wide and two chains and fifty links deep, be the same more or less, according to said map or survey, reference thereto being had: and all the right, title, claim, interest and demand of the said Jeremiah Burr, of, in, and to said above described premises, I shall expose to sale, as the law directs, at public vendue, at the Eagle Tavern, in the village of Lockport aforesaid, on Friday the 30th day of May next, at one o'clock in the afternoon of that day. Dated Lockport, April 17, 1833.

H. McNEIL, Sheriff.

Article no. 579   Subject: Advertisement
Ref. April 17, 1833; pg. 4, col. 1

ANTI-BILIOUS SPRING BITTERS.

These bitters strengthen the stomach, procure an appetite and assist digestion; are a most excellent preventive against Fever and Ague, and are the most pleasant and effectual remedy for the Jaundice. They fully warm the stomach and purify the breath; possessing mild and carminative properties, they are a most excellent medicine for Colics, Dysenteries, &c. &c., and for habitual costiveness are an infallible remedy.—They are superior to any other ever made, inasmuch as they possess a quality of destroying those inflammatory properties which so often accompany ardent spirits, and which prove so injurious when taken upon an empty stomach, and renders them a mild, wholesome, and invigorating detergent.—They are also extremely useful in cleansing the urinary passages, and are therefore well calculated for dropsical complaints: persons leading inactive lives will act wise by using this generous stomachic, as it enriches the blood and invigorates the whole system. These Bitters are warranted superior to any in the United States.

For sale, wholesale and retail, by the sole proprietor and manufacturer, G.W. MERCHANT, Chemist and Apothecary, Exchange Buildings, Lower Lockport.

Article no. 580   Subject: Advertisement
Ref. April 17, 1833; pg. 4, col. 1

CLOVER SEED
For sale by
SETH PARSONS & CO.
April 3d, 1833.

Article no. 581   Subject: Advertisement
Ref. April 17, 1833; pg. 4, col. 1

SPECIFIC DROPS.

A Positive Cure for the Fever and Ague.—The proprietor of this valuable and never failing remedy, in offering it to the public, feels it necessary to remark that it has never been known to fail in any one instance where it has been tried: and he would assure all those afflicted with the above complaint, that it is entirely free from any injurious ingredient whatever. The cure is speedy and effectual; 16 hours generally being sufficient to destroy the disease. This medicine is warranted, and if it should fail (which it has never been known to do yet,) the money will be refunded.

Prepared and sold by G.W. MERCHANT, Chemist and Apothecary, Lower Lockport. April 17, 1833.

Article no. 582   Subject: Advertisement
Ref. April 17, 1833; pg. 4, col. 1

Extract: To the Unfortunate.

C'est un fait connu de tout le monde et principalement des medecins que depuis quelques années il s'est opère un grand changement dans les soins administrés aux infortunés atteints de cette terrible maladie, (appelée vénérienne.) [Transcriber's notes: Accents did not appear in the original text, and have been supplied by the transcriber. Translation: "It is a well known fact generally, and principally among physicians for the last several years, that there has been a considerable development in the care administered to the unfortunates afflicted with this terrible malady (called venereal disease.)" This was the first sentence appearing in a substantially sized advertisement, all of which was printed in French, except for the last paragraph, viz.:] Where the person addresses by letter inclosing $5, the necessary medicines will be forwarded by mail, free of expense to the purchaser. Apply or address to

G.W. MERCHANT, Chemist and Apothecary,
Lower Lockport, N.Y.

Article no. 583   Subject: Advertisement
Ref. April 17, 1833; pg. 4, col. 2

Extract: Land Agency Office.

The subscriber has opened an Office in Dayton, Ohio, for the purpose of enabling persons from a distance, desirous of locating themselves in Dayton, or its vicinity, to purchase Lands or other real Estate, with greater ease. {Advertisement includes description of services offered.} The subscriber also being in the practice of Law, will attend promptly and faithfully to any business of a general nature which may be intrusted to him from abroad, and which agents are accustomed to transact, such as the collecting of demands due from persons in this vicinity, the paying of taxes, &c. JAMES A. SHEDD.

Application may be made to either of the following gentlemen, as references of character: [David Stone, or H.G. Phillips, Dayton; Wm. M'Lean, of the firm Reeves & M'Lean, Cincinnati; Jarvis Pike, Columbus; Henry Dana Ward, New York; Newkirk, White & Co., or M. Newkirk & Co., Philadelphia.] Dayton, March 19, 1833.

Article no. 584   Subject: Notice
Ref. April 17, 1833; pg. 4, col. 2

NOTICE.

The partnership heretofore existing between Daniel F. Rhoad and Jerome Petrie, under the firm of Rhoad & Petrie, has been dissolved. Lockport, April 5, 1833.

Article no. 585   Subject: Advertisement
Ref. April 17, 1833; pg. 4, col. 2

Saddle & Harness Making.

J. PETRIE begs leave to inform the public, that he will continue to carry on the above business, at the old stand of Rhoad & Petrie, sign of the Saddle, on Main-street, nearly opposite the Eagle Tavern, where he will keep constantly on hand

Saddles, Bridles, Harness, Trunks, &c.
of the best workmanship—and will be ready to execute with promptness all orders in his line. April 8.

Article no. 586 Subject: Notice
Ref. April 17, 1833; pg. 4, col. 2

PARTNERSHIP DISSOLVED.

The partnership heretofore existing between George T. Levalley and Nathaniel Forrester, in the lime burning business, was dissolved on the 12th of Feb. last, since which time the undersigned has had nothing to do with the concern. The accounts previous to the above date remain to be settled by the members of the old firm.

N. FORRESTER. Lockport[,] April 8, 1833.

Article no. 587 Subject: Advertisement
Ref. April 17, 1833; pg. 4, col. 2

Agents Wanted.

NOTICE.—The subscriber takes this method to inform persons QUALIFIED to become soliciting agents in the book business, that immediate employment can be given to As Many as shall apply for the terms of 4, 8 or 12 months.

The qualifications required of such as may wish to enter into this business, are merely that they are sober and candid in behaviour, genteel and conciliating in address, with a common amount of general information, and having the ability to give responsible names, with himself, to secure the payment for all books ordered.

The remuneration to agents shall be such as to engage the attention of all persons, commonly employed by the month. Such as are qualified, or have had Schools under their care, are the men who are preferred, as being peculiarly circumstanced to do well in this business.

For any, and all information, respecting the nature of the work, the mode of doing the business, and the probable amount of what an agent may clear a month; with the counties or county he may wish to canvass, write to Mr. Francis William, Albany, when instant attention will be bestowed, if post paid, and not otherwise.

Such as may notice this proposal, who feel conscious of the above qualifications, will do well not to neglect the opportunity, as the remuneration to be given is more captivating than may at first sight be supposed.

FRANCIS WILLIAM. March 14th, 1833.

Article no. 588 Subject: Notice
Ref. April 17, 1833; pg. 4, col. 2

INFORMATION

Is wanted of William Parker, formerly of England, where he left in 1818, and was living some time in Lockport, and between Lockport and Lewiston. Any information where said Parker, who has parents in Canada, can be found, will be very thankfully received by the subscriber, his brother, now residing with Gen. W.L. Churchill, Stafford, Genesee Co. N.Y.—and if he is living, and this meets his eye, he is requested to write to me immediately.

JAMES PARKER. Stafford, Gen. Co., April 2, 1833.

Article no. 589 Subject: Advertisement
Ref. April 17, 1833; pg. 4, col. 2

Rochester Fire Engine Manufactory.

The subscriber having manufactured one Fire Engine for the Corporation of this village, has been induced, at the earnest solicitation of his friends, to continue the manufacturing of them.—He has employed experienced workmen and is prepared to make to order, any number of Engines that may be wanted for a village or city. He will warrant his Engines to be superior in power and equal in durability to any manufactured in the United States. The following certificate from different members of the Fire Departments in this village will show the estimation in which the Engine, made for this place, is held.

Engines will be furnished at New-York prices, and delivered free of transportation at any village or city on the Canal or Lake in this State.

LEWIS SELYE.

Mr. Lewis Selye has built a Fire Engine for this village the past summer, and we consider it superior in workmanship, and at least Equal in Power to the New-York Engines made by Force or Smith, both of which are in use here.

JACOB THORN, President of the Village of Rochester.
Wm. H. WARD, Chief Engineer of Fire Department, Rochester.
THOMAS KEMPSHALL, Assistant Engineer.
BENJAMIN H. BROWN, 2d Engineer.
Wm. S. WHITTLESEY, Foreman of Fire Company No. 1.

P.S. Messrs. J. GRAVES & Co. having made 300 feet of Hose for the above Engine, which has proved to be equal, if not superior, to any manufactured in New-York or Philadelphia will contract to furnish any quantity at New-York prices. Rochester, March 27, 1833.

Article no. 590 Subject: Advertisement
Ref. April 17, 1833; pg. 4, col. 3

Massachusetts Patent Sawed SHINGLES.

The subscriber has in operation at Black Rock, head of Squaw Island, Andrus' Patent for manufacturing Shingles. 20 years' experience at the east, by those who have used them, has satisfactorily demonstrated that they are decidedly superior to the common Shingle. Also,

Sawed Lath, manufactured at the same place.

WALTER OSBORNE.

REFERENCE. William Forsyth, U.C.; Augustus Porter, Niagara Falls; House & Boughton, N.W. Gardner,

Lockport; U. Driggs, Tonewanta; H.B. Potter, S. Jordan, J.G. Driscoll, J. M'Knight, M. Baker, B. Rathbnn [sic], N. Rossiter, Buffalo.

Black Rock, Feb. 14, 1833.

Article no. 591 Subject: Advertisement
Ref. April 17, 1833; pg. 4, col. 4

MACKEREL.

10 Barrels, 8 half do. Mackerel—for sale by
ROGERS & BROWN. July 24.

Article no. 592 Subject: Advertisement
Ref. April 17, 1833; pg. 4, col. 4

PINE SHINGLES.

125 M. first rate Western Singles, for sale by
(July 24.) ROGERS & BROWN.

Article no. 593 Subject: Advertisement
Ref. April 17, 1833; pg. 4, col. 5

HATS!

An assortment of Hats, of superior workmanship and quality, manufactured in Lockport, by T. & J. Birdsall, kept constantly for sale at the fashionable Clothing Store of

G.S. PLACE. Lockport, May 31, 1831.

Article no. 594 Subject: Advertisement
Ref. April 17, 1833; pg. 4, col. 6

FARM FOR SALE!

A Farm of 127 acres, lying near this village on the Canal, of which 35 acres is under good improvement, we will sell on the most favourable terms, if application is made soon. We will assign the article which has yet 4 years to run, or give a warranty deed as shall best accommodate the buyer. Any person wishing to procure a convenient, and good farm will do well to examine this before purchasing elsewhere.

SETH PARSONS & Co. Lockport, March 25th, 1833.

Article no. 595 Subject: Advertisement
Ref. April 17, 1833; pg. 4, col. 6

Rogers & Brown,

Have just received as large and as well selected a stock of

Fall and Winter Goods,

as was ever offered in this County: All, or any of which, they will sell at as low prices as they can be purchased in the western country.—Their old customers and others are invited to call and examine their stock, which offers great inducements to purchasers. Lockport, January 2, 1833.

Article no. 596 Subject: Natural Phenomena
Ref. August 7, 1833; pg. 1, col. 3

Singular Phenomenon.—A correspondent of the *Bulletin*, gives the following account of an uncommon occurrence which took place in Genesee county, on the 20th of June.

Between two and three o'clock in the morning there was heard by several of the inhabitants of the town of Java and Sheldon, Genesee co. a remarkable roaring resembling that of a "rushing mighty wind," accompanied with a trembling motion of the earth for a considerable extent. It was so considerable, that some removed the glass and earthenware from their shelves to prevent its breaking. In the morning there was discovered on the farm of Mr. J. Sykes, in the north part of the town of Java, a remarkable breach in the earth, extending from Seneca creek west, across a small flat of a few rods extent, up the side of a hill, the slope of which was about 40 or 50 rods in length. It was 20 rods wide at the end next the creek, 13 at the middle and 16 at the upper end, where the earth was sunk from 20 to 25 feet, while it was raised about 20 feet above the bottom of the creek at its lower end, making the highest point at the creek nearly as high as the lowest depression at the other extremity. The bed of the creek was raised about 20 feet and carried about three rods beyond its former situation. The ground was thrown into ridges from 2 to 10 feet high. A considerable part of the surface has entirely disappeared, presenting in its stead several strata of different kinds of earth. Trees, stumps, and logs, were carried 12 or 15 rods. A small grove of timber, some of which was 20 inches through, was carried the above distance; some standing, some broken down, and some torn up by the roots. In some instances, logs and other ponderous substances, that were in contact, were separated 7 or 8 rods, and others before at a distance, were thrown together. There are many conjectures concerning it, but no one can satisfactorily account for it.

Article no. 597 Subject: Education
Ref. August 7, 1833; pg. 2, col. 3

Lewiston Academy.—By an advertisement in our paper of this week, it will be seen that the summer term of this institution will close on the 22d inst., when various exercises, demonstrative of the proficiency of the students, will be gone through with. This Academy already enjoys a high reputation, and we call the attention of our citizens to the projected examination on the 22d, as one which will no doubt prove very interesting, and as affording evidence of the propriety of additional efforts being made to cherish this growing seminary, the influences of which cannot be otherwise than salutary to the community. [Transcriber's note: This article appears in the Editorial columns.]

Article no. 598 Subject: Transportation
Ref. August 7, 1833; pg. 2, col. 3

The Canal.—The state of the Canal is worse than it has been in any previous years, despite the large sums that have been squandered upon it the present season. Boats are daily aground in the vicinity of this place, notwithstanding the vast quantity of water in the feeder—lake Erie!—which supplies this section of the canal. In view of the facts here stated, the question naturally presents itself, is there no way by which the navigation can be improved, and a saving made of the sums which are annually thrown away in the shape of repairs? We answer, there is. Let honest and competent men be put in charge of the canal, and give them a carte blanche upon the treasury. When this is done, the canal will be put in a condition, not only to facilitate commerce, but to save yearly twice the interest of the money that will be requisite to put it in a good state of repair, and keep it so. But while thirty-third rate lawyers, who have not brains enough to get a living at their trade,—but who nevertheless are thoroughgoing chaps at the polls and political hurrahs,—are intrusted with the management of the public works, so long will every thing be kept at sixes and sevens. [Transcriber's note: This article appears in the Editorial columns.]

Article no. 599 Subject: Agriculture
Ref. August 7, 1833; pg. 2, col. 3

Goodsell's *Genesee Farmer.*—This is the title of an Agricultural paper, published at Rochester, by Mr. N. Goodsell, which has reached its fifth number. It bids fair to be another valuable auxiliary to the cause of Agricultural science, and we cannot but wish that the best success may attend the labours of the enterprising editor. The paper is printed in the quarto form, at $2 per year, in advance. We hesitate not to recommend it to farmers generally.

Article no. 600 Subject: Politics
Ref. August 7, 1833; pg. 2, col. 3

Extract: A mark of wisdom.—It is with sincere pleasure that we transfer to our columns the annexed article from the *Utica Elucidator* of Tuesday week. To our Masonic fellow citizens in every part of the United States, we would say—"Go thou and do likewise."
Decline of Freemasonry.—It is with pleasure that we announce to the public that the Masonic hall on Catharine street, in this city, in which the disciples of Hiram Abiff have long been wont to meet in secret conclave, has been recently disposed of for some more worthy purpose. {Article includes discussion of the decline of freemasonry in the city of Utica.} [Transcriber's note: This article appears in the Editorial columns. Length, 4 paragraphs.]

Article no. 601 Subject: Transportation
Ref. August 7, 1833; pg. 2, col. 3

We earnestly hope the following contemplated reduction of Tolls on the Erie and Ohio Canals, will be effected:—
From the *Argus.*
New-York and Ohio Canals.—We are authorised to state that Judge Tappan and Mr. Kelly, a committee of the Canal Commissioners of Ohio, had a meeting with a committee of the canal board of this state, at the canal room, on Tuesday last, that it was agreed by them to recommend to their respective boards a reduction of 25 per cent. on the toll on merchandize transported on the canals of the two states. Should the recommendation be adopted, the reduction would take effect after the expiration of the present year. [Transcriber's note: This article appears in the Editorial columns.]

Article no. 602 Subject: Transportation
Ref. August 7, 1833; pg. 2, col. 5

"Long Freights."—In a stroll upon the docks, we observed considerable lots of Merchandise shipping upon the Erie Canal, for Merchants in the state of Tennessee. This is the fruits of a too long delayed reduction of Tolls. Three years ago our small-light rulers attempted to increase, instead of diminish the rates of toll on the Erie Canal; but fortunately for the state, this suicidal policy was resisted by the intelligence and firmness of the Anti-Masonic members of the Legislature.—*Albany Jour.*

Article no. 603 Subject: Court
Ref. August 7, 1833; pg. 2, col. 6

The Hon. Nathan Williams, Judge of the 5th Circuit, has finally completed his 60th year, and is about to resign his office. Samuel Beardsley will probably be the successor. This will leave a vacancy in Congress, to be filled at the ensuing election.—*Al. Jour.*

Article no. 604 Subject: Education
Ref. August 7, 1833; pg. 2, col. 6

Lewiston Academy.
The Summer Term of this institution will close on Thursday the 22d of August. Examination will commence on Thursday, 20th inst. [sic], and continue through three days. On Thursday afternoon an address by J.H. Quinby; in the evening, the play *Damon and Pythias* followed by the farce *Animal Magnetism*. The next term will commence on Monday 23d of September.
G. REYNOLDS, Secretary.
Lewiston, August 7th, 1833.

Article no. 605	Subject: Military

Ref. August 7, 1833; pg. 2, col. 6

BRIGADE ORDERS.
State of New-York, 5th Brigade, July 25th, 1833.

The commissioned officers, non-commissioned officers, and musicians of the 5th Brigade, in the 24th Division of Infantry, of the Militia of this State, are hereby ordered to rendezvous at the times and places hereinafter stated, armed and equipped as the law directs, for the purpose of training, disciplining and improving in martial exercise.

Those of the 163d Regiment at the village of Lewiston, on Wednesday and Thursday, the 21st and 22d days of August next.

Those of the 180th Regiment at the Court-House Square, in the village of Lockport, on Thursday and Friday, the 22d and 23d days of August next.

Those of the 210th Regiment at Morehouse's Corners, in Hartland, on Friday and Saturday, the 23d and 24th of August next.

The several parades will be formed at nine o'clock, A.M., of each day.

And the several Regiments composing said Brigade, are herehy [sic] ordered to rendezvous at the times and places hereinafter stated, armed and equipped as the law directs, for inspection, review and martial exercise, viz:

The 210th Regiment at Morehouse's corners, in Hartland, on Wednesday the 18th day of September next.

The 180th Regiment at the Court-House square in the village of Lockport, on Thursday the 19th day of September next.

The 163d Regiment in the village of Lewiston, on Friday the 20th day of September next.

The respective lines of the several Regiments to be formed at 9 o'clock, A.M. of the day appointed.

By order of Brig. Gen. A.H. PORTER.
W. HUNT, Brigade Inspector.

Article no. 606	Subject: Advertisement

Ref. August 7, 1833; pg. 2, col. 6

PARLEY's Magazine, Nos. 7, 8, 9;
The People's do. , " 7, 8, 9,
National Portrait Gallery, No. 4, containing fine Portraits of Daniel P. Tompkins, Henry Clay, and Gen. William Moultrie; just received by
Augut [sic] 6.   N. LEONARD.

Article no. 607	Subject: Advertisement

Ref. August 7, 1833; pg. 3, col. 1

—,000 [partially illegible] Bushels Wheat WANTED.
The Lockport Mills, formerly belonging to [—; illegible due to tear in page] L.A. Spalding and subsequently rented for a term [illegible] years by L.A. & A.H. Spalding, no exertions [illegible] be wanting on their part, in the management of [illegible] extensive establishment, to give perfect satisfaction to the farmers, and the public generally. Having engaged a first rate custom Miller, and A.H. Spalding having for a number of years attended particularly to grinding, they feel confident, that no better custom work can be done in this or any other country, than they are prepared to do.

Particular pains will be taken to accommodate aged or infirm persons or boys, who may wish to have grists ground at these mills.

Cash paid for wheat, at the highest market prices, or wheat received in store at all times. A share of public patronage is respectfully solicited.

A.H. SPALDING & Co.
Lockport, 8th month, 7th, 1833.

Article no. 608	Subject: Advertisement

Ref. August 7, 1833; pg. 3, col. 1

Extract: Lockport Book Store.
Late Publications Just Received. {Advert includes extensive list of books.} [Titles begin with, Records of travels in Turkey and Greece, &c., and of a cruise in the Black Sea with the Caspian Sea, in the years 1829, 30, and 31, by Adolphus Slade, 2 vols.; and end with, Blake's Universal Geography for Schools and Academies.]
August 6.   N. LEONARD.

Article no. 609	Subject: Advertisement

Ref. August 7, 1833; pg. 3, col. 1

CHEAP EDITION of the works of Sir Walter Scott, which will embrace all his Poems, Novels, Histories, Biographies, Essays, and fugitive compositions: as well as the Biography and Private Correspondence now in the course of publication in New-York, in parts: each part embracing as much matter as is contained in two volumes of the present editions of the Waverly Novels, which will be put at the unprecedented low prices of thirty-seven and a half cents each part—ten parts are already published, comprising 1st, Waverly; 2d, Guy Mannering; 3d, Antiquary; 4th, Rob Roy; 5th, Black Dwarf and Old Mortality; 6th, Heart of Mid Lothian; 7th, Bride of Lammermoor; 8th, Ivanhoe; 9th, Monastery; 10th, Abbott; for sale single or in setts by
August 6.   N. LEONARD.

Article no. 610	Subject: Notice

Ref. August 7, 1833; pg. 3, col. 1

One Penny Reward!
Ran away from the subscriber on Sunday the 21st inst., William Mekum, an indented apprentice to the farming

business. Had on when he went away a black roundabout jacket, light fustian pantaloons, dark vest, a leather cap, and cowhide shoes; he was 15 years of age, is a little freckled, and rather small for his age. This is to forbid all persons harbouring or giving him credit on my account, as I will pay no debts of his contracting.

JAMES E. HAWLEY.

Pendleton, Niagara County, July 30, 1833.

Article no. 611 Subject: Notice
Ref. August 7, 1833; pg. 3, col. 1

Lost Pocket-Book.

Lost, on Tuesday the 23d inst., somewhere between Lockport and Royalton, a large sized calf skin Pocket-Book, containing three notes signed by James Pixley and payable to Austin Wallis, dated the 15th day of April, 1833: two of them of $200 each, and the other $280. Also, three notes signed by Wm. Taylor and payable to Austin Wallis, dated in April, 1832: two of them $45 each, and the other $5, due 1st January, 1833. On one of them is an endorsement of $25; also, one other note signed by Benjamin Purdy, payable to Austin Wallis, six months after date, amount $45; also, one other note signed by Archibald Taylor, and payable to John Maker or bearer, and due 1st January, 1834, amount about $31: also, some other small notes and obligations of value only to the owner. Whoever will return said pocket-book and notes, or give information where they may be found, shall be handsomely rewarded.

The public are hereby cautioned against purchasing any of the above mentioned notes.

AUSTIN WALLIS. Royalton, July 29, 1833.

Article no. 612 Subject: Notice
Ref. August 7, 1833; pg. 3, col. 1

Extract: SHERIFF'S SALE.

By virtue of an execution issued out of the Supreme Court of Judicature of the State of New-York, and to me directed and delivered, against the goods and chattels, lands and tenements, real estate and chattels real, of Robert Campbell and Anthony Slingerland, I have seized and taken, all the right, title, claim, interest, estate or demand, of the said Robert Campbell and Anthony Slingerland, of, in and to all the one undivided third part of all that tract of land situate, lying and being in the town of Porter, county of Niagara, and State of New-York, known as lots number twenty-three and twenty-eight, in township number fifteen, and ninth range of townships, of the Holland Company's Land, so called, {Notice includes description of boundaries,} containing two hundred acres, be the same more or less: all which said property, together with all the right, title, claim, interest or demand of the said Robert Campbell and Anthony Slingerland, of, in or to all and singular the appurtenances thereunto in anywise appertaining, I shall expose to sale, as the law directs, at the tavern or inn, in the village of Youngstown, in the town of Porter and county of Niagara, now kept by Lorenzo A. Kelsey, 23 September 1833. Dated August 7, 1833.

H. McNEIL, Sheriff. L.H. WALKER, Under Sheriff.

Article no. 613 Subject: Advertisement
Ref. August 7, 1833; pg. 3, col. 2

Dry Goods—Wholesale.

The subscribers have now for sale, in their stores at Niagara and York, a large and varied stock of

Staple and Fancy Dry Goods,

at unprecedented low prices.

They beg to give notice, that their Fall Stock is arriving, and will be shortly open for inspection at their establishments above noted.

WM. GUILD, Jun. & Co. Niagara, 31st July, 1833.

Article no. 614 Subject: Advertisement
Ref. August 7, 1833; pg. 3, col. 2

To Capitalists!
VALUABLE PROPERTY FOR SALE.

The subscriber offers for sale the undivided three fourths part of the Lockport Sash Factory.

This property is most eligibly situated on the natural basin, at the foot of the combined locks, in the flourishing and rapidly increasing village of Lockport, and is constantly supplied with an ample quantity of water to drive the machinery requisite for the manufacturing of Sash, Pails, and Tubs. To capitalists this property offers advantages which are not often to be met with in any section of the State or Union. The growth of the village and surrounding country is such as to furnish a ready market for almost any quantity of sash that could be manufactured—to say nothing of the facilities offered by the canal for sending the articles either east or west. The only motive which induces the subscriber to offer this property for sale, knowing as he does its great value, is the want of means to carry the establishment on as extensively as it ought to be. Those therefore who wish to enter into such a business, will find the opportunity here offered them, well worthy their prompt attention. The terms of sale will be made easy and reasonable. Refer to L.A. Spalding or the subscriber.

D.A. THOMPSON. Lockport, July 24th, 1833.

N.B. Connected with this establishment will be sold a patent right for manufacturing and vending sash, exclusively, for the counties of Niagara, Erie and Orleans.

The *Rochester Inquirer* and *Ithaca Chronicle* will publish the above to the amount of $2, and charge this office.

Article no. 615 Subject: Notice
Ref. August 7, 1833; pg. 3, col. 2

SHERIFF'S SALE.

By virtue of two executions issued out of the Supreme Court of Judicature of the state of New York, and to me directed and delivered, against the goods and chattels, lands and tenements, real estate and chattels real, of Silas Hopkins of my bailiwick, I have seized and taken all that certain tract or parcel of land, situate in township number fourteen, in the eighth Range in the town of Lewiston in the county of Niagara and State of New York, being seventy-six acres off the north end of the middle third part of lot number thirty-eight, all which I shall expose to sale as the law directs, at Public Auction or vendue, at the Lewiston Hotel, now kept by Isaac Colt, jr., on Friday the 6th of September next, at 2 o'clock in the afternoon of that day. Dated Lewiston, 24th July, 1833.

H. M'NEIL, Sheriff. R. FANNING, Deputy.

Article no. 616 Subject: Notice
Ref. August 7, 1833; pg. 3, col. 2

NOTICE.

Bond & Favor have concluded to give up business in the Mercantile line; therefore, the partnership heretofore existing is mutually dissolved.

STEPHEN B. BOND. JOSEPH FAVOR.
July 24, 1833.

Article no. 617 Subject: Advertisement
Ref. August 7, 1833; pg. 3, col. 2

100,000 Feet clear Canada Pine Lumber, and a general assortment of common stuff, on hand, at the subscriber's lumber yard.

L.A. SPALDING. Lockport, 7th mo. 17, 1833.

Article no. 618 Subject: Notice
Ref. August 7, 1833; pg. 3, col. 2

$5 Reward.

STRAYED or stolen from the subscriber on the 1st inst., a dark brown or black Mare, five years old, trim built, small limbs, switch tail, natural trotter, no shoes on, supposed to be a small scar on the back caused by the saddle, and one quite small on the neck, caused by bleeding; these scars may now not be visible, however: these are the only particulars that can now be recollected by the owner. Said mare is judged to be between 13 and 15 hands high, carries her head up, and has quite a coltish look. Whoever takes up, returns, or gives information where she may be found, shall receive the above reward and all charges paid.

CHARLES PRATT, Somerset, or
ACHILLES M. PRATT, Johnson's creek, Niagara co.
July 12, 1833.

Article no. 619 Subject: Notice
Ref. August 7, 1833; pg. 3, col. 2

$5 Reward!

LOST, on Saturday morning abut 9 o'clock, a silver Swiss watch, about five miles west of Lockport, on the Mountain Ridge road, near widow Thompson's. Whoever will return the watch to the owner at widow Thompson's, or leave it at Shepard's or Prentice's shop, shall receive the above reward.

BARRIT BURCHARD. Cambria, July 17, 1833.

Article no. 620 Subject: Advertisement
Ref. August 7, 1833; pg. 3, col. 2

FANNING MILLS.

The subscriber having for years witnessed the imperfect manner in which the wheat brought to this market has been cleaned, and knowing the loss sustained thereby to the purchaser as well as farmer, and believing the reason of this loss to be attributed to the great variety of miserably constructed Fanning Mills which have been crowded upon the farmers, has made arrangements with FRANCIS L. LE ROY, to manufacture and keep on hand a quantity of

Superior Fanning Mills,

for special use of the farmers of this county. They are made with great care, and differently arranged from any now used in this county, (excepting those made after the same pattern.) By being properly tended, they will clean sixty bushels of wheat per hour. By the arrangement of the screen, they separate, completely, the wheat from the tares, and deposit cockle and chess each by itself.

To the neat practical farmer, these mills are the kind wanted, and will soon make a saving, over the mills in common use, sufficient to pay their cost.

These mills are warranted to be of superior construction and workmanship, and to perform well.

Mills repaired, and other patents altered to the plans of those above mentioned, when their construction will admit of it.

Seives [sic] and Screens constantly on hand, and manufactured in the neatest manner, to suit mills of any size for Wheat, Corn or Barley. The shop is near the Flouring Mill formerly belonging to the subscriber.

L.A. SPALDING. Lockport, 7th month, 31st, 1833.

N.B. Terms of payment made easy to those wishing credit.

Article no. 621 Subject: Notice
Ref. August 7, 1833; pg. 3, col. 2

STRAY COW.

Strayed, or stolen from the commons in this village on the 5th July inst., a reddish Brown Cow, 5 years old last spring, brockled face, bugg horns, a long bushy tail, and a little white on the belly. No other marks recollected. She was in milk when lost. Whoever will return said cow, shall receive five dollars reward, and the thanks of the subscriber, together will all necessary charges.

JONATHAN SIMONS.
Lockport, 24th July, 1833.

Article no. 622 Subject: Advertisement
Ref. August 7, 1833; pg. 3, col. 3

Extract: NEW PUBLICATIONS,
just received at the Lockport Book Store:

{Advertisement includes list of about 20 books.} [Titles begin with, Life and writings of John Jay, and end with, Views in New York city and its environs, Nos. 1 to 6.] Together with most of the late Novels—received this day and for sale by

June 24, 1833.   N. LEONARD.

Article no. 623 Subject: Advertisement
Ref. August 7, 1833; pg. 3, col. 3

Extract: New Works,
Just Received at the New Book Store:

{Advertisement includes list of about a dozen books.} [Titles begin with, Boswell's Life of Samuel Johnson, LL.D. a new edition, with numerous additions and notes, by John Croker, LL.D. in 2 vols.; and end with the following titles: Mrs. Edgeworth's works, Boys' and Girls' Library, Christian Lyre, Young Man's own Book, Young Ladies' own Book, Singer's own book, Humourist's own Book, &c., &c.]

H.A. SILL. Lockport, June 26th, 1833.

Article no. 624 Subject: Advertisement
Ref. August 7, 1833; pg. 3, col. 3

NEW ESTABLISHMENT.

The subscriber would inform the inhabitants of Lockport, and the public generally, that he is commencing the business of

Book Binding

in this place, where he will manufacture and keep on hand,

Ledgers, Day-Books, Record Books, and Blank Books of every description. Blank Books made to order of any required size and pattern. Persons wishing to have Books, Pamphlets, &c. bound, may depend upon having them done in the best manner and on short notice, by leaving them at the Book Store of H.A. SILL.

Lockport, June 25th, 1833.

Article no. 625 Subject: Notice
Ref. August 7, 1833; pg. 3, col. 3

NOTICE is hereby given, in pursuance of the statute in such cases made and provided, that by virtue of the provisions and directions contained in the last Will and Testament of Jehiel Comstock, deceased, all the right, title, and interest of him the said deceased, in and to all that certain piece or parcel of land, situated and being in the town of Royalton, in the county of Niagara, and being part and parcel of lot number one, in the seventh section of township number fourteen, in the fifth range of townships of the Holland Land Company's Land, (so called,) and being bounded north and west by lands now in the possession of Martin Kinsley, east by lands of Joshua Dunbar, and south by lands in possession of one Ira O. Williams, containing fifty acres more or less, will be sold at Public Auction by the undersigned, executor of the last Will and Testament of the deceased, on the premises, on the 26th day of August next, at ten o'clock in the forenoon of that day. The interest of said deceased is to be sold, being a right of purchase under and by virtue of a contract or article of agreement with the Holland Company. The terms will be made known at the time of sale. Dated July 4th, 1833.

SAMUEL WARNER, Executor.

Article no. 626 Subject: Advertisement
Ref. August 7, 1833; pg. 3, col. 3

Extract: NEW BOOKS,
Just Received, by H.A. SILL, at the New Book Store, in front of L.A. Spalding's office. {Advertisement includes list of about twenty books.} [Titles begin with, Pencil Sketches, or outlines of Character and Manners, by Miss Leslie; and end with, The Summer Fete, by Thomas Moore.] July 10, 1833.

Article no. 627 Subject: Advertisement
Ref. August 7, 1833; pg. 3, col. 3

Valuable Village House and Lot for Sale.

The beautifully situated House and Lto [sic] on the corner of Walnut and Cottage streets, now occupied by A.W. Douglass, for sale on liberal terms. Its situation will command good rent, if the purchaser does not wish to occupy it.

The owner of this property wishes to purchase a farm, for which cash will be given for the balance, in exchange for the house and lot mentioned. Apply to

L.A. SPALDING. Lockport, 7 mo. 8, 1833.

[Transcriber's note: Three more advertisements follow for this vendor, in the same column, for: Pine shingles; Red cedar posts; and, Pine Eve troughs.]

Article no. 628   Subject: Advertisement
Ref. August 7, 1833; pg. 3, col. 3

Apprentice Wanted.

A Lad, 15 or 16 years old, of respectable parentage and good habits, is wanted as an apprentice to the Sash-Making and Glazing Business. Apply to the subscriber at his sash factory.

D. GREENVAULT. Lockport, July 17, 1833.

Article no. 629   Subject: Advertisement
Ref. August 7, 1833; pg. 3, col. 4

NEW BOOK STORE.

The subscriber respectfully informs the inhabitants of Lockport, and its vicinity, that he is now opening, in the store in front of L.A. Spalding's office, on Main-street, an entire new stock of

Books and Stationary [sic],

Comprising a general assortment of Theological, Medical, Classical, Miscellaneous, School and Blank Books, which are offered, wholesale and retail, on the most reasonable terms—such as he hopes will entitle him to a share of public patronage.

All orders from town or social Library Companies, merchants and individuals, will be promptly attended to.

A very liberal discount will be made to Library Companies and Merchants.

Those wishing to purchase, will find it to their advantage to call.

H.A. SILL. Lockport, June 12, 1833.

[Transcriber's note: Another advertisement appears for this vendor, in the same column, for: "Paper hangings and trimmings."]

Article no. 630   Subject: Advertisement
Ref. August 7, 1833; pg. 3, col. 4

Boots and Shoes at the Green Store.

The subscribers have just received from New-York, an extensive assortment of

Ladies', Gentlemens' [sic] and Children's

Boots and Shoes, which they offer for sale at reduced prices, at wholesale and retail.

J.M. HAMILTON & Co. June 12, 1833.

Article no. 631   Subject: Advertisement
Ref. August 7, 1833; pg. 3, col. 4

DOCT. HILL

has opened an office next door to the Frontier House, directly over the general stage-office, where he may be consulted at all times.

Lewiston, June 12, 1833.

Article no. 632   Subject: Advertisement
Ref. August 7, 1833; pg. 3, col. 4

UPPER LEATHER.

500 Sides first quality Upper Leather, for sale cheap at the Green Store.

J.M. HAMILTON & Co. June 12, 1833.

Article no. 633   Subject: Advertisement
Ref. August 7, 1833; pg. 3, col. 4

Extract: MEDICINES.

Drugs, Medicines, Paints, Oils, Dye-Stuffs, Glass-Ware, Brushes, Perfumery, Patent Medicines, &c. &c., for sale wholesale and retail, at the sign of the Big Mortar, Lockport, at reduced prices; among which are the following: {Advertisement includes long list of items for sale, arranged alphabetically, from Antimony to White Vitriol.} The above articles are warranted to be genuine. Physicians and country dealers will find it to their advantage to call before they purchase elsewhere.

ROYAL SHARP, Druggist. Lockport, June 12, 1833.

Article no. 634   Subject: Advertisement
Ref. August 7, 1833; pg. 3, col. 5

WOOL.

The subscribers will pay cash for any quantity of Fleece or Pulled Wool, common or Merino, delivered at the shop of Samuel Works, in Lockport lower town.

S. WORKS, J.K. SKINNER. Lockport, June 12, 1833.

Article no. 635   Subject: Advertisement
Ref. August 7, 1833; pg. 3, col. 5

CIGARS.

A Lot of superior cigars, just received and for sale low, at the New-Book Store by

Lockport, June 18th, 1833.   H.A. SILL.

Article no. 636   Subject: Advertisement
Ref. August 7, 1833; pg. 3, col. 5

NEW STORE and NEW GOODS.

ROYAL SHARP, respectfully informs Physicians, Painters, Cloth-Dressers, and the inhabitants of Lockport and vicinity generally, that he is now opening, in the New Store next door east of Lyman A. Spalding's Office, on Main-street, at the sign of the Big Mortar,—a general, well selected and extensive assortment of

Drugs, Medicines, Paints, Oils, Dys-Stuffs [sic],
Perfumery and Confectionary, &c.

All recently purchased, and of very superior quality. Said goods will be sold wholesale or retail, very low for cash.

To prevent the injurious consequences to health which the injudicious administration of medicine so often produces, R.S. can be consulted at the shop at all times, and will give advice in all cases of disease requiring medicine gratuitously.

As mistakes in the sale of medicine are often fatal, a Clerk well acquainted with Drugs and Medicines has been employed—and by much care and strict attention, he hopes to merrit [sic] the patronage of the public. June 5, 1833.

Article no. 637   Subject: Advertisement
Ref. August 7, 1833; pg. 3, col. 5

TEAS.
12 Chests young Hyson   Tea,
10 half do. do.   do   do.
6 [Chests] Hyson Skin   do.
2 do.   Old Hyson   do.
2 cases   Imperial   do.

The above Teas are of a very superior quality, and will be sold by the chest or at retail, at very low prices, by ROGERS & BROWN. June 5, 1833.
[Transcriber's note: Several more, small advertisements appear for this vendor, in the same column, for: 850 pieces calico; Irish linens; Palm leaf hats; Bleached sheetings and shirtings; French printed muslins; 100 Ginghams; and, Fruit.]

Article no. 638   Subject: Advertisement
Ref. August 7, 1833; pg. 3, col. 5

NEW GOODS.
HOUSE & BOUGHTON are now receiving a large assortment of New Goods. June 5.

Article no. 639   Subject: Advertisement
Ref. August 7, 1833; pg. 3, col. 5

50 Doz. Palmleaf Hats, received and for sale by HOUSE & BOUGHTON. June 5.

Article no. 640   Subject: Advertisement
Ref. August 7, 1833; pg. 3, col. 5

Trimmings and Bindings.
Shoe makers will find a good assortment of the above articles at the Green Store.
J.M. HAMILTON & Co. June 12, 1833.

Article no. 641   Subject: Advertisement
Ref. August 7, 1833; pg. 3, col. 5

LEATHER, BOOTS & SHOES.
The subscribers have on hand an extensive assortment of the above articles, of their own manufacture, and of a superior quality, which they offer for sale in large or small quantities, at such prices as cannot fail to suit those who call and examine them.
J.M. HAMILTON & Co. June 12, 1833.

Article no. 642   Subject: Advertisement
Ref. August 7, 1833; pg. 3, col. 5

IRON AND NAILS.
For Sale in large or small quantities, at the lowest rates by
June 11. SETH PARSONS, & Co.

Article no. 643   Subject: Advertisement
Ref. August 7, 1833; pg. 3, col. 5

EAGLE TAVERN, Lockport.
This Establishment was opened by the subscriber the latter part of the last season. It is entirely new, and one of the most commodious, extensive, well finished and furnished Public Houses in the western country. It is located in the centre of the village, a few rods above the combined locks, fronting the canal. From the walk on the top of the piazza, there is a good view of the upper and lower towns, the locks, the deep cutting though the rock, and the surrounding country. Standing near the bank of the canal, to which there are stairs immediately in front, under cover, and lighted during the night, and being open at all hours, makes it the most convenient point to take or leave the canal, and which can be done without inconvenience at any hour of the night, or during storms.

From this house stages arrive and depart daily to and from Niagara Falls, Lewiston, Youngstown, Rochester and Batavia. Extra carriages can be procured at any time for either of the above places.

The House being new and conveniently arranged, having a number of private parlours, with and without bed rooms attached, and standing at an interesting section of the great artificial channel through the mountains, renders it a desirable resting place for travellers and parties of pleasure.

The subscriber makes no pledges for himself, his servants, his viands, or his bar, but knowing his interests are in accordance with the comforts and convenience of his customers, he will endeavour to deserve the public patronage.
J.W. WITBECK.
Lockport, Niagara County, N.Y. June, 1833.

Article no. 644   Subject: Advertisement
Ref. August 7, 1833; pg. 3, col. 5

SOAP AND CANDLES.
The Subscribers keep on hand the above articles to sell, by the box, at Factory prices.
June 11. SETH PARSONS & Co.

Article no. 645 Subject: Advertisement
Ref. August 7, 1833; pg. 3, col. 5

MUSIC,

Vocal, and Instrumental, consisting of Songs, Duetts [sic], Glees, Trios, Catches, Marches, Waltzes, etc. Just received and for sale at the New-Book Store, by

H.A. SILL. June 19.

Article no. 646 Subject: Advertisement
Ref. August 7, 1833; pg. 3, col. 5

REMOVAL.
JOSIAH TRYON has removed his
Clothing Store

into the eastern end of the brick block, south side of the canal, and next door to Cranson and Kniffin's hardware store, where he will endeavor to attend promptly to all calls in his line of business. He has on hand a good stock of

Broad cloths, superior Velvet Cords, and Beverteens, together with most all articles appertaining to his business. His work will be done in the best style.

All persons indebted to him, whose demands are now due, must call and settle the same without delay, otherwise necessity will require that they be put in suit immediately, though the task is an unpleasant one to him.

Lockport, July 3, 1833.

Article no. 647 Subject: Advertisement
Ref. August 7, 1833; pg. 3, col. 6

More New Goods!!

HOUSE & BOUGHTON have this day received, an additional supply of Prints, Printed Muslins, Pink Chambrays, and Pinkplaid Ginghams.

Extract Ginghams, new patterns, elegant—2 pieces black and white French Muslins, a new article, beautiful patterns.

June 26.

[Transcriber's note: This advertisement was followed by three more for the same vendor, in the same column, for: Summer goods; Fresh teas; and, Cheap goods.]

Article no. 648 Subject: Advertisement
Ref. August 7, 1833; pg. 3, col. 6

BEAR'S OIL.

A Lot of genuine Bear's Oil, prepared by Sears, Rochester, just received and for sale at the Hair Dressing Establishment of W. FOX. June 5, 1833.

Article no. 649 Subject: Advertisement
Ref. August 7, 1833; pg. 3, col. 6

Fashionable Clothing Store.
E.J. PLACE

Informs the public, that he is now opening, at his Store on Main-street, corner of Cottage-street, in addition to his former stock, a choice lot of

Ready Made Clothing,

Consisting of Coats, Pantaloons, Vests, &c., &c., made in the latest fashion, and of the best quality and workmanship.

He has also on hand a good stock of Cloths, Vestings, &c., which he will make up to order, at the shortest notice in a workmanlike manner. He will also make garments of all kinds for those who choose to furnish cloth themselves.

N.B. As it is his intention constantly to keep on hand a good assortment of articles in his line, those wishing to purchase, would do well to give him a call previous to buying elsewhere.

Cutting done at short notice, and warranted to fit, if properly made up.

Lockport, May 29th, 1833.

Article no. 650 Subject: Advertisement
Ref. August 7, 1833; pg. 3, col. 6

IRON,

An extensive assortment, for sale by
SETH PARSONS & Co. Dec. 18.

[Transcriber's note: This advertisement was followed by another for the same vendor, in the same column, for: "Shoes and boots, in great variety, &c."]

Article no. 651 Subject: Advertisement
Ref. August 7, 1833; pg. 3, col. 6

Salt! 300 Bbls. Onondaga salt for sale at the lowest market price, by ROGERS & BROWN. Jan. 9, 1833.

[Transcriber's note: Several more advertisements appeared in the same column from the same vendor, for: Pine shingles; Fish; Good Leghorn Hats; Broad cloths; and, Dunstable hats.]

Article no. 652 Subject: Advertisement
Ref. August 7, 1833; pg. 3, col. 6

G.S. PLACE, Merchant Tailor,

Invites the attention of all those who have cloth to cut and make into clothing, to call at his fashionable

Clothing Store,

one door east of Rogers & Brown's, in T. Smith's stone building, where he is ready to wait upon all those that want their clothing made with neatness and despatch.

Article no. 653 Subject: Advertisement
Ref. August 7, 1833; pg. 3, col. 6

Extract: MEDICAL WORKS for sale by N. LEONARD.

{Advertisement includes list of about twenty books.} [Titles begin with, Eberle's Practice of Physic, and end with, Spencer's Essays, a late work.] N.B. Physicians in the country can be supplied to order. June 19.

Article no. 654	Subject: Advertisement
Ref. August 7, 1833; pg. 3, col. 6	

Valuable Real Estate for Sale.

The subscriber offers for sale the valuable Store and lot of ground, two doors west of the Eagle Tavern, in Main-street, Lockport. The Store is of brick, 3 stories high, and of front sufficient for two stores of fifteen feet each. It has been built but 4 years, and is constructed of the best materials.

There is also on the rear of the lot, on Crooked Alley, a two-story Dwelling House, well calculated to accommodate three small families.

Also, other dwelling houses and lots, situated in eligible parts of the village.

All the above property will be sold at a bargain.—One third of the purchase money to be paid down.

For further particulars apply to the subscriber on the premises, or to Gardner and Morse, Attorneys, Lockport.

B.H. WHITCHER. Lockport, June 12, 1833.

All persons indebted to the advertiser are requested to make payment on or before the 1st of September. This request must be complied with. B.H.W.

Article no. 655	Subject: Advertisement
Ref. August 7, 1833; pg. 4, col. 1	

Facts Speak for Themselves!!

I cheerfully certify, that I obtained of Mr. Merchant a vial of his Specific Drops, for a labourer on the Canal, who was severely attacked with the Fever and Ague, which perfectly cured him, although he was continually exposed to cold and wet for nearly two months, he remained perfectly free from any symptoms of the disease. I would therefore respectfully recommend it to the attention of the public.

ASHER TORRANCE. Lockport, May 1, 1833.

This may certify, that about the first of April last, I was attacked with the Fever and Ague very severely. I was so weak while under the influence of the disease, as scarcely to be able to stand. I then purchased a vial of Mr. Merchant's Specific Drops, and by the use of it I am confident it has cured me, and I would recommend it to the public as a valuable medicine.

JOHN VAN WIE. Lockport, May 10, 1833.

I do hereby most cordially certify, that several weeks since I was severely attacked with the Fever and Ague, and by the use of one bottle of Mr. Merchant's Specific Drops I was entirely cured, and have had no symptoms of the disease since: I do therefore recommend it to all those affected with the Fever and Ague, as a safe, sure, and valuable medicine.

C.H. M'CLEARY.
Lockport, May 14, 1833.

Article no. 656	Subject: Advertisement
Ref. August 7, 1833; pg. 4, col. 1	

More New Books at the Lockport Bookstore.

N. LEONARD is now receiving his spring supply of School and Miscellaneous Books. Also, a good assortment of Blank Books, first quality of paper and binding. May 14.

Article no. 657	Subject: Advertisement
Ref. August 7, 1833; pg. 4, col. 2	

Extract: DR. THOMAS WHITE's
Vegetable Toothache Drops.

The only specific ever offered to the public, from which a permanent and radical cure may be obtained of that disagreeable pain the toothach [sic], with all its attendant evils: such as fracturing the jaw in extracting of the teeth, which often proves more painful than the toothach itself; and cold passing from the decayed teeth to the jaw, thence to the head, producing a rheumatic affection, with many other unpleasant effects; such as a disagreeable breath, bad taste in the mouth, &c. &c., all of which are produced from foul or decayed teeth. I am happy to have it in my power to offer to the world a remedy, that will not only remove the pain nine times out of ten, if properly applied, but preserve the teeth from further decay, and arrest the disease in such as are decaying and have not commenced aching, restoring them to health and usefulness. {Advertisement includes certificates of attestation, or testimonials, provided by Wm. I.A. Birkey, Surgeon Dentist, Philadelphia; Dr. W. Judkins, Mt. Pleasant; and, Jonathan Dodge, New-York City.} For sale by SOUTHWORTH & REYNALE, and George W. MERCHANT, Druggists, Lockport.

Article no. 658	Subject: Advertisement
Ref. August 7, 1833; pg. 4, col. 3	

Extract: Massachusetts Patent Sawed SHINGLES.

The subscriber has in operation at Black Rock, head of Squaw Island, Andrus' Patent for manufacturing Shingles. 20 years' experience at the east, by those who have used them, has satisfactorily demonstrated that they are decidedly superior to the common Shingle. Also, Sawed Lath, manufactured at the same place. WALTER OSBORNE.

Reference. William Forsyth, U.C.; Augustus Porter, Niagara Falls; House & Boughton, N.W. Gardner, Lockport; U. Driggs, Tonewanta; H.B. Potter, S. Jordan, J.G. Driscoll, J. M'Knight, M. Baker, B. Rathbnn [sic], N. Rossiter, Buffalo.

To satisfy the public as to the goodness and utility of this Shingle, the manufacturer would refer to the following Certificates of gentlemen who are well known in this community: {Advert includes certificates, or testimonials, from Wm. Forsyth, Bertie, U.C.; Harry Thompson, Black Rock; J.G. Driscoll, Buffalo; S. Jordan, Buffalo, and concludes with the following certificate:}

This may certify that I have lately purchased of Walter Osborne, about thirty-five thousand of his Sawed Shingles, and although I have paid a higher price by the M. for them, (two dollars at the mill) than is usually charged for common shaved shingles; yet from them all being good and suitable for use, and requiring much less time and nails to lay them: also, being jointed and butts squared, I have no hesitation in giving it as my opinion, that they make a much better, cheaper, and make a better looking roof than any other shingles commonly in use in this part of the country.

AUGUSTUS PORTER. Niagara Falls, May 7, 1833.

Article no. 659   Subject: Advertisement
Ref. August 7, 1833; pg. 4, col. 3

PEARLASH.
Wanted immediately, 1,000 lbs. good Pearlash, by G.W. MERCHANT. May 29.

Article no. 660   Subject: Advertisement
Ref. August 7, 1833; pg. 4, col. 3

DRUG STORE REMOVED!
Southworth and Reynale have removed their Drug Store to the store lately occupied by Bond and Favor, on the north side of Main-street, and nearly opposite their old stand—where they are now receiving and opening a large and fresh assortment in their line. May 15.

Article no. 661   Subject: Advertisement
Ref. August 7, 1833; pg. 4, col. 4

MILLINERY GOODS.
The subscribers have a large stock of the above goods, at wholesale or retail—Viz:—Blond Lace, Do. Edging, Straw Trimming, Foundation, Florence, a great variety of Bonnet Silks, Ribbons, Reeds, Wire, Chip, &c. &c., for sale at as low prices as at any house west of Albany.
ROGERS & BROWN. June 5.

Article no. 662   Subject: Advertisement
Ref. August 7, 1833; pg. 4, col. 4

STATIONARY [sic].
N. LEONARD, has constantly on hand and for sale at wholesale or retail, Wrapping, Cap and Letter Paper, Coloured Letter and Note Paper, Quills, Ink and Ink Powder, Inkstands, Wafers, Red Wax, Slates and Pencils, together with a large assortment of Blank Books, of almost every variety of ruling and binding, "at low prices."

Article no. 663   Subject: Advertisement
Ref. August 7, 1833; pg. 4, col. 5

A CARD.
The Subscribers owe an apology to their numerous customers, and the public generally, for not having previously announced the arrival and reception of their large and splendid assortment of

SPRING AND SUMMER GOODS.
This delay has been owing solely to the great demand for our goods—and we have not time, even now, to specify the precise number of "pieces of Calico," or "Palm Leaf Hats," we have received, or have now on hand.—We give place in this respect to our neighbours, who doubtless have more leisure time than we have, but we deem it sufficient to mention, and it is all we can say at this time, that our supply is abundant, and we are constantly receiving additions suited to the wants of our customers. We invite all wishing to purchase good and cheap goods to call and examine our stock and prices.
June 11. SETH PARSONS & Co.

Article no. 664   Subject: Advertisement
Ref. August 7, 1833; pg. 4, col. 5

FOR SALE.
A First rate two horse Waggon for sale by
SETH PARSONS & Co. July 2.

Article no. 665   Subject: Advertisement
Ref. August 7, 1833; pg. 4, col. 5

GRIND STONES.
The subscribers have a quantity of the above article on hand, which they offer for sale at reduced prices.
ROGERS & BROWN. Lockport, May 8.

Article no. 666   Subject: Advertisement
Ref. August 7, 1833; pg. 4, col. 6

NEW GOODS!
ROGERS & BROWN are now receiving their usual extensive supply of Spring and Summer Goods,

Consisting of Dry Goods, Groceries, Hardware, Crockery, &c. &c., which they pledge themselves to sell at as low prices as any other establish[ment] in the Western Country. They would particularly invite their old customers, and others, to call and examine a better and cheaper stock of goods than was ever before offered for sale in this market. June 5.

Article no. 667   Subject: Politics
Ref. September 4, 1833; pg. 2, col. 4

Extract: The *Balance* says, that a Convention having been called for the 8th Senatorial District, the "Republicans of the Western counties should be up and doing!" We assure the forty editors, that the republicans will be "up and doing," without their troubling themselves in the least in the matter, and that they will also elect, by an overwhelming majority, an "efficient and intelligent man, of sound political principles, who will act with the True Democracy," maugre all the efforts of "the party" west of the Genesee. ... But, says the *Balance*, "the antimasons of the Legislature have always formed themselves into a political clan on most public questions; and by arraying themselves against the rest of the state, have placed their constituents in a worse situation than if they had been unrepresented altogether. Without any numerical force, they are commonly so stiff and perverse in their peculiar opinions, that they have little or no intercourse with the majority of the legislature. Hence they are altogether destitute of standing and influence." This philippic is the coinage of a knave. ... In this view, how pitiful—how inexpressibly contemptible and mean—is the paragraph that would rob them of standing and influence and character, or that would ascribe to them the "collarship" which so notoriously characterizes the partizans of the dorminant [sic] party. [Transcriber's note: This article appears in the Editorial columns.]

Article no. 668   Subject: Politics
Ref. September 4, 1833; pg. 2, col. 5

We hope our readers will bear in mind that the county meeting for the appointment of a delegate to represent this county in the Senatorial Convention, meets this evening at Mr. Jennings'. We trust the meeting will be a full one. [Transcriber's note: This article appears in the Editorial columns.]

Article no. 669   Subject: Miscellany
Ref. September 4, 1833; pg. 2, col. 5

The *Orleans American* requests us to copy the following, promising to requite the favour. We give place to the article in the hope that the delinquent may see the necessity and propriety of immediately paying over. We thank the *American* for his offer to reciprocate the favour, but hope we shall not soon be under the necessity of calling on him for "pay in kind"!

Black List.—The practice of publishing black lists of subscribers who defraud printers out of their just dues, is becoming quite general, and is attended in many instances, with good effects. The practice we think a salutary one, and accordingly, we would caution the public against trusting one William Angel, who lately left the town of Clarendon for a residence in the north-east part of Niagara County, as unworthy of confidence. He is indebted to us for the *Orleans American*, as Post Rider, $6.29. And from the manner of his leaving, and the promise he made to us respecting the demand, we have no doubt that it was his deliberate intention to defraud us of our dues. But if he will now pay the demand, we shall be glad to make the fact and his reasons for the neglect, (if he has any good ones) as public as we do the delinquency.

Article no. 670   Subject: Politics
Ref. September 4, 1833; pg. 2, col. 6

SENATORIAL NOTICE.

The Antimasonic Republican citizens of Niagara county are requested to meet in general convention, on Wednesday the 4th day of September next, at 7 o'clock, P.M., at the house of Samuel Jennings, in the village of Lockport, for the purpose of appointing a delegate to represent this county in the Senatorial Convention to be held at Batavia in September next.

JOHN GOULD, E. RANSOM, Jun., GEO. REYNALE. County Central Committee. August 28.

Article no. 671   Subject: Advertisement
Ref. September 4, 1833; pg. 3, col. 1

BEADS.

The subscriber has just received at the Toy and Seed Store, a very fine assortment of
        Seed and Cut Glass Beads.
Also,—Bead Needles and Bead Silk.
JOHN B. SMITH. Lockport, August 28th, 1833.

Article no. 672   Subject: Notice
Ref. September 4, 1833; pg. 3, col. 1

Notice.

All persons indebted to the estate of Jehiel Comstock, deceased, are notified to make immediate payment; and all persons having claims against said estate, are required to present the same for settlement, on or before the first day of November next.

SAMUEL WARNER, Executor.
Dated Royalton, August 28, 1833.

Article no. 673   Subject: Advertisement
Ref. September 4, 1833; pg. 3, col. 1

To Farmers—Barley Wanted!

The subscriber wishes to contract with farmers for 1500 or 2000 bushels of Barley, to be delivered on or about the 25th September next, at the Lockport Brewery, for which the highest market price in cash will be paid.

DAVID PYE. Lockport, August 28, 1833.

Article no. 674   Subject: Advertisement
Ref. September 4, 1833; pg. 3, col. 1

Valuable Farms for Sale.

The subscriber offers for sale, a valuable farm situated in the town of Royalton, about 3 1-2 miles southwest of

Middleport, containing 136 acres, of which about 70 are cleared and in a good state of cultivation. The buildings consist of a comfortable log house and good framed barn. There is also a good young orchard of about 300 bearing trees, of the different kinds of fruit.

Also, one other Farm, adjoining the above, containing 85 acres, of which about 60 are cleared. The buildings are a log house, with a framed addition, and a good framed barn. There is also an orchard of about 100 bearing apple trees, the greater part of which are engrafted.

The above property will be sold on advantageous terms. Apply on the premises to either of the undersigned, for further particulars.

JACOB DEPUY, Wm. DEPUY.

Royalton, Aug. 21st, 1833.

Article no. 675   Subject: Notice
Ref. September 4, 1833; pg. 3, col. 1

Strayed or stolen,

From the subscriber on the 20th ult., from the commons in this village, a deep red Cow, with no horns, 8 years old this spring. She gave but a small quantity of milk when she was missing, being farror [sic]. Whoever will deliver said Cow to the owner, or give information where she may be found, shall receive a suitable reward and all reasonable charges paid.

CHARLES JOINER. Lockport, August 21, 1833.

Article no. 676   Subject: Advertisement
Ref. September 4, 1833; pg. 3, col. 1

E. J. PLACE, is now receiving a large supply of coarse and fine pleated and plain stocks, which will be sold cheap for cash, or approved credit.

Country produce taken in exchange for work and clothing.

Lockport, August 21, 1833.

Article no. 677   Subject: Education
Ref. September 4, 1833; pg. 3, col. 1

Select Classical School.

J.B. CHASE will re-commence his School on Monday, the second of September next. He has purchased very extensive philosophical Apparatus and has made arrangements for increasing it as patronage and other circumstances may require. Lockport, Aug. 21, 1833.

Article no. 678   Subject: Advertisement
Ref. September 4, 1833; pg. 3, col. 1

GRECIAN LACES AND FOOTINGS.

A Good assortment of Grecian and Blond Laces and footings. Thread and Bobbinet Edgings, just received and for sale by HOUSE & BOUGHTON. Aug. 21.

Article no. 679   Subject: Notice
Ref. September 4, 1833; pg. 3, col. 1

Notice.

All persons indebted to the subscriber by Note or book account, which is due or been standing over six months, will call and settle the same forthwith and save expense. Those who neglect this notice, will find costs made soon, unless paid. August 14, 1833. G.S. PLACE.

Article no. 680   Subject: Advertisement
Ref. September 4, 1833; pg. 3, col. 1

APPRENTICE WANTED!—

To the Tin, Sheet Iron and Copper Manufacturing business. A lad of good habits, of respectable parentage, and between 14 and 17 years of age, will obtain a good situation by applying to the subscribers.

COOPER & GILBERT. Lockport, July 24.

Article no. 681   Subject: Advertisement
Ref. September 4, 1833; pg. 3, col. 1

Cash for Rags.

Cash and the highest price paid for Rags, at the New Book Store, by H.A. SILL. Lockport, August 14th, 1833.

Article no. 682   Subject: Advertisement
Ref. September 4, 1833; pg. 3, col. 1

DUTCH MADDER
of a superior quality, for sale by
R. SHARP. Lockport, August 14th, 1833.

[Transcriber's note: Two more advertisements follow for this vendor, in the same column, for: Drugs, medicines and glass ware; and, Junk bottles for sale, at the sign of the Big Mortar.]

Article no. 683   Subject: Advertisement
Ref. September 4, 1833; pg. 3, col. 1

SUPERIOR LATH.
400,000 Patent Machine Cut Lath for sale by
V. SPALDING. August 14, 1833.

Article no. 684   Subject: Advertisement
Ref. September 4, 1833; pg. 3, col. 1

Extract: Vegetable Rheumatic Drops,
OR SURE REMEDY.

Many articles are before the public, as a cure for that most obstinate and tormenting disease the Rheumatism, and from close observation, we are led to believe they have to a very great extent, failed to produce that desirable result: and may it not be attributed to the fact that articles said to cure almost every disease with which our frail bodies are attacked, and in their preparation that object is kept in view, viz: to have the medicine a cure for all diseases.

The Vegetable Rheumatic Drops are offered to the public as a sure remedy for Chronic and Inflammatory Rheumatism; and as no case is known where a perfect cure was not effected, we are justified in declaring it a valuable medicine for that painful disease, and for no other is it recommended. A few from the many testimonials of its efficacy are given below: {Advert includes testimonials from Aaron Holdridge, Columbus, Ohio, and from Rodney Spalding, Marion, Ohio.}

Take notice that the bottles are stamped "Vegetable Rheumatic Drops;" and the wrapper is signed O. & S. Crosby & Co. with red ink: none other are genuine. Price Fifty Cents. For sale by

SOUTHWICK & REYNALE, Druggists, Lockport.

Article no. 685 Subject: Advertisement
Ref. September 4, 1833; pg. 3, col. 2

COOPER & GILBERT,
Wholesale and Retail Dealers in Stoves, Hollow-ware, Tin, Sheet-Iron and Copper Ware. Store on Main-street. Lockport, Aug. 14, 1833.

Article no. 686 Subject: Advertisement
Ref. September 4, 1833; pg. 3, col. 2

CHEAP FOR CASH.
2,000 garments of Ready Made Clothing, for sale cheap for cash, by G.S. PLACE. August 14.

Article no. 687 Subject: Notice
Ref. September 4, 1833; pg. 4, col. 3

State of New-York, Secretary's Office.
Albany, August 10, 1833.
Sir—I hereby give you notice, that at the next general election in this State, to be held the on 4th, 5th and 6th days of November next, a Senator is to be chosen in the eighth Senate District, in place of Albert H. Tracy, whose term will expire on the last day of December next.

Notice is also given, that at the said election the following proposed amendments to the Constitution of this State will be submitted to the people, viz:
1. "For electing the Mayor of the city of New-York by the electors thereof."
2. "For authorizing the legislature to reduce the duties on salt."

JOHN A. DIX, Secretary of State.
To the Sheriff of the County of Niagara.

N.B. The inspectors of Election in the several towns in your county will give notice of the election of Member of Assembly, and for filling any vacancies in County Offices which may exist.

A general election is to be held in the county of Niagara, on the 4th, 5th and 6th days of November next, at which time will be chosen a Senator, one Member of Assembly, and one Sheriff, as mentioned in the notice of the Secretary of State, of which the above is a copy. Dated Lockport, August 28, 1833. H. McNEIL, Sheriff.

Article no. 688 Subject: Politics
Ref. September 11, 1833; pg. 2, col. 3

Eighth District.—The Antimasonic Republican Convention to nominate a candidate for Senator of this district, meets at Batavia on the 4th October next. We trust that the present incumbent, Hon. A.H. Tracy, who does so much honour to the state, and the district in particular, will again be put in nomination. The District might be searched through, and it would be no disparagement to the other talented men with which, we are happy to say, it abounds, to state, that his superior could not be found, as it regards talents, republican principles, and amiability and purity of private character. We admire and respect the man, both in his public and private capacity, should it be afforded us, of once again yielding him our feeble support. [Transcriber's note: This article appears in the Editorial columns.]

Article no. 689 Subject: Politics
Ref. September 11, 1833; pg. 2, col. 3

MASONICO-REGENCIANA—from the *Lockport Balance*. The forty editors are talking about the call of a county convention to nominate a Senatorial Delegate! "We hope to see this call responded to by a full representation from all the towns. The republicans of the county of Niagara may now enter the field under favourable auspices, and with strong homes of ultimate success."

"The serious inroads which were made upon the strength of our opponents, at the last election, give promise of a thorough revolution of popular feeling, by which the men and the measures of the republican party shall be vindicated and sustained even in the strong holds of federalism and political antimasonry."

"For the last few years the republicans of the western counties have contended against fearful odds. An excitement, just and laudable in its origin, was perverted from its honest and legitimate purpose, to the selfish schemes of political aspirants; and the democracy was prostrated and overwhelmed by that sentiment of indignation which should never have extended itself beyond the violation of the law. The mass of our people had no other object but to see the laws vindicated and the guilty brought to punishment. That object has been attained. Justice has had her course. The laws have been duly administered.—Courts and juries have faithfully done their duty. Freemasons, obedient to public opinion, have abandoned their lodges, and the institution has virtually ceased to exist among us."

"Our political struggles hereafter must be between the supporters of the doctrines which triumphed in the last election, and those who are at heart opposed to the democratic ascendancy."

"It is to be an unequivocal contest between democracy and federalism."

"Anti-masonry cannot much longer have any part or lot in the matter: for the good reason that the sources of anti-masonic enthusiasm have been dried up by the operations of time and the ample vindication of public justice in the judicial administration of the laws of the land."

"The prospect is more bright and animating.—Those who have faithfully defended the standard of democracy in the dark days which have now gone by, as we hope forever, should come forward with renewed energies, prepared for bold and decisive exertion."

"Let us recollect that we have heretofore contended for political existence against the most formidable combination of art, fanaticism, and fraud, which was ever brought to bear against men contending for the rights and equality of the people."

"From this retrospect let us look forward to the future and press onward to the victory which promises at no distant day to reward our efforts."

These are, without exception, the best jokes we have read for an age! [Transcriber's note: This article appears in the Editorial columns.]

Article no. 690 Subject: Accident
Ref. September 11, 1833; pg. 2, col. 4

Accidental Death.—On Saturday afternoon last, Mr. Daniel Swanson, carpenter, fell from a scaffold, while at work on the cornice of the new Methodist Chapel, now building in this village, and fractured his skull so badly that he survived the fall but forty minutes. The distance which he fell was about forty-two feet.

Article no. 691 Subject: Politics
Ref. September 11, 1833; pg. 2, col. 4

COUNTY MEETING.

At a meeting of the Antimasonic Republicans of the County of Niagara, convened pursuant to notice at the House of Samuel Jennings, in Lockport, on the fourth day of September, 1833, for the purpose of appointing a delegate to represent this county in the Senatorial Convention to be held at Batavia, Seth Parsons was called to the chair, and H.J. Stow appointed secretary.

On motion, it was resolved, that Elias Ransom, Jr. Esq., be the said delegate to represent the county in the said convention.

On motion, it was resolved, that the Central County Committee be authorised to fill the vacancy, should any occur, in the said representation.

S. PARSONS, Chairman. H.J. STOW, Secretary.

Article no. 692 Subject: Government
Ref. September 11, 1833; pg. 2, col. 4

Extract: The following is from the *Long Island Star*. The propositions are well worthy the consideration of the public generally, and we trust they will receive all the attention they merit.

Appeal to Editors. We take the liberty respectfully to call the attention of our brother Editors throughout the State of New-York, to the great error now existing in the Election law of this state, in requiring three days to hold the general election in November every year. We request them to examine the subject, and have no doubt they will discover—That one day is sufficient to take in all the votes in every town in this state, &c. {Article includes discussion of arguments.} It is for the Editors of newpapers to examine this matter, and give correct impressions to the public. If a change is deemed proper, it can easily be effected by proper application to our next legislature. [Transcriber's note: This article appears in the Editorial columns.]

Article no. 693 Subject: Notice
Ref. September 11, 1833; pg. 2, col. 5

The *Lowell Journal* advertises a runaway by the name of Timothy Kendall, who has absconded from Dunstable, leaving an amiable and virtuous wife, three small children, and an aged and decrepid father, and carrying off with him a girl named Abby Winship, about 20 years of age. He is said to have defrauded his neighbours and the public out of a large sum of money—being generally supposed to have carried away from three to four thousand dollars with him. Kendall is about 40 years of age, 5 feet, 9 or 10 inches high, thin built, brown hair, light eyes, down cast look, walks erect and quick; is a good singer, plays well on a flute and clarionet, great snuff taker, free and easy in conversation, and well calculated to deceive.

Article no. 694 Subject: Transportation
Ref. September 11, 1833; pg. 2, col. 6

Steamboat on the Genesee River. The spirit of improvement and enterprise which has ever distinguished the citizens of Rochester, is still buoyant and indomitable.—It is but a few days since, that we noticed the filling up of the stock of the Tonewanda Rail Road. Now we are informed that a Steamboat is immediately to be placed on the Genesee River, to ply between Rochester and Geneseo. It has been satisfactorily ascertained that the River can easily be made navigable.—*Al. Jour.*

Article no. 695   Subject: Court
Ref. September 11, 1833; pg. 2, col. 6

More Counterfeits.—A stranger called at a store in this village yesterday, and requested an exchange of United States bills for those of Canada. The merchant fortunately had but ten dollars Canada, for which he received in exhange a $5 bill of the U.S. Branch Bank, at Portland, and another of the same amount of the Catskill Bank, both of which he soon discovered were counterfeit. Three dollar counterfeit bills of the Utica Bank are in circulation in this vicinity.—*Roch. Dai. Adv.*

Article no. 696   Subject: Miscellany
Ref. September 11, 1833; pg. 3, col. 1

One more of the Tea Party. In your last evening's *Transcript* there was a notice from the *Otsego Republican*, that there was living in that county a Mr. Hewes, supposed to be the only survivor of the memorable tea party. There is now living in Wardsborough (Vt.) Mr. Samuel Hammond, a native of Newton, (Mass.) 87 years old, but still healthy and vigorous, who was one of that party.—*Transcript.*

Article no. 697   Subject: Marriage
Ref. September 11, 1833; pg. 3, col. 1

MARRIED.—In Somerset, on the 1st inst. by Elder J.N. Wilson, Mr. David Prusia, of Yates, Orleans co., to Miss Sibyl Shelden, of the former place.

Article no. 698   Subject: Notice
Ref. September 11, 1833; pg. 3, col. 1

Goods at Cost!!
The entire Stock of Goods, Debts, &c. of Bailey H. Whitcher, having been assigned to the subscriber for the benefit of his (the said Whitcher's) creditors: Notice is hereby given, that the goods will be sold, either by wholesale or retail, at cost. Those who wish to purchase goods low, are invited to call and purchase.
—Also,—
All who are indebted to said B.H. Whitcher, are hereby notified that immediate payment must be made. It is hoped that all concerned will attend without delay, and save trouble and cost.
SETH PARSONS, Assignee.
Lockport, Sept. 7th, 1833.

Article no. 699   Subject: Social Welfare
Ref. September 11, 1833; pg. 3, col. 1

County Superintendents.
A Meeting of the Board of Superintendents of the Poor of the county of Niagara, will be held at the Poor House on Tuesday the 24th of September inst., at 9 o'clock, A.M., for the purpose of auditing and settling accounts relative to the county poor, and for the transaction of such other business as may be brought before the board. By reference to an Act of Legislature of this State, passed February 23d, 1832, it is made the duty of the county Superintendents to audit and settle all accounts of Overseers of the Poor, Justices of the Peace, and all other persons, for services relating to the support, relief, or transportation of county paupers.
G. BACON, Clerk to Superintendents.
Lockport, Sept. 11, 1833.

Article no. 700   Subject: Advertisement
Ref. September 11, 1833; pg. 3, col. 1

WANTED—A Journeyman Book Binder.
H.A. SILL. Lockport, September 11th, 1833.

Article no. 701   Subject: Politics
Ref. November 6, 1833; pg. 1, col. 1

Extract: NIAGARA COUNTY.
Antimasonic County Convention.
At a Convention of Delegates representing the Republican Antimasons of the several towns in the County of Niagara, assembled pursuant to public notice, at the house of Samuel Jennings, in the village of Lockport, on Monday, 21st inst., Eliakim Hammond, Esq., of the town of Cambria, was called to the Chair, and A.H. Moss, of the town of Porter, chosen Secretary. The Convention being thus organized, the following delegates produced their credentials and took their seats: [Listed, below.] The Convention then proceeded to a ballot for a candidate for the office of a member of Assembly ... {Article includes numerous Resolutions and a lengthy address to the Free and Independent Electors of Niagara County.} [These were followed by appointments to Town Committees and Vigilant Committees, listed below. Length of article, four columns.]

[Transcriber's note: Refer to key for numbered codes, after list of names.]

Adams, Jason (1)   Aldrich, Johnson (2)
Andrews, Abel B. (3)   Bailey, Joseph S. (4)
Baker, Charles (5)   Barker, David (6)
Barnes, Stephen (7) (8)   Beach, Philip, Jr. (8)
Beamer, James (9)   Benedict, George R. (10)
Bills, Thomas (11)   Birdsall, Joseph, jun. (11)
Brasington, Lewis (12)   Brong, Jacob (13)

Carlton, David (13)
Carpenter, Warren (15)
Castle, Ezra (11) (37)
Clark, B. (16) (36)
Clarke, Sylvester P. (18)
Cole, Dyer (19) (20)
Cooke, Bates (20) (24)
Cooke, Lothrop (21)
Crapsey, Daniel W. (22)
Davenport, Benjamin S. (13)
Davis, Nathaniel (23)
Deklyn, F.M. (3)
Depue, Jacob (15)
Edminson, Andrew (3)
Fanning, R. (24)
Fenn, Ethan (10) (20)
Fleming, Robert, Hon. (25)
Freeman, Asher (10)
Freeman, William (15)
Gould, David (8)
Gray, Arthur (9)

Hartley, Jesse (3)
Hayes, Stephen (1)
Hinman, Horace (15)
Hurd, Erastus (15)
Ives, Atwater (23)
Keyes, Henry (18)
Kilbourn, David (9)
Kitridge, Abner (11)
Kuney, Benjamin S. (13)
Leland, Otis (11)
Manley, Samuel (9)
McCormick, James (12)
McNall, John (15)
Mitchell, Charles F. (20) (26) (29)
Moot, Jacob (30) (32)
Newman, Almeron (28)
Oliver, Daniel (7)
Orton, Myron (31)
Parsons, Aaron (17)
Plater, Eli (24)
Pratt, Charles (2)
Race, Ira (30) (32)
Raymond, E.W. (13)
Reynale, George (33)
Roberts, T.T. (14) (33)
Robinson, Riley (23)
Simonds, Austin (3)
Skeel, Christopher H. (27)
Smith, Jacob, jun. (13)
Stahl, Enoch (33)

Carpenter, [Ben.] (14) (33)
Carrington, Asa (15)
Chapin, Theodore H. (13)
Clark, H.W. (17)
Cleveland, A.H. (12)
Compton, Jacob (9)
Cooke, Isaac, jun. (21)
Craig, John (15) (22)
Crosier, William (8)
Davis, James (5)
De Veaux, Samuel (17)
Deming, Allen L. (15)
Downer, Roswell (2)
Edmunds, Edwin (11)
Farrington, John (12)
Fisk, E.H. (11)
Foster, Lemuel (15)
Freeman, Joel (13)
Galusha, Daniel (6)
Gould, John (26)
Hammond, Eliakim (7) (20) (31)
Hathaway, Sylvester R. (8)
Herington, James (20) (37)
Hurd, Eli (22)
Hurd, R. Leonard (9)
Keeny, George (12)
Kidder, Benjamin (9)
Kinyon, Allen (27)
Knowles, William (5)
Lawson, James (13)
Lockwood, Samuel (28)
Martin, Caleb (6)
McLeland, Richard L. (15)
Merritt, S.S. (28)
Molyneux, William (8)

Moss, A.H. (20) (30) (32)
Nigill, David (16) (36)
Oliver, Philander (8)
Outwater, John (28)
Pickard, Lawrence (18)
Plum, Havely (11)
Pratt, Francis O. (4) (20)
Ransom, Elias, jun. (26)
Raynor, Henry (15)
Richards, Roswell (3)
Robinson, John (21)
Shock, Philip (29)
Sinclair, Eben (3)
Smith, Abraham (28)
Spalding, L.A. (29)
Stahl, William (13)

Sutherland, Joel (9)
Thomas, Eben (15)
Toland, James (1)
Towsley, William (8)
Van Horn, Cornelius (28)
Wakeman, Stephen, jun. (13)
Watson, Ira (9)
Webber, Thomas (31)
West, Ira (23)
Worden, Semy (16) (36)

Teachout, Abram (27)
Thompson, Isaac (12)
Tower, Otis (23)
Tracy, Albert H., Hon. (35)
Vromer, Sydney (12)
Ward, N.M. (20) (36)
Weaver, William (37)
Wentworth, Nathan (13)
Williams, John (13)
Wright, Henry (11)

Key:
(1) Appointed to the Central Committee for the village of New Fane.
(2) Appointed to the Vigilant Committee for the village of Somerset.
(3) Appointed to the Vigilant Committee for the village of Pendleton.
(4) Delegates for the village of Somerset.
(5) Appointed to the Central Committee for the village of Wilson.
(6) Appointed to the Central Committee for the village of Somerset.
(7) Delegates for the village of Cambria.
(8) Appointed to the Vigilant Committee for the village of Cambria.
(9) Appointed to the Vigilant Committee for the village of Lewiston.
(10) Delegates for the village of Royalton.
(11) Appointed to the Vigilant Committee for the village of Hartland.
(12) Appointed to the Vigilant Committee for the village of Porter.
(13) Appointed to the Vigilant Committee for the village of Lockport.
(14) Appointed to the Central Committee for the village of Lockport.
(15) Appointed to the Vigilant Committee for the village of Royalton.
(16) Delegates for the village of Niagara.
(17) Appointed to the Central Committee for the village of Niagara.
(18) Appointed to the Central Committee for the village of Pendleton.
(19) Delegate for the village of Wilson.
(20) Appointed to a Committee to report Resolutions and Address expressive of this meeting.
(21) Appointed to the Central Committee for the village of Lewiston.
(22) Appointed to the Central Committee for the village of Royalton.
(23) Appointed to the Vigilant Committee for the village of Wilson.

(24) Delegates for the village of Lewiston.
(25) To be presented to the citizens of Niagara County as a suitable person to represent them in the next session of the Legislature of the State of New-York.
(26) Appointed to the County Central Committee.
(27) Appointed to the Central Committee for the village of Hartland.
(28) Appointed to the Vigilant Committee for the village of New-Fane.
(29) Delegates for the village of Lockport.
(30) Delegates for the village of Porter.
(31) Appointed to the Central Committee for the village of Cambria.
(32) Appointed to the Central Committee for the village of Porter.
(33) Recommended as a suitable candidate for the office of Sheriff.
(34) Appointed to the Central Committee for the village of Lockport.
(35) Nominated as a candidate for Senator for the Eighth District.
(36) Delegates for the village of Niagara.
(37) Delegates for the village of Hartland.

Article no. 702   Subject: Politics
Ref. November 6, 1833; pg. 1, col. 3

Extract: To the Free and Independent Electors of Niagara County: Fellow-Citizens—Having nearly arrived at that period of the year when the elective franchise devolves alike on us all, your Democratic Antimasonic Representatives feel desirous to close their auspicious labours by addressing you on the subject which brought them together, in the hope that it may be both useful to you and to themselves. {Article includes a lengthy Address.} [Submitted by:] E. Hammond, Chairman, and A.H. Moss, Secretary. [Length, 2 columns.]

Article no. 703   Subject: Politics
Ref. November 6, 1833; pg. 2, col. 3

WHIG TICKET.
Antimasonic Republican Nominations.
Eighth District.
For Senator—Albert H. Tracy.
Niagara County.
For Assembly—Robert Fleming.
For Sheriff—George Reynale.

Article no. 704   Subject: Politics
Ref. November 6, 1833; pg. 2, col. 3

Extract: THE ELECTION.
Before this sheet reaches all our readers, the present contest will probably have been ended. As, however, it will meet the eye of a large number of our friends, we improve the opportunity once more earnestly to urge them to turn out, with their wonted spirit and zeal, in support of the antimasonic nominations. ... We trust every antimason—every citizen who honours the laws and their just administration—every freeman whose heart is wrapt up in the prosperity and dignity of the country—either has or will do his duty at the present election. [Transcriber's note: This article appears in the Editorial columns. Length, 1/2 column.]

Article no. 705   Subject: Politics
Ref. November 6, 1833; pg. 2, col. 3

The *Balance* of last week whines most piteously about the defection in the ranks of the Regency Party—interlarded very plentifully with dictatorial disquisitions about the right of people to vote as they please! We are ashamed of ye, neighbours! This is no time to cry craven. You must not admit the startling truth that your party is racked and rent, but swear most roundly that it is the antimasons who are "knocked into the middle of next week." It may be too late to do this for effect this election—but then a lie for the old Handmaid is never without odour—never out of season! Moreover, you should never let your wrath so far get the better of your caution, as to induce you to expose any of the secret tactics of "the party." Depend upon it, your leaders will not thank you for your indiscretion in proclaiming that the drill-book of your faction forbids that any of the hewers of wood and drawers of water for the Simon Pure "Republican Party" should be allowed to slip their collars, be they ever so much overloaded. This was a nice tit-bit of discipline to be rolled beneath the tongues of the elect of the party, for their nourishment, and not to be betrayed to your bearers of burdens. But you have let out the secret, and you see the very jacks kick up at it. They won't go that load! [Transcriber's note: This article appears in the Editorial columns.]

Article no. 706   Subject: Politics
Ref. November 6, 1833; pg. 2, col. 4

It is a difficult matter to please our opponents. Sometimes our sheet is "too personal," for these mild gentlemen—and then again we have "too little pepper and mustard" in it to suit their taste! Because, forsooth, we last week forebore treading too hardly upon the poor miserable worms (we speak after the manner of politicians) who have been commanded to suffer their names to be used by the "Regular" Masonic-Regency party for the offices of member of assembly and sheriff, the sapient maker of the address which emanated from the

Irregular-Masonics who assembled at the Central House, has gravely surmised that it was because we were fearful that the characters of the antimasonic candidates might be too severely handled!—and this wise conceit is given a body to also at the very moment when every sworn calumniator in the ranks of "the party" was busily employed in spreading, from Dan to Beersheba, the most gross slanders against our friends! Verily, the wisdom of our opponents passeth all understanding! It were a joke indeed that we should be mum, lest the masonic slander-mill should be set to work at winnowing the reputations of these men, when a hundred liars' tongues—and among them, perchance, those of the very men who put forth the address in question—were as busy as maggots in a cheese in destroying the fair fame of their neighbours! The transcendent light of the lodge-room only could have enabled these geniuses extraordinary to smell out such a reason for our forbearance! [Transcriber's note: This article appears in the Editorial columns.]

Article no. 707   Subject: Politics
Ref. November 6, 1833; pg. 2, col. 4

One of the tales by which the enemy are endeavouring to circumvent the antimasons, is the assertion that Messrs. Tracy and Fleming are freemasons! This is the most petty falsehood that we have lately come across. But it is indicative of the character and present condition of the masonic institution. Freemasonry was a liar from the beginning—but when her votaries, her grand high priests and grand kings, were wont to promenade our streets in their gilded mitres and crowns, and their tinselled and tinkling robes, she was bold and audacious in her movements, aiming at high emprises, and scorning the petit-larceny efforts that now mark her course: but since her worshippers embrued their hands in the blood of an offending brother—since public opinion has driven the pasteboard coronets and crimson robes of state from off the stage, and the "illustrious princes" of the order have been obliged, like the accursed of the earth, to crawl into dens and by-places to hatch their plots against the peace and happiness of the people—the acts and doings of the old Handmaid have assumed a corresponding meanness—the order has sunk into the very dregs of contemptiblity—and there we are content to let it remain. [Transcriber's note: This article appears in the Editorial columns.]

Article no. 708   Subject: Politics
Ref. November 6, 1833; pg. 2, col. 4

The efforts of the masonic party to defeat the election of Mr. Reynale—or rather to lessen his majority, for defeat him they cannot—are untiring. They leave nothing undone or unsaid, to accomplish their purpose.

Why is this? The answer is ready. He has been an unwavering antimason from the earliest rise of the party to the present—never flinching from the performance of any duty which the good of the cause required at the hands of an honourable and patriotic citizen. This is an offence which they cannot forget. He has been a thorn in the side of the old Handmaid, and her idolizers seek to return the compliment by defaming him in every possible way. But "let the grey mare go through!" We guess her backers will find her race was a bootless one. Antimasons are not apt to turn their backs upon their friends at the bidding of their designing antimasonic neighbours—nor do they feel particularly called upon to believe the tales which they are sure to trump up about election times. They have had too many specimens of masonic swearing in this quarter, to be inclined to put too much faith in their political missiles. Their efforts, therefore, against Mr. Reynale, we are happy to say, "will not amount to the general issue!" [Transcriber's note: This article appears in the Editorial columns.]

Article no. 709   Subject: Politics
Ref. November 6, 1833; pg. 2, col. 4

Were we the masonic candidate for member of Assembly, we would certainly commence an action for damages against the Editor of the *Balance*.—It is enough to be set up as a pin on a political nine-pin alley to be bowled down with the first ball, without being held up as a laughing stock for friend and foe. It is enough to make a cynic "snort right out," to hear the *Balance* men talk like a lawyer, about Hiram Gardner "raising the dignity of Niagara county in the Legislature!" Why the surrogate must almost "jump right on eend" [sic] himself at such stuff. We could no more swallow such a bolus, than we could one of assafoetida. But some folks have strong stomachs, and can stand any thing. But, as we before said, if the *Balance* folks lied about us as they do about Judge Gardner, they should hear from us pretty considerably quick, "in the name of the people of the state of New-York," &c., &c. How like a flat the "Grand King" must feel! [Transcriber's note: This article appears in the Editorial columns.]

Article no. 710   Subject: Fishing
Ref. November 6, 1833; pg. 2, col. 6

NOTICE—Is hereby given that the undersigned, freeholders and inhabitants of Somerset, in the county of Niagara, intend to apply to the Judges of the Court of Common Pleas of said county, at the next term of said Court, to be holden at the Court House in Lockport, on the first Tuesday in January next, for an order to prevent fishing with nets, seines, or otherwise, in the Golden Hill

Creek, or in the waters of Lake Ontario, at any place within eighty rods of the entrance of the said Creek into the Lake.

JOSEPH S. BAILEY, PHILANDER HOPKINS,
ASA HARINGTON, TITUS C. PRATT,
JOSEPH EVLAND, STEPHEN DENISON,
ETHAN DENISON. Oct. 23.

Article no. 711	Subject: Politics
Ref. November 6, 1833; pg. 2, col. 6	

TO THE ELECTORS OF THE COUNTY OF NIAGARA.

Fellow-Citizens:—I offer myself before you a Candidate for the office of Sheriff, at the ensuing election. I am personally acquainted with the majority of Electors of this county whose votes I solicit; and this acquaintance with them was formed in the discharge of duties in an office subordinate to that which I now solicit. The public have had ample opportunity to judge of the manner in which those duties were performed; and with that knowledge, and the additional assurance that industry and fidelity will be exercised in the discharge of the duties of the office which I solicit, I am content to rest my claims.—I am not unaware that the manner in which I present myself before you has not been recently pursued in this section; but I know that the unprejudiced of all political parties are, as they should be, convinced that the principles by which the few leaders of each of our political parties are governed, are incorrect and injurious to public interest—That the Electors are convinced of its incorrectness, and will act upon the principle of the inquiries, not whether he is of this, or that, or the other party, but upon the great and distinguishing principle—Is he honest? Is he capable? and will he discharge the duty with which we invest him, faithfully and uprightly?

I can do no more than repeat the pledges given above, "my former services and the manner in which they have been performed," and the assurance that neither perseverance nor fidelity shall be wanting in the discharge of either the public or individual business which shall devolve upon me, in case of an election to that office. Under these circumstances I request the support of the independent electors of the county.

STEPHEN B. BOND. Lockport, Oct. 9th, 1833.

Article no. 712	Subject: Marriage
Ref. November 6, 1833; pg. 2, col. 6	

MARRIED—in Buffalo, on the 31st ult., by the Rev. Mr. Eaton, Mr. Wm. L. Parsons, Merchant, of this place, to Miss Mary A. Holt, of that city.

Article no. 713	Subject: Education
Ref. November 6, 1833; pg. 2, col. 6	

SELECT SCHOOL.

The subscriber having returned to the place, intends to reopen his school on the 6th inst., in the upper room of a building opposite House & Boughton's, heretofore acquired by Mr. Charles Belden. The room is sufficiently large to accommodate forty scholars. His terms of tuition remain as they have been—

For Reading, Writing, Arithmetic, Geography and English Grammar, $2,50

For History, Natural Philosophy, and Rhetorick, $3,00

For Logic, Moral Philosophy, Chemistry and the Latin Language, $3,50

D. FERRIS. Lockport, Nov. 2, 1833.

Article no. 714	Subject: Advertisement
Ref. November 6, 1833; pg. 2, col. 6	

SUPERIOR WORKMANSHIP.

STEPHEN MARCH having rented the stone Blacksmith Shop, near Spalding's Mills, is ready to do any work in his line on short notice, and in a superior manner.

EDGE TOOLS

of all kinds made in the best style, and warranted. Steel Eleptic Springs for carriages made or repaired; and any other kind of work in Iron or Steel, done on reasonable terms. A share of the public patronage is respectfully solicited.

Most kinds of country produce received in payment.
Lockport, Nov. 2, 1833.

Article no. 715	Subject: Advertisement
Ref. November 6, 1833; pg. 2, col. 6	

TAILORING.

The subscriber respectfully informs the inhabitants of Lockport and its vicinity, that he has commenced the above business in House & Boughton's brick block, (up stairs,) three doors east of the Eagle Tavern, where he will be ready to attend to all calls in his line. All work entrusted to his care will be done in good style and on reasonable terms.

N.B. Cutting done on short notice, and warranted to fit if properly made. Most kinds of country produce received in payment. L.N. STRAW. Lockport, Oct. 29, 1833.

Article no. 716	Subject: Advertisement
Ref. November 6, 1833; pg. 2, col. 6	

WANTED

Immediately, four journeymen to the tailoring business, to whom steady employment will be given through the winter.

E.J. PLACE. Lockport, Oct. 30, 1833.

Article no. 717 Subject: Advertisement
Ref. November 6, 1833; pg. 3, col. 1

Extract: IRON AND STEEL.

WM. HUMPHREY is now receiving, and offers for sale, at the sign of the Padlock, Lockport, Lower Town, the following assorted lot of Iron and Steel, viz: [Listed, a couple of dozen articles, beginning with, P.S.I. Old Sable Russia Iron, and ending with, German, Swedes and Spring Blistered and Cast Steel.] Oct. 29, 1833.

Article no. 718 Subject: Advertisement
Ref. November 6, 1833; pg. 3, col. 1

GUN SMITHERY.

50 Remington's, Sill's and Miller's Rifle Barrels. 150lbs. Brass and Steel Gun Mountings,—Also, Percussion and Flint Locks.—Powder, Lead, &c. &c. for sale at the sign of the Padlock, (Lower Lockport,) by WM. HUMPHREY. Oct. 29.

Article no. 719 Subject: Advertisement
Ref. November 6, 1833; pg. 3, col. 1

JOINERS' TOOLS.

Jtst [sic] received, the largest and most splendid assortment of Joiners' tools (of I.R. Collins' manufacture, Utica,) ever heretofore offered in this market, and for sale at the sign of the Padlock.

Lockport, (Lower Town,) Oct. 29th, 1830. [sic]

Article no. 720 Subject: Advertisement
Ref. November 6, 1833; pg. 3, col. 1

SCHOOL BOOKS.

N. LEONARD is now receiving direct from New York, a large supply of School Books, of the latest editions and the most approved kinds.—He is prepared to furnish teachers and others on the lowest terms, and they will find it to their advantage "to call and see." (Oct. 29.)

Article no. 721 Subject: Notice
Ref. November 6, 1833; pg. 3, col. 1

STRAYED into the pasture of the subscriber about the 15th of Sept. a gray mare about four years old, shod all round.

Also,—a bay mare about 12 or thirteen years old, with shoes on her forefeet, a white spot on the side about the size of a dollar. The owner is requested to prove property and take them away.

JOHN L. ACHMECK. Lockport, Oct. 21, 1833.

Article no. 722 Subject: Notice
Ref. November 6, 1833; pg. 3, col. 1

NOTICE.

Ran away from the subscriber, about two weeks since, a bound servant girl, called Dianthe Roberts. All persons are forbid harbouring or trusting said servant girl, at their peril. Whoever brings her back shall receive one cent reward, but no charges.

JOHN GOULD. Cambria, Oct. 21, 1833.

Article no. 723 Subject: Advertisement
Ref. November 6, 1833; pg. 3, col. 1

TOKEN, FOR 1834,
Just received, at the New Book Store.
Oct. 22. H.A. SILL.

[Transcriber's note: This advert was followed by another for the same vendor, in the same column: "Family Bibles."]

Article no. 724 Subject: Advertisement
Ref. November 6, 1833; pg. 3, col. 1

Extract: THE FAMILY MAGAZINE, or Weekly Abstract of General Knowledge. A Weekly, Literary and Scientific periodical, consisting of eight pages super-royal, 8 vol. to a No. {Advertisement includes further description of subject matter.} Terms—One dollar and fifty cents, payable in advance. Published at 233 Broadway, New-York, by ORIGEN BACHELOR, Ed'r. & Prop'r. Applications for the Magazine will be promptly attended to, by NOAH FULLER, Agent for the Proprietor. Lockport, Sept. 22, 1833.

Article no. 725 Subject: Notice
Ref. November 6, 1833; pg. 3, col. 1

NOTICE.

Those persons who are indebted to me by note or book account, are informed that their respective dues must be paid immediately, that I shall not remit in the least of my exertions to collect, and that unless they are paid in a reasonable time they will be put in other hands for collection. I therefore wish that this notice may be fairly understood, for I intend there shall be no mistake or equivocation.

J.M. PARKS. Lockport, October 8, 1823. [sic]

Article no. 726 Subject: Advertisement
Ref. November 6, 1833; pg. 3, col. 1

BRAN by the Ton, at
SPALDING'S MILLS.
Lockport, 9 mo. 18th, 1833.

Article no. 727   Subject: Advertisement
Ref. November 6, 1833; pg. 3, col. 2

Extract: Just received and for sale by
G.W. Merchant—An extensive and choice selection of Drugs, Medicines, Perfumery, Fancy Articles, Paints, Dye Stuffs, &c. &c.

Among which are {Advert includes list of several dozen articles, ranging from cocoa, table oil and tapioca, to morphine, strychnine and paints.} G.W.M. tenders his grateful acknowledgments to his former customers for their very liberal patronage, and begs leave to assure them and the public that nothing shall be wanting on his part to ensure a continuance of their favor. He is determined to sell as cheap as can be bought in the country, of the same quality. Great pains have been taken in the selection of his articles—and from his thorough knowledge of the business in which he is engaged, acquired by years of close and unremitting application, he flatters himself that his knowledge and skill in his vocation will be useful to those physicians and others who wish to purchase good articles—to find which is extremely difficult, since so many impositions in the way of impure and adulterated articles are practiced upon some of those who buy to sell, who instead of being able to judge of the quality from chemical tests, can hardly distinguish cream of tartar from Tartar Emetic. Hence the practitioner many times, who has not time to analyze, is defeated in his object. The public and particularly the faculty, are respectfully desired to call and examine his stock. Any articles sold not proving as good as recommended will be gratefully received and the pay refunded.

N.B. Chemicals and compounds of every description manufactured and for sale as above, at New York prices.

Particular attention will be paid to prescriptions from physicians, and family orders as usual. Medicine will be personally delivered at any hour of the night.

Lockport, October 16, 1833.

Article no. 728   Subject: Advertisement
Ref. November 6, 1833; pg. 3, col. 2

Extract: The following Fall and Staple GOODS,
just received and for sale by
Wm. Guild, Junr. & Co. at York and Niagara, viz:

{Advertisement includes list of several dozen articles, ranging from broad cloths, cassimeres and sattinets, to beverteens, tartans and camblets.} White and Tarred Cordage, assorted sizes; 2,000 two and three (stout) bushel Bags, and an assortment of other Dry Goods.

All purchased for Cash, before the late rise in England, and will be sold low. Niagara, 11th September, 1833.

Article no. 729   Subject: Notice
Ref. November 6, 1833; pg. 3, col. 2

Extract: SHERIFF'S SALE.

By virtue of an execution issued out [of] the Court of Common Pleas for Niagara County, to me directed and delivered, against the goods and chattles [sic], lands and tenements, of Eber Griswold, of my bailiwick, I have seized and taken all that certain peice [sic] or parcel of land, situate, lying and being in the village of Lockport, in the county of Niagara, and state of New York, being part and parcel of farm lot number twelve, in the fourteenth township, and sixth range of townships, of the Holland Land Company's Land, (so called,) and which said peice [sic] or parcel of land [was mapped by Jesse P. Haines, surveyor, and which map was filed in the office of the Clerk of the County of Niagara] is known and distinguished as village lot number fifteen, on [the] north side of Caledonia street, in the village of Lockport, east of Transit street, in said village, and on the westerly side of the Erie Canal, {Notice includes further description of land,} containing half an acre of land, be the same more or less, ... being the same peice [sic] of land that was conveyed to the said Eber Griswold by Jared Comstock and wife, by Deed bearing date 14 October 1822, and recorded in Niagara County Clerk's Office, in book of Deeds number one, on pages 247 and 248:—

Also,—all that certain peice [sic] or parcel of land situate, lying and being in the village of Lockport, &c., and being part or parcel of farm lot number twelve [as above, &c., and which was mapped for Asher Saxton and Henry S. Platt, and which map was filed in the office of the Clerk of the County of Niagara, and is known and distinguished] as being village lot number sixteen, on the west side of Saxton street, and bounded as follows {Notice includes description of boundaries;} All which said property I shall expose, to sale, together with the appurtenances thereunto in anywise belonging, at the Eagle Tavern, in Lockport, now kept by J.W. Witbeck, 14 December 1833. Dated Oct. 28th, 1833.

H. McNIEL [sic], Sheriff.

Article no. 730   Subject: Notice
Ref. November 6, 1833; pg. 3, col. 3

Extract: List of letters remaining in the Post Office at Pendleton, September 30, 1833. [List of names, below.] S.P. CLARKE, P.M. October 8, 1833.

Andrews, Liman, Rev.	Brainard, Martha
Buck, Harvey	Clarke, George P.
Curtis, Baily	Darling, William
Eaton, Jeremiah S.	Folger, Montraville
Griffin, Benedick W.	Holly, James C.
Holstead, Gardner	Jervis, Archibald

Jones, Absalom
Kline, David
Rugg, Luke
Tracy, John F.
Wilson, John
Wyman, Joseph

Kinient, Alfred
McZenan, John
Sykes, Wealthy Ann
Wilkenson, S.
Wilson, Reuben

Article no. 731   Subject: Advertisement
Ref. November 6, 1833; pg. 3, col. 3

I wish to inform that part of community in Lockport and its vicinity, who have got their eyes open, and have found, by sad experience, that they cannot find in the Apothecary shop that medicine which is congenial to their constitutions, that if they will call one door east of the Central House, in the upper town, I will accommodate them with the sure and safe medicine which the God of nature has provided and placed in our country for our use. I intend to keep on hand a general assortment of
BOTANICAL MEDICINE.
with which I think I shall be enabled to give general satisfaction to those that wish to try the virtue of the Botanic System. I shall at all times be ready to wait on those that call.
DOCT. H. LONG. Lockport, October 8, 1833.

Article no. 732   Subject: Advertisement
Ref. November 6, 1833; pg. 3, col. 3

FOR SALE BY THE SUBSCRIBERS AT
YORK AND NIAGARA,
50 crates Fine and Common Crockery, assorted.
50 casks Glass Ware, comprising Tumblers, Wine Glasses, quart and pint Decanters.
A large assortment of
Men's, Women's and Children's Boots and Shoes.
A large assortment of
Sole and Upper Leather,
Soap and Candles,
Pot, Post and Fools-cap paper,
Grey and Brown Wrapping do.
400 quarter casks Merrick's and Hays'
Gunpowder, F. FE and cannister;
And the following Shott's Company's Castings, viz:
400 single and double Canada Stoves, 27, 30, 33 and 36 Inch,
2,000 Camp Ovens, 12 a 15 Inch,
3,000 Bellied Pots, 2 1-2 a 7 Gallons,
600 Sugar Kettles and Pot-ash Coolers,
100 Pot-ash Kettles, weighing 4 a 12 cwt.
Assorted casks of tinned and un-tinned folding handed Tea Kettles, Goblets and Stew-pans—all sizes,
Imperial Weights,
20 quarter Casks and Hhds. Madeira Wine,
10 Casks Bottled Madeira.
WM. GUILD, Jr. & Co. Niagara, 12th September, 1833.

Article no. 733   Subject: Education
Ref. November 6, 1833; pg. 3, col. 3

Notice.
Several young men of sufficient learning, abilities, &c., and who have had some experience in school keeping, will probably find employment as teachers of common schools in our town the ensuing winter:—And as the citizens of our town have voted to raise all the money which the statute allows for the support of common schools,—to wit, double the amount we received from the state treasury—they will probably receive ready pay when their services shall be completed. We give this notice, in hopes of calling the attention of young men of superior talents, and who are in all respects well qualified to teach children and youth all the necessary branches of Education.
LEVI LEONARD, R.J. M'LELAND,
DECIUS S. FENN, SIMON BIXBY,
SAMUEL WARNER, JAMES BAKER,
Commissioners and Inspectors of Common Schools.
Royalton, Sept. 28th, 1833.

Article no. 734   Subject: Advertisement
Ref. November 6, 1833; pg. 3, col. 3

LEATHER, BOOTS & SHOES.
A First rate assortment of Sole Leather, Upper, Leather, Calf, Kip and Morocco Skins. Boots, Shoes, &c. for sale as usual, at the Green Store by ROGERS & Co.

Article no. 735   Subject: Advertisement
Ref. November 6, 1833; pg. 3, col. 3

Wanted.
A Boy about 16 years of age, as an apprentice to the Book Binding Business. Apply immediately.
H.A. SILL. Oct. 1st.

Article no. 736   Subject: Advertisement
Ref. November 6, 1833; pg. 3, col. 3

OATS
Will be received in payment for subscriptions due on the *Niagara Courier*, if delivered by 1st November next.
Oct. 2d, 1833.

Article no. 737   Subject: Notice
Ref. November 6, 1833; pg. 3, col. 3

Dissolution
The firm of J.M. Hamilton, & Co. was dissolved on the 31st day of August last, by mutual consent.
ROGERS & BROWN[,] J.M. HAMILTON.
Lockport, September 17, 1833.

NIAGARA COURIER, LOCKPORT, N.Y. (1828–1833): TRANSCRIPTS, EXTRACTS AND INDEXES

Article no. 738   Subject: Advertisement
Ref. November 6, 1833; pg. 3, col. 3

Coopering.

The subscriber still continues to carry on the Coopering business, in all its branches, and will be found in the shop at all hours, ready to execute all orders in his line of business, that he may be favoured with at the shortest notice, therefore a share of the public patronage is respectfully solicited.

R. VAUGHAN, Agent. Lockport, 18th Sept., 1833.

Article no. 739   Subject: Advertisement
Ref. November 6, 1833; pg. 3, col. 3

150 Barrels.

The subscriber has on hand one hundred and fifty pork barrels, of the first quality, which he will sell for cash or country produce: Owing to the scarcity of the article, it is an object for those in want of barrels this fall, to secure them immediately.

GEORGE S. PLACE. Lockport, 18th Sept., 1833.

Article no. 740   Subject: Advertisement
Ref. November 6, 1833; pg. 3, col. 3

Equitable Fire Insurance Co.
City of New-York.

The undersigned having been appointed agent of the above Company, for the county of Niagara and its vicinity, is authorized to issue policies of assurance against loss or damage by fire, on the most favourable terms. For the information of the public, it may be well to state, that this institution, so far as it is known, enjoys a high character for fairness and liberality.

W. HUNT. Lockport, Sept. 25, 1833.

Article no. 741   Subject: Advertisement
Ref. November 6, 1833; pg. 3, col. 5

Extract: More New Books.

Just received at the "Lockport Book Store." {Advertisement includes list of a couple dozen books.} [Titles begin with, Transatlantic Sketches, comprising scenes in North and South America, by Capt. Alexander; and end with, Parley's Magazine, Nos. 10, 11, 12, 13.]

Oct. 1st. N. LEONARD.

Article no. 742   Subject: Advertisement
Ref. November 6, 1833; pg. 3, col. 5

FALL GOODS!

ROGERS & BROWN are now receiving a splendid assortment of Fall Goods, (direct from New-York,) consisting in part of

English Merinoes, French do., Merino Circassian, Common do., Broadcloths, Home made Cloths, Domestic Flannels, Cassimeres, Callicoes & Ginghams, Italian Silks, Gros de Swiss Silks, " " Naples do. Coloured and Black, Florence do., Brown Shirtings and Sheetings, Bleached Shirtings and Sheetings, Black and Coloured Cambrics, Batting and Wadding, Bonnet Ribbons, Taffeta do.; Red, White and Yellow Eng. Flannels; Hosiery, Gloves, &c.; Pongees, Leghorn Hats, Cambric, Jaconet, Swiss and Mull Musins [sic], &c. &c.

—Also—

Groceries, Crockery and Hardware.

N.B.—The above enumerated Goods, with a very great variety of others, will be sold low. Purchasers are respectfully invited to call and examine for themselves.

Lockport, Sept. 25, 1833.

Article no. 743   Subject: Notice
Ref. November 6, 1833; pg. 3, col. 5

Look at This!

All persons indebted to the late firm of J.M. Hamilton & Co. whose notes or accounts are due, are requested to make immediate payment to the subscribers at the Green Store, as the dissolution of partnership has rendered it necessary that the books should be settled.

Sept. 25. ROGERS & Co.

Article no. 744   Subject: Advertisement
Ref. November 6, 1833; pg. 3, col. 5

Ohio Castings.

20 Tons just received from the Arcole Furnaces, consisting of

Stoves, Hollow-Ware, Cart, and Waggon Boxes,
all which are of S. Wilkeson & Sons' late improved Patterns. For sale at the sign of the Padlock.

WM. HUMPHREY.

Lockport, Sept. 18th, 1833. (Lower Town.)

Article no. 745   Subject: Temperance
Ref. November 6, 1833; pg. 3, col. 5

Temperance Almanacs,
For 1834,
For sale by the gross, dozen, or single, by
(Sept. 25.) H.A. SILL.

Article no. 746   Subject: Advertisement
Ref. November 6, 1833; pg. 3, col. 6

ALMANACS FOR 1834.

The Western, Temperance, Christian, German and Pocket Almanacs, just received and for sale by the gross, dozen, or single copy, by N. LEONARD. Oct. 29.

Article no. 747   Subject: Advertisement
Ref. November 6, 1833; pg. 3, col. 6

WANTED,
A Journeyman Book Binder.
H.A. SILL. Oct. 8.

Article no. 748 Subject: Advertisement	Article no. 749 Subject: Advertisement
Ref. November 6, 1833; pg. 4, col. 1	Ref. November 6, 1833; pg. 4, col. 3

LITHONTRIPTIC WATER.

A positive and pleasant remedy for the Strangury, Gravel and Stone, or other urinary complaints.

It has been generally supposed that the Stone could not be cured without a surgical operation; but as it is an undeniable fact, established by its extensive use in Europe, that the Lithontriptic Water possesses so powerful a property of obviating so painful an operation, that it is the duty of any person possessed of such an invaluable secret to offer it for the relief of those afflicted with that troublesome disease. This medicine has been satisfactorily employed in England by a large number of respectable individuals, in many of whom, the symptoms of the disease were the most acute and distressing[.] In America it has been truly successful, a few bottles were first imported for the use of a gentleman in the city of Boston, and so decided was the relief obtained, that measures were taken to procure the original receipt, according to which the Medicine now offered to the public, is prepared. Among those who have been relieved by the Lithontriptic Water, the proprietor is at liberty to mention to the public, Mr. Arial N. Brown of Lockport, Maj. Daniel Jackson of Watertown, Mass. and many other respectable gentlemen in the city of Boston of whom the liberty has not yet been asked.

The subscriber lately obtained the receipt of a highly respectable physician in the vicinity of Boston, who assures him that he had used it in practice without a single failure. Prepared and sold by

G.W. MERCHANT, Chemist and Apothecary.

Lockport, Lower Town, Oct. 16, 1833.

Vienna or Dutch Pills,
An Unrivalled Family Medicine.

These Celebrated Pills were originally prepared by Joseph Keyser, at Vienna, the capital of Austria, upwards of fifty years ago; and such was their beneficial effects that their composition and the mode of making them was purchased by the French Government, and has since been acknowledged by some of the most eminent medical gentlemen in Europe, to be, without exception, a most effectual remedy in various diseases, and well calculated to prevent disorders generally.

As there are many puffing impositions on the public, in introducing various Patent Medicines, and others, with statements of remarkable cures never made, yet certified by feigned names, &c. &c., render it difficult for the proprietors to do justice to the public in offering a sufficient motive to induce them to make a trial of the virtues of this most invaluable medicine, but at the same time they do boldly challenge this article for general use and utility against any other article of this nature whatever, heretofore offered, and call upon sceptics to analize [sic] and examine it, and if its composition is not calculated to effect all that is here asserted, unhesitatingly publicly to expose it as a spurious and deceptive article. For sale by,

ROYAL SHARP, Druggist. Lockport, Oct. 8, 1833.

2. INDEX OF NAMES

Abbey, 93
Abiff, 600
Achenback, 160
Achmeck, 721
Adair, 164
Adams, 69, 72, 95, 118, 134, 134, 153, 160, 172, 297, 701
Agur, 134
Aiken, 462
Aikin, 86, 461
Aikins, 576
Aimes, 152
Albany Argus, 560
Albany Eagle Air Furnace and Machine Shop, 414
Aldrich, 701
Alger, 160
Allcot, 573
Allen, 69, 71, 72, 134, 164, 255, 329, 362, 395, 415, 422
Almy, 252
Alverson, 86
Alvord, 148, 160, 179, 422
American Colonization Society, 329
Anderson, 70, 152
Andrews, 252, 426, 701, 730
Andrus, 70, 573
Angel, 669
Angevine, 325
Anguish, 160
Anquish, 422
Anson, 134
Anti-Masonic Convention, 45, 62, 65, 93, 94, 95, 96, 126, 135, 145, 148, 162, 168, 170, 172, 174, 179, 183, 189, 190, 234, 303, 305, 337, 396, 397, 398, 399, 401, 422, 430, 491, 498, 499, 547, 551, 600, 670, 688, 691, 701, 702, 703, 704, 706, 707, 708

Arbuckle, 116
Arbuthnot, 164
Armstrong, 74, 164
Arnold, 93, 322
Ash, 179, 422
Ashley, 73
Associate Reformed Church, 504
Atwater, 134
Auburn Prison, 475
Austen, 422
Austin, 69, 152, 160
Axtell, 410
Babcock, 93
Bachelor, 724
Backus, 93, 305
Bacon, 20, 93, 118, 157, 179, 294, 309, 362, 518, 699
Baer, 422
Bailey, 160, 422, 701, 710
Baker, 69, 75, 148, 160, 179, 184, 337, 382, 396, 422, 590, 701, 733
Baldwin, 160, 163
Ballou, 93
Bancroft, 81, 480
Baney, 454
Bangs, 234
Barber, 69, 70, 160
Barker, 69, 260, 701
Barlow, 46
Barmen, 71
Barmore, 163
Barnard, 69
Barnes, 69, 72, 160, 297, 422, 701
Barnum, 68, 69
Barr, 160
Barris, 422
Barrow, 515
Bartholomew, 73
Bartlett, 573

Barton, 71, 101, 134, 152, 165, 187, 336, 382
Bascom, 93
Bass, 69
Bates, 69
Bathgate, 69
Batty, 365
Baxter, 69
Beach, 134, 365, 701
Beals, 237
Beals, Wilkeson & Co., 432
Beamer, 422, 701
Bean, 184
Bear's Tavern, 505
Beardsley, 603
Beare, 160
Beatty, 152
Becker, 573
Beckwith, 234, 378
Beebee, 512
Beekman, 93
Belden, 480, 713
Bell, 69
Bellack, 70
Benedict, 69, 422, 569, 701
Benjamin, 166, 369
Bennet, 160
Bennett, 141
Bently, 163
Benton, 297
Bernard, 93
Bibbins, 69
Bickford, 422
Bigelow, 160
Bills, 179, 701
Birdsall, 70, 277, 297, 593, 701
Bissel, 134, 160
Bissell, 73, 386, 436, 442, 488, 518
Bixby, 46, 733
Bladen, 164

Blaisdel, 160
Blakesly, 47
Blanchard, 69, 163
Blanck, 69
Blecker, 427
Bleecker, 329
Bleyne, 164
Blincea, 74
Blood, 160
Blossom, 134
Blowers, 573
Bois, 337, 396
Boles, 422
Bolles, 101, 111
Bomen, 72
Bond, 284, 365, 366, 616, 711
Bond & Favor, 533, 660
Boots, 71
Bosworth, 272, 374, 422,
Boughton, 25, 87, 145, 148, 148, 160, 169, 172, 179, 297, 337, 396, 405, 405, 422. *See also* House & Boughton.
Bowen, 338
Bower, 72
Bowerman, 163
Bowers, 152
Bowman, 160, 163
Brackenridge, 69
Bradner, 179
Bradnor, 72
Brae, 134
Brainard, 730
Brang, 69
Brasington, 701
Bratt, 177
Bridsall, 422
Briggs, 85, 133, 160, 181
Bristoll, 422
Britton, 153
Brong, 701
Bronson, 70, 72, 152, 163, 297, 303, 422
Brooks, 194

Brothers, 237
Brown, 46, 69, 74, 134, 152, 160, 164, 179, 217, 223, 269, 307, 323, 359, 365, 422, 517, 589, 748
Browning, 160
Bruce, 77, 119, 134
Bruin, 153
Bryan, 96, 120, 127, 163, 234
Buchanan, 422
Buck, 57, 160, 730
Buel, 93, 160, 554
Buell, 339
Bugbee, 422
Bullen, 422
Bullock, 75
Bunce, 234
Burchard, 274, 619
Burdick, 160
Burgess, 152, 153
Burner, 160
Burnet, 297
Burns, 160
Burr, 71, 72, 152, 337, 363, 396, 422, 578
Burrow, 120
Burwell, 492
Bush, 69, 422
Butler, 69, 93, 297, 303, 329
Butts, 163
Cabot, 72
Cadwallader, 1, 120, 161, 182, 422, 428, 429, 539, 540, 557, 736
Caine, 164
Calhoun, 118
Calkins, 69, 196
Cambrelling, 297
Campbell, 7, 422, 612
Canal Bank of Lockport, 452
Canal Board, 495, 500, 558
Canfield, 93, 160, 164, 422
Carl, 69, 160
Carlton, 701
Carpenter, 69, 362, 422, 701
Carr, 69

Carrington, 71, 160, 422, 701
Carroll, 168
Carter, 93
Cary, 46, 93, 96, 127, 134
Castle, 422, 701
Caten, 93
Catlin, 148, 172, 176, 179, 268, 277, 277, 279, 280, 296, 404, 548
Center, 42, 78, 105, 371
Chaffe, 284, 366
Chaffee, 422
Chamberlin, 160
Chapin, 160, 294, 422, 701
Chapin & Hart, 3
Chaplin, 179, 422
Chapman, 91, 101, 109, 114, 165
Chappell, 160
Charlow, 72
Chase, 5, 75, 163, 219, 294, 425, 442, 465, 466, 516, 538, 677
Chatlin, 160
Cheeney, 553
Cherry, 163
Chesapeake and Ohio Canal, 136
Chesebro, 134
Child, 237, 367
Childs, 15, 70, 93, 297
Chipman, 134, 184
Chubbock, 71
Chubbuck, 70
Church, 71
Churchill, 70, 164, 588
Clapp, 71
Clapsaddle, 148, 179
Clark, 69, 148, 152, 153, 160, 169, 179, 297, 329, 402, 422, 554, 573, 701
Clark Fairman & Co., 512
Clarke, 61, 73, 93, 215, 234, 378, 422, 573, 701, 730
Clay, 118, 331
Cleaveland, 422. *See also* Cleveland.
Clement, 163

Clements, 69
Cleveland, 701. *See also* Cleaveland.
Clinton, 69, 427
Cochran, 410
Cochrane, 556
Coe, 46, 134, 149, 297, 508
Coffin, 70
Colbert, 494
Colbertson, 153
Colby, 422, 461, 462
Cole, 422, 573, 701
Coleman, 203
Collar, 179
Collins, 69, 93, 160, 719
Collins & Hannay, 234
Colt, 615
Colville, 179
Comen, 72
Compton, 69, 74, 152, 304, 379, 422, 701
Comstock, 8, 84, 89, 93, 282, 284, 327, 365, 366, 367, 368, 422, 472, 625, 672, 729
Conkey, 160
Converc, 160
Conway, 152
Cook, 69, 70, 71, 139, 148, 152, 153, 160, 172, 179, 337, 375, 376, 396, 422
Cooke, 4, 10, 18, 21, 36, 46, 88, 93, 172, 254, 263, 305, 314, 422, 461, 462, 701
Cooke & Stow, 226, 250, 469
Cooley & Lathrop, 27
Coombee, 184
Coon, 93
Cooper, 70, 134, 468, 528, 561
Cooper & Gilbert, 680, 685
Corey, 113
Corn, 378
Corning, 297, 414
Corning, Norton & Co., 414
Cornish, 160
Cortlandt, 193

Corwin, 69
Cotheal, 337, 396, 422
Cotton, 55, 69
County Poor House, 169
Covey, 160
Covill, 276
Craig, 69, 75, 422, 701
Crandal, 72
Crandall, 93
Crandell, 89, 378
Crane, 69
Cranson, 160
Cranson & Kniffin, 646
Crapsey, 75, 422, 701
Crary, 93, 148, 172, 179
Crawford, 72
Crocker, 69
Crooks, 70, 164
Crosby, 684
Crosier, 304, 701. *See also* Crozier.
Cross, 69
Crossen, 160
Croswell, 401
Crozier, 179. *See also* Crosier.
Crysler, 74
Cuddeback, 422
Cudworth, 69
Cullings, 69
Culver, 508
Currier, 69
Curry, 149
Curtenius, 396, 422
Curtis, 69, 120, 730
Curtiss, 422
Cushman, 337
Cushman & Falconer, 385
Cusick, 70
Cutler, 163
Cuykendall, 569
Cuyler, 237, 297
Dack, 71
Dady, 160
Dalliba, 337

Daly, 250
Dalzell, 160
Daniels, 480
Darling, 297, 362, 378, 730
Darrow, 119, 134
Dart, 163
Dauchy, 69
Davenport, 701
Davidson, 69
Davies, 148
Davis, 69, 70, 71, 93, 148, 152, 163, 179, 422, 701
Daws, 160
Day, 120, 160, 260
Dayharh, 378
Dayton, 480
De Freest, 396, 422. *See also* Defreest.
De Graff, 297
De Veaux, 14, 28, 32, 58, 107, 148, 179, 260, 422, 701
De Witt, 303, 329
Dean, 93, 184, 234
Deaves, 152
Defreest, 337. *See also* De Freest.
Deklyn, 701
Delavan, 435
Demaree, 422
Deming, 701
Demmon, 160
Denison, 70, 354, 710
Dennison, 106
Denny, 183
Depue, 304, 701
Depuy, 71, 674
Devereux, 153
Dewey, 152, 234, 422, 461, 462
Dexter, 160
Dicinger, 160
Dickerson, 48, 70, 179, 422
Dickinson, 277
Digee, 160
Dilley, 492
Dillon, 160
Dimmack, 70

Dimond, 64
Diossy, 153
Dix, 477, 687
Dixon, 93, 378
Dodge, 134
Donnar, 160
Doshon, 69
Doss, 152
Doty, 74, 148, 160, 169, 179, 422
Doud, 69
Doughten, 362
Douglass, 148, 160, 627
Downer, 422, 701
Doyle, 134
Drake, 163
Draper, 98, 160
Driggs, 71, 590
Driscoll, 590, 658
Dubois, 337, 396, 422
Dukehart, 234
Dunbar, 625
Dunham, 93, 337, 396, 422
Dunkan, 152
Dunkin, 70
Dunlap, 337, 396, 422
Dunlap & Craig, 75
Dunnet, 160
Dunscomb, 153
Durand, 152
Durham, 153
Dutton, 163
Dwight, 46
Eager, 454
Earl, 70, 148, 179
Earll, 297, 500
Eastman, 160
Eaton, 302, 712, 730
Eaton & Brown, 307
Eddy, 69
Edgerton, 69
Edmerson, 573
Edminson, 701
Edmiston, 378
Edmunds, 701

Edmundson, 23
Edson, 160
Edward, 152
Eggleston, 234
Ellicott, 178, 371
Elliot, 160
Elliott, 252
Ellis & Shotwell, 234
Ellmaker, 189, 331, 396, 422
Ellsworth, 69
Ely, 93, 305
Emmons, 153
Empry, 71
Ensworth, 134
Erie Canal, 497, 598, 601, 602
Estes, 74, 250
Evans, 64, 311
Evland, 710
Fairbanks, 160
Fairchild, 70
Fairman, 512
Falconer, 385
Fallen, 152
Fannerty, 368
Fanning, 67, 278, 325, 615, 701
Farewell, 134
Farman, 71
Farmers' Mills, 313, 386, 411
Farrel, 93
Farrell, 160
Farrington, 701
Favor, 533, 616. *See also* Bond & Favor.
Faxton, 234, 275
Fay, 297
Feaghn, 153
Feenan, 70
Feeter, 297
Fellows, 7, 16, 120, 132, 214, 294, 341
Feltus, 137
Fenn, 71, 143, 148, 163, 179, 422, 701, 733
Fenner, 278

Ferguson, 93, 152
Ferris, 713
Ferriss, 175
Fick, 139
Field, 93
Fields, 179
Finch, 160
Firman, 17, 70
First Presbyterian Church, Lockport, 556
Firth, 70
Fisk, 372, 410, 701
Fitch, 93, 96, 127, 305
Fitzpatrick, 160
Flagg, 128, 303, 370, 477
Fleming, 41, 120, 134, 148, 375, 382, 701, 707
Foley, 160
Folger, 73, 730
Folsom, 312
Foot, 69, 303
Forbes, 422
Forbs, 72
Force, 74
Ford, 63, 71, 144
Forrester, 586
Forsyth, 590, 658
Foster, 69, 160, 163, 701
Fowler, 69, 74
Fox, 69, 82, 134, 248, 383, 648
Frask, 158
Frayne, 160
Freasher, 153
Freeman, 69, 148, 152, 160, 169, 179, 422, 701
French, 93, 116
Frink, 237
Frisbie, 297
Frost, 72
Fuller, 160, 724
Gallup, 555
Galt, 104
Galusha, 422, 701
Gardner, 59, 74, 81, 97, 106, 110, 113, 124, 158, 160, 191, 219,

Gardner, continued, 297, 312, 318, 367, 373, 375, 376, 377, 549, 590, 709
Gardner & Morse, 654
Garley, 160
Garlick, 69, 152
Garlinghouse, 147
Garnsey, 148, 172, 410
Garrison, 70
Garrow, 297
Garsey, 179
Gary, 160
Gaskill, 69
Gates, 163, 422
Gay, 101, 337, 396, 422
Gaylord, 72
Gebhard, 337, 396, 422
Geddes, 303
Geer, 69
Genesee Farmer, 566
Germain, 63
Gibbins, 183
Gibbs, 69, 160, 380, 419
Gibson, 439
Giddins, 119, 134, 234, 294, 430, 446, 530
Gilbert, 160, 528, 680
Gillet, 410, 574
Gillett, 93
Gilson, 355
Gleason, 178
Glime, 72
Goddard, 177
Golden, 69
Goodeno, 178
Gooding, 271, 313, 365, 369, 480, 481
Goodsell, 599
Gordon, 75
Gould, 48, 69, 273, 422, 508, 670, 701, 722
Grace, 152
Graham, 152
Grainger, 118. *See also* Granger.

Grand Jury of Ontario County, 331
Grandin, 297
Granger, 93, 120, 135, 172, 337, 396, 422. *See also* Grainger.
Grant, 152, 153, 160
Graves, 69, 71, 163, 589
Gray, 134, 148, 179, 701
Green, 72, 93, 134, 153, 163
Greenman, 71, 163
Greenvault, 380, 419, 628
Greenwood, 72
Gregory, 160, 489
Griffen, 163, 396, 422. *See also* Griffin *and* Grifen.
Griffeth, 164
Griffin, 134, 730. *See also* Griffen *and* Grifen.
Griffith, 152, 237
Griffith, Brothers & Son, 237
Griffiths, 86
Grifin, 72. *See also* Griffen *and* Griffin.
Grigg, 234
Grinnell, 70
Griswold, 160, 422, 729
Groves, 69
Grow, 423
Grunway, 153
Guild, 613, 728, 732
Guthrie, 93
Hackett, 69
Hadley, 164
Hagar, 381
Haick, 160
Haight, 297
Haines, 40, 42, 57, 98, 105, 282, 284, 327, 363, 365, 367, 374, 409, 472, 473, 550, 578
Halcomb, 71
Hall, 69, 73, 93, 134
Halsey, 273, 274
Hamilton, 630, 632, 640, 641, 737, 743
Hammon, 65

Hammond, 126, 148, 179, 422, 696, 701, 702
Hancock, 260
Hancox, 492
Hand, 257
Hanford, 134
Hannam, 46
Hannawell, 184
Hannay, 234
Hard, 93, 396, 422
Hardy, 70
Harington, 710. *See also* Harrington, Herington, *and* Herrington.
Harrington, 74, 164. *See also* Harington, Herington, *and* Herrington.
Harrison, 152, 160, 234, 422
Hart, 3, 160, 163
Hart, Griffith & Co., 237
Hartley, 422, 573, 701
Harton, 71
Harvey, 70, 164
Harwood, 71, 160, 163
Hascall, 93
Hase, 148
Hasset, 160
Hatch, 120, 422
Hathaway, 42, 86, 105, 337, 365, 367, 396, 422, 472, 550, 701
Hatter, 160
Haven, 69
Haviland, 69, 163
Hawes, 160
Hawkins, 69
Hawks, 47, 69, 93, 337, 396, 422
Hawley, 69, 133, 160, 303, 337, 396, 422, 610
Hawley & Ralston, 219
Hay, 69
Hayden, 46
Hayes, 179, 422, 701
Hayward, 134
Hazeltine, 93, 148
Heartwell, 95

Heing, 153
Helm, 153
Hemenway, 272
Heminway, 160
Henderson, 73, 573
Henry, 160
Herington, 422, 701. *See also* Harington, Harrington, *and* Herrington.
Hernandez, 153
Heron, 22
Herrick, 164, 561
Herrington, 575. *See also* Harington, Harrington, *and* Herington.
Hess, 179
Heveland, 71
Hewes, 696
Hewitt, 85
Hibbard, 160
Hildreth, 160
Hill, 69, 91, 114, 129, 203, 631
Hillyard, 69
Himman, 69, 74, 164, 332, 422, 480, 701
Hitchcock, 422, 480
Hoag, 152
Hodge, 153
Hodges, 160
Hoffman, 153, 562
Hogan, 555
Holden, 71
Holderman, 70
Holdridge, 163
Holland Land Company, 178, 311, 462
Holland, 160
Hollenback, 69
Holley, 402
Holly, 730
Holmes, 70, 148, 172, 179, 262, 356, 378, 422
Holstead, 730
Holt, 712
Holway, 70

Hopkins, 69, 93, 152, 153, 173, 303, 339, 365, 369, 374, 615, 710
Hopkinson, 153
Horton, 163, 203
Hoskins, 93, 99
Hosley, 70
Hotchkin, 46
Hotchkin & Starr, 46
Hotchkiss, 70, 134, 260
Hotchkiss & Woodward, 152
Houghton, 69
Houk, 70
House, 65, 126, 148, 179
House & Boughton, 25, 29, 34, 35, 37, 156, 198, 200, 204, 222, 228, 244, 282, 286, 287, 295, 327, 420, 421, 444, 445, 447, 456, 458, 459, 463, 471, 514, 534, 537, 590, 638, 639, 647, 678, 713, 715
Houstater, 179, 422
How, 152, 153
Howay, 70
Howder, 84
Howe, 573
Howell, 70, 134, 153, 337, 396, 422
Hubbard, 134, 153, 160, 163
Hubbell, 297
Hucher, 153
Hudson, 69
Huested, 160
Hughes, 56, 69, 227
Hull, 153, 163
Humphrey, 93, 206, 211, 453, 717, 718, 719, 744
Hunt, 297, 554, 605, 740
Huntington, 337, 396, 401, 422
Hurd, 69, 179, 365, 422, 701
Hustler, 375
Hutchins, 163, 410
Hutchinson, 337, 396, 422
Hutley, 153
Hyde, 164, 492

Ingersoll, 297
Ingols, 69
Irwin, 70, 72
Isengham, 71
Ives, 160, 164, 701
Jackson, 118, 134, 163, 331
Jacob, 70
Jacobs, 153
James, 297
Jeffrey, 422
Jenkins, 564
Jenks, 69, 93
Jenney, 69
Jennings, 40, 69, 76, 100, 126, 129, 142, 148, 170, 269, 282, 284, 323, 327, 365, 366, 457, 668, 670, 691
Jenvell, 163
Jervis, 730
Jessup, 237
Jinny, 160
Johnson, 69, 148, 152, 160, 163, 276, 297
Johnston, 179
Joiner, 675
Jones, 41, 71, 160, 163, 730
Jonley, 70
Jordan, 590, 658
Judd, 160
Kavannah, 184
Kearn, 61
Keeny, 701
Kelley, 69, 160
Kelly, 70, 160, 280, 601
Kelsey, 163, 250, 376, 612
Kempshall, 589
Kempville Hotel, 529
Kendall, 693
Kent, 69, 70, 152, 160, 337, 396, 401, 422
Kenyon, 179. *See also* Kinyon.
Ketchum, 134
Keyes, 422, 701
Keyser, 303
Kidd, 152

Kidder, 69, 701
Kilbourn, 701
Kimball, 69
Kimberley, 69
Kimberly, 57, 160
King, 69, 74, 134
Kingsley, 134
Kinient, 730
Kinnis, 160
Kinsley, 69, 625
Kinyon, 148, 179, 422, 701. *See also* Kenyon.
Kishlar, 378
Kissam, 153
Kite, 422
Kitredge, 422
Kitridge, 701
Kizer, 69
Kline, 179, 574, 730
Kniffin, 646
Knight, 71
Knoll, 422
Knowles, 422, 701
Knox, 71, 410
Kuney, 701
Lacey, 337, 396, 422, 508
Lacy, 93
Laing, 69
Landers, 422
Lane, 69
Lathrop, 27, 69
Lattee, 70
Law, 94
Lawrence, 69, 422
Lawson, 134, 701
Lay, 69
Layton, 160
Leavenworth, 69, 160
Lee, 71, 163, 280, 422
Leland, 422, 701
Lemman, 69
Lendrum, 374
Lenox, 69
Leonard, 98, 134, 153, 202, 210,

Leonard, continued, 218, 230, 246, 288, 289, 298, 324, 340, 347, 352, 357, 382, 393, 407, 417, 422, 464, 484, 485, 520, 521, 544, 606, 608, 609, 622, 653, 656, 662, 720, 733, 741, 746
Leslie, 69
Levalley, 365, 586
Levenworth, 573
Leverett, 443
Levy, 153
Lewis, 30, 69, 73, 93, 152, 160, 378, 394, 507
Lewiston Academy, 155, 382, 597
Lewiston Hotel, 250
Leyburn, 69
Lincoln, 134
Lindsley, 163
Liscomb, 519
Littlefield, 205
Livingston, 46, 337, 396, 422
Livingsworth, 86
Lock Hospital, 314
Locke, 69
Lockport Balance, 191, 402, 559, 667, 689, 690, 705, 709
Lockport Bank, 468, 488
Lockport Book Store, 408, 449, 608, 622, 656, 741
Lockport Brewery, 673
Lockport Classical School, 294
Lockport Drug Store, 348
Lockport Furnace, 241
Lockport Mills, 130, 607
Lockport Sash Factory, 614
Lockport Tannery, 213, 229, 253, 389
Lockport Temperance Society, 425
Lockwood, 163, 212, 236, 343, 344, 531, 701
Long, 103, 160, 731
Loomis, 73, 134
Lord, 120, 337, 396, 422

Love, 93
Loveland, 163
Lowry, 148
Loyd, 164
Lusk, 69, 160, 164
Lutten, 69
Lutts, 164
Lyman, 337
Lynch, 23
Lyon, 75, 163
Lysinger, 160
M'Alister, 93
M'Allister, 93
M'Bride, 134. *See also* McBride.
M'Cleary, 655. *See also* Maclary.
M'Collum, 146, 480. *See also* McCollum.
M'Elrath & Bangs, 234
M'Kain, 40
M'Kean, 40, 56
M'Kinstry, 337, 396. *See also* M'Kinstry.
M'Knight, 590. *See also* McKnight.
M'Lean, 583. *See also* McLean.
M'Leland, 733. *See also* McLeland.
M'Martin, 337, 396. *See also* McMartin.
M'Nall, 160, 297, 615. *See also* McNall.
Mabee, 163
Macan, 549
Mack, 152
Mackham, 152
Maclary, 163. *See also* M'Cleary.
Maclouch, 184
Madison, 378
Magrath, 152
Mahr, 160
Makee, 71
Maker, 611
Manchester, 163
Manley, 701
Manly, 422

Mann, 160, 297
Many, 414
Many & Ward, 414
March, 714
Marcy, 71, 402, 404
Marsh, 160, 234
Marshall & Dean, 234
Martin, 701
Martling, 554
Marvin, 93, 134
Mason, 93, 120, 160, 284, 365, 366, 501
Mass, 164
Mather, 134, 160, 337, 396, 422
Matthews, 69, 134
Maxwell, 134
Mayell, 303
Maynard, 69
McArthur, 422
McAvoy, 160
McBride, 74. See also M'Bride.
McClennen, 153
McClue, 422
McCollough, 152
McCollum, 152. See also M'Collum.
McCormack, 71
McCormick, 422, 701
McCracken, 152
McKeever, 160
McKinstry, 422. See also M'Kinstry.
McKnight, 160, 422. See also M'Knight.
McKnitt, 72
McLaren, 504
McLaughlin, 422
McLean, 164. See also M'Lean.
McLeland, 70, 422, 701. See also M'Leland.
McLeod, 160
McMartin, 422. See also M'Martin.
McMonagle, 69

McNall, 71, 422, 701. See also M'Nall.
McNeil, 179, 269, 323, 325, 363, 370, 372, 409, 473, 522, 550, 578, 612, 687, 729
McNitt, 73
McRoberts, 52
McZenan, 730
Medbery, 492
Mehene, 70
Mekum, 610
Mepler, 152
Merchant, 163, 168, 567, 570, 571, 577, 579, 581, 582, 655, 657, 659, 727, 748
Merriam, 152
Merrit, 410
Merritt, 71, 422, 701
Merry, 153
Michell, 163
Middle District Bank, 402
Mighells, 69
Miles, 69
Millard, 104, 160, 278, 422
Miller, 70, 93, 152, 160, 337, 396, 422
Millerd, 69
Milliken, 378
Millikin, 179, 372
Milling and Forwarding Coalitions, 508
Mills, 72, 75
Minor, 179, 431, 539, 540, 541, 542, 543
Mitchell, 160, 386, 411, 422, 701
Mixer, 337, 396, 422
Moffat, 23
Moffatt, 93
Mohr, 70
Molineux, 134
Molyneux, 21, 403, 701
Moore, 69, 163, 573
Moot, 701
Morehouse, 70
Morgan, 61, 95, 134, 147, 297, 422

Morgan & Winslow, 237
Morris, 93, 153, 183, 337, 422
Morrison, 72, 74, 134
Morse, 153, 160, 164, 654
Moseley, 134
Mosely, 120, 422
Moss, 179, 422, 701, 702, 703
Mower, 93
Moyer, 160
Mudge, 422
Mudget, 203
Muir, 303
Mullon, 70
Munger, 160
Munro, 160
Murgatroyd, 153
Murray, 376
Myars, 160
Myers, 160, 483
Mystery Advertiser, 490
Nash, 56
Neal, 52, 160
Needham, 160
Nelson, 69
New Book Store, 623, 626, 629, 635, 645, 681, 723
New York State Temperance Society, 435
Newcomb, 422
Newkirk, 583
Newkirk, White & Co., 583
Newman, 69, 148, 179, 422, 701. See also Numan.
Niagara County Temperance Society, 480, 509
Niagara Courier, 1, 161, 182, 428, 429, 557, 736
Nickerson, 297
Nigill, 701
Niles, 69
Noag, 160
Norcross, 422
North, 231
Northam, 53, 69, 75, 97, 124, 252, 467

Northrup, 203
Norton, 148, 152, 170, 172, 179, 275, 278, 329, 396, 414, 422, 480
Nova Scotia, Bishop of, 153
Numan, 160. *See also* Newman.
O'Flyng, 339
Odle, 378
Ohio Canal, 121
Olds, 69
Oliphant, 160
Oliver, 148, 179, 422, 701
Olmstead, 46, 93, 134
Olmsted, 8, 132, 154, 167
Olney, 69
Olnry, 160
Ontario Female Seminary, 171
Orcutt, 163
Orleans American, 669
Orton, 71, 160, 179, 422, 701
Osborn, 134
Osborne, 590, 658
Osmer, 70
Ostrander, 422
Otis, 69, 160
Ousterhout, 74
Outwater, 422, 701
Owen, 70, 422
Packard, 234
Paddock, 234
Page, 278
Paige, 422
Paine, 72
Palmer, 69, 237
Pardee, 72
Pardy, 422
Park, 70
Parker, 69, 74, 122, 134, 148, 153, 472, 588
Parkhurst, 134
Parks, 160, 294, 725
Parmenter, 69, 160
Parsoll, 93
Parsons, 6, 12, 13, 39, 69, 83, 90, 92, 160, 170, 179, 209, 214,

Parsons, continued, 224, 238, 280, 285, 315, 318, 338, 345, 351, 373, 387, 395, 397, 422, 434, 437, 438, 470, 480, 501, 532, 536, 580, 594, 642, 644, 650, 663, 664, 691, 698, 701, 712
Parsons & Phelps, 455
Parsons Gooding & Co., 271, 313, 386
Partial, 160
Patterson, 365, 472
Pattison, 69
Pearce, 69
Pease, 69, 422
Peck, 69, 72, 93, 160, 179, 481
Peckham, 93
Peet, 134
Pendleton Temperance Society, 426
Pennell, 134
Per Lee, 337, 396, 422
Percival, 93, 234
Perrin, 71
Perry, 71, 74, 116, 134, 160, 513
Petrie, 584, 585
Phelps, 455
Philips, 160
Phillips, 22, 40, 54, 76, 100, 101, 104, 108, 109, 111, 128, 134, 140, 148, 165, 172, 178, 179, 365, 404, 422, 472, 583
Philosophical Institute of Canandaigua, 171
Phinney, 69
Pickard, 378, 701
Pierce, 69, 72, 74, 93, 163, 402
Pierson, 160
Pike, 492, 583
Pinney, 75
Pixley, 71, 611
Place, 195, 221, 291, 292, 293, 310, 349, 358, 440, 448, 451, 546, 593, 649, 652, 676, 679, 686, 716, 739
Plater, 701

Platt, 134, 262, 356, 365, 729
Playter, 152, 461
Plum, 701
Pollay, 69
Pomeroy, 144
Pond, 160
Pool, 70, 422
Pope, 102
Porter, 43, 69, 71, 72, 101, 153, 165, 260, 480, 590, 605, 658
Porter, Barton & Co., 152
Potter, 160, 179, 337, 396, 422, 590
Pound, 237
Pratt, 75, 152, 153, 163, 422, 618, 701, 710
Prentice, 26, 170, 179, 199, 216, 240, 242, 243, 416, 619
Prentiss, 234
Prescott, 164
Price, 69, 134
Priest, 69
Prime, 160
Prought, 69
Prusia, 697
Purdy, 611
Putman, 74
Pye, 673
Quade, 69
Quadee, 74
Quinby, 604
Quinn, 153
Race, 701
Raimant, 160
Ralle, 188
Ralston, 219, 294
Randall, 69, 160
Raney, 160
Ranny, 71
Ransom, 2, 47, 57, 65, 93, 126, 148, 179, 284, 365, 366, 422, 670, 691, 701
Rathbun, 590
Rawson, 134
Raymond, 70, 422, 701

Raynor, 701
Rea, 160
Read, 93
Reed, 134
Reeves & M'Lean, 583
Remele, 71
Remely, 71
Rensselaer, 506
Republican Young Men, 118, 120
Rew, 70
Reynale, 11, 19, 56, 71, 148, 163, 179, 348, 371, 422, 433, 657, 670, 701, 708
Reynale & Stewart, 131
Reynolds, 69, 70, 410, 422, 604
Rhoad, 584
Rice, 69, 72, 153, 160, 163
Richards, 69, 160, 422, 701
Richardson, 33, 69, 93, 160
Richmond, 160
Ridner, 208, 307
Riff, 72
Riggs, 153, 163
Robards, 160
Robbins, 69
Robbinson, 152
Robbs, 152
Roberts, 71, 74, 160, 163, 492, 573, 701, 722
Robinson, 75, 153, 160, 422, 701
Robison, 93
Robson, 207, 511
Rochester, 120
Rodgers, 160
Rogers, 50, 60, 64, 69, 115, 153, 160, 179, 213, 220, 229, 253, 258, 389
Rogers & Brown, 217, 223, 233, 245, 249, 270, 283, 321, 342, 361, 364, 384, 390, 448, 450, 468, 523, 524, 526, 527, 535, 545, 572, 591, 592, 595, 637, 651, 652, 661, 665, 666, 737, 742
Rogers & Co., 734, 743

Root, 61, 69, 70, 71, 369
Rose, 180, 297, 337, 396, 422
Rosevelt, 297
Ross, 69, 70, 71, 179
Rossiter, 590
Rouse, 117
Rowe, 69
Rowly, 163
Rugg, 730
Rumery, 422
Rummerfield, 152
Rush, 118, 172, 183
Rushmore, 290
Ryckman, 250
Ryen, 70
Sackett, 297
Sadler, 42, 105
Sage, 69, 70, 152
Salisbury, 72
Sanborn, 94
Sanders, 134, 152, 160. *See also* Saunders.
Sargent, 123
Sark, 72
Saunders, 69, 181, 277. *See also* Sanders.
Savage, 184, 329
Sawyer, 75, 134
Saxton, 148, 172, 179, 729
Scarborough, 69, 70, 152
Schenck, 432
Schermerhorn, 237, 297
Schuyler, 277
Schyler, 148, 179
Scobey, 69
Scott, 410, 422, 467
Scovell, 365
Scoville, 54
Scrantom, 482
Scullion, 160
Searle, 153
Sears, 69, 196, 648
Seaver, 153
Seceding Masons, 46

Sechler, 71, 371
Seele, 74
Seeley, 70, 422
Seever, 418
Selye, 589
Sergeant, 331
Seward, 120
Sexton, 237, 401
Seymour, 237, 297
Shankland, 160
Sharp, 69, 633, 636, 682, 749
Sharpe, 525
Shaver, 69
Shedd, 583
Sheffield, 163
Shelden, 697
Sheldon, 71, 93, 179
Shepard, 70, 160, 619
Sheppard, 93
Sherman, 69
Sherwood, 297
Shields, 69
Shipman, 378
Shock, 701
Shoemaker, 337, 396, 422
Short, 134
Shotwell, 234
Shumway, 120
Sibley, 134
Sill, 69, 623, 624, 626, 629, 635, 645, 681, 700, 723, 735, 745, 747
Silsby, 69
Simmons, 179, 492
Simonds, 69, 160, 701
Simons, 621
Simpson, 160
Sinclair, 701
Sincler, 573
Sitterington, 69
Skeel, 701
Skinner, 53, 77, 354, 634
Skinner & Dewey, 234
Slade, 69
Slayton, 66, 76, 100, 140, 160

Sleight, 234
Sleighton, 101
Slidell, 153
Slingerland, 612
Sloan, 69
Sly, 232
Smita, 69
Smith, 23, 69, 70, 81, 93, 134, 152, 153, 159, 160, 163, 164, 179, 194, 217, 250, 282, 297, 303, 327, 329, 337, 358, 375, 396, 406, 422, 436, 441, 448, 461, 473, 483, 488, 514, 652, 671, 701
Smith & Southwick, 264
Smith & Southworth, 252
Snyder, 69, 163
Society of Friends, 45
Soper, 160
Southwick, 93, 148, 172, 179, 503
Southworth, 160, 252, 294, 348, 480
Southworth & Reynale, 657, 660, 684
Spalding, 24, 98, 130, 201, 235, 237, 239, 247, 255, 256, 299, 317, 319, 320, 346, 350, 362, 365, 374, 391, 392, 413, 422, 480, 509, 510, 525, 533, 568, 607, 614, 617, 620, 627, 683, 701, 726
Spalding's Mills, 726
Spencer, 70, 303, 337, 396, 422, 529
Spooner, 73
Sprague, 139, 163, 169
St. Peter's Episcopal Church, 301
Stafford, 211, 316, 360, 388, 394, 528, 538
Stage, 163
Stahl, 69, 422, 701
Stahler, 69
Staht, 160
Stanard, 306
Stanley, 46
Stark, 69, 160

Starr, 46
Stearns, 112
Stebbins, 297
Steele, 93
Steele & Faxton, 234
Steeprock, 553
Stevens, 69, 75, 163, 337, 396, 422, 483
Stevenson, 70, 153
Steward, 507
Stewart, 131, 153, 252, 422
Stickney, 241
Stiles, 160
Stocker, 71
Stockham, 93
Stocking, 160
Stoddard, 93
Stone, 70, 134, 150, 163, 239, 422, 491, 583
Story, 70
Stoughtenburg, 297
Stoughton, 165
Stow, 118, 160, 226, 297, 336, 422, 691
Stowell, 163
Stranks, 69
Straw, 152, 715
Stryker, 297
Stuart, 71
Sturges, 203
Sullivan, 152
Summers, 152
Sumner, 93
Sutherland, 70, 422, 701
Swaim, 134
Swain, 74
Swanson, 690
Sweet, 93
Swift, 152
Sykes, 596, 730
Syks, 73
Sylvant, 71
Symonds, 160, 164
Taggart, 194, 267, 275, 276

Talbot, 93
Tappan, 507, 601
Tariff Convention, 300
Taylor, 69, 134, 164, 178, 179, 377, 422, 573, 611
Teachout, 422, 701
Terry, 160
Thacher, 422
Thaxter, 153
Thayer, 163, 426
Thayre, 378, 573
The State University of New York, 496
Thirstenan, 410
Thomas, 153, 160, 252, 422, 701
Thompson, 42, 54, 57, 74, 104, 105, 118, 120, 153, 164, 172, 237, 272, 273, 274, 282, 327, 363, 422, 573, 614, 619, 658, 701
Thomss, 69
Thorn, 589
Thorn & Frink, 237
Thrall, 69
Throop, 281, 478
Thurston, 69
Tibbles, 69
Tillotson, 69
Timerman, 410
Timmerman, 308
Titus, 63, 71, 152
Tobey, 163
Toland, 701
Tompkins, 179
Toner, 164
Toole, 70
Torrance, 655
Totton, 70
Tower, 179, 422, 701
Townsend, 148, 153, 179, 197, 255, 337, 376, 564
Townsend & Barton, 152
Townson & Bronson, 70
Towsley, 422, 701
Tracy, 69, 303, 337, 497, 687, 688, 701, 707, 730

Trall, 99
Tripp, 160
Trowbridge, 123, 160, 294
Truman, 70
Tryon, 70, 148, 152, 155, 179, 227, 646
Tucker, 9, 49, 51, 151, 160, 337, 353, 396, 404, 422, 436, 480, 488, 509, 544
Tucker & Price, 69
Tuckerman, 153
Turk, 337, 396, 422
Turner, 119, 134, 163, 308
Tuthill, 46
Tuttle, 160, 337, 396, 422
Tyler, 59, 70, 71
U.S. Branch Bank, 695
Underwood, 160, 410
Utter, 93
Valentine, 179. *See also* Volentine.
Valentine & Jenkins, 564
Van Allen, 462
Van Brunt, 261
Van Buren, 331, 422, 551
Van Camp, 160
Van Dyke, 93
Van Horn, 148, 178, 277, 278, 279, 280, 422, 701
Van Horne, 179
Van Tassel, 197
Van Velzer, 160
Van Volkenburgh, 378, 422
Van Vothenburgh, 73
Van Wie, 655
Vanderpool, 554
Vannorsel, 152
Vanslike, 179
Vanslyke, 378
Vaughan, 738
Veile, 303
Village of Lockport, 326
Virle, 163
Volentine, 71. *See also* Valentine.
Vroman, 164, 422

Vromer, 701
Wadsworth, 46, 70, 168, 172, 237, 502
Wakeman, 422, 701
Waldbridge, 134
Walden, 172, 179
Waldo, 160
Waldron, 188
Walker, 69, 134, 148, 160, 179, 422, 612
Walker & Matthews, 69
Wall, 71, 163
Wallis, 611
Walton, 297
Ward, 162, 168, 343, 344, 414, 422, 531, 583, 589, 701. *See also* Many & Ward.
Ware, 44, 422
Waring, 337, 396, 422
Warner, 69, 160, 378, 625, 672, 733
Warren, 70, 297
Wart, 573
Washburn, 70, 318, 373, 472
Waterman, 422
Waters, 93
Watson, 10, 701
Watterson, 160
Weaver, 70, 701
Webber, 422, 701
Webster, 69, 152, 329
Weed, 93, 96, 127, 134, 305
Weelbur, 160
Welch, 74, 160
Wellman, 72, 153
Wells, 118, 163, 234
Wentworth, 701
West, 69, 72, 422, 701
Westbrook, 188
Weston, 160
Whaley, 69
Wheeler, 71, 160, 508
Whetlock, 184
Whippey, 409
Whippry, 160

Whitcher, 31, 294, 654, 698
Whitcher & Porter, 43
Whitcom, 72
White, 111, 149, 152, 153, 160, 381, 401, 583
Whitewell, 72
Whiting, 134
Whitnell, 153
Whitney, 72, 107, 108, 111, 147, 152
Whittlesey, 93, 305, 589
Whitton, 160
Wichell, 69
Wichterman, 422
Wilbur, 337, 396, 422
Wilcox, 152, 454
Wild, 554
Wiley, 163
Wilkenson, 730
Wilkeson, 96, 127, 152, 297, 432
Wilkins, 164
Wilkinson, 297
Willard, 329
Willcox, 70
William, 587
Williams, 69, 70, 71, 74, 93, 110, 148, 153, 160, 164, 179, 234, 300, 422, 603, 625, 701
Willink, 272, 373
Willis, 160
Willits, 69
Willson, 70
Wilmarth, 69, 160
Wilson, 160, 378, 573, 697, 730
Wilts, 69
Wiltsie, 72
Winchell, 423
Winchip, 422
Winer, 79
Wingart, 573
Wingert, 378
Winn, 378
Winship, 693
Winslow, 237
Wirt, 189, 331, 396, 422

Witaker, 153
Witbeck, 369, 371, 372, 373, 374, 409, 472, 473, 550, 643
Witmer, 91, 114
Wood, 153, 337, 396, 422
Woodard, 69, 160. *See also* Woodward.
Woodcock, 163
Woodruff & Hotchkiss, 70
Woodward, 40, 56, 69, 152, 153, 160, 174. *See also* Woodard.
Woolcott, 160
Woolworth, 163
Worden, 38, 72, 153, 160, 422, 701
Workman, 72
Works, 93, 305, 422, 480, 512, 634
Worthington, 71
Wray, 153
Wright, 70, 120, 134, 160, 163, 203, 259, 303, 367, 404, 477, 701
Wright, Young & Co., 402
Wyman, 730
Yates, 152, 297, 329
Yerington, 422
Yerington & Stickney, 241
Yerrington, 148, 179
York, 152, 160
Young, 80, 160, 402. *See also* Wright Young & Co.
Youths' Temperance Society, 434
Zachariah, 410

3. INDEX OF SUBJECTS

Accident, 116, 505, 690
Advertisement, 1, 2, 3, 4, 5, 6, 7, 8, 9, 10, 11, 12, 13, 14, 15, 16, 17, 19, 20, 21, 22, 23, 24, 25, 26, 27, 28, 29, 30, 31, 32, 33, 34, 35, 36, 37, 43, 49, 50, 51, 55, 58, 60, 78, 79, 80, 82, 89, 90, 102, 112, 115, 129, 130, 131, 142, 151, 154, 155, 156, 161, 162, 166, 167, 176, 177, 182, 195, 196, 198, 199, 200, 201, 202, 204, 206, 207, 208, 209, 210, 211, 212, 213, 214, 215, 216, 217, 218, 219, 220, 221, 222, 223, 224, 226, 227, 228, 229, 230, 233, 234, 235, 236, 237, 238, 239, 240, 241, 242, 243, 244, 245, 246, 247, 248, 249, 252, 253, 254, 255, 256, 257, 258, 261, 262, 263, 264, 270, 271, 283, 285, 286, 287, 288, 289, 291, 292, 293, 294, 295, 298, 299, 306, 307, 308, 309, 310, 312, 313, 315, 316, 317, 319, 320, 321, 324, 340, 341, 342, 343, 344, 345, 346, 347, 348, 349, 350, 351, 352, 353, 354, 355, 356, 357, 358, 359, 360, 361, 362, 364, 380, 381, 383, 384, 385, 386, 389, 390, 391, 392, 393, 394, 395, 407, 408, 411, 414, 416, 417, 419, 420, 421, 423, 437, 438, 439, 440, 441, 442, 443, 444, 445, 446, 447, 448, 449, 450, 451, 453, 455, 456, 457, 458, 459, 460, 463, 464, 466, 467, 469, 470, 471, 482, 484, 485, 488, 490, 510, 511, 512, 513, 514, 515, 519, 520, 521, 523, 524, 525, 526, 527, 528, 529, 531, 532, 534, 535, 537, 539, 540, 541, 542, 543, 544, 545, 546, 547, 568, 569, 570,

Advertisement, continued: 571, 572, 576, 577, 579, 580, 581, 582, 583, 585, 587, 589, 590, 591, 592, 593, 594, 595, 606, 607, 608, 609, 613, 614, 617, 620, 622, 623, 624, 626, 627, 628, 629, 630, 631, 632, 633, 634, 635, 636, 637, 638, 639, 640, 641, 642, 643, 644, 645, 646, 647, 648, 649, 650, 651, 652, 653, 654, 655, 656, 657, 658, 659, 660, 661, 662, 663, 664, 665, 666, 671, 673, 674, 676, 678, 680, 681, 682, 683, 684, 685, 686, 700, 714, 715, 716, 717, 718, 719, 720, 723, 724, 726, 727, 728, 731, 732, 734, 735, 736, 738, 739, 740, 741, 742, 743, 744, 746, 747, 748, 749

Agriculture, 185, 379, 431, 479, 494, 497, 508, 564, 565, 566, 599

Anti-Masonic movement, 45, 46, 61, 62, 65, 93, 94, 95, 96, 110, 126, 127, 135, 145, 148, 162, 168, 170, 172, 174, 179, 183, 189, 190, 210, 234, 303, 305, 337, 396, 397, 398, 399, 401, 403, 422, 430, 449, 491, 498, 499, 547, 551, 600, 602, 667, 670, 688, 689, 691, 701, 702, 703, 704, 705, 706, 707, 708, 709

Chancery, 367, 442

Children, 555

Court, 44, 63, 64, 117, 119, 134, 146, 147, 184, 296, 492, 498, 553, 554, 562, 603, 695

Crime, 330, 475, 561, 563

Death, 137, 150, 187, 193, 405, 502

Editorial, 302, 403, 430, 478, 559
Education, 171, 205, 382, 465, 474, 496, 530, 597, 604, 677, 713, 733
Fire, 301
Fishing, 710
Government, 477, 560, 692
Health and medicine, 314, 328, 332, 333, 334, 335, 336, 338
History, 188, 548
Insolvent debtors, 41, 59, 106, 110, 113, 357, 533, 548
Land and property, 427
Lockport Balance newspaper, 191, 402, 559, 667, 689, 705, 709
Manufacture, 300, 432
Marriage, 47, 139, 149, 194, 273, 274, 275, 276, 304, 339, 483, 697, 712
Military, 605
Miscellany, 125, 138, 669, 696
Mortgage sales, 42, 53, 56, 57, 98, 105, 107, 218, 246, 250, 256, 268, 282, 284, 327, 366, 369, 371, 374
Natural phenomena, 596
Notice, 18, 38, 39, 40, 41, 42, 48, 52, 53, 54, 56, 57, 59, 66, 67, 68, 69, 70, 71, 72, 73, 74, 75, 76, 77, 81, 83, 84, 85, 86, 87, 88, 91, 92, 98, 99, 100, 101, 103, 104, 105, 106, 107, 108, 109, 110, 111, 113, 114, 126, 127, 128, 132, 133, 140, 141, 143, 144, 152, 153, 157, 158, 159, 160, 163, 164, 165, 175, 178, 180, 181, 197, 203, 225, 231, 232, 250, 259, 260, 268, 269, 272, 277, 278, 279, 280, 281, 282, 284, 290, 311, 318, 322, 323, 325, 326, 327, 363,

153

Notice, continued: 365, 366, 367, 368, 369, 370, 371, 372, 373, 374, 375, 376, 377, 378, 387, 388, 394, 397, 406, 409, 410, 412, 413, 415, 418, 428, 429, 436, 452, 454, 461, 462, 468, 472, 473, 486, 489, 507, 516, 517, 522, 533, 536, 538, 549, 550, 557, 558, 573, 574, 575, 578, 584, 586, 588, 610, 611, 612, 615, 616, 618, 619, 621, 625, 672, 675, 679, 687, 688, 698, 721, 722, 725, 729, 730, 737

Politics, 62, 65, 93, 94, 95, 96, 118, 120, 123, 135, 145, 148,

Politics, continued: 168, 170, 172, 173, 174, 179, 183, 189, 190, 191, 192, 303, 305, 331, 337, 396, 398, 399, 400, 401, 402, 404, 422, 433, 491, 499, 551, 600, 667, 668, 670, 689, 691, 693, 701, 702, 703, 704, 705, 706, 707, 708, 709, 711

Religion, 45, 61, 97, 124, 266, 267, 481, 503, 504, 556

Slavery, 329

Sheriff's sales, 40, 54, 76, 77, 100, 101, 104, 108, 109, 111, 165, 178, 269, 323, 325, 363, 365, 372, 409, 472, 473, 550, 578, 612, 615, 729

Social welfare, 169, 487, 518, 699

Societies, 46

Suicide, 122

Temperance, 425, 426, 434, 435, 480, 493, 501, 506, 509, 552, 745

Transportation, 121, 136, 186, 251, 297, 424, 476, 495, 500, 598, 601, 602, 694

Weather, 265

Wills and estates of deceased persons, 10, 91, 114, 157, 180, 272, 318, 368, 373, 376, 377, 575, 625, 672

4. SUPPLEMENTARY INDEXES

4.1 CHANCERY
Bissell, F., 442
Chase, E.I., 442
Child, Jonathan, 367
Comstock, Darius, 367
Comstock, Jared, 367
Comstock, Nathan, 367
Gardner, H., 367
Haines, Jesse P., 367
Hathaway, Otis, 367
Wright, Hiram, 367

4.2 INSOLVENT DEBTORS
Bond & Favor, 533
Corey, Levi L., 113
Dennison, Asahel J., 106
Fleming, Robert, 41
Gardner, Hiram, Judge of the Court of Common Pleas, 59, 106, 110, 113, 549
Jones, Jesse G., 41
Leonard, H., 357
Macan, George, 549
Spalding, L.A., 533
Tyler, Augustus, 59
Williams, William, 110

4.3 MORTGAGE SALES
Benjamin, John A., 369
Bond, William M., 284, 366
Bosworth, Boardman H., 374
Buck, Moses H., 57
Catlin, Henry, 268
Center, J., 42, 105, 371
Chaffe, Amasa, 284, 366
Comstock, Jared, 284, 366
Comstock, Nathan, 282, 327
Cooke & Stow, 250
Daly, John, 250
De Veaux, Samuel, 107
Draper, Luke, 98
Ellicott, Joseph, 371
Estes, Andrew, 250
Gooding, John, 369
Haines, Jesse P., Surveyor, 42, 57, 98, 105, 282, 284, 327, 374
Hathaway, Sylvester R., 42, 105
Hopkins, H.K., 374
Hopkins, Henry K., 369
House & Boughton, 282, 327
Hughes, William, 56
Jennings, Samuel, innkeeper, 282, 284, 327, 366
Kelsey, Gideon L., 250
Kelsey, Lorenzo A., 250
Kimberly, Homer, 57
Lendrum, James, 374
Leonard, Chauncey, 98
Leonard, N., 218, 246
Lewiston Hotel, 250
M'Kean, James, 56
Mason, James F., 284, 366
Nash, Cotton, 56
Northam, Festus, 53
Ransom, E., 57, 284, 366
Reynale, George, 56, 371
Root, Portous R., 369
Ryckman, John J., 250
Sadler, Warren, 42, 105
Sechler, William M., 371
Skinner, Allen, 53
Skinner, Annis, 53
Smith, Hezekiah H., 250
Smith, Isaac W., 282, 327
Spalding, L.A., 256
Spalding, Lyman, 98
Spalding, Lyman A., 374
Thompson, David A., 282, 327
Thompson, S.B., 42, 105
Thompson, Samuel, 57
Whitney, Parkhurst, 107
Witbeck, J.W., tavern keeper, 369, 371, 374
Woodward, Carlos B., 56
Woodward, Corydon C., 56
Woodward, Wareham M., 56

4.4 SHERIFF'S SALES
Angevine, Ferris, 325
Barton, Benjamin, 101, 165
Batty, Job, 365
Beach, Ambrose, 365
Bolles, Nathaniel, 101, 111
Bond, William M., 365
Brown, Charles, 269, 323
Brown, Eseck, 365
Bruce, Eli, 77
Burr, Jeremiah, 363, 578
Campbell, Robert, 612
Chapman, David, 101, 109, 165
Chapman, Stephen, 109, 165
Colt, Isaac, 615
Comstock, Jared, 365, 472, 729
Comstock, Nathan, 365
Ellicott, Joseph, 178
Fanning, R., 615
Fanning, Rufus, 325
Fisk, Orrin, 372
Galt, John, 104
Gay, Aden, 101
Gay, Ziba, 101
Gleason, Ezra, 178
Goodeno, John, 178
Gooding, John, 365
Griswold, Eber, 729
Haines, Jesse P., Surveyor, 40, 363, 365, 409, 472, 473, 550, 578
Hathaway, Otis, 365, 472, 550
Hopkins, Hiram B., 365
Hopkins, Silas, 615
Hurd, Davis, 365

Sheriff's sales, continued:

Jennings, Samuel, innkeeper, 40, 76, 100, 269, 323, 365
Kelsey, Lorenzo A., 612
Levalley, George, 365
M'Kain, James, 40
M'Kean, James, 40
M'Neil, H., 615. *See also* McNeil.
Mason, James F., 365
McNeil, H., Sheriff, 269, 363, 409, 550, 578, 612, 729. *See also* M'Neil.
McNeil, Hiram, Sheriff, 323, 325, 372, 473. *See also* M'Neil.
Millard, Almon H., 104
Millikin, Asa, 372
Parker, Halstead H., 472
Patterson, Joseph, 472
Patterson, Joseph H., 365
Phillips, John, Sheriff, 40, 54, 76, 100, 101, 104, 108, 109, 111, 165, 178, 365, 472
Platt, Henry S., 365, 729
Porter, Augustus, 101, 165
Ransom, Elias, 365
Saxton, Asher, 729
Scovell, Seymour, 365
Scoville, Seymour, 54
Skinner, Allen, 77
Slayton, Harvey, 76, 100
Sleighton, John W., 101
Slingerland, Anthony, 612
Smith, Anson, 473
Spalding, Lyman A., 365
Stoughton, John W., 165
Taylor, Christopher L., 178
Thompson, Samuel B., 54, 104, 363
Van Horn, Daniel, 178
Walker, L.H., 612
Washburn, Daniel, 472
Whippey, George S., 409
White, Berryhill H., 111
Whitney, Parkhurst, 108, 111
Witbeck, J.W, tavern keeper, 372, 409, 472, 473, 550
Woodward, Carlos B., 40
Woodward, Corydon C., 40
Woodward, Wareham M., 40

4.5 WILLS AND ESTATES

Bacon, Asa, 157
Bacon, Betsey, 157
Bacon, Gillet, 157
Bosworth, Bordman H., 272
Chapman, David, 91, 114
Comstock, Jehiel, 625, 672
Comstock, Thomas, 368
Cook, Bates, Attorney at Law, 10, 375, 376
Dunbar, Joshua, 625
Fannerty, Patrick, 368
Fleming, Robert, 375
Gardner, Hiram, Judge of the Court of Common Pleas, 318, 373, 375, 376, 377
Hemenway, Alanson, 272
Hemenway, Electa C., 272
Herrington, David, 575
Herrington, James, 575
Herrington, Jonathan, 575
Herrington, William, 575
Hill, Ezekiel, 91, 114
Hustler, Katharine, 375
Kelsey, Martha, 376
Kinsley, Martin, 625
Murray, James, 376
Parsons, Seth, 318, 373
Rose, George P., 180
Rose, Jairus, 180
Smith, Willard, 375
Taylor, Joash, 377
Taylor, Miles N., 377
Thompson, Samuel B., 272
Townsend, Jacob, 376
Warner, Samuel, 625, 672
Washburn, Daniel, 318, 373
Watson, Alexander, 10
Williams, Ira O., 625
Willink, Wilkem, 272
Willink, William, 373
Witbeck, J.W., 373
Witmer, Abraham, 91, 114

4.6 REFERENCES TO WOMEN

Note: Use the article numbers, cited in the index entries below, to refer to the related transcription or extract in Chapter 1, *Transcripts and Extracts*.

Format: Surname, Forename, Title; Town, State; Article no.; Subject; Brief description.

[Unnamed]; Albany, New York; Article no. 555; Children; son of Col. Hogan, keeper of the jail, aged about three years, was missing; another child pointed out to his mother the hole into which Col. Hogan's son had fallen.

[Unnamed]; Buffalo, New York; Article no. 505; Accident; young Dutch woman died almost instantly of a fall at her place of employ, Bear's Tavern.

[Unnamed]; Canandaigua, New York; Article no. 171; Education; reprint from the *Ontario Repository* newspaper, about the new Ontario Female Seminary in Canandaigua.

[Unnamed]; state of New York; Article no. 496; Education; the Regents of the University of New York distributed funds to the Ontario Female Seminary.

[Unnamed]; Temple, New Hampshire; Article no. 116; Accident; an unnamed female "who by great caution and presence of mind, succeeded in stopping the horses, until some persons who saw them pass came to her relief."

Adams, Sophia; Lockport, New York; Article no. 160; Notice; on the list of people for whom letters remain in the Post Office at Lockport.

Anderson, Elizabeth; Lewiston, New York; Article no. 152; Notice; on the list of names for whom letters remain in the Post Office at Lewiston.

Anderson, Elizabeth W.; Lewiston, New York; Article no. 70; Notice; on the list of letters remaining at the Post-Office in Lewiston.

Ashley, Sarah; Pendleton, New York; Article no. 73; Notice; on the list of letters remaining at the Post-Office at Pendleton.

Bacon, Betsey; Lockport, New York; Article no. 157; Notice; estate of Asa Bacon, deceased; Betsey Bacon, Administratrix, and Gillet Bacon, Administrator.

Baker, Elizabeth W.; Lockport, New York; Article no. 160; Notice; on the list of people for whom letters remain in the Post Office at Lockport.

Barnes, Miss A.; Niagara Falls, New York; Article no. 72; Notice; on the list of letters remaining at the Post-Office at Niagara Falls.

Beckwith, Widow J.; Pendleton, New York; Article no. 378; Notice; on the list of letters remaining in the Post-Office at Pendleton.

Blakesly, Miss Laura; Lockport, New York; Article no. 47; Marriage; to Mr. Cephas Hawks.

Blanchard, Lovina; Lockport, New York; Article no. 69; Notice; on the list of letters remaining at the Post-Office in Lockport.

Boughton, Emma Hickox; Lockport, New York; Article no. 405; Death; daughter of George H. Boughton, Esq., in the fifth year of her age.

Brackenridge, Maria; Lockport, New York; Article no. 69; Notice; on the list of letters remaining at the Post-Office in Lockport.

Brainard, Martha; Pendleton, New York; Article no. 730; Notice; on the list of letters remaining in the Post Office at Pendleton.

Browning, Hannah; Lockport, New York; Article no. 160; Notice; on the list of people for whom letters remain in the Post Office at Lockport.

Bryan, Lucy; Royalton, New York; Article no. 163; Notice; on the list of people for whom letters remain in the Post Office at Royalton.

Buell, Miss Julietta E.; Royalton, New York; Article no. 339; Marriage; to Henry K. Hopkins, Esq., of Lockport, Attorney at Law.

Burr, Miranda; Royalton, New York; Article no. 71; Notice; on the list of letters remaining at the Post-Office in Royalton.

Burr, Sally; Niagara Falls, New York; Article no. 72; Notice; on the list of letters remaining at the Post-Office at Niagara Falls.

Cabot, Miss E.L.; Niagara Falls, New York; Article no. 72; Notice; on the list of letters remaining at the Post-Office at Niagara Falls.

Cabot, Miss S.C.; Niagara Falls, New York; Article no. 72; Notice; on the list of letters remaining at the Post-Office at Niagara Falls.

Caine, Sophia; Youngstown, New York; Article no. 164; Notice; on the list of people for whom letters remain in the Post Office at Youngstown.

Calkins, Miss; Lockport, New York; Article no. 196; Advertisement; millinery and mantua-making, in partnership with Mrs. Sears.

Carr, Betsey; Lockport, New York; Article no. 69; Notice; on the list of letters remaining at the Post-Office in Lockport.

Chamberlin, Widow; Lockport, New York; Article no. 160; Notice; on the list of people for whom letters remain in the Post Office at Lockport.

Chatlin, Elizabeth; Lockport, New York; Article no. 160; Notice; on the list of people for whom letters remain in the Post Office at Lockport.

Clark, Miss Achsah L.; Troy, New York; Article no. 554; Court; plaintiff in slander suit against John O. Martling; trial resulted in a verdict of $1200.

Clark, Miss Eliza; Troy, New York; Article no. 554; Court; mentioned in the slander suit brought by Miss Achsah L. Clark against John O. Martling.

Comstock, Mrs. Jared; Lockport, New York; Article no. 365; Notice; Sheriff's Sale of land in Lockport, bounding a tract of land deeded to Joseph H. Patterson by Jared Comstock and wife.

Comstock, Mrs. Jared; Lockport, New York; Article no. 472; Notice; Sheriff's Sale of a certain tract of land in Lockport, conveyed by Joseph Patterson to Jared Comstock and wife.

Comstock, Mrs. Jared; Lockport, New York; Article no. 729; Notice; Sheriff's Sale of land in Lockport, conveyed to Eber Griswold by Jared Comstock and wife.

Crandal, Eliza; Niagara Falls, New York; Article no. 72; Notice; on the list of letters remaining at the Post-Office at Niagara Falls.

Depue, Miss Jane; Cambria, New York; Article no. 304; Marriage; to Benjamin D. Compton, of Lewiston.

Depuy, Mrs. Rebecca; Royalton, New York; Article no. 71; Notice; on the list of letters remaining at the Post-Office in Royalton.

Dexter, Margann; Lockport, New York; Article no. 160; Notice; on the list of people for whom letters remain in the Post Office at Lockport.

Dixon, Susan; Pendleton, New York; Article no. 378; Notice; on the list of letters remaining in the post-office at Pendleton.

Doshon, Julia; Lockport, New York; Article no. 69; Notice; on the list of letters remaining at the Post-Office in Lockport.

Driggs, Miss Starbing; Royalton, New York; Article no. 71; Notice; on the list of letters remaining at the Post-Office in Royalton.

Dunscomb, Eliza; Niagara Falls, New York; Article no. 153; Notice; on the list of people for whom letters remain in the Post Office at Lewiston.

Ferguson, Harriet; Lewiston, New York; Article no. 152; Notice; on the list of names for whom letters remain in the Post Office at Lewiston.

Fick, Miss Sarah; Middleport, New York; Article no. 139; Marriage; to Isaac N. Cook, both of Middleport, in Niagara County.

Gaylord, Theodosia; Niagara Falls, New York; Article no. 72; Notice; on the list of letters remaining at the Post-Office at Niagara Falls.

Gibson, Miss; Middleport, New York; Article no. 439; Advertisement; millinery and mantuamaking, Middleport.

Gilson, Miss; Middleport, New York; Article no. 355; Advertisement; millinery and mantuamaking, Middleport.

Grant, Mrs. P.; Niagara Falls, New York; Article no. 153; Notice; on the list of people for whom letters remain in the Post Office at Lewiston.

Graves, Miss Martha M.; Royalton, New York; Article no. 71; Notice; on the list of letters remaining at the Post-Office in Royalton.

Graves, Martha M.; Royalton, New York; Article no. 163; Notice; on the list of people for whom letters remain in the Post Office at Royalton.

Green, Miss Martha; Niagara Falls, New York; Article no. 72; Notice; on the list of letters remaining at the Post-Office at Niagara Falls.

Green, Miss Sarah; Niagara Falls, New York; Article no. 72; Notice; on the list of letters remaining at the Post-Office at Niagara Falls.

Halcomb, Mehitable; Royalton, New York; Article no. 71; Notice; on the list of letters remaining at the Post-Office in Royalton.

Hall, Mary W.; Ontario County, New York; Article no. 134; Court; witness called in, *The People vs. Eli Bruce, Orasmus Turner, and Jared Darrow, for Conspiracy, &c.*, at the Ontario Sessions held 20 August 1828; was the wife of the jailer.

Hart, Tryphena; Royalton, New York; Article no. 163; Notice; on the list of people for whom letters remain in the Post Office at Royalton.

Harwood, Adeline; Lockport, New York; Article no. 160; Notice; on the list of people for whom letters remain in the Post Office at Lockport.

Harwood, Maria; Royalton, New York; Article no. 71; Notice; on the list of letters remaining at the Post-Office in Royalton.

Hawley, Betsey; Lockport, New York; Article no. 160; Notice; on the list of people for whom letters remain in the Post Office at Lockport.

Hawley, Electa; Lockport, New York; Article no. 160; Notice; on the list of people for whom letters remain in the Post Office at Lockport.

Hemenway, Electa C.; Lockport, New York; Article no. 272; Notice; Administratrix of the real estate of Alanson Hemenway, deceased; co-Administrator with Bordman H. Bosworth.

Henry, Semantha F.; Lockport, New York; Article no. 160; Notice; on the list of people for whom letters remain in the Post Office at Lockport.

Holden, Miss Anna C.; Royalton, New York; Article no. 71; Notice; on the list of letters remaining at the Post-Office in Royalton.

Holt, Miss Mary A.; Buffalo, New York; Article no. 712; Marriage; to Wm. L. Parsons, Merchant, of Lockport.

Holway, Sarah; Lewiston, New York; Article no. 70; Notice; on the list of letters remaining at the Post-Office in Lewiston.

Hoskins, Mrs. Huldah; Article no. 99; Notice; a plea to the public, in search of her two sons, William and Calvin Hoskins.

Howell, Mrs.; Niagara Falls, New York; Article no. 153; Notice; on the list of people for whom letters remain in the Post Office at Lewiston.

Hubbard, Phebe; Lockport, New York; Article no. 160; Notice; on the list of people for whom letters remain in the Post Office at Lockport.

Hughes, Susannah; Lockport, New York; Article no. 69; Notice; on the list of letters remaining at the Post-Office in Lockport.

Hull, Mary; Royalton, New York; Article no. 163; Notice; on the list of people for whom letters remain in the Post Office at Royalton.

Hull, Mrs.; Niagara Falls, New York; Article no. 153; Notice; on the list of people for whom letters remain in the Post Office at Lewiston.

Hustler, Katharine; Lewiston, New York; Article no. 375; Notice; Surrogate's Notice, probate of will of Katharine Hustler, deceased, before Hiram Gardner, Esquire, Surrogate of the county of Niagara.

Hyde, Sarah S.; Youngstown, New York; Article no. 164; Notice; on the list of people for whom letters remain in the Post Office at Youngstown.

Johnson, Mrs. Amanda; Lockport, New York; Article no. 276; Marriage; to Benjamin Covill, of Lockport.

Kelly, Semanthy; Lockport, New York; Article no. 160; Notice; on the list of people for whom letters remain in the Post Office at Lockport.

Knight, Almira; Royalton, New York; Article no. 71; Notice; on the list of letters remaining at the Post-Office in Royalton.

Lay, Hannah; Lockport, New York; Article no. 69; Notice; on the list of letters remaining at the Post-Office in Lockport.

Lenox, Catharine; Lockport, New York; Article no. 69; Notice; on the list of letters remaining at the Post-Office in Lockport.

Long, Sally; Lockport, New York; Article no. 103; Notice; caution to the public; Sally Long had left the "bed and board" of her husband, Benjamin Long, of Lockport.

Lusk, Rebecca; Youngstown, New York; Article no. 164; Notice; on the list of people for whom letters remain in the Post Office at Youngstown.

Makee, Miss Abijal; Royalton, New York; Article no. 71; Notice; on the list of letters remaining at the Post-Office in Royalton.

Manchester, Eliza; Royalton, New York; Article no. 163; Notice; on the list of people for whom letters remain in the Post Office at Royalton.

McKnight, Mary; Lockport, New York; Article no. 160; Notice; on the list of people for whom letters remain in the Post Office at Lockport.

North, Phoebe; Somerset, New York; Article no. 231; Notice; caution to the public; Phoebe North eloped from her husband, Moses North, of Somerset.

Norton, Miss Thirza; Lockport, New York; Article no. 275; Marriage; to Edwin L. Faxton, of Lockport.

Parker, Huldah; Youngstown, New York; Article no. 74; Notice; on the list of letters remaining at the Post-Office at Youngstown.

Perry, Sarah; Lockport, New York; Article no. 513; Advertisement; vendor of a large farm, situated about a mile and a half east of the village of Lockport, a short distance south of the Batavia road.

Pratt, Elizabeth; Royalton, New York; Article no. 163; Notice; on the list of people for whom letters remain in the Post Office at Royalton.

Prought, Nancy; Lockport, New York; Article no. 69; Notice; on the list of letters remaining at the Post-Office in Lockport.

Robbs, Hester; Lewiston, New York; Article no. 152; Notice; on the list of names for whom letters remain in the Post Office at Lewiston.

Roberts, Dianthe; Cambria, New York; Article no. 722; Notice; a bound servant girl, who ran away from John Gould, of Cambria.

Rogers, Hannah; Niagara Falls, New York; Article no. 153; Notice; on the list of people for whom letters remain in the Post Office at Lewiston.

Sage, Mary A.; Lockport, New York; Article no. 69; Notice; on the list of letters remaining at the Post-Office in Lockport.

Sears, Mrs.; Lockport, New York; Article no. 196; Advertisement; millinery and mantua-making, in partnership with Miss Calkins, in Lockport.

Seever, Mrs. John; Hartland, New York; Article no. 418; Notice; caution to the public; husband refused to contract for the debts of his wife.

Shelden, Miss Sibyl; Somerset, New York; Article no. 697; Marriage; to David Prusia, of Yates, Orleans County.

Sill, Mary; Lockport, New York; Article no. 69; Notice; on the list of letters remaining at the Post-Office in Lockport.

Simonds, Harriet; Lockport, New York; Article no. 160; Notice; on the list of people for whom letters remain in the Post Office at Lockport.

Sly, Mary; Town not stated, New York; Article no. 232; Notice; eloped from her husband, Eli Sly.

Smith, Miss Elizabeth; Cambria, New York; Article no. 194; Marriage; to Otis Brooks, of Cambria.

Smith, Sarah; Lewiston, New York; Article no. 152; Notice; on the list of names for whom letters remain in the Post Office at Lewiston.

Smith, Miss Sarah; Rochester, New York; Article no. 483; Marriage; to Robert H. Stevens, Esq.

Steeprock, Mrs. John; Batavia, New York; Article no. 553; Court; July, 1832 trial of John Steeprock, an Indian, for the murder of his wife.

Stocking, Clarissa; Lockport, New York; Article no. 160; Notice; on the list of people for whom letters remain in the Post Office at Lockport.

Stone, Mrs. Rhoda; state of N.Y.; Article no. 150; Death.

Summers, Mary; Lewiston, New York; Article no. 152; Notice; on the list of names for whom letters remain in the Post Office at Lewiston.

Sykes, Wealthy Ann; Pendleton, New York; Article no. 730; Notice; on the list of letters remaining in the Post Office at Pendleton.

Syks, Emeline; Pendleton, New York; Article no. 73; Notice; on the list of letters remaining at the Post-Office at Pendleton.

Taylor, Ellen; Youngstown, New York; Article no. 164; Notice; on the list of people for whom letters remain in the Post Office at Youngstown.

Thompson, Miss Adeline; Cambria, New York; Article no. 274; Marriage; to John Burchard, of Lima, Livingston county.

Thompson, Miss Nancy; Cambria, New York; Article no. 273; Marriage; to William Gould, of Cambria.

Thompson, Widow; Cambria, New York; Article no. 619; Notice; reward posted by Barrit Burchard, for silver Swiss watch lost near widow Thompson's.

Toole, Mary S.; Lewiston, New York; Article no. 70; Notice; on the list of letters remaining at the Post-Office in Lewiston.

Totton, Sally; Lewiston, New York; Article no. 70; Notice; on the list of letters remaining at the Post-Office in Lewiston.

Tryon, Mary Ann; Lewiston, New York; Article no. 152; Notice; on the list of names for whom letters remain in the Post Office at Lewiston.

Turner, Celicia; Royalton, New York; Article no. 163; Notice; on the list of people for whom letters remain in the Post Office at Royalton.

Virle, Louisa C.; Royalton, New York; Article no. 163; Notice; on the list of people for whom letters remain in the Post Office at Royalton.

Weaver, Laury; Lewiston, New York; Article no. 70; Notice; on the list of letters remaining at the Post-Office in Lewiston.

Wellman, Emily; Niagara Falls, New York; Article no. 72; Notice; on the list of letters remaining at the Post-Office at Niagara Falls.

Wellman, Emily; Niagara Falls, New York; Article no. 153; Notice; on the list of people for whom letters remain in the Post Office at Lewiston.

Weston, Sally Ann; Lockport, New York; Article no. 160; Notice; on the list of people for whom letters remain in the Post Office at Lockport.

White, Miss Mary; Lockport, New York; Article no. 149; Marriage; to Nathaniel Coe, of Portage, Allegany County.

White, Mary; Lockport, New York; Article no. 160; Notice; on the list of people for whom letters remain in the Post Office at Lockport.

Wingart, Elizabeth; Pendleton, New York; Article no. 573; Notice; on the list of letters remaining in the Post Office at Pendleton.

Wingert, Elizabeth; Pendleton, New York; Article no. 378; Notice; on the list of letters remaining in the post-office at Pendleton.

Winship, Abby; Dunstable, Massachusetts; Article no. 693; Notice; carried off by a runaway, named Timothy Kendall, who absconded from Dunstable, leaving "an amiable and virtuous wife, three small children, and an aged and decrepid father."

Summary statistics, references to women:

Table 4. References to women by subject.	
Type of notice	No.
Letters for pick-up at post-office	83
Marriage	13
Advertisement	6
Ran away, eloped	6
Court	3
Sheriff's Sale	3
Accident (includes 1 fatality)	2
Death	2
Education	2
Estates of deceased persons	2
Murder (alleged)	1
Plea, in search of missing family	1
Probate of will	1
Unnamed heroine	1
Other	2
Total	128

5. MICHENER CADWALLADER

Michener Cadwallader was born in 1798 in Huntingdon, Pennsylvania, the son of John Cadwallader II and Catharine Proctor. His paternal grandfather was Colonel Thomas Proctor, an Irishman, who commanded the Pennsylvania artillery during the Revolutionary War. His maternal grandfather was John Cadwallader, an attorney in Baltimore.

Early in his career, Mr. Cadwallader was the publisher of a periodical journal entitled, *The Archives*; in this pursuit, he was occupied with the study of State papers under the control of Congress. He moved to Lockport, New York with the intention, apparently, of launching the *Niagara Courier* newspaper as an organ of the anti-Masonic movement. In addition to providing generous broadsheet space for this purpose, Mr. Cadwallader also took aim at his opponents, in particular, the editor of the *Lockport Balance* paper (for which articles, refer to index entries for "Lockport Balance," in Chapter 2, *Index of Names*).

After selling the *Niagara Courier* in 1834, Michener Cadwallader moved to Buffalo. There, he took up the reins of the *Buffalo Journal* daily newspaper—regarded as a "staunch Whig paper"—from 1834–36, in partnership with Mr. David M. Day and Dr. Henry R. Stagg. Later, Mr. Cadwallader pursued a career in government with the city of Buffalo, first as City Clerk, 1846–47, and then as City Comptroller, 1848–53.

Michener Cadwallader married Mary Ann Cooper Brower (1795–1866) in New York in 1824. The couple had three daughters, Catherine (1830–), Elizabeth (1833–) and Emma (1838–), all born in the state of New York.

Mr. Cadwallader died on February 9, 1864, and was buried at Forest Lawn cemetery in Buffalo.

BIBLIOGRAPHY

Barber, Gertrude A., compiler. *Extracts of marriages from the Brooklyn Eagle (volumes 1-14, 1841–1880) and the New York Evening Post (volumes 1-7, 1801–1837) newspapers.* Transcription of notice, published April 10, 1824: "Thursday evening by Rev. Dr. Kuypers, M. Cadwallader, late of Huntingdon, Pa., to Mary Ann C. Brouwer, of this city." Ancestry, by subscription, http://www.ancestry.com (accessed July 11, 2011).

Boone, Jay. "Mary Ann Brower Cadwallader." Photograph of gravestone (Forest Lawn Cemetery, Buffalo, Erie County, New York, USA; Plot: Section G); Find a Grave Memorial #54534696, created July 5, 2010. Find a Grave, http://www.findagrave.com (accessed July 11, 2011).

Cadwallader, Michener, ed. *Niagara Courier* newspaper. Lockport, New York: M. Cadwallader, June 26, 1828–November 6, 1833.

Follett, Frederick. *History of the Press of Western New York.* Rochester, New York: Jerome & Brother, Daily American Office, 1847.

French, J.H. *Gazetteer of the State of New York.* Syracuse, New York: R. Pearsall Smith, 1860.

Gales and Seaton. *The Debates and Proceedings in the Congress of the United States, Eighteenth Congress, First Session*, Volume 1. Washington, D.C.: University of North Texas (UNT). UNT Digital Library, http://digital.library.unt.edu (accessed July 11, 2011).

Salisbury, Guy H. "Early History of the Press of Erie County." *Publications of the Buffalo Historical Society, Volume II*. Buffalo: Bigelow Brothers, 1880.

"The Buffalo Journal." *The New-Yorker.* New York, N.Y.: H. Greeley & Co., July 7, 1838.

The Commercial Advertiser Directory for the City of Buffalo. Buffalo, New York: Jewett Thomas & Co., 1850.

United States, Bureau of the Census. *Seventh Census of the United States (1850).* Washington, D.C.: National Archives and Record Service (Records of the Bureau of the Census, Record Group 29, National Archives microfilm M432-501, page 217A, image 441). Ancestry, by subscription, http://www.ancestry.com (accessed February 2, 2011).

Wein, Roy. "Mitchenor A. Cadwallader." Photograph of gravestone, with biographical notes (Forest Lawn Cemetery, Buffalo, Erie County, New York, USA; Plot: Section G); Find a Grave Memorial #45782931, created December 25, 2009. Find a Grave, http://www.findagrave.com (accessed July 11, 2011).

www.ingramcontent.com/pod-product-compliance
Lightning Source LLC
Chambersburg PA
CBHW080546170426
43195CB00016B/2689